THE HANDBOOK OF

TELEMARKETING

THE
HANDBOOK
OF
TELEMARKETING

Strategies for
Implementation
and Management

MICHAEL STEVENS

The Decisions Group
Direct Marketing Services

KOGAN
PAGE

The author welcomes correspondence from suppliers of products and services and other organisations with interests in telephone marketing and related activities for possible coverage in subsequent editions of this book. Correspondence should be sent to Michael Stevens at the publisher's address below.

First published in 1991

Kogan Page Limited
120 Pentonville Road
London N1 9JN

© Michael Stevens 1991

British Library Cataloguing in Publication Data
A CIP record for this book is available from the British Library.
ISBN 0 7494 0089 7

Typeset by J&L Composition Ltd, Filey, North Yorkshire
Printed and bound in Great Britain by Biddles Ltd,
Guildford and Kings Lynn

Contents

List of Figures

List of Tables

Foreword

I am delighted to have the opportunity to introduce *The Handbook of Telemarketing* to sales and marketing professionals the world over.

Telemarketing is perhaps the least understood of the advertising and marketing mediums. I am sure the book will go a long way towards rectifying this. It guides the reader through all the thought processes necessary for a full appreciation of the medium, tackles the thorny issue of 'agency or in-house', gives a detailed assessment of staffing and other practical considerations, helps the reader set his or her targets and analyse results and provides a number of fascinating case studies.

A brief summary of the legal and self-regulatory rules with which all practitioners should be familiar, and an exhaustive appendix, rounds off a most comprehensive coverage of the subject in a very readable form. The tables of valuable information alone are worth the book's cover price.

The very qualities of telemarketing that make it such an effective tool are liable to generate criticism if not employed ethically. That is why the BDMA sets such great store by proper and effective self regulation, of which the BDMA Guidelines (Appendix B) are a prime example. The sharper the tool the greater the precision with which it should be used and I have every expectation that this *Handbook* will contribute greatly to a more complete acceptance of this truism.

Colin Fricker
Director General
British Direct Marketing Association

Preface

Reading this book will help you to understand why the telephone was the fastest growing marketing medium in the UK during most of the 1980s. Companies throughout the world are becoming increasingly aware that using the telephone in a planned and controlled way as an integral part of their sales and marketing strategy can boost their efficiency, increase profitability and create competitive advantage. Those who fail to recognise and take advantage of these opportunities will undoubtedly suffer as their competitors reap the benefits of telephone marketing.

This book provides step-by-step guidance on how to get the best out of what is arguably the most flexible tool available to sales and marketing professionals. It brings together all the information you need to capitalise on the commercial benefits of telephone marketing, helping you to:

- recognise opportunities for using telephone marketing, covering a wide range of applications as well as strategic opportunities, such as the Single European Market, and new information technologies;

- compare the economics of using a telephone marketing agency and setting up in-house;

- select and brief an agency;

- set up an in-house telephone marketing operation, covering all aspects of planning, selecting equipment, and selecting, recruiting, training and motivating staff;

- plan, implement and manage a telephone marketing campaign;

- take advantage of the long-term opportunities for developing telephone marketing activities on a strategic basis;

- understand current legislation and good practice initiatives relating to telephone marketing in the UK, Continental Europe and the US;

- learn by the example of companies who have already used telephone marketing to gain competitive advantage.

The book will be invaluable to anyone who wants to gain a better understanding of how to use telephone marketing effectively, from those who are just starting out in their careers and want a thorough grounding in the subject, to seasoned professionals who simply want to widen and update their knowledge.

Acknowledgements

This book contains the fruits of many people's labours. I am very grateful to The Decisions Group for placing at my disposal the expertise of their staff which has been built up over nine years in the direct communications business. My sincere thanks to all those who made themselves available, often at short notice, to share their knowledge and to review parts of the text. Two individuals deserve special mention – Karen Darby, who introduced me to the world of telephone marketing several years ago and inspired this book, and Katharine Bollon, who devoted an enormous amount of time to coordinating research and collating information for the book.

I would also to like thank Colin Fricker and Tessa Kelly at the British Direct Marketing Association, who provided information for, and reviewed, the chapter on legislation and good practice initiatives; and Melanie Hannah, at Ogilvy & Mather Direct – Teleconsult, for her advice on selecting a telephone marketing agency.

Introduction: What is telephone marketing?

Telephone marketing is the *planned* and *controlled* use of the telephone for sales and marketing purposes.

This simple definition is widely accepted as being an accurate reflection of the wide range of activities which constitute telephone marketing. While there are many other definitions, this one incorporates the key phrase 'planned and controlled'.

The telephone has become an increasingly important method of direct communication for marketing because it has unique characteristics. Unlike other direct marketing media, such as mail, the telephone allows immediate two-way communication. With a large mailshot, for example, the message may have been carefully planned to encourage people to buy, but its immediate effectiveness is unknown and may not be known for weeks. Once posted, it is too late to change any of the things which can influence the effectiveness of direct mail – the message, the target audience, the timing of the offer, its appeal, and so on. With telephone calls, however, each contact that is made provides feedback which can be recorded, measured and analysed to help gauge the effectiveness of the message, the level of interest among the target audience, and all the other variables, on an ongoing basis. Different combinations can be tested, with the flexibility to make changes at any stage of a campaign, until a formula is found which achieves optimum results. Costs can also be monitored and compared with results, providing a continuous measure of cost-effectiveness, and only the number of calls required to achieve the desired result need to be made, for example to book a specific number of appointments for a field sales force. So the use of the telephone, like other direct marketing media, can be planned to achieve specific objectives, but it also allows for greater flexibility in its implementation. The telephone is unique in that the immediate feedback enables calling to be closely controlled in order to help ensure that these objectives are achieved in the most cost-effective way.

Telephone marketing is still often confused with telesales, but there are some important differences, the major one being this element of planning and control. Traditionally, telesales has often been poorly planned, with callers themselves deciding who they are going to call and what they are going to say. Without structure and consistency to the calling it cannot be accurately measured and controlled, and there is little or no opportunity to evaluate and improve upon results.

Secondly, direct selling is only one in a large number of marketing applications for the telephone. It can also be used, alone or in combination with other marketing methods, to help achieve the full spectrum of sales and marketing objectives, from evaluating new markets to improving investor relations.

The industry

Telephone conversations have made a contribution to sales and marketing activities ever since the telephone was introduced into the business world, but it was not until 1962, in the US, that telephone marketing appeared in a recognisable form. Although this activity was concentrated on direct selling by telephone, businesses were beginning to use it in a more controlled way to achieve pre-set objectives. This was more than a decade before these methods were being used in Europe.

The good telephone marketing agencies have always been at the forefront of development and the professional use of the medium, and they can take a large part of the credit for the current sophistication of the industry, and for helping to encourage its use throughout the business world. The first UK agency was established in the late 1970s and the next decade saw explosive growth in both the number of agencies and in the amount companies were spending on in-house telephone marketing activities.

According to research commissioned by the Colorgraphic Group*, published in 1990, the UK agency sector grew by 435 per cent between 1985 and 1989, when it was valued at £75m. Over this period it was the fastest growing method of marketing communication. Although the growth rate slowed in 1990, due to natural levelling in a now established industry, the downturn in the economy and high set-up costs, it is still expected to increase by 165 per cent, to a value of around £200m, by 1995.

There are no figures available for the growth rate of the company sector over a similar period. However, a 1988 survey† of the UK industry by the British Direct Marketing Association (BDMA) revealed that 52 per cent of the organisations with at least two exchange lines covered by the survey spontaneously claimed to use telephone marketing, rising to 97 per cent when prompted with a list of possible applications. Over half of those with more than 10 telephone lines use dedicated telephone marketing staff, and companies with more than 20 lines were each making an average of 78,000 telephone contacts per calendar month. Calculating an accurate value for their total expenditure on telephone marketing is impossible, but the report gave a tentative estimate in excess of £5bn in 1988.

Not all Western European countries have experienced the same growth in telephone marketing. For example, while Germany leads Europe in the number of telephone marketing agencies, followed by France and then the UK, in terms of total revenue Germany is believed to rank fourth, after France, the UK and Holland. This is possibly because of German legislation prohibiting 'cold' calling.

National differences in the way the use of the telephone is viewed, culturally as well as commercially, can naturally have a major influence on the industry's growth. In some of the Scandinavian countries, for example, all forms of telecommunication are given a high priority in

---

* *Direct Response – The Market Map*, A quantitative analysis of the UK direct response industry, 1990. Commissioned from Research Associates by the Colorgraphic Group.
† *Survey of the UK Telephone Marketing Industry (1988)*, prepared by the Telephone Marketing Committee of the British Direct Marketing Association, 1990.

business; one reason being that the harsh winters make travel difficult and limit face-to-face meetings. This may help to account for the fact that the value of the agency sector per capita of population in Sweden exceeds that in the UK by a healthy margin, possibly around 40 per cent, with a similar situation existing in Finland. Comparative expenditure in Holland is even higher, at around twice that in the UK, reflecting a greater appreciation of the power of telephone marketing in that country.

When it comes to a 'telephone culture', however, no country compares with the US, where consumers generally consider the telephone to be an essential communications tool for their day-to-day existence. According to the US *Direct Marketing* magazine, a total of US$45bn was spent on telephone marketing in 1988 – twice the amount spent on direct mail. A more recent estimate, from staff at the US Direct Marketing Association and published in *Marketing Director International*, puts the 1990 total US spend on telephone marketing at around US$370bn.

Figures which include corporate spend on in-house telephone marketing can only ever be 'guesstimates'. Apart from difficulties in obtaining data from the corporate sector, the telephone has become such an everyday business tool that it is difficult to draw the line between its planned and controlled use for telephone marketing, and the more *ad hoc* contribution it makes to sales and marketing activities. However, the magnitude of these figures shows that the telephone is becoming an increasingly important means of communication in corporate sales and marketing strategies.

Success story

The increased use of telephone marketing over the past decade has been stimulated by a wide range of factors acting to sustain growth of the industry. These include:

- a growing diversity in the products and services available;

- increasing competition;

- market fragmentation, with a move away from mass marketing and a growing emphasis on marketing to individual consumers and businesses;

- the increasing cost of advertising media;

- the falling costs and increasing sophistication of computing, enabling automated data analysis and handling for one-to-one communications on a large scale;

- upward-spiralling costs of conventional selling, such as maintaining a field sales force or local branches;

- the introduction of special telephone services, such as 0800 numbers; and

- the increased use of credit cards.

Research carried out in 1989, by The Decisions Group in conjunction with *Marketing* magazine, found that, among a cross-section of British companies in different industries, the most popular techniques for achieving a dialogue with customers and prospects were direct mail, followed by telephone marketing and then sales promotion, because they achieve the best results. Although growth of the telephone marketing industry began to slow in 1990, there are signs that it is more resilient than other marketing methods in an economic downturn. Large increases in the cost of media advertising, for example, have forced many companies to look at other methods of marketing communication, like the telephone, where results can be accurately monitored and measured, and where costs are accountable.

One of the most significant recent trends in marketing has been the growing use of databases to help plan, implement and measure the effectiveness of marketing activities. Detailed and accurate information on customers and prospects has become an increasingly valuable commodity with advances in the technology available to exploit it. Database-driven marketing, where the data is continuously enriched and refined, automates the process of delivering a personalised marketing message to individuals at a time when it will have the most productive impact. The telephone has played an important role in the growth of database marketing, both as a cost-effective means of gathering and maintaining accurate information on customers and prospects, and as a way of exploiting it with precisely targeted calls. The greatest impact of the telephone, however, has been in its integrated use with other marketing methods as a part of an overall strategy for building, developing and exploiting a marketing database.

More and more companies are considering the benefits of telephone marketing right at the beginning, when planning the strategy for achieving their sales and marketing objectives, in order to find the most effective way of gathering, managing and exploiting information about their markets. This trend will continue to grow as more companies wake up to the benefits of database marketing and the role that the telephone can play.

Advancing information technology, combined with falling computing costs, is likely to bring about a revolution in information management for sales and marketing in the 1990s. Technology already plays a highly significant role and, according to the Colorgraphic research, the market for software, hardware and associated training for direct marketing is likely to double between 1990 and 1995. Moriarty and Swartz* of Harvard University identified a trend in the US in 1989, already making itself felt in the UK, towards the greater use of information technology in sales and marketing. Advanced marketing and sales productivity (MSP) systems, they say, can improve productivity by automating selling and direct marketing support tasks, and the collection and analysis of information to improve the quality of decision-making. With sales and marketing costs averaging between 15 and 35 per cent of total corporate costs, they suggest that this is the next frontier for automation, and report examples of sales increases ranging from 10 to more than 30 per cent, with investment returns often exceeding 100 per cent. With the increasing importance of sales and marketing services, combined with an economic downturn, the productivity improvements arising from automation provide a major opportunity for the 1990s. In many of the systems which provide an integrated environment for sales and marketing information management, the telephone plays a pivotal role. Although the initial costs of such systems are high, the investment can be justified quickly because results and benefits are easily measured and analysed.

However, entry into telephone marketing does not demand a major investment in sophisticated technology. Apart from being able to take advantage of a substantial number of excellent agencies, there is a widening range of sophisticated but relatively inexpensive software for

---

* 'Automation to Boost Sales and Marketing', by Rowland T Moriarty and Gordon S Swartz, *Harvard Business Review*, January–February 1989 (reprint number 89105).

telephone marketing, which can run on PCs, while some companies operate successfully using paper-based systems.

The telephone marketing industry has matured rapidly in recent years, with a rise in the sophistication of techniques and standards of professionalism. While it still attracts a degree of scepticism, arising mainly from a lack of knowledge and understanding, it looks set to provide expanding opportunities, throughout the 1990s, for gaining competitive advantage, particularly when used as an integral part of the overall sales and marketing strategy. Companies who ignore these opportunities risk losing out to their competitors.

1

The Principles of Telephone Marketing

With the freedom of choice between an ever-increasing range of competing products and services, consumers and businesses are demanding more and more of the companies from whom they will buy. They want to be treated as individuals, and have their personal preferences and needs catered for efficiently, and with deference to their freedom to shop elsewhere. The overriding concern of all businesses today is therefore to seek out those individuals interested in their products and services, encourage them to become customers and then keep them, developing a long-term relationship to increase their buying value. Although many different methods can be employed to achieve this objective, the cornerstone of such a strategy is regular, accurately targeted communication by whatever means is most effective at the time, whether that is mail, the telephone or a personal visit. Of all the direct marketing media, the telephone is the one most suited to establishing a dialogue with customers, finding out more about their needs and preferences, and developing a long-term profitable relationship.

The telephone provides direct access to all businesses and a growing majority of consumers, and obviously it can be used both for making (outbound) and receiving (inbound) calls. However, it is such a commonplace, everyday piece of business equipment that it is often treated as something more akin to the office photocopier than a powerful means of communication. It requires planning and skill to get the best results from a telephone call, and yet the majority of business communication over the telephone lacks both. In some areas this can have a seriously damaging effect on the company's image, marketing efforts and resulting profitability.

Take, for example, the handling of enquiries made by telephone. If the person calling is not yet a customer this is the point at which a new customer can be won – or lost forever – depending on how effectively the call is handled and how well it meets the needs of the enquirer. Worse still, an existing, high-spending customer could be lost to a competitor. Although not all types of calls have such high potential for success or failure, almost every organisation, from the largest multinationals to the smallest enterprises, can benefit by adopting the principles and practices of telephone marketing. Whether they are talking with other businesses, consumers, or both, the applications of telephone marketing are so varied and flexible that it can be used, for example, to:

- research, evaluate and test new markets;
- identify prospects and their potential value;
- generate leads and make appointments for sales people;
- sell products and services;
- service existing customers;
- launch new products or services;
- handle responses generated by advertising;
- process orders and enquiries;
- handle complaints;
- build, maintain and exploit marketing databases;
- invite people to events;
- update mailing lists;
- communicate important company/product/service information;
- either raise awareness or funds.

Organisations which undertake any of these or similar marketing-related activities could find that adopting a telephone marketing approach, alongside other methods, will improve the cost-effectiveness of their marketing efforts. It can help to win customer loyalty and new business, create new opportunities and boost profitability. However, while it is a very powerful marketing tool, the telephone is not the most appropriate medium in every situation because it has certain disadvantages.

Advantages and disadvantages of telephone marketing

Getting the maximum benefit from using the telephone in marketing requires an understanding of its advantages and disadvantages, which are summarised in Table 1.1. Only then can it be selected on the basis of being the best method for achieving a particular objective and used in the most effective way.

Table 1.1 The main qualities of telephone marketing

Telephone marketing	
Advantages	*Disadvantages*
Targeted	More expensive than
Personal	some other techniques
Interactive	Comparatively low volume
Immediate	Intangible
High quality	Sometimes intrusive
Flexible	Easily misused
Measurable and	
accountable	
Testable	
Intrusive	
Cost-effective	

Advantages

The characteristics of telephone marketing which can give it an advantage over alternative methods are as follows.

It is targeted When telephone marketers make a call they can be certain of whether or not the intended contact has been reached, so the marketing message is always delivered to the correct person. With business-to-business calling, even when a contact name is not known, the telephone can be used to find the name of the decision-maker or to gather other useful information about the company.

It is personal   The telephone is the most personal means of communication after face-to-face contact. Calls are specifically targeted so the marketing message can be personalised for each individual, incorporating into the conversation information which is directly relevant to them and their needs. By establishing a dialogue it provides the opportunity to answer questions, overcome objections, respond to buying signals or different levels of interest and even take account of individual personalities. Each conversation collects more information so that subsequent contact, whether by telephone or any other method, can be more highly personalised.

It is immediate   Every telephone call gets an immediate result of some type, be it an unobtainable or wrong number, someone who would like to be called back, or a negative or positive response. Every one of the possible responses can be used to decide what action should be taken next to maximise the value of each individual. Because the response is immediate, the results of a telephone marketing campaign can be continuously monitored, measured and analysed to help improve its effectiveness. The immediacy of the telephone may also appeal to customers and prospects. British Telecom research, for example, claims that 6 out of every 10 adults in the UK would prefer to respond to an offer by telephone rather than by using a Freepost coupon.

It is interactive   Because a telephone conversation is two way, telephone marketers can guide each conversation to help obtain the information or response they require. Every contact made gathers useful information, even if the response is something like, 'No, we are already using another supplier'. No other medium apart from face-to-face contact, which is the most expensive, offers the opportunity to elicit and record personal *ad hoc* responses. Because calls are specifically targeted, individual comments can be noted and added to the database for use later in planning and carrying out other sales and marketing activities. A company currently using another supplier, for example, may be contacted again when a special offer is being made. With business-to-business calls, even if the intended contact is not reached, valuable information can be obtained quickly from the switchboard operator, for example other contact names or company sites.

It is high quality   The personalised information that can be gained from a telephone conversation allows every contact to be screened, for example finding out whether they use the types of product supplied by the company and graded according to their potential value. Follow-up action can then be prioritised, perhaps arranging an immediate appointment with someone who is ready to buy, noting that the person would like to be called back in three months' time, or registering their dissatisfaction with distribution and passing on the information for action by the relevant department. Other direct marketing methods cannot guarantee such accurate screening and grading.

It is flexible Telephone marketing can be used for many different purposes and each campaign can be tailored and continuously refined to achieve maximum results. The message can be tailored to the individual; there are no geographical constraints; calls can be timed to provide maximum response rates and to suit each contact; immediate feedback from calls can be used to change the approach and so on.

It is measurable Every aspect of a telephone marketing campaign can be continuously monitored and measured, for example the number of:

- calls made per hour (call rate);
- contacts made with decision-makers (contact rate);
- contacts unavailable;
- telephone numbers unobtainable;
- positive responses, with reasons;
- negative responses, with reasons.

Ongoing analysis of this information can be used accurately to gauge the effectiveness of different approaches and to help identify why they do or do not work. A large proportion of unobtainable or wrong telephone numbers, for example, would indicate that the contact list being used is old. On the other hand, if the contact rate is very low compared with the call rate, perhaps the timing of calls is not appropriate. Immediate action can be taken to modify a campaign to produce optimum results.

It is accountable Accurate and detailed measurement of results means that the return on investment in a campaign, or even its individual elements, can be continuously monitored. This information can be used as a basis for comparing the cost-effectiveness of telephone marketing with other methods of achieving the same objectives.

It is testable Accurate measurement of campaign results enables testing of different approaches to gauge their relative effectiveness. Campaigns are commonly tested, by running a 'mini' or 'test' campaign, to measure the relative value of different sources of contact names (or 'leads'), different types of offer and so on. These tests can be conducted quickly and, because results are available immediately, decisions can be made on how to produce optimum results from the campaign, often while it is in progress.

It is intrusive It is hard to resist answering a ringing telephone and, once answered, a skilful telephone marketer is well prepared to answer any objections people may raise against continuing the call. In some situations, however, the intrusive nature of a ringing telephone can be a disadvantage (*see* p. 31).

It is cost-effective All of the above qualities combine in a medium which is highly cost-effective when used in the right application and in the right way.

Disadvantages

The drawbacks of using telephone marketing are as follows.

It is more expensive than some other techniques Telephone marketing is labour-intensive. Add to that the cost of the telephone calls themselves and the cost per contact can amount to very many times more than a mailshot or media advertising, and there are very few economies of scale. The purpose, content and targeting of calls must therefore be carefully planned to achieve maximum benefit in minimum time.

It is comparatively low volume Media advertising and direct mail can reach huge numbers of people in a single 'strike'. In comparison, a telephone marketer may be able to make perhaps 30–40 contacts per day, depending on the purpose of the call.

It is intangible A telephone conversation provides no opportunity to show products or sales literature, or for the telephone marketer to read any visual cues to gauge the reaction of contacts or assess their situation. Effective two-way communication relies solely upon the skills of the telephone marketer in being able to paint a verbal picture of what is being offered, and to listen and quickly analyse and respond to individuals' feelings and needs. In addition, there is no immediate opportunity for either party to make any written under-taking, for example to give a legally binding quotation or to sign an order, although verbal agreements may be confirmed subsequently in writing. Similarly, the telephone obviously cannot be used for things like product demonstrations, although it is invaluable for arranging qualified appointments.

It is sometimes intrusive   Most people have experienced the irritation of receiving calls at home from companies they have never heard of, at inconvenient times, or offering products or services for which they have no use or interest. Cold calling (ie having had no prior contact) can easily become intrusive, particularly to consumers. This need not be the case, however, if calls are accurately targeted, made at a reasonable time, and the contact is asked at the beginning whether it is convenient.

It is easily misused   One of the telephone's greatest strengths, being a very personal and powerful medium of communication, can also be a drawback. It is all too easy to create a negative impression if a call is not conducted skilfully and professionally.

All these factors need to be considered carefully in deciding when is the most advantageous time to use telephone marketing, as well as in planning how to make the most effective use of it. The aim should be to choose applications where capital can be made of the advantages, and the disadvantages can either be avoided or their effects minimised by careful planning. Telephone marketing is ideal, for example, in applications where information needs to be exchanged quickly, such as in making appointments for a sales team, or where the personal touch is vitally important, such as in dealing with complaints. It is not well suited to applications where, for example, long or complex explanations must be given, such as detailed technical specifications of products, or where a demonstration may be required, such as in selling high-value capital equipment (although it can be used to set up a demonstration).

How does it fit into the marketing mix?

When companies draw up their strategy for marketing themselves and their products or services, it may include many different short- and long-term objectives, together with details of target markets, pricing structures, new products, distribution methods and so on. In deciding how they will achieve these objectives they can choose from an enormous range of marketing activities falling into categories like advertising, sales promotion, direct marketing, PR and exhibitions. The overall aim is to gain maximum benefit from the budget and this is achieved by careful selection of the various marketing activities (or the marketing mix) which they will use.

Although individual marketing activities may be used to achieve particular objectives, they are much more effective when used in an integrated way. Mailshots, for example, commonly produce around a 2 per cent response rate. Although this can be cost-effective, combining telephone marketing with a mailshot can increase the response rate to 12–15 per cent or more. A similar synergy is seen with many combinations of activities. Taking it a step further, *all* the activities in the marketing mix should be planned and implemented to act as one integrated whole, feeding off each other to produce optimum results at the lowest possible cost. In terms of direct marketing activities, this is achieved through the effective management of information on customers and prospects, gathering and exploiting it in the most efficient, productive way. This is where the telephone is a particularly flexible and powerful complement to other activities. Getting the best out of telephone marketing, and the other activities it is working with, means planning its use as an integral part of the overall marketing strategy.

Isn't it expensive?

Telephone marketing appears expensive, at first, when you consider that a single telephone call to a customer or prospect may cost between £7 and £10 (the approximate cost of a 10-minute call, at peak rate, including telephone metered units, staff costs and overheads). However, when comparing it with other methods of achieving the same objective, the picture can be very different. It has been estimated* that in 1989 it cost £52,500 a year to keep a sales person

---

* See Table 2.2 on p. 55.

on the road. A member of a field sales team could make between 4 and 6 sales calls per day which, if spending 215 days on the road, would cost from £40 to £60 each. Having the field sales force visit all prospects and all customers, at this level of cost, is definitely not the most cost-effective way of deploying this expensive resource. Although the telephone should not be viewed as a substitute for the field sales team, there are many ways in which it can support and augment them. Take the following situations as examples.

New leads   A sales executive has the names of five people who might possibly become customers and visits each one of them. Only three are interested in the product and only two make a purchase, including one who wants to 'try out' the product. The total cost of those two sales, including one to someone who is less likely to make a repeat purchase, could be as high as £300. An alternative approach would have been to telephone each lead. These calls could have been used to ascertain their buying potential, ie to qualify them, to decide whether it would be worthwhile having someone visit them and, if it is, to book appointments for the sales executive.

Regular, low-spending customers   Individually, these customers represent a small amount of revenue, but together they may constitute a very significant proportion of the company's turnover. It is unlikely that the sales team could afford the time to visit all of these customers on a regular basis, if at all, and yet regular contact with them is essential because:

- everyone likes to feel that their custom, however little in value, is appreciated;

- they may occasionally have questions they want answered, perhaps about volume discounts or a query on an invoice, which do not merit them making a telephone call but which, unanswered, are a source of dissatisfaction;

- when stocks begin to get low they may buy from the most convenient source, which could be a competitor visiting or telephoning them at the right time.

So, while it is not cost-effective for the sales force to visit them, some form of regular contact with these customers may be essential to retain their business. The answer is regular calls from the telephone marketing team, who could each make around 30–40 contacts per day, using the calls to encourage repeat orders, promote special offers, sell in new products, answer any questions the customers have, and generally make them feel that the company values their business.

These are just two of several situations in which the telephone can be used to help a field sales team make more cost-efficient use of their time (other situations will be examined in Chapter 2). There are comparable benefits to be gained, though not in the same ways, with all applications of telephone marketing. Therefore, rather than being an expensive medium for marketing communications, using the telephone can help to cut costs when used effectively in the right application.

How can these benefits be achieved?

Any organisation could be taking advantage of the benefits of telephone marketing within weeks of making a decision by employing the services of a specialist agency. Its full integration into the marketing mix, through which maximum benefit is achieved, can take many months of planning, but there are many applications which can be put into effect quickly, some in just a few days if necessary.

Using a good agency has two major benefits – it does not require long-term commitment and their expertise guarantees the best chances of success. Most companies who are using telephone marketing first experienced its benefits through work carried out for them by an agency. While some continue to use an agency, others decide that there are advantages to setting up their own dedicated telephone marketing unit in-house. However, these are companies who have made the decision to use the medium and continue to use it because they have found it successful. On the other hand, there are also a very small minority of companies who have made that decision, albeit not always for the right reasons, and who have found it unsuccessful and have not used it again.

Many people, including some seasoned marketing professionals, are wary of telephone marketing and the BDMA survey* in 1988 helped

---

* *Survey of the UK Telephone Marketing Industry (1988)*, prepared by the Telephone Marketing Committee of the British Direct Marketing Association, 1990.

to pinpoint some of the attitudes which exist towards the medium. Telephone marketing agencies were asked what they considered were the major barriers to its greater use by their clients. The three most common responses were as follows.

Lack of knowledge and understanding of techniques   Over one-third of agencies (35 per cent) felt that clients did not even understand the basic techniques of telephone marketing, let alone what it can achieve and how it is used. According to the report:

> They [the clients] do not understand that the telephone can be used as a marketing tool. There is a prevailing view that everyone thinks he knows how to use the phone. 'It is just making phone calls with no added value: there is no strategy, no planning, it sort of happens spontaneously', as one telemarketer summed it up.

Cost   This was mentioned by 29 per cent of agencies, who felt that clients tended to think of making telephone calls as an expensive means of communication, because they looked at the total costs without appreciating the value of the direct and indirect benefits.

The image of telephone marketing   As little as five years ago telephone marketing had a very serious image problem, particularly among consumers receiving calls from companies selling things like double glazing and insurance. Although the number of professional users now greatly outweighs the 'cowboys', 25 per cent of agencies felt that clients still often associate telephone marketing with this type of image.

In an overview of their survey of companies using telephone marketing in-house, the BDMA report says:

> In summary, there is evidence of an overwhelming need for better understanding, education and overall professionalism in the use of telemarketing within the company environment. This is independently confirmed by the agencies.

Companies cannot benefit from telephone marketing if they choose not to use it because they don't understand how it works, nor will they achieve the full benefit of it if they do not learn how to use it professionally. The remaining chapters of this book set out to help in that learning process and show how to use this powerful marketing tool to gain competitive advantage.

2

Applications and Opportunities

One reason why telephone marketing has grown so rapidly is that it has a greater degree of flexibility than any other direct marketing medium. Whenever an organisation wants to establish a dialogue with customers, prospects, suppliers, opinion-makers, or anyone else who may have an impact on its commercial success, the telephone can play a key role in the communications strategy.

The applications and opportunities are wide and varied, ranging from short-term tactical communications to the long-term strategic development of profitable business relationships. Timely, personalised marketing messages can be delivered direct to all sectors of both consumer and business-to-business markets, through either outbound or inbound calls. At the same time this gathers feedback from the marketplace to help refine marketing methods and plan future strategies. Telephone marketing may be used as the sole method of achieving a particular objective, or in combination with other marketing media, such as direct mail.

But telephone marketing is not a panacea. Using it cost-effectively, and ensuring maximum benefit, requires the right application, chosen for the right reasons and implemented professionally. Competitive advantage and improved profitability are there for the asking, but this can only be achieved with an understanding of how to use the telephone as a marketing tool. It is most effective when integrated into the overall sales and marketing strategy, capitalising on its particular benefits to meet specific objectives.

Inbound and outbound calls

Because of the live interaction, both inbound and outbound calls have an element of control which enables either of them to be used in a

Table 2.1 Inbound/outbound telephone marketing applications

Inbound	Inbound and outbound	Outbound
Lead qualification	Appointment making/ diary management	Lead generation and qualification
Catalogue/ brochure fulfilment	Direct sales/order taking	Pre-mail
Data capture	Customer care	Pre/during/post advertising
Credit servicing	Shareholder communications	List building/testing
Dealer location	Crisis management	Database building/ maintenance
	Fund/awareness raising	Invitation to events
	Traffic generation (retail, events etc)	Market evaluation and test marketing
	Post mail	Market research
		Subscription/ membership renewals
		Account/customer servicing
		Credit jogging

broad range of applications to help meet many types of marketing objective. These applications are summarised in Table 2.1.

Inbound calls are usually generated by publicising a telephone number that callers can use for a specific purpose, such as requesting information, placing orders or making complaints. An increasing number of advertisements in the media include a dedicated telephone number, providing a convenient and immediate means of contacting an organisation. These have proved highly successful. Giving a telephone number along with a post-reply coupon, for example, can result in many more telephone calls than written replies. Conversions to sales from telephone responses can also be higher than with coupons. The more quickly people receive a response, for example a sales brochure, the more likely they are to respond positively; this is further encouraged when the people answering the calls create a positive impression of the organisation.

Outbound calls are easier to control than inbound, in one sense, because it is easier for the organisation to predict, and therefore plan for controlling, the likely course of the conversation. The use of resources can also be planned and controlled more easily. If the telephone does not ring with an inbound call, the telephone marketer either sits idle or finds something else to do. However, outbound callers cannot guarantee the willing attention of the recipient, unlike inbound calls. In addition, the organisation has to identify who to call – a contact list – in a way which achieves the largest possible proportion of positive responses.

The BDMA survey in 1988 revealed that the number of calls made in the UK is fairly evenly split between outbound and inbound calls. However, the balance of expenditure on the two types of call differs between telephone marketing agencies and in-house usage. Outbound calls accounted for about 70 per cent of in-house expenditure, while for agencies the expenditure is much higher on inbound than outbound calls. This highlights the tendency towards a more strategic use of in-house telephone marketing, such as field sales support, and a more supportive role for agencies through activities such as response handling.

Despite this differentiation, there are many objectives which can be achieved by either type of call, and each call may have more than one objective. Inbound calls requesting information, for example, could also be used to generate leads for a sales force. Similarly, outbound appointment booking calls can also be used to evaluate potential markets or to solicit interest in receiving company literature. Tailoring telephone applications, and integrating them into the marketing strategy at an early stage can therefore provide a cost-effective solution to many marketing needs.

Integrating telephone marketing

Telephone marketing is a powerful medium when used by itself, but when used in combination with other marketing activities it can often produce dramatic results, increasing the effectiveness of the campaign through synergy (see Figure 2.1). Combining the telephone with direct mail generally produces the most striking increase, although it can also be highly effective in combination with other marketing activities. Success depends largely on the way in which the methods are combined and used. The effectiveness of a highly appealing press advertisement, for example, would fall if readers' calls are not handled efficiently; results will also fall if an advertisement does not generate many calls, however well those received are handled. Similarly, the

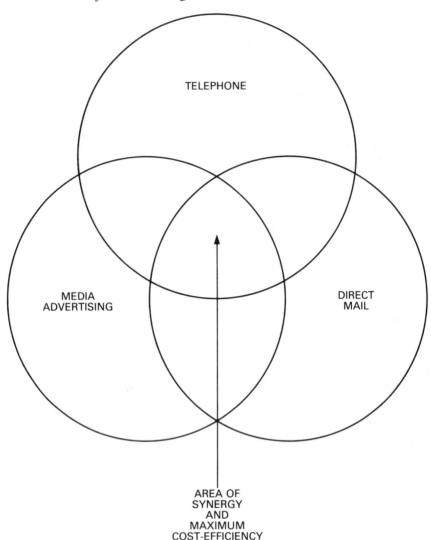

Figure 2.1 Integration of marketing activities

timing of a mail/call combination has to be carefully coordinated to produce optimum results. Ways in which the telephone can be integrated with other marketing activities include the following.

Direct mail

List building/testing This is where the telephone is used to create a list of contacts or to check the details on an existing list. The benefits include:

- a high number of calls per hour (ie call rate), because information can be obtained quickly at switchboard level (thereby minimising costs);

- a better chance of the mailing being read by the intended person, thereby increasing the response rate;

- reduced wastage of mail, which is particularly useful if a high-cost item is being sent, for example a product sample, and the annoyance factor (on receiving 'junk mail') is also reduced;

- creating a good image with correctly addressed, personalised mailings;

- the accuracy of bought-in lists can be tested;

- information can be gathered to build up a picture of decision-maker hierarchies within certain company types;

- additional information gained (for example other contacts, locations) can be used for subsequent approaches;

- the cost of follow-up is reduced because the mailing is more accurately targeted.

Pre-mail hype This is where the aim is to identify and contact decision-makers prior to them receiving a mailing. Using the telephone can:

- arouse curiosity or build interest;

- lay the foundation for a positive response perhaps by conveying a positive impression of the idea/concept;

- create an expectation;

- obtain commitment, for example by informing individuals they will be called again, after the mailing or event, for their comments;

- grade the potential of contacts – low-interest contacts may be deleted from the mailing list, medium-interest contacts may be mailed but only followed up at a later date, while those showing highest interest are mailed and followed up within days;

- increase the response rate;

- reduce the cost of follow-up.

Mailshot follow-up   The telephone can be used to follow up people who have responded to the mailing, to qualify their interest, to assess and/or maximise impact, to take the next action, or to follow up non-respondents to find out why they didn't respond and prompt a reply. The benefits include:

- an increase over mail-alone response rates of 500 per cent or more;

- an opportunity to assess the quality of response;

- grading each contact according to potential, so that further action can be prioritised.

Typical uses of telephone follow-up to a mailing are direct selling, arranging product demonstrations and setting appointments for a sales force.

In some applications, such as seminar booking, a three-stage, call/mail/call strategy is often used, combining many of the benefits of pre- and post-mail calls. If an organisation has an accurate 'profile' of likely customers and an accurate mailing list it can fairly confidently mail first and follow up with a phone call. If, on the other hand, either of these factors are uncertain, the telephone can be used either to test a proportion of the list, to gauge its accuracy and contacts' interest or to update the full list. A company supplying industrial machinery which is prospecting for new business, for example, may find it more cost-effective to call prospects first to obtain details of the decision-maker, what machinery the company currently uses, their budget for new equipment, and so on, before mailing. A follow-up call could then capitalise on the fact that the prospect has shown an interest, and has seen the appropriate literature, and is therefore more likely to agree to see a sales representative or attend a seminar.

Advertising

The telephone can be used to measure or increase the effectiveness of press or broadcast advertising, as follows.

Prior to the advertising campaign   This can be used to aid media selection, for example by asking buyers which publications they usually read and why, and to focus attention.

During the campaign   To assess awareness or maximise on advertising impact, which is especially useful for new product launches.

Post campaign To answer responses and follow up the interest generated, and to gauge the response to the advertisement to help plan future campaigns.

Sales

Integration of the telephone with sales activities is described in detail later, but it can provide support for the following.

Customer servicing Existing customers can be called on a regular basis to identify needs, sell add-ons, assess long-term potential and encourage customer loyalty.

Major accounts Large organisations often have complex structures for decision-making. The telephone can be used to identify the decision-making process (for example the role of specifiers, committees and boards) and all the opportunities for multiple sales to the same organisation. The sales force can then be supplied with a comprehensive 'dossier' on each company before their visit.

Customer events The telephone can be used to invite valuable customers to PR-type events or to get potential customers to attend new product demonstrations.

Resource back-up For example, to compensate for sickness/holidays of the sales force, or alternating visits with telephone calls to maximise the sales resource.

Surprisingly, the BDMA survey found that only one-third of companies with dedicated telephone marketing staff combined it with other marketing activities (usually direct mail or press advertising), and this tended to be the larger companies. However, this need not be the case; the integrated approach is used in many applications on a smaller scale.

The following descriptions of individual applications give some idea of the flexibility of telephone marketing, although they are by no means exhaustive.

Building and maintaining marketing databases

The telephone is playing an increasingly important role in gathering and maintaining the accuracy of information on customers and prospects for marketing databases. These databases have become one of the most valuable tools available to marketing departments as the information stored and the way it is used has become more diverse and sophisticated.

The value of marketing databases rests on two important principles: customers are more likely to favour those suppliers who treat them as individuals and show that they want to cater for their specific needs; and the more companies know about the characteristics of their customers (a profile – who buys what and why etc), the better they can serve existing customers, and the more accurately they can identify prospects and new markets.

Computer systems can hold, analyse and sort vast amounts of data on customers and prospects. By accumulating detailed information, such as the sex, age, lifestyle, hobbies, occupation, income and type of home (for consumers), and industry, size, budget, number of sites and employees (for businesses), companies are able to identify and grade the potential value of existing and potential customers. Using the database to track and analyse customer and prospect activity, companies can predict their likely needs at any given time and target them with timely, personalised communications. Optimising sales and marketing activities in this way is called database marketing, which is described in more detail in Chapter 9 (*see* pages 361–81).

The availability of increasingly sophisticated software for analysing and targeting markets enables the database to be used as the basis for all of a company's sales and marketing activities. However, the usefulness of a database depends on the accuracy of the information it contains. It has to be gathered carefully and 'cleaned' regularly to maintain its accuracy; cleaning the database is particularly important where data may change often, such as with names and job titles in business-to-business markets.

Data can be obtained and updated in various ways (for example transactions and other contact with customers, renting or buying mailing lists, mailshots, directories and questionnaires), but the telephone is the quickest and most reliable method. Because it is conversational, companies can gain a better understanding of the needs of individual contacts and respond more quickly and accurately as these needs change, for example by discovering who is not buying and why they are not buying. Compared with a response rate of perhaps only 2 per cent for direct mail, using the telephone generally obtains feedback from 80–90 per cent of the people called. Although not all of these people will convert (buy the product), they do provide valuable information for the database. Because it is interactive, data already held can quickly be checked and confirmed.

Compared with other data-gathering methods the telephone can be relatively expensive, but all types of calls can serve to gather useful information. Data capture and checking is therefore now usually incorporated into telephone marketing campaigns as a secondary objective, although it is sometimes used purely for information gathering. Building and maintaining the database, as a by-product of both inbound and outbound telephone marketing calls, then becomes much more cost-effective. Even when used for passive information gathering (ie as the primary objective), a telephone call can serve other purposes, for example customer care.

A telephone marketing operation can also benefit directly from the database. Obviously it enables better targeting of calls, delivering a relevant message to each contact at the right time. In situations where urgent action is required, for example a product recall, the database provides contact details so that calls can start within 24 hours. And many computerised telephone marketing systems enable telephone staff to interface directly with the database. With incoming calls, for example, they can instantly call up customer records on the computer screen and respond to them as individuals, thus enhancing the relationship.

List building, cleaning and testing

Inaccurate contact lists can greatly reduce the cost-effectiveness of a direct marketing campaign, whatever medium is being used. In direct mail, for example, incorrect names, addresses or job titles, misspelt names, and individuals' changing circumstances can all make response rates plummet, as well as reflecting poorly on the efficiency of the organisation doing the mailing.

Using the telephone to collect and update information on contacts may, at first, appear expensive. However, it is quicker than by mail, and proves more cost-effective, because of the higher response rate and almost complete accuracy.

List building consists of collecting information on a target market, either to add to an existing list or to build a new list. The extent of the information obtained varies, but will at least include the name, address and postcode, and telephone number (known as the NAT) of the contact. In business-to-business applications, the contact name and job title, size and type of company, and perhaps also the number of sites and additional contacts (such as influencers, specifiers and users) would also be obtained.

List cleaning consists of checking and updating an existing list, with information similar to list building, to ensure it is accurate. The recommended frequency for cleaning a list is about every six months, although the necessity for cleaning varies, depending on the likely extent of changes in contact details.

The telephone is also a quick and efficient method of testing the accuracy of a list when this is not known, ie when it was last cleaned. For example, what proportion of the list actually are, as claimed, retired couples between the ages of 65 and 75? By telephoning a proportion of the list, usually about 10 per cent, their details can be checked and the accuracy of the list measured. Testing can be particularly important with bought-in lists, where the date of the last cleaning may not be known. Some other uses for testing are described in Chapter 8 (*see* pages 341-48).

Market evaluation and test marketing

Almost any feature of a market can be gauged by telephone – reaction to a product launch, buying habits and intentions, company buying cycles, geographical bias, the appeal of pricing structure and so on. It is a quick and flexible way of building up an accurate picture of a market, and can be cost-effective if a good contact list is used in combination with the right strategy and tactics. Because it is inter-active, specific feedback can be obtained on how well the company's products or services meet the needs of customers and prospects. Contact names and telephone numbers for gaining feedback on a product can be obtained through various mechanisms, such as on-pack promotions and guarantee or registration cards. It is also possible to identify new market trends and provide valuable information for business development, for example new products and marketing strategies.

Market evaluation is easily combined with other applications. A company prospecting for new business, for example, may buy in a list of contacts with characteristics similar to existing valuable customers. The telephone can be used to test or clean the list at the same time as evaluating their interest and grading their buying potential in order to prioritise them for future marketing activities. At the same time, the calls may be used to generate leads for the sales force.

Testing awareness and penetration of an advertising campaign is another useful application, especially where there is a commitment to high expenditure over an extended period. Because feedback is immediate, resources can be concentrated quickly on those sectors of the relevant media giving the best value for money.

Market research

Market research, either qualitative or quantitative, in both business-to-business and consumer markets, can be conducted very effectively over the telephone. It is faster and much less expensive than other forms of market research, and questions can be altered rapidly to incorporate new requirements, for example if a new factor or trend is revealed which requires further investigation. In 1988, according to the Association of Market Survey Organisations, telephone research accounted for 16 per cent of all market research interviews.

Market research differs from market evaluation in that research data, for example a company's product usage, is not directly used subsequently for sales activities. Telephone research can be used alone or in combination with fieldwork (street or door-to-door interviews) or postal (questionnaire) interviews. The information gathered can be invaluable in planning future strategies and selecting specific marketing activities. It may be used, for example, to measure product awareness and attitudes, market needs, brand preferences, customer satisfaction and so on, as a preliminary to direct mail or product development.

Market research companies in the UK have recently begun to show an interest in automatic data collection, a computerised research technique developed and widely used in the US. This consists of a selected panel of people who regularly telephone the researching company and respond to questions posed by a computer. These systems can employ voice recognition or multi-frequency telephone dial tones and have the advantage that they do not require interviewers, and the data is automatically stored on the computer. It is faster, more flexible and costs much less than traditional telephone research.

It should be noted that there are strict codes of conduct governing market research, for example those of the UK Market Research Society (*see* Chapter 10, pages 395-6). In particular, information which will be used for targeted sales activities must not be obtained under the guise of market research.

Invitations to events

The costs of all elements of staging an event, such as venue and audio-visual hire, catering and downtime of sales personnel, continue to rise. It is therefore increasingly important to ensure maximum benefit is achieved. Whether the event is for customers, prospects or other audiences, like the media, the optimum number of the right type of people need to attend. The objectives of the event will determine the criteria for selecting attendees, but ensuring that the best 'value' prospects attend (especially avoiding freeloaders) still requires careful screening. The telephone has proved to be the most effective way of screening, confirming attendance and, if required, arranging meetings with company representatives.

The telephone is generally combined with postal invitations in two ways – call-mail-call, or mail-call – and both may be followed by a 'catering' call. The catering call is made just a few days before the event, asking individuals to confirm their attendance so that the company can cater for the correct number. It is very easy for someone to say 'yes' when asked if they would like to attend a particular event, simply to get rid of the person on the telephone, when they have no intention of attending, but they are more likely to be honest when confronted with the prospect of causing unnecessary wastage. In terms of the true number who will attend, the call-mail-call combination is normally accurate to about 90 per cent. The mail-call combination, on the other hand, tends to be much less successful because, without prior telephone screening, the mailing cannot be so accurately targeted.

A further advantage of early screening is that the best prospects can be identified and singled out as targets for the sales team. If the company has a good customer and prospect database, or if useful information about the contact has been obtained during screening, this can be used by the sales personnel at the event to show an interest in their particular needs. Even those who do not wish to attend can provide useful information, such as their interest in the company's products or services, other market information and, of course, why they do not wish to attend.

After the event, the telephone is again the most cost-effective way of continuing the dialogue with attendees. This should be undertaken within a week and can be used to gauge reaction to the event, arrange appointments with the best prospects, ask others if they would like any further information and arrange a time for later contact. People who do not show up at the event can also be contacted by telephone to determine the reason and, if appropriate, arrange for them to attend a subsequent event or meet a company representative.

Response handling

The use of a telephone number as a mechanism for customers and prospects to respond to advertisements and direct mail has been growing rapidly in recent years. This is thanks partly to the proliferation of credit cards and to reduced cost or free telephone calls through 0345 and 0800 numbers (*see* 'Telephone services', pages 63–73). Companies advertising in this way benefit from speed and convenience for the caller, striking while their interest is still high. Orders can be taken over the telephone and at the same time secondary objectives can be pursued, such as up-selling or gathering market data. Where information has been sent in response to enquiries, contacts should be followed up after an appropriate interval to gauge their potential, try to convert the enquiries to sales, or at least to show continued interest. Follow-up activities are equally as important as the advertisement. Every call provides an opportunity for promoting the organisation and establishing a profitable business relationship.

Public offers of shares in national industries, such as British Gas, the water authorities and regional electricity companies, have used the response line mechanism with great success; Firstdirect, the 24–hour home banking division of Midland Bank, relied heavily on this method; motor manufacturers have advertised telephone numbers to provide callers with information on their nearest dealer, and to arrange a test drive at a convenient time and location.

A telephone response line can also be used as part of a customer care programme by publicising the 'phone number of a product advice/ technical support centre, for example in instruction manuals. This provides reassurance to customers and, if they need to make a call, quicker resolution of any problems they experience. The result is a happier customer and one who is more likely to deal with the company again. ICL, the computer company, has a team of telephone diagnosticians to deal with fault reports from customers. Using a sophisticated computerised diagnostic tool, they can check whether a fault does exist – since many calls are due to users' lack of knowledge. If there is a fault, the diagnosis ensures that an engineer arrives at the customer's premises with the right parts.

In situations where there is an urgent need to recall products, or provide replacement parts, an advertisement with a telephone number provides a means to rectify the problem quickly and allay concern among customers, distributors, retailers or anyone else affected.

The effectiveness of many of these applications relies upon a combination of factors, each of which is essential to success. These include the type of offer being made, the seriousness of the enquiry (which is encouraged by accurate targeting), a rapid response to the call (for example the despatch of a brochure) and professional handling of the call (for example the ability to recognise a sales opportunity or give appropriate advice).

Direct sales and account servicing

A field sales force is a company's most expensive resource and the cost has increased to such an extent that most companies have had to reduce the size of their sales team and/or boost their efficiency. The first option carries the danger of not providing adequate cover, while individual efficiency can only be increased to a certain extent. Telephone marketing provides a number of solutions both for increasing sales force efficiency and for enabling the company to provide the same cover with a smaller sales force, while still ensuring effective customer service and customer contact.

Lead generation and qualification

In an ideal situation, a sales team will only be visiting people who have a need for the company's products or services and therefore will be receptive to the sales message. Lead generation consists of telephone screening leads and establishing buying potential. The source of leads may be a bought-in list of prospects, contacts from incoming enquiries and coupon responses, or any other source where their value as potential customers is not known.

The telephone is the only way to screen and grade leads accurately, apart from expensive face-to-face contact. It is also immediate, which is particularly important if the prospects have shown an interest by contacting the company. By grading the contacts, future sales and marketing activities can be prioritised to ensure efficient use of the resources available. Leads can be graded into three groups, requiring different follow up:

- those with an immediate need, or key account customers – immediate action, for example setting up an appointment with a sales person;

- those with an interest in purchasing, but not immediately, or medium-sized account holders – a customer service-type call plus mail follow-up;

- those with an interest in purchasing in six months or so – contact again prior to the likely purchase date, having told them to expect a call.

Lead qualification, which is often combined with lead generation, assesses the immediate sales potential of each contact and agrees with them the next action, for example an appointment with a member of the sales team. It is important that the qualifying criteria are clearly established and agreed, for example companies which are suitably large in terms of budget or number of employees. Using the telephone to generate qualified leads increases the available selling time of the sales team dramatically. Combined with appointment booking, it can increase their productivity by as much as 20 per cent.

Appointment making/diary management

If telephone marketers book qualified appointments the field sales force can spend their time more profitably – in selling and looking for new business. A by-product of this application is valuable sales management information, such as accurate monitoring of the results of each team member's sales appointments and regional variation in market response. For example, one office equipment supplier used an agency to book qualified appointments for its sales force in two regions of the UK, and expected a 15 per cent conversion rate (calls to appointments). The agency achieved 23 per cent, with the appointments resulting in £½ million worth of sales and securing an annual revenue of nearly £1m.

Servicing small, medium-sized and marginal accounts

Regular calls by the sales force to these accounts are generally unnecessary. It is far more cost-effective for them to concentrate on key accounts and new business, and use a trained telephone marketing team to service other accounts. One caller can achieve perhaps 30–40 sales contacts per day, depending on the complexity of the sale, the time taken to reach decision-makers and so on, compared with perhaps 4–6 per day for field sales personnel.

The telephone is also an ideal medium where, for some reason, such as a holiday or illness, the regular sales person is unable to visit customers. Although not necessarily resulting in a sale, a telephone call will reassure customers that their business is still valued and help dissuade them from looking elsewhere for a supplier.

Servicing key accounts

Although the sales force will almost invariably handle key accounts in person, telephone calls to major customers in between visits can provide ideal support. Such calls provide an opportunity to respond to any interim needs of the customer, reflect the high priority given them by the company and help to prepare both sides for sales visits in order to ensure that the outcome is mutually beneficial.

Reactivating lapsed or neglected accounts

The most productive prospects are likely to be previous customers who, for some reason, no longer buy from the company. Whatever the reason – whether a *faux pas* by the company, sale of the business, a change in buying policy, poaching by a competitor, dissatisfaction with the product – a telephone call is an inexpensive way to identify the reason for the lapse, if it is not known, and to restimulate interest. A mailshot, perhaps informing them of a special promotion or free trial offer, is an ideal way of opening this dialogue.

Similarly, small revenue or irregular customers often get neglected during the pursuit of new business and the servicing of major accounts. Keeping these customers is vital and there is always the possibility of them increasing their business as they grow or develop.

Customer care and loyalty building

It costs many times more to acquire a new customer than it does to keep an existing one, but it is all too easy to neglect even large revenue customers between purchases. Regular telephone contact is the most cost-effective way for companies to let their customers know they 'care' and every opportunity should be taken to build and maintain their loyalty. There are many opportunities to use both inbound and outbound calls where customer care is either a secondary or a 'disguised' objective, for example:

- *customers phoning to* enquire about other products or services, check stock availability, enquire about product specifications or suitability, complain or report problems, or query a transaction, perhaps delivery or an invoice;
- *the company phoning to* ensure customer satisfaction with a product or service, identify what new or improved products or services the customer would like, or issue an invitation to an event.

The telephone is more personal than mail and enables an immediate response to customer needs – customer care-type calls can often result in additional sales. It can also be cheaper, when all the costs of receiving and replying to mail are weighed.

Soliciting new customers/prospecting

Calls made to prospects chosen at random from the telephone directory, for example by replacement window companies, continue to tarnish the image of telephone marketing in the minds of consumers. However, cold calling can be carried out professionally and cost-effectively by telephone – it simply involves making the right offer to the right people at the right time.

The telephone, integrated into direct selling activities, is highly flexible. Every call can be tailored to make a personal approach to each contact, establishing and building individual business relationships. Telephone activity can also be increased or decreased quickly, according to need, to ensure that the best use is made of resources, for example stepping up lead generation for the sales force during unexpectedly quiet periods. Targeting is the key to success. The database should be updated and analysed constantly to ensure that resources are allocated in the most efficient way.

In summary, using the telephone for direct sales and sales support enables companies to maintain a high level of contact with customers and more accurately to measure, as well as reduce, the cost of sales. Customers also benefit from the speed and greater convenience, for example a quicker response when stocks are low. According to a 1989 report commissioned by Datapoint (UK)*, companies can increase the productivity of their sales force by more than one-third by providing in-house telephone marketing support. Table 2.2 shows the comparative costs of maintaining field sales and telephone marketing personnel.

Shareholder communications

The late 1980s saw an explosion in takeovers and acquisitions in the UK, when not even the most stable of companies were immune from hostile bids. The threat is now likely to increase throughout Europe and could reach fever pitch as a result of the dramatic political changes in Eastern Europe and the advent of the Single European Market. The US and the Far East have already shown their eagerness to establish a presence in Europe through acquisitions and mergers. European companies are following the same route as a way of protecting their market share, making their national brands more international, and capitalising on the expanding market.

In the US, where the threat of takeover is almost commonplace, companies have developed highly sophisticated shareholder communications programmes as a way of reducing their vulnerability. Shareholders are contacted regularly on issues which may influence how they would vote on matters affecting the company, with the telephone playing an important role in combination with direct mail and media advertising. Private shareholders are seen to be equally as important as the large institutional investors, since their collective vote can often determine the balance of power.

Even though there are telephone marketing agencies offering

---

* *Telephone Marketing vs Direct Sales Force Costs*, by Melanie Howard, August 1989. A report commissioned by Datapoint (UK) Ltd.

Table 2.2 Comparison of telephone marketer and direct sales personnel costs

Sales person	*Costs per annum (£)*
Direct:	
Basic salary	17,500
Plus NI and pension	5,000
On-target commission	10,000
Car (inc depreciation etc)	5,500
Expenses (travel and entertainment)	5,000
Perks, inc BUPA and life assurance	2,500
	£45,500
Indirect:	
Management time, accommodation, secretarial support, heating, lighting, recruitment, training, stationery, photocopying	7,000
TOTAL	**£52,500**
Telephone marketer	*Costs per annum (£)*
Direct:	
Salary	12,000
Plus NI and pension	2,400
On-target commission	3,500
Perks (BUPA etc)	2,500
	£20,400
Indirect:	
Clerical support, management time, accommodation, heating, stationery, office supplies	8,500
TOTAL	**£28,900**

Source: *Telephone Marketing vs Direct Sales Force Costs*, by Melanie Howard, August 1989. A report commissioned by Datapoint (UK) Ltd. Reprinted with permission.

expertise in shareholder communications, this is still a highly under-valued and under-used application. While many companies now recognise the power of the telephone in gaining and keeping customers, few seem to view shareholder communications in the same light. Yet, in proportion, shareholders have more power to determine the future of the company.

The telephone is the ideal complement to direct mail and media advertising. Valuable information can be obtained – such as opinions on corporate strategy, direction and takeovers – at the same time as delivering or reinforcing corporate messages, and quickly and effectively answering queries and allaying fears. Maintaining an accurate database of shareholders (for example the number and type of shares held, and the level of past and pledged support) enables communications to be highly personalised. When the need arises, the company can quickly contact its most influential supporters by telephone, delivering an important message and gauging reactions. In some situations, such as the time constraints on takeover bids (see Table 2.3), speed may be vital.

The telephone has many other similar applications, for example inviting key shareholders to an emergency general meeting or eliciting proxy votes, or building a database of high-potential investors prior to share flotations. However, there are strict laws in the UK governing shareholder communications of this type. In the case of takeovers, for example, all aspects of the campaign have to be passed by the Takeover Panel. Telephone scripts and any literature sent out must be vetted carefully to ensure that the campaign complies with the various regulations, for example the City Code on Takeovers, Mergers and Substantial Acquisitions and the Financial Services Act (1986) (both examined in Chapter 10). Even so, as companies recognise the increasing need to protect themselves from predators, the telephone is likely to become a more familiar element in corporate communications with investors.

Crisis management

The number of consumer scares in the UK appeared to reach an unprecedented level in 1989, exaggerated, no doubt, by widespread media coverage. Salmonella in eggs, listeria in pâté and other chilled foods, glass in baby food, contaminated drinking water and, more recently, BSE ('mad cow disease') all raised public alarm and led to

Table 2.3 Example of using the telephone for shareholder communications

Communications during the bid period		
Day	Stage of bid	Action
	Announcement	Initial strategy formulated/discussed
0	Offer document posted	
1	Shareholders able to accept bid	Research reaction to bid
14	Deadline for defence	Analyse shareholder register
21	First closing date and disclosure of acceptances	
30	All defence documents presented may withdraw	Commence calling Open helpline
42	Shareholders who have accepted offer	
46	Final bid (predator purchases more than 30%)	Recall 'undecided' shareholders, latest
57		calling completed by day 57
60	Bid declared unconditional or it will lapse	

Source: *The Direct Communications PORTFOLIO*, The Decisions Group, 1990.

calls for tighter controls by government and manufacturers/producers. At the same time, there was widespread criticism that these events either should not have been allowed to happen or action should have been taken earlier to minimise the danger to consumers.

There is no doubt that a consumer scare, particularly when reinforced by bad press, can have a disastrous effect. Sales of Perrier water, for example, plummetted after the benzene contamination incident. Months later, world sales were reported at still only 60 per cent of their pre-scare level – with some retailers refusing to stock the product. Media coverage can often compound, or even create, consumer fears when they do not carry the full story, such as in the case of reporting the findings of the latest health studies. Take the case of polyunsaturated margarines. Despite the volume of evidence showing the health benefits of a greater proportion of polyunsaturated fats in the diet, on one occasion controversy arose leading to bad press coverage and it was left to manufacturers to present the positive health aspects to consumers.

Corporate crisis management strategies are now relatively common in the UK, but the telephone is not usually an integral element of the communications strategy. In the US, however, it has become quite common for companies to call on the expertise of telephone marketing agencies to field calls from worried consumers, and to make calls to distributors, retail outlets and others who can help minimise the damage to sales when such an incident happens.

Although its use in the UK is not widespread, there are at least two agencies which offer a specialist service for telephone-based crisis management, either handling calls themselves or setting up an in-house operation, and either providing their own staff or training company staff. There have been several examples of hot-lines set up to allay consumer fears. The Foodline, for example, was set up in 1989. Funded by a consortium of supermarkets, it is staffed 24 hours a day by specially trained operators who can answer questions about food contamination. An example of how a helpline can be used is given in the Comet case study in Chapter 11 (*see* pages 427–33).

Communication by telephone stands a much better chance of satisfying individuals' immediate needs than any other medium. Whether they wish to seek information or advice, ask for replacement of faulty goods or simply vent their anger, a dedicated telephone number provides direct access to people who are specially trained to create the best possible image for the company.

In the event of a crisis, telephone activity can begin within hours, provided contingency strategies and tactics have been planned (or within days if an inbound number is being advertised). The immediate questions that need to be answered in a crisis situation include the following.

- Who is affected and how many are they (for example customers, wholesalers and retailers)?

- What impact will this situation have on the company image?

- What action is required for each group affected?

- Is there capacity for existing resources to cope adequately with this demand?

- What specific messages need to be delivered?

- What is the best way to communicate these messages (ie inbound/ outbound calling, media advertising, direct mail)?

- What are the best tactics for each group affected (for example pre-emptive calls explaining the problem and offering to rectify it; a hotline number advertised in the media; personal calls by the sales force; agency or in-house)?

- Who should be contacted first (for example the largest revenue earners, key distributors)?

Crisis management by telephone also provides the opportunity to gather additional information for the database, for example market opinion and trends, thus reducing the real cost burden. Once the immediate crisis has passed, 'normal' telephone marketing calls made by the company can be used to help rebuild confidence. If business has been lost, these groups should be specifically targeted with the most appropriate sales and marketing activities.

With increased emphasis on customer service, combined with the rising incidence of product tampering and a highly reactive media, the telephone is a natural component of any corporate crisis management strategy.

Fund/awareness raising

The telephone has proved a very effective medium for fund raising, whether by charities or other institutions, and is becoming more popular in the UK since the relaxation of restrictions on their advertising. Donations may be made directly or they may come via the sale of special goods or tickets to events, and calls can double as a publicity tool highlighting recent activities and successes. This application is popular in the US, where it is used to call and thank large donors, and to solicit donations from existing and potential donors. Inbound calls can be encouraged by offering a free call or one charged at the local rate.

The provision of dedicated inbound numbers for raising awareness of company products and services is also becoming more popular in the UK and has a variety of applications. One major record retailer, for example, has advertised a number for consumers to call and listen to a selection of music from hit albums. Similarly, a dedicated line could be used to provide recorded information on products and services – perhaps those which are currently available on special offer. With the growing awareness of special telephone services (for example Freefone and 0800), and increasingly sophisticated technology for providing information services, this application could become one of the biggest growth areas in telephone marketing.

The applications of telephone marketing are being continuously refined and expanded. The BDMA survey, which provided a snapshot of the UK industry in 1988, revealed that companies still had a long way to go in fully exploiting the potential of the telephone as a marketing tool (Table 2.4). Awareness is increasing, however, and with more and more companies investing in telephone marketing, both with agencies and in-house, the rate of development of applications is likely to increase.

The single European market and 1992

Competition will increase dramatically, though not necessarily immediately, once the remaining barriers to trade have come down across Europe by the end of 1992. While much has already been written and discussed about the opportunities this offers businesses, the most immediate action required is to implement strategies for protecting their existing market share. Many of the telephone applications already described in this chapter have a major role to play.

In terms of capitalising on the opportunities, by 1992 there will be an estimated 200 million plus telephones in European homes and offices, and this will be one of the most cost-effective ways of penetrating these markets. For companies who do not have the resources to establish local offices, or who need to allocate those resources elsewhere, it will probably be the only cost-effective method. With the possibility of international call costs from the UK

Table 2.4   Prompted in-house use of the telephone in marketing applications

How UK organisations were using telephone marketing in 1988		
	Overall (52% of sample)	*Using dedicated, trained staff (32% of sample)*
Outbound		
Appointment setting	72%	66%
Order taking (including re-selling, up-selling, cross-selling)	60%	62%
Lead generation/screening/ qualification (including list building)	38%	47%
Traffic generation (retail/ showrooms/exhibitions etc)	19%	16%
Publication subscription renewal	13%	12%
Membership renewal and reactivation	12%	14%
Account/customer servicing (including customer care programmes)	63%	58%
Customer database extension	37%	39%
Prospect database building	32%	38%
Credit jogging	60%	43%
Charity/political donations	22%	24%
Market research/sales surveys	9%	7%
Inbound		
Order taking (including up-selling, cross-selling and response conversion)	78%	73%
Brochure fulfilment/literature requests	61%	50%
Arranging appointments	86%	59%
Dealer location/traffic generation	26%	22%
Customer care hotline (problem line)	49%	54%
Customer enquiries (general)	91%	83%
Database building/updating	35%	36%
Credit servicing	41%	33%
Charity donations	15%	9%

Source: *Survey of the UK Telephone Marketing Industry (1988)*, prepared by the Telephone Marketing Committee of the British Direct Marketing Association, 1990. Reprinted with permission.
Sample: Overall, 52% of the 509 organisations interviewed claimed to use telephone marketing (ie planned and controlled); 32% claimed to use dedicated, trained and supervised staff for telephone marketing activities.

falling (*see* page 380), telephone marketing could become an even more attractive proposition.

There are many hurdles to be overcome in reaching across Europe by telephone, even though the potential rewards are high. The first step will be for companies to identify the different markets for their products or services; this is not straightforward at present, because of the varying styles of market research in different countries (although the telephone can play a role here). Then companies will have thoroughly to research the cultural differences impinging on sales promotion, and either train or recruit staff with the appropriate sales and language skills. Language training schools in the UK have already responded by offering specialist business language courses tailored to different industries and markets. Companies will also have to be knowledgeable about local legislation governing telephone marketing, such as data protection, and national good practice initiatives.

Telephone marketing agencies, whose business is expanding through-out Western Europe, are working to provide a service to clients which removes many of these headaches for them. The UK agency Telemarketing Link (TML), for example, launched a multi-lingual service in September 1989, recruiting French, German, Italian, Spanish and Dutch-speaking staff, to help companies who do not have the in-house resources to take advantage of the international opportunities. Several other leading agencies also offer a multi-lingual service. The Decisions Group, together with two other UK agencies, Merit Direct and McColl McGregor, have taken another approach and have established plans for a pan-European strategic telephone marketing service. Campaigns would be co-ordinated from the UK, where all the planning would be done and the necessary support systems established. The information required to run the campaign would then be sent over the telecommunications network to an agency, or agencies, in each target country, who would make modifications, if required, to ensure that it ran successfully in their own country. Each agency would send the results of the campaign back to the UK to be collated and analysed. This approach provides more comprehensive support in overcoming the barriers arising from the varying cul-tures, business practices and legislation in different countries. Several leading agencies have, and others will be establishing, branches in other European countries, or signing reciprocal deals with native agencies, to help clients take advantage of the opportunities in Europe.

Research from the Colorgraphic Group* confirms a growing interest in agency-based international outbound campaigns. The demand for international contact lists is also growing, although this is coming mainly from the USA where companies are particularly anxious not to be excluded from the potentially lucrative European market.

A service which would prove useful in penetrating European markets is the use of an International 0800, enabling customers across Europe to telephone free direct to a central point in the UK. However, this is an expensive option because of the need to have staff with the appropriate language skills on call almost around the clock. One solution which several agencies are exploring is the use of computer voice-recognition systems. These can be programmed to respond in the required languages and can overcome the language barriers for at least some telephone marketing applications.

All types of pan-European marketing face enormous difficulties, but direct marketing is particularly vulnerable. The prospect of European data protection legislation, examined in Chapter 10, means that companies could be restricted to contacting only those people with whom they have had prior contact. Post-1992, we are likely to see a period of rapid growth in international telephone marketing, but it will be those companies who have already implemented strategies for winning customers and encouraging their loyalty, thus side-stepping restrictive legislation, who will benefit most.

Telephone services

The introduction of two special telephone services by British Telecom (BT) in 1985, began a revolution in inbound telephone marketing which has now become the biggest single area of industry growth. The two services, LinkLine and Callstream, use special telephone number prefixes to denote different call charge structures. Subscribers can advertise numbers with these prefixes to encourage inbound calls, which are either free, subsidised or charged to the caller at a premium rate. More recently, BT has introduced Advanced LinkLine to offer even greater flexibility for inbound call handling.

---

* *Direct Response – The Market Map*, a quantitative analysis of the UK direct response industry, 1990. Commissioned from Research Associates by the Colorgraphic Group.

In this section we look at the facilities provided by these different services, while the costs, waiting times and criteria for deciding which service to use are examined in Chapter 4 (*see* pages 175–80).

LinkLine

The prefixes used in this service are 0800 (a free call) and 0345 (charged at the local rate), and it is increasingly common to see advertisements bearing these numbers. Even people who feel highly aggrieved about the quality of products or services they have bought will often feel it is too much trouble to search out an address and write, or find a telephone number and persevere until they get through to the right person. There is even less chance, therefore, of customers contacting a company to place an order or to obtain product advice or information, unless it is made extremely easy and convenient for them. Costs are easily accountable and call volumes can provide a measure of advertising effectiveness. When used to provide product advice or technical support, they can often save a considerable proportion of service call-outs by resolving problems during the call.

Whatever reason a company has for generating incoming calls, advertising a LinkLine number provides a solution. To accommodate those people who may not wish to use the telephone, there is the option to add a coupon and/or a Freepost address. Users of the service have the option either of receiving calls on their normal exchange lines or having a dedicated line.

One stated purpose of LinkLine was to help small businesses compete on more equal terms with larger companies who could afford to maintain local offices. However, they are of greater significance and value to both large and small companies. LinkLine numbers were generating around 12 million calls a year by 1991 and BT predicted that this would double in the following two years.

LinkLine 0800 (Toll-free) Callers can dial direct from anywhere in the UK, free of charge, using numbers with the 0800 prefix, while call costs are borne by the renter. Despite the cost, especially when appealing offers generate a large response, this service can prove very cost-effective by providing high visibility and a large number of contacts for future use.

LinkLine 0345 Callers can dial direct from anywhere in the UK for the price of a local call using an 0345 number, and the renter pays some of the call charge. Providing an 0345 number avoids customers or prospects being deterred by long distance charges. The cost per call to the renter is lower than with LinkLine 0800, although it is currently much less widely used than that service.

BT has divided the UK into eight zones for the LinkLine 0800 and 0345 services, and calls made within each zone can be routed to one or more convenient locations, for example where calls can be handled most efficiently, even though one telephone number has been advertised nationally. There are three different LinkLine price options (examined in Chapter 4), and two of these enable companies to use their normal telephone lines. This means that the lines carrying inbound LinkLine calls can also be used for normal inbound and outbound traffic, as well as providing access to the full range of features available through the new digital exchanges, for example call forwarding.

The most effective LinkLine numbers are likely to be those which are easily remembered, and this is where telephone marketing agencies, as potentially large users of the service (*see* page 177), can sometimes offer added value to clients.

Advanced LinkLine

This new service, launched by BT at the end of January 1990, uses the same two prefixes as LinkLine (to which users must first subscribe), but provides far greater flexibility in call handling. It offers a range of features enabling companies to choose exactly how incoming calls are routed. These include:

- routeing each call to the office nearest the caller – using the same prefix, which can be advertised nationally, different services can be provided in each area according to local market needs;

- outside business hours (at night, over the weekend or both) all calls can be automatically re-routed to one office;

- incoming calls can be automatically shared among offices in proportion to the load each one can handle, or routed according to a pre-set pattern by time of day or day of the week;

- if lines at one office are engaged, calls can either be held until a line is free, or automatically re-routed to a free line elsewhere;

- calls can be answered with a recorded message offering a choice of service – using a dial tone telephone callers simply press a number to select the service they require and the call is routed to the appropriate department; this facility enables different aspects of the business (for example sales, service, enquiries) to be integrated and serviced under a single telephone number;

- callers' messages can be recorded and retrieved later;

- pre-set plans to cope with specific telephone needs (for example during an emergency, after a particularly successful promotion or a change in distribution policy) can be implemented within about 30 minutes.

These features further enhance the cost-effectiveness of telephone marketing operations, for both large and small companies, by making best use of available resources. BT provides a consultancy service to analyse how a company handles its incoming calls and recommends appropriate Advanced LinkLine features.

Callstream

Callstream, using numbers prefixed with 0898, is a premium rate service whereby callers pay a higher call charge (currently 34p per minute cheap rate and 45p at all other times). Part of the income is retained by BT and the remainder goes to the line renter or service provider. It is used primarily by companies providing information services (usually recorded), via the telephone, for which callers are paying through their telephone bill.

BT offers both a basic facility, whereby they supply only the network service and a managed service, where the line renter supplies the messages and BT operates the answering system. Status reports are provided for both services, providing a day-by-day analysis of the number of calls received and the revenue due to the line renter, which are compiled and sent once a week. A managed service is also available on a bureau basis from a number of companies, some addresses of which are given in Appendix C. BT also offers a special facility within the managed service called the Mass Access Service. This enables a line renter to run high-profile campaigns, generating a large volume of responses, where up to 500 lines may be required for a short time.

There has been an explosion in the use of 0898 numbers and

they generate enormous revenues (a projected £260m per annum by 1993). However, they have not been without their problems. Consumer outcry over enormous bills run up by children calling various premium rate services caused BT to 'pull the plug' on providers of certain services. These have now been reinstated, but all service providers are now governed by a very strict code of practice (*see* Chapter 10, pages 386–7).

The majority of services currently provided on 0898 numbers are not strictly telephone marketing applications, except in the sense of generating revenue for the service provider. They range from up-to-the minute share prices and cricket scores to overtly sex-oriented recorded messages and live 'chatlines'. However, they do have valuable applications in supporting and promoting products and services, for example after-sales service, competitions and quizzes, list building and test marketing, particularly when combined with computer voice-recognition systems. Competitions and quizzes are probably the most popular current applications; callers have the opportunity to 'win' a prize or free gift and are therefore less deterred by the cost of the call. The provision of information on products, services or any other topic which can promote the company in the marketplace, is likely to grow in the future.

The revenue obtained from the 0898 services helps to offset some of the cost of the promotion. Incorporating secondary objectives, such as market research, helps further to make it more cost-effective. Computer voice recognition is being used increasingly in this type of application, bringing further cost reductions; the element of interactivity also supposedly increases caller interest. Such is the potential of this type of application that there are now sales promotion companies which specialise in interactive computer tele-phone promotions.

International 0800

This is the international equivalent of LinkLine 0800. Callers can dial direct to the UK from abroad without going through the operator (many other countries have similar services using different prefixes). One number is given from each country; calls are free to the caller from most countries, although in some they may have to pay a nominal charge of no more than the cost of a local call. This is a huge incentive to make contact with a company abroad, providing the offer is right.

Paying for international calls may sound highly expensive, but it is a way of promoting the company abroad without the high cost of maintaining local offices, and it helps to create the impression of an 'international' organisation. It can also be used to test new overseas markets to determine whether or not it is worthwhile setting up abroad or appointing agents.

FreeFone

With this service, callers dial 100 for the operator and, when the call is answered, ask for 'FreeFone Joe', or whatever name the company wishes to use. The operator then connects the caller to the company. These calls are free of charge to the caller. The time and place of origin of calls are logged by the operator and a report sent to the service renter, providing valuable marketing information such as differences in regional response and the impact of local advertising. Two other advantages are that it is generally much easier for callers to remember a name than a telephone number, and it serves a branding function, by incorporating the company or product name.

Call Forwarding

This is another BT service which enables companies to publicise a local telephone number, without the need to have a local answering facility or one which is permanently staffed, and have calls automatically re-directed, when necessary, to wherever there are staff to answer them. Calls are automatically intercepted and callers hear a recorded message explaining that the call is being re-routed. This enables companies to provide their customers with a local contact number and ensure that their calls are always answered with the minimum of inconvenience to them.

Mercury Communications, currently the only other major service provider in the UK telecommunications market, already has some services equivalent to those from BT and is planning to extend its range. Its premium rate service, for example, uses the prefixes 0881 and 0839, while toll-free numbers commence with 0500. The company introduced a new service in January 1991, providing a 'hotline' feature on Mercury payphones in UK post offices. Five extra buttons on the telephones can be rented, branded with a company name, and used by consumers to make a free call direct to the company. Electronic posters have been in use at post offices for some time, and companies therefore have the opportunity to advertise and provide a telephone direct response mechanism on a very local basis. If the hotline feature is successful it will be extended to all Mercury payphones.

As other players enter the UK telecommunications market the range and sophistication of services on offer is likely to rise, while costs will fall as a result of increased competition. Existing services already greatly enhance the range and flexibility of options in applying telephone marketing, and the future can only bring greater opportunities.

Computerised systems

The application of information technology to assist telephone marketing operations is still in its infancy, but it is advancing rapidly. Even so, some of the systems currently available are sophisticated and offer wide-ranging benefits and opportunities, including improved productivity, greater flexibility, better management information and control, and new and improved profit-generating services.

Computer Assisted Telephone Interviewing (CATI)

The introduction of computer software applications programmes specifically designed to aid telephone interviewing is largely responsible for the rapid increase in the sophistication of telephone marketing. There is a growing range of good programmes on the market, each supplier offering a slightly different product but all providing the basic features required to run a successful telephone marketing operation. As an example, the features offered by one such package, TOPCAT™, distributed in Europe by Norsk Data Ltd, are shown in Table 2.5.

Software for telephone marketing is becoming increasingly sophisticated, with a trend towards programmes which can be more easily tailored by users to integrate and co-ordinate all their sales and marketing activities. However, computerisation is not the key to making a telephone marketing operation successful, although it can greatly enhance the efficiency of an already well-run operation (for example, it has been estimated that automatic dialling can result in a

Table 2.5 Key features of TOPCAT – typical computer-assisted telephone marketing software

Key Features of TOPCAT

Outbound and inbound call management.
Set up and maintain calling schedules.
Automatic call selection, dial and re-scheduling, eg at a time more convenient for the recipient.
Instant on−line access to full customer histories and a library of reference (eg sales) literature.
Updating customer information during calls.
Checking a company's calling history.
Script management:
  • full and partial scripting; automatic prompted scripting, eg for less experienced callers
  • script creation, testing and editing.
Database design, creation and maintenance:
  • define data structures and screen layout
  • import and export data in any format, eg from and to main database
  • new file creation
  • data entry and updating
  • list merging and purging (deduplication)
  • incorporate market information
  • coding, eg by customer/prospect profile, area, customer history, call results
  • list records meeting specified criteria
  • on-line search facilities, eg local dealer location
  • automatic lead generation
  • lead tracking
  • market research.
Automatic mailshot creation and maintenance, eg personalised communication and automatic follow-up.
Supervising a number of projects simultaneously.
Re-scheduling projects to accommodate changing workload.
Password control with different levels of access.
Real-time monitoring and measurement, eg caller performance by individual and team.
Sales territory planning and allocation.
Automatic sales force diary management.
Sales force performance and target monitoring – continuously, weekly, monthly.
Reporting, eg
  • call outcome
  • caller performance and call progress by individual and team
  • campaign results
  • successful contact rate by customer, sales person, area, time of day
  • unsuccessful contacts by reason
  • *ad hoc* report design.
Electronic mail.
Add-on modules for sales order entry and stock control.

Reprinted with the permission of Norsk Data Ltd.

25–40 per cent increase in operator productivity by improving speed and avoiding dialling errors).

Automatically Dialled, Recorded Message Players (ADRMPs)

ADRMPs automatically dial numbers on a contact list and play a recorded message when the call is answered. Currently these systems are not approved for use in the UK, although the BDMA's *Telephone Marketing Guidelines* (*see* page 385) do not exclude their use, provided they are introduced by a human operator, thus giving contacts the opportunity to refuse the call. If, and when, these systems are approved there undoubtedly would be very strict controls on their application.

Automatic or Power Dialling

Although automatic dialling from contact lists held on a company's computer is a valuable feature of modern telephone marketing software, systems are also available which will automatically generate and dial telephone numbers at random or in sequence, ie new contacts. BT, the Office of Fair Trading (OFT) and the BDMA's Telephone Committee are opposed to the use of such equipment.

The OFT, in a 1984 report on telephone selling, said it would remain 'strongly opposed to the introduction of automatic dialling equipment in the UK unless there are adequate facilities to enable people to avoid receiving such calls should they so wish'. The BDMA's *Telephone Marketing Guidelines* reflect these sentiments, suggesting that, 'sales and marketing calls should not be generated by random or sequential dialling manually or by computer'. However, since accurate targeting is a key feature of good telephone marketing, these systems, choosing contacts at random, actually have no benefits to offer the telephone marketing professional.

Voice Recognition Systems

The technology for recognising and processing the human voice is already available, although there is a limited range of systems available. However, computer voice recognition is on the verge of a major breakthrough and the next few years are likely to see increasingly sophisticated systems and applications. Greater accuracy and flexibility, easier programming and improved quality will be the major areas of improvement. The technology required for recognising telephone dial tones is less sophisticated, but most research and development appears to be concentrating on dual-purpose systems.

The application of these systems can be divided broadly into three areas:

- *audiotex*, utilising the premium rate service to provide information services, such as for entertainment, live sports commentary and interactive services;

- *transaction processing*, such as credit card purchases, including theatre seat or holiday booking, and home banking;

- *telephone marketing*, for sales support and promotion, such as order taking, market research, list building and hotline support.

Early commercially available voice recognition systems had limited capabilities, for example recognising single digit numbers, 'yes' and 'no' and a limited number of other words, or reacting to any sound made by the caller to select alternatives presented by the computer. However, the technology is becoming more sophisticated and research is well advanced on systems which will be able to simulate relatively complex conversations with callers. This has great significance for telephone marketing, both in terms of cost reduction and the range of applications. The specifications and facilities offered by current voice interactive computer systems vary. As an example, however, the features offered by the Hi-Call system from Telsis Limited, based in Hampshire, UK, include:

- up to 30 simultaneous live lines, 1,000 programmes or services, 32,000 announcement files of almost 100 hours total duration;

- single keystroke programming;

- voice detection, dial tone and speech recognition options;

- remote update and system management via telephone;

- caller recording, with powerful management and information downloading facilities;

- up to 30 live inputs simultaneously, such as for continuous sports commentaries or 'interrupts' like news bulletins at pre-set times;

- connection to databases or other computer systems;

- full management information.

There are a number of agencies developing telephone marketing applications for voice processing. Estimates on cost savings and potential applications vary. One agency estimates that the cost of an inbound campaign could be reduced by about 70 per cent, and that 60–70 per cent of such campaigns could be handled in this way. Although the latter figure appears extremely optimistic, it is predicted that applications using this technology could account for 10 per cent of the European telecommunications market by 1993.

These systems are expensive to buy and, in some applications, expensive to maintain. High-volume usage, in the right application, is therefore required to justify purchase. However, as systems become more sophisticated and costs eventually begin to fall, more companies are likely to find their application cost-effective.

Deciding how to apply telephone marketing

While telephone marketing offers many exciting opportunities, it can be far less cost-effective in achieving certain objectives than other sales and marketing activities. The greatest benefits are to be found in using the telephone as an integral part of the overall sales and marketing strategy, and capitalising on its specific benefits while avoiding applications where its weaknesses are emphasised. Deciding when and how to use it requires a careful consideration of what the organisation is trying to achieve, now and in the long term. Current activities and future objectives need to be analysed to identify whether, and where, the telephone could offer advantages over, or when combined with, other methods. This involves answering questions like the following.

- What are the company's current and future markets?

- How does/will the company communicate with these markets to achieve its various objectives?

- What are the current costs, for example of making a sale, or gaining a new customer?

- What are the costs likely to be for entering new markets?

- Could any of these costs be reduced by utilising the benefits of telephone marketing?

- Could the telephone provide additional information on contacts, compared with existing methods, which would make it more cost-effective?

- What are the opportunities for integrating it with other sales and marketing activities?

The 'ladder of loyalty' in Figure 2.2 shows the overall aim of using telephone marketing, or any sales or marketing activity, which is to establish and develop profitable relationships. Obviously this needs to be done in the most cost-efficient way, and the same detailed cost/

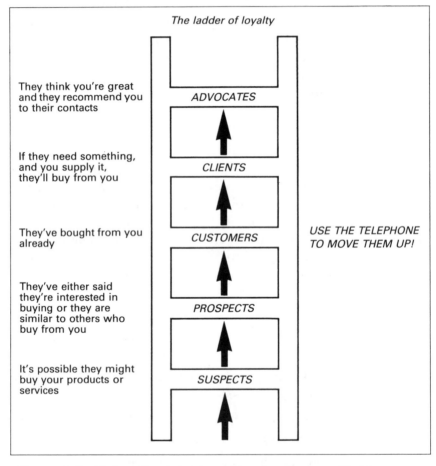

Figure 2.2 Using the telephone to develop profitable relationships (After the Loyalty Ladder developed by Murray Raphel and Ray Considine)

benefit analysis that goes into planning other activities should be applied to telephone marketing.

Cost is obviously a major consideration. Telephone contact with a switchboard operator may cost about £2, while with a decision-maker it escalates to £7–8 or more. However, in some situations there is no alternative to using the telephone:

- where the required level of contact with customers and prospects cannot be achieved in any other way;

- where no other method can effectively penetrate, for example remote areas;

- where immediate action is essential, for example product recall;

- where receipt of an urgent message has to be guaranteed;

- where the company has to create a local presence in order to break into a new market, but does not have the resources for large-scale media promotion.

Costs could still seem prohibitive, even when the telephone offers the only solution. But the flexibility of telephone communication means that secondary objectives can be incorporated to improve the cost/benefit ratio.

Perhaps the biggest single mistake made by companies inexperienced in telephone marketing is that they view it in isolation, often using it to solve an immediate problem and with little forward planning; there is no strategy and no opportunity for cross-fertilisation and synergy with other methods. Even when it is not combined directly with other marketing activities, such as direct mail, the telephone can yield valuable information to improve their efficiency, provided this is incorporated into the campaign objectives. Similarly, the complementary activity can improve the effectiveness of telephone marketing.

Telephone marketing has become highly sophisticated and expertise is required to optimise the benefits. Agencies are, quite naturally, eager to demonstrate these benefits to clients, and will usually suggest to those new to the medium that they 'test' the application with the agency. This brings the expertise of the agency to bear on the planning and execution, and provides the client with a taste of what they could possibly achieve in-house. In Chapter 3 we examine the role of agencies, their selection, and the pros and cons of using an agency or setting up in-house.

3

Agency or In-house?

Once a decision has been made to use a particular application of telephone marketing there is no simple answer to the question whether to employ an agency or to do it in-house. Both have their advantages and disadvantages which must be weighed up according to the needs and preferences of the organisation, the application, the resources required and those available.

The growing number of agencies in the UK and the rising expenditure on their services demonstrates the increasing level of interest in trying out telephone marketing. However, more and more companies are setting up in-house units. Having run campaigns with an agency and discovered the power of the medium, many decide that there are long-term advantages to developing a permanent in-house resource. Consequently, there are now many agencies which can provide comprehensive consultancy and training services to help companies establish a successful in-house operation with minimum risk to their investment and marketing effectiveness.

Choosing between an agency and in-house is not always an either/ or decision. Companies which have set up in-house may still employ an agency when they want to develop a new application. This ensures that the necessary expertise is available to optimise the success of the campaign, and provides a learning opportunity for the company. The efficiency and productivity of many in-house units is also maintained by the ongoing use of agency training resources. Similarly, if a company decides to establish or upgrade a marketing database, to be used in conjunction with telephone marketing, there are agencies that can help.

Deciding if and when to use an agency can be straightforward, or it may present a real dilemma. This chapter aims to make the decision easier, by examining the pros and cons of agency and in-house telephone marketing, the agency services available, the questions to be answered in selecting the right service and the right agency, and explaining how to get the best out of the agency that is chosen.

The role of telephone marketing agencies

The sophistication of telephone marketing is increasing rapidly and the specialists – the agencies – are at the forefront of developments. Inevitably, therefore, they play a key role in helping businesses to exploit the medium to its full potential.

The agency role has been expanding rapidly over the past five years. Established agencies have been capitalising on their experience of what it takes to set up and run a successful telephone marketing operation by offering additional services such as training, consultancy and database marketing. The BDMA survey in autumn 1988 revealed that the total UK agency revenue was about £60m per year, being £40m from telephone marketing and £20m from other services. These figures were expected to rise by 40 per cent by autumn 1989. As more and more companies set up in-house, the proportion of revenue gained from services other than telephone marketing is likely to increase, as will their diversity. And the marketplace is benefiting directly from these changes. Apart from the wider range of expertise available, agencies which are not totally dependent upon telephone marketing for their revenue are more able to provide genuinely unbiased advice on the best way to meet particular marketing objectives.

The following sections outline the four key areas in which agencies can provide a service, namely telephone marketing, database marketing, training and consultancy. Not all agencies offer all of these services, nor do all those that offer them have the same levels of expertise or resources.

Telephone marketing

In the early years of telephone marketing in the UK, when it was a relatively untried medium and few had invested in an in-house unit, agencies obviously provided the only resource for most companies. Now the situation is quite different. The BDMA survey revealed that UK agencies were making an estimated 14.4m telephone contacts per year which generated a revenue of £40m. This compares with a tentative estimate of £5bn expenditure on the full range of in-house telephone marketing activities.

The survey also revealed some notable differences in the nature of agency and in-house operations. Within agencies, for example:

- about 60 per cent of calls were outbound, 40 per cent inbound − nearly two-thirds of contacts were with prospects and the remainder with clients' existing customers;

- 68 per cent of contacts were business-to-business and 32 per cent consumers;

- about 80 per cent of contacts (both inbound and outbound) were concentrated within the three most popular applications − brochure fulfilment, appointment setting and lead generation;

- the most frequently offered outbound services were lead generation, appointment setting and market research;

- the most frequently offered inbound services were brochure fulfilment and customer enquiries.

The results of the survey of in-house telephone marketing were summarised in Table 2.4 (*see* page 61). Briefly, the picture looked like this:

- of the 509 organisations surveyed, 52 per cent spontaneously claimed to use the telephone in a planned and controlled way for marketing activities, of which 32 per cent claimed to use dedicated, trained and supervised staff, this being much more likely in larger organisations;

- other businesses accounted for the greater proportion of contacts, particularly for outbound applications − these were more likely to be existing customers rather than prospects (the reverse of the agencies);

- the most widely used outbound applications were appointment setting, account/customer servicing, order taking and credit jogging;

- the most widely used inbound applications were general customer enquiries, arranging appointments, order taking, brochure fulfilment and credit servicing.

These findings point to a basic difference in role between agencies and in-house units. Most agencies tend to play more of a supportive role, for example servicing one-off projects, solving immediate problems, and providing additional prospect and market information. In-house operations, on the other hand, tend to be concentrated on maintaining and servicing existing business.

Obviously this distinction is not complete. Some companies use agencies to help with the long-term, strategic development of their business. This happens especially where, despite a commitment to using telephone marketing in the long term, it is not cost-effective to set up in-house. Similarly, some in-house resources, particularly those which lack the full commitment and support of the management, may be used only on a tactical level, as and when there is an obvious and pressing need for telephone marketing, for example to provide leads for the sales force during otherwise 'quiet' periods.

The range and mix of telephone marketing services offered by agencies varies tremendously. Some deal almost exclusively with inbound calls, for example, while others deal with outbound, and some provide both. The same is true of business-to-business versus consumer calling and of manual versus computerised systems. The range of applications offered, described in Chapter 2, also varies. Some offer a broad range while others specialise in a select group. There are also an increasing number of agencies which are developing the expertise to specialise in particular vertical markets, such as finance and high technology, and in particular applications, such as crisis management and shareholder communications. Ancillary services, such as mailing fulfilment and large volume data entry, are also offered by some agencies, either directly or through subcontractors.

The first contact a company has with an agency is often when they are taking their first step into telephone marketing. Under these circumstances, the agency will probably want to explore telephone marketing in the broader context of the company's operations, not just the intended application. By understanding their short- and long-term objectives and marketing plans, the agency will be able to offer the company the benefit of their experience in exploiting the medium to the best advantage.

Most agencies will suggest testing a campaign prior to full 'roll-out'. Even companies with in-house resources will often use an agency to test new campaigns, particularly when it is something outside their experience. Testing has a number of benefits:

- agency expertise helps to achieve the maximum benefit, for example the ideal application and media combination;

- it demonstrates, at relatively low cost, whether or not the type of campaign will work, and provides suggestions on alternative ways of achieving the same objective;

- it helps to set staffing levels and to fine-tune the campaign, for example scripts and administrative systems;

- it provides an indication of call and conversion rates, costs per positive result or per call, and likely return on investment;

- it provides 'benchmark' results to measure and improve the efficiency of other campaigns;

- it requires relatively low commitment.

Many agencies offer a 'test package', which consists of a mini-campaign costing perhaps in the region of £4–6,000 for 100 hours of calling. The size of the test recommended varies with the complexity of the campaign and the number of elements to be tested, which could include, for example, lead sources, target markets, contact levels, marketing mix, the offer, the approach and timings. The cost of a test package from a good agency might cover the following.

Set-up Researching the target market and suitable lists; designing the campaign structure, the contact strategy (for example whether to call or mail first) and advising on integration with other media; a minimum training period for the callers working on the campaign, covering products/services, the company, its market and competitors; preparation of a script or framework for calls, a full list of features, benefits, unique selling points and common objections and how to counter them; producing documentation for recording contact information, and implementing information flow systems.

Management support A project manager to run the campaign and ensure that the client's objectives are achieved and quality standards are maintained; an account manager to provide daily feedback, if required, on campaign results and advise on the direction of the campaign; and the opportunity to visit the agency to meet the callers and listen to calls.

Calling A fixed number of calling hours.

Quality checking A team leader re-calling a percentage of calls to examine the results and ensure their complete accuracy; checking of all contact records for quality and minimum standards of information.

Reporting results A detailed report summarising and interpreting the campaign results and providing future guidelines and recommendations (*see* pages 350–1 for typical content).

Additional fees may be incurred for items such as list purchase, data entry, fax, photocopying and delivery.

The cost of a full campaign will obviously vary tremendously, depending on the particular application and its size. Example charge ranges for two applications are shown in Table 3.1. Where the agency has already tested the campaign, the costs for roll-out should be reduced proportionately to take account of the work already completed, for example design of the script and data capture document.

Before running a test or a full campaign an agency will want to ensure that client expectations are realistic. They will ask what it currently costs to obtain an order (or other positive result) using existing methods, and the client's target cost. They will be able to say, from experience, what call rates can be achieved for different applications, and the likely conversion rates of calls to positive results, and can judge whether the current or target costs can be realistically achieved or improved upon using telephone marketing. If the agency is unsure of the call rate they will generally suggest a range, although after running a test they will know what can be achieved.

One of the great benefits of using agencies is their ability to resource these services within hours. In order to accommodate the fluctuating demands of their clients, some agencies maintain a register of fully trained non-permanent staff who can be called upon at short notice. One agency, for example, made 5,000 calls for a client over a single weekend, having received only three hours' warning.

For companies which have a relatively short-term requirement for additional in-house resources or expertise, for example to cope with busy periods or with a crisis, or to develop and test new procedures, some agencies offer an on-site support service. Instead of the company having to recruit, or transfer, and train additional staff, the agency will provide skilled callers, supervisors and managers, at very short notice, to work at the client's premises. Where an agency has helped a company set up in-house, it can, if required, place one of its

Table 3.1 Example of UK agency charges (range) for an inbound and an outbound campaign

---

Example agency campaign charges (range, as at December 1990)

Inbound

AIM: To staff a bank of 0800 lines on a monthly basis. Taking name, address and telephone details and subsequently fulfilling these with a personalised letter and brochure.

Set-up fee to include design of script and data capture
document, briefing and training of staff. Booking of lines
(suggest a bank of 6 lines). One-off payment — £ 1,500–1,750

Handling fee @ £15–17.80 per hour per operator. Lines staffed
from 9am–9pm, Monday to Sunday = 84 hours per week per line
= 504 hours per week
= 2,016 hours per month
= @ £15–17.80 per hour - £30,240–35,884 per month
(otherwise 75p per) (payable 50% in advance)
response)

Brochure Fulfilment

Set-up data capture file – estimate 6 hours @ £45–65 per hour – £ 270–390
Data capture, per 000 — £ 500–650
Production of letters. Set up — £ 125–160
Printing, per 000 — £ 120–140
Digitised signature — £ 130–160
Brochure fulfilment @ 100 per hour @ £10–15 per hour — according
to response

Budget required (subject to a 10% management fee) — £32,885–39,134
+ variables*

* Any additional disbursements (eg post, fax, courier) charged @ cost plus 17.65%.
All costs usually subject to VAT.

Outbound

AIM: To contact communications managers in financial and shipping companies and make appointments for the sales force.

Set up. One-off payment — £ 400–525
Carding up 1,000 @ 175 per hour = 6 hours @ £10–12.50 per hour– £ 60–75
Calling 1,000 @ 5 calls per hour = 200 hours @ £30–35 per hour– £ 6,000–7,000
Data entry set up — £ 400–525
Data entry 1,000 @ 30 per hour = 34 hours @ £10–12.50 per hour– £ 340–425
Management fee @ 10% — £ 720–855

Budget required — £ 7,920–9,405
+ variables*

* Any additional disbursements (eg post, fax, courier) charged @ cost plus 17.65%.
All costs usually subject to VAT.

experienced account managers in the unit to oversee operations, perhaps during the first 6–12 months.

If a company is committed to a major ongoing telephone marketing programme, but does not want to set up in-house, some agencies will establish and run a dedicated unit at their own premises. Although this still represents a major investment by the client, it can have distinct advantages. Apart from not having to find a site for the operation, and not increasing the headcount, all the headaches of designing, implementing and running a telephone marketing unit are passed to the agency. Constant liaison, often including a company manager based at the agency, ensures that the company retains control of operations and that the unit is fully integrated with other sales and marketing activities.

Regular readers of the marketing press will know that new services are being launched all the time. Telephone marketing is still undergoing rapid change. Agencies are responding to the growth in in-house operations by providing new support services, as well as expanding the boundaries of the medium by developing new applications, techniques and strategies. One area of growth for agencies in the immediate future is likely to be inbound calling, as more companies turn to direct response advertising. It requires particular expertise to ensure that in-house inbound call-handling facilities are used efficiently, and companies who are using this method for the first time, or only use it sporadically, generally opt for using agency resources.

Only a few agencies in the UK are currently capable of handling high-volume inbound calling. However, they are well placed to service this rapidly growing need and many of those now offering only outbound calling are likely to move into this area. Apart from enabling companies to buy all their telephone marketing needs from one source, this will provide an element of creative cross-fertilisation and synergy. Many types of campaign will benefit as a result.

Database marketing

The BDMA survey revealed, in 1988, that the greatest area of growth for agencies was customer database development. The growing importance of database marketing, and the role that the telephone can play in building and maintaining a database, was outlined in Chapter 2. It was inevitable that some agencies would capitalise on their experience of this powerful combination to move into database marketing. Services that are now offered include:

- database creation and management;

- database and computer consultancy;

- analysis and reporting;

- direct mail and mailing fulfilment;

- data entry, postcoding and telephone number searching.

Agencies can build a database from scratch (installing a new system if required), enrich or restructure an existing database, integrate the database more fully with sales and marketing activities, or provide advice and help with a particular database marketing application. As with telephone marketing, this work can be carried out either at the agency or on the client's premises. It is not unusual for companies to employ an agency to build and permanently maintain on their premises relatively large databases which are fully integrated into the companies' sales and marketing strategies.

Training

Many people underestimate the skills required – in callers, supervisors and managers – to run a successful telephone marketing operation. Agencies have learnt through experience what skills are required, what type of training works best, how to deliver it and how often. A variety of services are on offer to help recruit, train and develop company staff to ensure optimum performance of an in-house unit is achieved and then continuously improved upon. There are tailored and public courses in telephone techniques, telephone sales, telephone marketing management, and 'train the trainer', as well as complete selection and recruitment services for all the staff required.

An agency will analyse training needs, recommend the best method of training and type of course and, if required, design a course to achieve the client's specific objectives. But finding staff and providing them with the necessary skills is only part of the story. Agencies know well the importance of staff confidence, commitment and motivation in maintaining high performance and, for this reason, companies now often employ them to provide regular ongoing training for staff. More detail on the methods and importance of selection, recruitment, training and development will be found in Chapters 5 and 6.

Consultancy

The major area of consultancy, carried out mostly by agency personnel, is in advising companies on how to get the best out of in-house telephone marketing, either starting from scratch or improving an existing resource. The number of agencies in the UK offering this type of consultancy is increasing quite rapidly, although the level of expertise varies. There is also a handful of independent consultants who, as well as offering this service, will provide advice on, and help manage, campaigns run for the client by an outside agency. As the number of agencies increases and telephone marketing becomes more sophisticated, it is likely that the demand for this latter type of service will increase.

Consultancy may be either tactical, providing a one-off, tailored solution for a particular situation, or it may be strategic, where the consultant develops a long-term relationship with the client and provides ongoing advice on how best to use telephone marketing for continuous development of the business.

The extent of consultancy required will depend on clients' knowledge of telephone marketing and their specific needs, but in-depth consultancy on setting up in-house could result in a report covering all of the following areas:

- business and financial objectives for the unit, with an overall plan of how they can be achieved;

- how the unit will sit within, and affect other parts of, the company structure;

- resources required
  - human resources
  - physical resources
  - telephone equipment
  - computerisation, if required
  - ergonomic environment;

- siting;

- departmental structure, including job specifications, lines of reporting, and communications within the unit and to and from other departments;

- operational systems and planning, for example procedures, scripts, call recording systems and how information should be processed, and manual or computerised calling;

- work planning, ie how to ensure efficient use of resources, avoiding peaks and troughs, and planning for future growth;

- support required, including administration and resources to meet the business generated;

- staff sourcing and selection, including attracting applicants, developing personality profiles and selection criteria, and interviewing strategies and techniques;

- training and development requirements, including appropriate career paths within the company;

- performance measurement, ie how individual, team and unit performance will be monitored, measured and evaluated;

- methods of testing to ensure viability and refine procedures;

- benchmarking – to set optimum attainable targets;

- possible applications and the revenue they can generate;

- ongoing review and development of the unit;

- costings, short and long term, in comparison with agency costs.

Every one of these areas is important in setting up an in-house unit and having an expert make recommendations on any one of them is a good reason for employing a consultant. Particularly for those companies wary of taking the first step, an expertly designed strategy for success provides peace of mind and is invaluable in helping convince the board to make the necessary investment, in terms of both finance and commitment.

It should be obvious, from the areas that may be covered, that a consultant needs to conduct a careful and thorough analysis of the client company. This may take anything from a couple of days to six weeks or more, depending on the size and complexity of the company, and their specific needs. During this time the consultant will visit many departments, perhaps at many sites, meet with staff, ask

Table 3.2 Example consultancy fees for setting up in-house

Consultancy quotation (range) – setting up in-house

Consultancy time, both on and off-site, is charged at a unit fee of £650–£1,000 per day. In addition, a 10 per cent management fee is levied.

Stage 1

To provide expert advice to the
preparation of the business plan. Estimate
4–8 days @ £650–£1,000 per day   : £2,600/4,000 – 5,200/8,000

Stage 2

To develop operational plans and systems
and to produce deliverables. Estimate
20–25 days @ £650–£1,000 per day   : £13,000/20,000– £16,250/25,800

Stage 3

To provide ongoing professional support
and review. Estimate 2–4 days per month
for 6 months @ £650–£1,000 per day   : £7,800/15,600– £12,000/24,000

Estimated budget   £23,400/39,600– £33,450/57,800

All fees subject to a 10 per cent
management charge.

Additional disbursements

Faxes, photocopying, delivery, postage,
public transport, mileage, accommodation,
subsistence, reasonable expenses etc

At cost plus 17.65 per cent handling fee.

Terms

All fees exclude VAT.
See individual terms and conditions.

Note: Consultancy fees can vary widely. Under all circumstances it is vital
to determine exactly what the charges cover and, when making
comparisons, to compare like with like, including the expertise of the
consultants.

searching questions and often request highly confidential and sensitive information. Financial and business objectives, corporate philosophy, customer base and markets, sales and marketing strategies, administrative systems, reporting structures and much more information may be required to make recommendations and draw up a working document for establishing an in-house unit.

An example of consultancy fees is given in Table 3.2. Costs ranging from £23–58,000 may seem excessive, but in-house telephone marketing represents a substantial investment in terms of both set-up and running costs. This could easily amount to over £400,000 for a non-computerised unit with six callers, in the first year alone (Table 3.3). Consultancy fees are a fraction of the losses that could be incurred if the unit failed to operate efficiently, so it is not surprising that more and more companies are taking advantage of this service. Research from the Colorgraphic Group (Table 3.4) predicts that UK agency revenue from this service will rise from around £3.75m in 1990 to £10.5m by 1995.

There are two other trends within the UK telephone marketing agency sector which are worthy of mention because they could have benefits for some clients.

Regionalisation   Over the past few years, the number of UK agencies outside London and the South East has been increasing rapidly. In 1988, according to the BDMA survey, 58 per cent of agencies were concentrated in this area. More recent estimates place the majority of agencies outside London and the South East, and this trend is continuing.

As telephone marketing becomes more widely accepted, there is a growing demand in the North of England which is being met by the formation of new agencies, by existing marketing services companies offering telephone marketing, and by London-based agencies opening regional centres. At the same time, costs in London and the South East have escalated dramatically. Combined with the growing scarcity of skilled staff, particularly callers, this has encouraged some agencies to move their base of operations to the North.

The chief benefit to clients is a reduction in costs while maintaining comparable quality. Another advantage, which can be significant, is the relative proximity of an agency, which facilitates close liaison during campaigns.

Table 3.3 Example costs of running an in-house telephone marketing unit

Annual costs of running an in-house outbound calling unit		
6 callers (@ £12–14,000 pa)	72,000	–	84,000
NI and pension contributions	14,400	–	16,800
BT units (rental and call charges)	55,000	–	65,000
	£141,400		£165,800
'Hidden' costs			
Manager (inc car and bonus)	28,000	–	32,000
Supervisor	18,000	–	20,000
Clerical support	23,000	–	25,000
Overheads	32,000	–	35,000
Equipment costs (variable)	–	–	–
Stationery, printing, etc	10,000	–	12,000
Incentives, bonuses	20,000	–	22,000
Perks (BUPA etc)	20,000	–	22,000
Excluding equipment costs	£151,000	–	£168,000
Total running costs	£287,400		£333,800
Additional 1st year costs			
Recruitment, training, advertising, consultancy	£ 44,000	–	£ 80,000

Additional variables

Telephone line installation and rental, list rental, additional staff facilities, association memberships, computerised telephone marketing system (software and hardware), call management facilities (eg ACD), capital equipment depreciation.

Note: Costs can vary widely, eg according to location (property costs and salaries), calibre of staff (salaries and training costs), equipment, consultancy fees etc.

Table 3.4 The agency sector of the UK telephone marketing industry

Activity	The UK agency sector 1990 % (£)	1995 % (£)
Consultancy (total)	17 (15m)	15 (30m)
Pure consultancy	20 (3.75m)	35 (10.5m)
Training	80 (11.25m)	65 (19.5m)
Outbound (total)	28 (25m)	30 (60m)
Customer care	10 (2.5m)	25 (15m)
Selling	20 (5m)	15 (9m)
Database development	30 (7.5m)	40 (24m)
Appointment setting/ lead generation	40 (10m)	20 (12m)
Inbound (total)	55 (50m)	55 (110m)
Customer care	20 (10m)	40 (44m)
Brochure fulfilment	80 (40m)	60 (66m)

Source: Direct Response – The Market Map, a quantitative analysis of the UK direct response industry, 1990. Commissioned from Research Associates by the Colorgraphic Group. Reprinted with permission.

Integration While most agencies currently play a largely supportive role, there are signs of a trend towards market specialisation and agencies being involved at an early stage of the client's strategic and business planning. Other marketing service industry sectors have followed this course, developing long-term relationships with clients, and similar benefits can be gained in telephone marketing. These include:

- greater understanding of the client business;

- optimum use of telephone marketing through full integration with other sales and marketing activities;

- integration with short and long-term business plans;

- a permanent, professional resource available, as and when required, without large investment or long-term commitment.

Agency or in-house – the advantages and disadvantages

Whichever option is chosen, agency or in-house, there will be disadvantages as well as advantages. Each will have a different mix of benefits and drawbacks according to the situation, which has to be analysed in order to strike the best balance. The following points can be used as a checklist to help in making a decision, although they are not exhaustive, and their relevance and implications may vary from company to company and campaign to campaign.

The advantages of agencies

The advantages are:

- limited financial commitment when employing an agency for one-off tactical campaigns;

- no fixed investment for a series of occasional campaigns;

- can provide cost-effective short-term support during busy periods (for example due to seasonal fluctuations) or when there is a gap in representation (because of holidays for example);

- one hundred per cent commitment;

- full resources of the agency always on call – need only use it when required;

- can develop a long-term relationship where telephone marketing is fully integrated with other sales and marketing activities;

- specialists in telephone marketing, with the expertise to create the most effective type of campaign for the situation;

- fully established management, control and monitoring procedures;

- no additional resources required, for example staff, hardware, telephone lines, premises;

- no additional overheads;

- can handle high-volume outbound or inbound campaigns;

- can accommodate urgent requirements;

- can test on a wide range of criteria before roll-out of a campaign;

- can easily provide calling after business hours and at weekends;

- can be used for straightforward applications currently conducted in-house (for example list building), releasing that resource for new campaigns which rely upon other company resources (for example expertise);

- can get campaigns up and running quickly;

- maintain a high level of efficiency.

The disadvantages of agencies

The disadvantages are:

- concern over the agency's ability to understand the business – lack of product knowledge etc;

- fear of losing control;

- expense;

- opens an additional channel of communication which could become blocked, cause delays etc.

Agencies can present many valid arguments to negate these perceived disadvantages. They would say, for example, that expense is relative. It is what you get for your money which matters when comparing in-house with agency and telephone marketing with other marketing methods. A good agency will always try to allay client fears over these disadvantages at their first meeting. Many companies, however, are still highly sceptical of the medium itself, and a decision is often made before they get to the stage of meeting agencies. Others simply would not employ an agency to undertake any work.

The advantages of in-house

When companies in the BDMA survey were prompted to give their reasons for setting up in-house, the factors mentioned most often were, in order: to keep profits in-house; cost; ease of access to customer data; better utilisation of staff; agency lack of understanding of their business; fear of losing control/remoteness of an agency. Overall, the benefits of setting up in-house include:

- easier communication;

- instant and more direct control;

- greater flexibility, provided the expertise is available;

- greater confidence, for example not having 'outsiders' dealing with customers;

- easier connection to on-line systems, for example databases;

- more detailed knowledge available on extremely complex products or services;

- successes are down to the company and no one else, which can help spur staff on to higher achievement;

- it can prove more cost-effective;

- it is easier to budget long term;

- in-house expertise can be developed.

The disadvantages of in-house

The disadvantages are:

- once made, the commitment to invest is inescapable;

- requires expertise to set up properly;

- specialised, efficient supervision and management is required, for example for maintaining high motivation and monitoring and analysing results;

- increased headcount and overheads;

- the resource needs to be fully employed, even during seasonal 'lows';

- holiday and sickness cover is required;

- the company has responsibility for individual, team and unit performance; failures are down to the company.

Agency personnel in-house

There is a third option, which combines some of the advantages and disadvantages of both agency and in-house operations. That is, using an agency to staff and run a campaign at a company site. The benefits should be clear, namely close control by company management, an opportunity for hands-on learning, constant liaison and reporting, immediate availability, and so on. However, there are also disadvantages, for example additional resources may be required (more space, more telephone lines), there is increased risk of 'interference' by company management and of alienating company staff by bringing in 'outsiders'. However, this may be the best solution where, for example:

- a campaign requires integration with company systems, for example on-line information;

- staffing levels need to be stepped up quickly, perhaps to meet a deadline, or to take full advantage of an opportunity;

- a campaign concerns issues which the company wants to keep from staff, perhaps a takeover bid;

- an unexpected campaign arises, for example to deal with a crisis;

- technical support or advice regarding company products or services may be required, for example where it may be necessary to transfer calls internally.

Which is the most cost-effective?

Many major companies have established in-house operations which are proving highly cost-effective, but this is not the solution for every company or every situation. An agency may be the solution where, for example:

- it is current company policy to limit capital investment or staffing levels;

- where developing and testing a new application would disrupt existing work;

- where special telephone services (such as LinkLine and Callstream) are required for a limited period or occasional campaigns;

- where there is a need for sporadic, high volume calling; or

- where the company wants to test how they could benefit from telephone marketing.

An agency may seem an expensive way of getting a job done; in the BDMA survey, the most frequent reason given spontaneously for setting up in-house was cost. However, any telephone marketing activity, whether in-house or agency, requires a high level of expertise to make it work effectively. Developing that expertise in-house is a lengthy and costly exercise, not to mention the expense of salaries, equipment and overheads.

The highest return on an investment in telephone marketing will be achieved by integrating it into the company's long-term plans, and fairly detailed business and financial analyses are required to decide whether these objectives could best be achieved using an agency or setting up in-house. If a consultant has been employed to carry out an in-depth feasibility study, this will result in recommendations on all the potential applications of telephone marketing and how they can be integrated into company operations. Obviously, by incorporating several objectives in a single campaign, it is possible to increase cost-effectiveness. Without the expertise of a consultant it is very easy to overlook the added value of, say, gathering market data when using the telephone for direct sales. The importance of this added value escalates rapidly the more telephone marketing is integrated with other activities.

Once the role of telephone marketing within the organisation has been defined, the relative costs and return on investment of using an agency versus in-house can be calculated by testing each of the main applications. A test of 100 calling hours, for example, could be used to make 500 appointment-setting calls, list build 1,500 company names and decision-makers, or make 475 market evaluation calls. Ideally, tests on each application should be carried out by two agencies to provide an accurate evaluation, and both agencies should be given exactly the same opportunity to produce results, ie the same brief.

The duration of a test, namely the number of calling hours, can have a critical impact on results and the perceived cost-effectiveness compared with other marketing methods. During a campaign the effective call rate (the number of decision-makers contacted each hour) and the conversion rate (positive call results) both rise. As a result, the cost-effectiveness of calling increases. In addition, campaign set-up costs

Table 3.5 Variation in results according to test duration

Appointment setting campaign				
Number of hours	Call rate/ hour	Number of calls	Success – conversion rate	Cost per appointment
25	3	75	10%	£253
50	4	200	11%	£123
75	4.5	338	13%	£79
100	5	500	15%	£57

are the same whether the test runs for 25 hours or 100 hours, and so the greater the number of calling hours the wider the spread of these costs. Table 3.5 provides an example of how cost-effectiveness can vary according to the duration of a test.

The information provided on the test campaigns should be fairly detailed, although this will vary according to the nature of the campaign and the client's specific objectives. A final report may contain the following information:

- a summary of campaign background, the source and number of leads, aims and objectives, and targets;
- duration of the test and number of callers;
- a breakdown of calls, for example
  - total diallings
  - total contacts
  - number of each type of positive response (order, or information request)
  - number of negative responses, with reasons (for example, already serviced)
  - call-backs
  - unobtainables;
- analysis of conversion rates;
- breakdown of results by scripted questions;
- analysis of achieved targets.

This information can be used to calculate the return on investment for the test campaign. The results of a direct selling test campaign, for example, might be as follows:

Duration of test (hours)	100
Contacts made	450
Contact rate (average per hour)	4.5
Positive results (sales)	94
Conversion rate	20.89%
Total campaign costs	£5,000
Cost per sale =	**£53.19**

Of course, this figure does not take account of the value of additional information gained, for example list updating – enabling more accurate targeting later), which is difficult to quantify but which reduces the effective cost. In addition, the relative cost of the test will be proportionately higher than a full campaign because of the one-off set-up fee charged by the agency (*see* Table 3.1) and the other factors mentioned earlier. The agencies should therefore be asked what they would charge for the full campaign. The conversion rate (contacts to positive results) in the test can be used to calculate the cost per positive result. When the agency results are received, average values should be taken for each application. Some variation is to be expected.

With some additional calculations, the agency figures can then be extrapolated to give a costing for the same applications run in-house. This requires a calculation of the cost of establishing and running an in-house unit. Example figures have been given in Table 3.3. Obviously, these will vary tremendously according to the size of the unit and the nature of the applications. A 40–line inbound operation, for example, would incur far greater costs in terms of equipment, telephone, staffing, direct response advertising and accommodation, than the outbound operation used in this example. It should be remembered, also, that costs such as overheads will not vary in direct proportion to the size of the unit. Taking the annual running costs as in the region of £310,000, excluding consultancy, the average cost per positive result can be calculated as follows:

Average contact rate (per hour)	4.5
Effective calling hours per week	27.5
Contacts per caller per week	123.75
Contacts per 43 weeks	5,320
Average conversion rate	20.89%
Successful calls per annum	1,111
For 6 callers	6,666
Cost per positive result =	**£46.51**
(£310,000 ÷ 6,666)	

In order to calculate accurately what revenue would be generated by an in-house unit, ideally a year's schedule of campaigns should be drawn up showing different applications, duration of campaigns and number of callers employed. This will enable optimum use to be made of callers' time, and costs per positive result can be calculated for each campaign. If the average value of a positive result is known, for example the average value of a sale, then the overall return on investment in the unit can be calculated for the year.

Although this method requires extensive planning, it has the advantage of allowing some of the added value of achieving secondary objectives within campaigns to be incorporated into the calculations. If a direct selling campaign also produces 800 new leads for the sales force, for example, the cost of a separate campaign to generate 800 leads represents added value.

Obviously, provision must be made for such things as lower contact rates during peak holiday periods and other predictable variations. It should also be borne in mind that the predicted return on investment will only be achieved if the in-house unit operates as efficiently as the agencies providing the test results; hence the value of employing a consultant to conduct a feasibility study and using agency training resources.

These calculations should provide a comparison of the cost per positive result and the percentage return on investment for each application, for both agency-run and in-house campaigns. The following decisions can be made based on these figures:

- whether agency or in-house is more cost-effective for each application;

- what applications could be run more cost-effectively by an agency, ie farmed out;

- the most profitable applications to run in-house;

- what mix of in-house applications would provide the greatest return on investment;

- whether an in-house unit would be a profit centre.

If a decision is made to use an agency for some or all of the intended campaigns, it is preferable to start a campaign straight after it has been tested, because the campaign is already set up and running, and the agency team will still be geared up to producing optimum results. The process of setting up in-house is described in Chapter 4.

Choosing an agency

As the industry grows, selecting the best available agency is becoming more difficult; there is a larger choice, more variety of services offered, and a wider differentiation in terms of the scope and extent of expertise available.

Selecting an agency should be a methodical process, whatever the service being sought. Using the wrong agency can lead to a poor first experience, disillusionment with telephone marketing and a lost opportunity to gain competitive advantage. Ideally, the agency should match the needs of the organisation in terms of short- and long-term sales and marketing objectives, preferred working style, and budget.

There are a handful of consultants in the UK who maintain up-to-date information on agencies, such as their specialisation and style of working, and who are experienced in advising on selection to meet particular needs. The following information is based on the selection strategy used by one of these consultants*. Selecting an agency for database marketing, consultancy or training differs in various respects from choosing one for telephone marketing, and these differences are outlined later.

The selection process

The basic procedure for selecting an agency, described in the following pages, consists of these stages:

1 Formulating the brief;
2 Tailoring selection criteria;
3 Matching agencies to the profile;
4 Telephone screening agencies;
5 Assessing responses to the written brief;

---

* Teleconsult, part of Ogilvy and Mather Direct, offers independent advice and consultancy on the strategic and tactical use of the telephone, with practical solutions tailored to meet companies' specific sales and marketing needs. Guidance on the implementation of telephone activity is provided, including the selection and use of the most appropriate agency(ies); Teleconsult maintains an up-to-date register of telephone marketing specialists, including the types of information covered in the section on 'selection criteria'. The company's address is given in Appendix A.

6 Selecting and visiting agencies;
7 Reviewing and appointing the agency(ies).

The selection process involves evaluating agencies against a variety of criteria which have been described separately, for clarity, beginning on page 103.

1 Formulating the brief The first step is to define the campaign concept and strategy in a written brief (the development of a campaign brief will be examined in Chapter 8). This will reveal what expertise and facilities are required in an agency, and will also be used later for assessing shortlisted agencies by asking them to respond to the brief with a written proposal. However, companies should expect to utilise the expertise of the agency they choose in developing and redefining the brief to ensure that the campaign will provide maximum benefit.

2 Tailoring selection criteria Looking through the selection criteria, described on pages 103-113, which are the important ones in the current situation? For example, is the size of the agency important to the company, and what size is preferable? What facilities will be required, for example an 0800 number or brochure fulfilment? The chosen criteria form a profile of the type of agency that is required.

3 Matching agencies to the profile At this stage, a comprehensive list of agencies should be compiled. A good source is the BDMA, which will provide a list of its members who all maintain the high ethical and professional standards laid down in the Telephone Marketing Guidelines. Other agencies may be located through advertisements in the marketing press (*see* Appendix C), personal contacts who may have used an agency and, particularly for companies located in the regions, the *Yellow Pages*. A list of UK agencies, up to date as at April 1991, is given in Appendix A. Lists of agencies in other European countries, who are members of their national trade association, should be available from the addresses listed in Appendix C. Another good source is the International Telephone Marketing Database (*see* Appendix A).

An initial shortlist of, say, ten agencies should be selected for telephone screening. Many can be eliminated using easily identifiable criteria, for example if the company intends to visit the agency regularly then location will obviously be important.

4 Telephone screening agencies Telephoning this initial shortlist, ideally speaking with the new business director or equivalent, can serve a number of purposes. It will help to demonstrate their approach and presentation, for example, and provide the opportunity to explore the selection criteria in more depth. Also, for an inbound campaign, finding out what range of telephone numbers they use will enable the company to make calls and test their efficiency, for example speed and quality of response, the way the call is handled and the time taken for any literature requested to arrive. Finally, if the agency sounds promising, information can be requested, such as a company brochure, terms and conditions, rates, a client list and so on. Unsuitable agencies should then be deleted from the list.

5 Assessing responses to the written brief The agencies remaining on the list, perhaps three or four in number, should be sent the written brief and asked to respond with a campaign proposal within a given timescale; note that it is vital to give each agency exactly the same information. Although it can save time to give this initial brief and discuss strategy face-to-face at the agency, this is likely to turn into a sales presentation which will make it extremely difficult to compare the agencies. It can also be confusing to visit one agency after another.

The responses, when received, should be evaluated against criteria such as:

- speed of response;
- format of presentation;
- accuracy and quality; and, **most importantly**,
- interpretation of the brief and recommendations.

6 Selecting and visiting agencies Responses to the brief should be analysed and perhaps two agencies selected, initially, to visit and complete the final assessment. These visits are to explore areas such as:

- telephone staff;
- account team personalities and experience;
- approach; and
- operational systems.

The visits are basically to check that the written responses are a true reflection of how the agencies would actually perform, and to go through the remaining selection criteria. Good agencies will be eager to discuss how the company could utilise telephone marketing in broad terms, as well as the proposed application. They will ask a lot of questions to ensure that the company is making best use of the medium and does not have unrealistic expectations.

7 Reviewing and appointing the agency(ies) If none of the agencies come near to meeting the selection criteria, then obviously the selection process should be repeated with a different list of agencies. Otherwise, the final assessment ought to be based on a test. It should be possible, from previous discussions with agencies, to rewrite the initial brief to incorporate some of the recommendations which have been made. Worthwhile agencies should be willing to take part in a split test – giving two agencies the same brief and comparing their performance in terms of cost per positive result. If there is a large margin between the two, say over 15 per cent, then the agency producing the best results should be chosen. If they produce similar results, the company should choose the one which offers the best prospects for developing a long-term working relationship.

Selection criteria

The selection criteria which are relevant will depend largely on the nature of the campaign defined in the brief, but they should also cover points such as the type of agency the company prefers to work with, the most convenient location, and so on. The following criteria are summarised in Table 3.6.

1. Capacity/facilities

Lines – type and scale Almost any agency could handle a test of, say, 500 calls. However, could they handle the roll-out of a full campaign, of perhaps 2,000 calls per month, with their current commitments? The number of lines the agency has available, therefore, can be important, depending on the nature and size of the campaign. If the company is looking for a long-term relationship with an agency, the capacity to handle future applications must also be considered.

For inbound applications it is very important that the agency

Table 3.6 Criteria for selecting a telephone marketing agency

Agency selection criteria	
Capacity/Facilities Lines: type and scale Staff levels and scale Current commitments Sites: scale and location Computerisation: type and scale Support facilities	*Work Profile* Business-to-business/ consumer Inbound/outbound Applications Industry Client base
Business Profile/Price Size Years of experience Solvency (turnover) Industry rating Independent/part of a group Location Membership of trade associations Rates/formula	*Approach* Style Management structure Training/briefing/reporting Professionalism Personalities Confidentiality

Source: Teleconsult (Ogilvy & Mather Direct). Reprinted with permission.

already has the type, and number, of lines required, because there are delays in obtaining certain special telephone services. In addition, if a large media campaign is planned, a memorable number or series of numbers may be desired, in which case the agency should be asked for its number ranges.

The key question is whether or not the agency can handle the proposed campaign, for example:

- Do they have available the type of lines required?

- Do they have the capacity available to handle the volume/rate of outbound calls to be made or inbound calls expected?

- Do they have experience of handling this volume of calls?

- Do they operate the lines at the times required, perhaps at weekends, or 24 hours a day?

Staff levels and scale   However small the intended campaign, it is important that the pool of available agency staff (ie not currently committed) is large enough to accommodate the campaign with capacity to spare. Again, it is important to consider whether these resources could accommodate the company's long-term needs.

Current commitments   If a company wants a campaign set up and running at short notice it may be that the agency has already allocated their best resources to current campaigns. To avoid this problem companies should give agencies sufficient notice so that they receive the best possible resources and service. The agency should therefore be asked the minimum turnaround time for setting up a campaign of the type intended.

Sites – scale and location   For some applications, and for some companies, the location of the agency can be important. Where a field sales or service force is involved, for example, perhaps in appointment setting, it is desirable for the callers to build up a rapport with them, ideally through face-to-face contact. Acrimony can develop if 'anonymous' people appear to be dictating to company staff when and where they should be going. This can be avoided if, first, the concept is properly explained to them and, secondly, they can meet the callers involved. An agency operating at more than one location may therefore offer advantages, provided the scale of operations at these sites is adequate.

Computerisation – type and scale   Agencies vary from 100 per cent computerisation to totally manual, paper-based systems. The cost of running an outbound test campaign, particularly if it is relatively small, is likely to be substantially less using a paper-based rather than a computerised system. This is because computer set-up costs are comparatively high, unless a large volume of calls are being made. On the other hand, computerisation does have the advantage of providing more sophisticated and thorough results analysis at relatively low cost. This can be particularly important in testing. If it is a high-volume test, or if it is very likely to lead to a full campaign roll-out, then the relative cost is not as high. The agency should be asked for their recommendations, together with an explanation of the benefits, of using paper-based and/or computerised systems for the proposed campaign. Where both are recommended, they should be asked about the percentage of calls to be handled by each, and why.

Support facilities   Can the agency handle mail fulfilment, order processing or whatever other services are required for the campaign? It is generally not desirable to have too many different suppliers involved because of possible delays in communication. In brochure fulfilment, for example, consumers may telephone in response to a television commercial and expect to receive information within a few days. If their order has to be passed from the agency to the client and then on to a fulfilment house, a delay of perhaps a week can create a very poor impression and possibly lose a sale. On the other hand, the sophistication of the service required may necessitate involving a specialist, or the scale may be such that only a specialist company can provide a cost-effective service.

2. Work profile

Business-to-business/consumer   Some agencies specialise in one area or the other, even though they may have experience in both sectors. It depends largely on whether they are predominantly inbound or outbound. What experience does the agency have in contacting the intended market, ie business-to-business or consumer and, in the case of the former, what vertical market (or industry) and levels of decision-maker?

Inbound/outbound   Again, most agencies specialise in one or the other, although some offer both. There are two schools of thought – one that inbound and outbound calling do not mix well in the same environment, and the other that the agency offering both will have a broader understanding of the medium and its applications. Prospective clients should make their own decision. There are a number of questions that may be relevant:

- which inbound/outbound services do they offer and what are their main activities?

- what proportion of their work is inbound/outbound, and how is their revenue split between the two?

- What are their normal hours of operation for inbound calling – hours per day, days per week?

- Does the inbound service allow them to answer by individual client name/telephone number?

Applications What experience does the agency have in the intended application and related areas? How broad or specialist are their capabilities? Do they provide facilities for brochure fulfilment and, if so, is this on-site or subcontracted? Direct selling requires a different kind of caller and environment than, say, market evaluation. For many applications it is important, therefore, to find out whether the agency has a broad understanding of the telephone used as a direct marketing medium rather than a sales tool. Overall, however, applications experience is perhaps not as important in selection as business-to-business/consumer, inbound/outbound and industry criteria.

Industry Many agencies are now positioning themselves as small, quality specialists in particular vertical markets, for example high-tech or finance. The downside is that, if an agency becomes too specialised in vertical markets, it will not always have the benefit of drawing on the experience of testing new applications and new approaches that comes from dealing with a good cross-section of industries.

Client base – accounts/conflicts Are blue-chip companies using them, suggesting that they provide quality telephone marketing? How many clients come back again and again, with whom the agency has accounts rather than handling one-off tactical campaigns? What percentage of their revenue is repeat business? Long-term, strategic use of the agency's resources suggest that they can create consistently good telephone marketing strategies and avoid becoming stale. Ideally, the agency would have a cross-section of blue-chip companies and many smaller companies as clients. Conflict with existing clients may be important to the company, although agencies can generally over-come the problem by assigning different account teams to the conflicting projects, or running them at separate sites, if they have more than one.

Finally, the company may decide to set up in-house once it has sampled success. Could the agency provide the necessary advice and support to help them to do this, in other words, consultancy and training? If not, a new agency would have to get to know the company from scratch.

3. Business profile/price

Size Telephone marketing agencies usually give clients a considerable amount of 'free' time in developing campaigns, ie they don't charge a consultancy fee. Being at the top of an agency's client list, in terms of revenue, generally increases the amount of input, attention and priority given to a campaign – because potential future revenue is high. There is something to be said, then, for not choosing one of the largest agencies. On the other hand, a large agency generally has the benefit of more experience. Therefore, a client on a small budget, for example, who needs to get maximum results first time and cannot afford to learn through experience, may want to choose an agency which has a proven formula for making the particular application work. So the greater experience of larger agencies can be of more benefit to the small client.

Large agencies specialising in inbound calls are usually computerised and tend to take a production line approach. This may not provide the creative environment required and does not always lend itself to frequent client liaison. Smaller agencies, on the other hand, tend to take a more personalised approach.

Years of experience The agency industry is becoming increasingly competitive and inevitably new agencies face stiff competition from those which are well established. Companies that do cease business appear to do so generally within two years. The most important factor, however, is the number of years of experience in telephone marketing of the people running the agency.

Solvency (turnover) In recent years many agencies, both large and small, have been faced with financial problems, and solvency may become particularly relevant for a very large roll-out campaign. This is one area where it is particularly useful to use a consultant to help select an agency. They have up-to-date information which generally includes financial stability.

Industry rating Charts which show the ranking of agencies can be misleading. Is it better to choose an agency which is top in turnover or top in the quality of service delivered? Reputation is far more important than industry rating.

Independent/part of a group   If the agency is part of a very large group, it is important to consider whether internal usage of their facilities will be given priority over client usage. On the other hand, if the agency is part of a group, they can often draw on wider experience and resources.

Location   Establishing a face-to-face dialogue with the agency is important, particularly at the test phase, so that the company can get first-hand experience. Location can therefore become an issue, particularly if the company intends to visit the agency regularly. In addition, however, agencies located outside London may have definite cost advantages – lower overheads and salaries – which are passed on to clients. Recruitment of callers is also easier – London agencies are finding it increasingly difficult to recruit the quality of telephone marketing staff they want, although it is easier to find better quality executive and management staff. Telecommunications services provided to agencies outside London also tend to be more efficient.

Membership of trade associations   Agencies should be asked what trade associations and professional bodies they or their personnel belong to. Members of the BDMA, for example, should offer a high standard of ethical and professional conduct. This can be especially important in sensitive areas of consumer work, such as the timeshare business.

Rates/formula   Cost is obviously an important consideration. There is no standard method of charging and, even though the industry is becoming increasingly competitive, charges can vary considerably. It is vital to look at how the agencies calculate their charges. Do they charge hourly or per call? And would the nature of the campaign provide an incentive for callers to produce quantity rather than quality? Do they charge per effective call, or for all calls, or a combination? What is the setting-up charge? Are British Telecom meter unit charges included, or extra? (Remember that, if inbound calls are charged per minute, which is usual, costs can quickly mount up even if the basic charge is only 40 pence.) Do they charge a fixed price per campaign? There are many permutations. Can they provide an accurate working budget, and do they charge for doing this?

Although a test can indicate the likely cost per effective call, costs can escalate instead of reducing when a campaign is rolled out. Every effort should be made to ensure that there are no 'hidden' charges.

Apart from methods of charging, the agencies should be asked whether they offer volume discounts, test and seasonal packages. Telephone marketing has its seasonality because there are times, during the summer and around Christmas and New Year, when decision-makers are not so accessible for outbound campaigns. It can be more cost-effective to buy their services at these times for applications such as list building or cleaning, where information can be obtained from someone other than the decision maker.

4. Approach

This is where a visit to the agency becomes essential. Apart from any formal presentation, just walking around an agency, observing and talking to staff, can reveal a great deal.

Style   A great deal can be picked up by walking around an agency. What sort of impression does it create? Does it feel like a marketing or a 'hard-sell' environment? Would the company feel comfortable working with the agency? Talking with agency personnel will help to reveal their enthusiasm, commitment and professionalism.

Management structure   Most of the benefits of telephone marketing are based on the high degree of control and reactivity that the medium allows. The agency should have a strong management and supermisory structure, and be willing to show prospective clients a chart of their account management structure, which would be a dedicated team for the proposed campaign. The calibre of management can be checked by asking to meet and talk with a supervisor and account manager from that team. Liaison is vital, so the agencies should be asked who would be the point of contact in the event of a query, or to check how the campaign is progressing, and whether they are always available or sometimes out on the road.

Training/briefing/reporting   This is the area where the level of the agency's quality management becomes apparent. What process do they go through in preparing for a campaign? What is the background of callers? How much training do they get before they go on the telephone? How do they train staff? These things can be confirmed by chatting with the callers. Most agencies will give their staff a specific briefing for each campaign and the client should be involved in this, although not necessarily to deliver it.

What methods do they use for quality control, such as verification calls, and what sort of standards would be applied in the proposed campaign? What reporting systems do they use? If these are computerised, what would happen in the event of a system crash? What examples can they show of other campaigns they have done? The agency should be willing to show dummy reports of the type they could produce, and these should be checked to see if they have the flexibility and content required.

Professionalism All contact with the agency – telephone, written and face-to-face – will give an indication of their professionalism.

Personalities Because the campaign will require close liaison, the prospective client should meet the staff who would handle the account to see if a good rapport is likely to develop.

Confidentiality This can be more important to some companies than others. Many companies like the PR and coverage they get when their campaigns are promoted. The agency should bring case histories and experience to bear in discussing new campaigns, but they should seek client approval before revealing details. Professional integrity is highly important, however, whether or not the company wants its campaigns to remain confidential.

Finally, the agencies should be asked for the names of clients who can be approached for references. These can be followed up with a telephone call to those clients to discuss what they thought worked well in their campaign and what could have been improved. Most agencies will offer the names of a few relevant clients after consulting them for permission. If an agency refuses to provide any names they must have good reasons – equally as good as those for the prospective client going elsewhere.

Selecting other agency services

Many of the criteria for selecting telephone marketing services may also apply in selecting consultancy, database marketing and training services. However, there are some essential differences and additional areas that should be considered. These are as follows.

Consultancy   Advising a company on the most effective way of using telephone marketing in-house requires an in-depth knowledge of their business. Consultants require access to many departments, and often highly confidential and sensitive information such as budgets and long-term business strategies. In selecting someone the company feels they can trust with this information, the individual becomes much more important. This is particularly true if the consultant is not a part of an agency and cannot be judged by *their* reputation.

Potential client conflict and confidentiality are also more critical. Agencies can overcome this problem by allocating a different account handling team or using different sites, but an independent consultant, after spending perhaps three weeks inside a company, will remember clearly every detail of that business. There is also a larger potential for conflict, because the information obtained by the consultant could be of competitive value to companies which are not even in the same business or market. So the questions of client conflict and confidentiality have to be explored very carefully. In addition, of course, an independent consultant may lack the back-up resources available through an agency consultant.

Near the top of the list of selection criteria are the consultants' understanding of the strategic use of telephone marketing as an integral part of company operations. They must be specialists and have the appropriate credentials.

Database marketing   The criteria for selecting a telephone marketing agency to provide database marketing will depend on the specific service required. One of the most important criteria for creating or developing a database is the agency's ability to understand the client's existing information systems. While telephone marketing agencies are knowledgeable about the use of the telephone in building and maintaining databases, database marketing *per se* is a relatively new area for them, and their relevant experience and expertise should be examined carefully. What specialist personnel do they have? Have they done anything comparable for other clients?

Training   There are some organisations other than agencies which provide telephone marketing training, although they often do not offer such a wide range of courses. The selection criteria are the same for both and include some of those mentioned for telephone marketing, for example facilities, capacity, current commitments, work profile, client base and fees. However, there are some additional areas that should be explored, such as the content of courses and the training methods employed, whether courses can be tailored to the company's needs, and whether they can be delivered in-house. Chapter 6, on training and development, gives more detail on the content and availability of courses.

Briefing in a campaign

An experienced agency should be skilled at guiding clients through the briefing process and will ask for information of the type detailed below. This list is not exhaustive, but it illustrates what information a company can be expected to provide. Briefing an in-house telephone marketing unit will cover much the same information, particularly when the unit works for many different internal 'clients'. (This is examined in more detail in Chapter 8.)

Not all this information will be required for every type of application. The following key has been used to show what is likely to be relevant for each one, although this may vary, perhaps depending on whether telephone marketing is being integrated with direct mail.

LB = List building   *AS* = Appointment setting
List cleaning   Direct sales
List verification   Seminar bookings
                                  Public relations
                                  Accounts servicing
                                  Shareholder communication

ME = Market evaluation
Lead qualification
Lead generation
Market research

Bracketed codes, for example *(ME)*, indicate that, for this particular application, the information is not essential, but it would be useful. Although the information may appear irrelevant, there are good reasons why an agency and, equally, an in-house unit may request it. First, it is important that the callers feel confident, and having sufficient background information so that they can answer any queries from contacts is one way of building confidence. Secondly, they may be calling a very inquisitive market. In a sensitive area such as defence, for example, contacts will be unwilling to reveal information if they do not feel confident in the authenticity of the call and its stated objectives. The same is often true in highly competitive markets. The more pertinent background information callers have, the more likely they are to achieve a positive result.

Client background

Details of the company, past and present – LB, ME, AS   An agency needs to gain a 'feel' for the company. Is it a new, ambitious company with radical ideas which might want to try something innovative? Or is it more conservative and needing to maintain that image? The agency will usually ask to look through corporate literature.

Details of product/service/event – (ME), AS   What is the company trying to achieve, for example to sell a product or service, or book an event? Details are required, such as price lists, an outline of unique selling points, details of the event etc.

Details of the market place – (ME), AS   This should cover the current and future customer base (with reasons for choosing future prospects), competitors (so that the opposition is known), and likely objections to the company product/service/event and how they can be overcome. Objections are likely to be more important in some applications than others. In direct sales, for example, perhaps the targeted market generally dislikes buying over the telephone. Or with market evaluation, perhaps the area is highly competitive or innovative, and contacts are reticent about revealing valuable information.

Campaign details

Aims and objectives of the campaign – LB, ME, AS   What is the company's definition of success for the campaign? What has to be achieved to satisfy people that it has been a success? This is especially important for in-house units, since other departments will inevitably feel that it is a drain on their own resources and need to be shown concrete proof of its cost-effectiveness. There are a number of areas to cover.

- What information is to be captured?

- Broadly, how should this be achieved? What impression does the company want to create? What type of approach should be used, bearing in mind the application, in order to build a rapport with the target audience? This will help to determine the type of script to be used.

- How will the information be recorded? If the information is going to be data-entered it will need to be clear, precise and easy to enter. If it is going to a sales person it will need to have some sales bias. How will the person who receives the information be using it, and how should the method of recording accommodate their particular needs?

- How frequently will data and results be reported? How are the different responses going to be grouped, for example the codes to be used – 'ORD' for orders, 'AS' for already supplied etc?

- How will it be reported at the end? This is one of the most difficult things to decide at this stage, but it is vitally important to clarify what information the final report will contain and how it will be presented. Although the primary aim may be to achieve a 5 per cent conversion to sales, for example information on the other 95 per cent of contacts is invaluable. What needs to be recorded and reported on them, for example reasons for not buying, regional variations etc? Once this information has been defined, all other aspects of the campaign will form around it and be reported at the end.

Other factors

Order form and liaison – AS   For applications such as direct sales, appointment setting, seminar booking and brochure fulfilment, details of 'orders' will have to be communicated to a particular person(s). Who will this be? How will the information be passed on? When does it need to be passed on to ensure that the next step can be fulfilled on, or by, the right date?

Representatives' diary availability and liaison – AS   When booking appointments, who does the telephone marketing supervisor or project manager liaise with to find out which days they are available? How and when do they liaise?

Media schedules and liaison – ME, AS These are extremely important in applications which are generating inbound calls through media advertising. What ads are being placed, through which media, and when? What is the likely level of response, for example is it a full page ad in the national press or a quarter page in small circulation trade journals? This information will help to determine the likely daily response level and the level of staffing required. Media schedules have a great tendency to be changed and liaison is essential to ensure that, if there is a change, the telephone marketing element is rescheduled accordingly. Who is the contact for media schedules?

Mailing schedules and liaison – ME, AS Mailing schedules can be even more unpredictable than media schedules. Who is doing the mailing, and who is the contact? What is the first day the mailing is likely to arrive? How quickly are people likely to respond, for example does the mailing contain a limited period special offer? Are there any imminent disputes that could hold up delivery?

Targets

The following information may be applicable in all situations: *LB, ME and AS*.

Number of leads How many targeted leads are actually available? It is common for clients to think they have a sufficiently large contact list, either in-house or which has been bought in, only to find that a fair proportion of them are unsuitable, for example because they do not fit within the target market. Or perhaps some of the expected sources, perhaps regional or local offices, do not have the expected numbers available.

Presentation of leads How will these leads be delivered to the agency or in-house unit, for example on labels, in books, on disk or magnetic tape? The telephone marketers may need to make provision for the leads to be processed to suit their operational systems. For example, are they paper-based or computerised? If computerised, what are the preferred formats?

Quality of leads How up to date is the list? How quickly does the information on this type of lead usually change? Business-to-business markets, for example, change more quickly than consumer markets, and there is more rapid change within certain sectors of these markets.

Information on leads What proportion of the leads have all the information required, for example name, job title, post code, telephone number. Post codes are sometimes vital. Sales territories are often allocated according to post codes and in appointment setting campaigns callers need to book the right representative in the right area.

Source of leads Where did these leads originate? How was the information obtained and by whom? Apart from giving a feel for the market being called, and an indication of lead quality, this information may be necessary to ensure that the list can be used legally, ie in compliance with the Data Protection Act 1984 (examined in Chapter 10).

Number of workable leads The number of usable leads can drop dramatically if a large proportion on the list require telephone number searches. Similarly, if six lists have been bought in from different list brokers, after de-duplicating one against the other (ie removing all duplicates), a much smaller list will result.

Number of mailings How many people have been/will be mailed? When were they/will they be mailed? Is there a response coupon/an inbound number? How well targeted is the mailing? A copy of the mailpiece should be given to the agency.

Number of calls How many calls will have to be made? If the calls are going to be made during a campaign period of, say, two weeks, it is unlikely that callers will get through to all the contacts. Some may be on holiday, at conferences, always in meetings and so on. July, August and December are notoriously difficult times to get hold of people in business-to-business markets. Also, the higher the level of the decision-maker, the more difficult they are to contact and some types of jobs preclude easy contact. Outside holiday periods, and assuming that the contacts are not top management, around 70 per cent of contacts are likely to be reached – although this can vary considerably. A margin of **30–50** per cent additional leads, or more, will therefore be required.

How many calls are likely to be received, for example in response to direct mail? This is a much more difficult question to answer and one where an agency or consultant can usually provide guidance. Many factors come into play, such as the nature of the offer made, the media used, how effective the advertisement is, the accuracy of targeting, and so on.

Number of appointments/sales, attendees/completes How many successful calls are required, for example number of appointments or completed questionnaires, or the value of sales?

Call rate At this stage it is possible for the agency to estimate roughly the number of calls that can be made per hour (call rate), which will depend on the application/extent of the script, target market and so on.

Conversion rate The rate of conversion of decision-maker contacts to orders, appointments or whatever, will depend on a variety of factors such as the quality of leads, the application and the offer being made. An agency will often suggest a range of realistic call and conversion rates on the understanding that these may be revised once a campaign is under way. They will also say if the client has unrealistic expectations of the outcome of a campaign.

Deadlines and scheduling

Leads arriving – LB, ME, AS When will the leads be available?

Client approval of campaign details – ME, AS How quickly will approval be given once the script, data capture documents and so on, have been submitted. Clearly, the speed with which the campaign can be started will depend on the number of people required to give approval and the speed of the decision-making process. If approval of the campaign details is required from an outside agency, such as the Takeover Panel for shareholder communications, this could add a further delay. This type of approval also lapses after a finite time, so speedy approval by the company becomes even more critical.

Callers' brief – (ME), AS Most agencies like the client to be present at, and often take part in, the briefing of callers. Will the client be available, and prepared, when required?

Callers de-brief – (ME), AS The first de-briefing of callers often takes place on the afternoon of the second day of a campaign, and perhaps again the next day. This is a time when progress is reviewed and any fine-tuning of the campaign (for example the script) is worked out between the callers and the supervisor or manager. Agencies often ask clients to attend to field questions from callers; at the same time, it gives the client another oppor-tunity to get to know the agency team. Where a campaign is being run in-house, it may be relevant to have the internal 'client' attend the de-briefing.

Last call – LB, ME, AS When will the last call be made? This may be critical in some applications, for example appointment setting or direct sales, where successful calls require action by people other than the telephone marketers.

Communications/reporting – LB, ME, AS How will progress be reported daily, how frequently and to whom? Will that person be available and when?

Report presentation – LB, ME, AS The timing of delivery of the final report, with campaign results and analyses, may be crucial. If it is a newsworthy poll or market research, for example, the company may want to ensure that it is available in time to be broadcast on the 6.00pm news on a particular day, or for the next day's national press. Or, if the campaign is something new, perhaps the results have to be presented to the board on a particular day. Poor scheduling, or simply a delay in the presentation of final results, can negate one of the prime objectives of a campaign.

Definition of success

As mentioned previously, this is applicable in all situations, *LB, ME,* and *AS*. Although the aims and objectives should already have been clarified, it is important to know where the line will be drawn between an acceptable and an unacceptable outcome. If something unforeseen happens, the telephone marketers need to know at what stage it is preferable to 'pull the plug' on a campaign, rather than incur further costs. This does happen with a very small percentage of campaigns, despite fine tuning.

A thorough briefing, whether with an agency or in-house, provides the basis for a successful campaign. However, a balance has to be struck between too much information, which can cloud the important issues, and too little, which does not optimise the potential of the campaign, and could even lead to serious failure.

Briefing for database marketing may need to be equally as thorough, for example where the agency is establishing and maintaining a marketing database for the client. If a good agency has been chosen, they will be experienced in guiding the client through this briefing process. For consultancy on setting up in-house, briefing is more of an ongoing process, although the consultant will require an initial statement of the client's objectives. Similarly, an agency designing a bespoke training course will require clear objectives from the client.

Follow-through

Once a campaign is up and running there should be regular, preferably daily, contact between the client and agency for reporting on progress, and to ensure that any minor problems can be resolved quickly. The client may be asked to be present at the early de-briefing sessions, when possible changes for fine-tuning the campaign will be worked out. If the campaign is run over an extended period the client should have regular review meetings with the team to discuss progress. Results should be checked, as they are received, against the initial projections made by the agency to ensure that targets are being met and that all the information required is being collected. The client can make random checks by calling a small number of the people contacted, for example to find out how the call was handled, whether the information recorded was accurate and so on. Any shortfall in standards should be reported immediately to the agency. When buying other services clients should pay similar attention to the achievement of agreed objectives.

Following one simple rule will ensure that a company makes the best possible use of agency and/or in-house resources – *if in doubt, get expert advice*.

4

Setting Up a Telephone Marketing Unit

Establishing a telephone marketing unit in-house represents a major investment, not only financial but also in terms of management commitment to the possibly widespread changes required to integrate telephone marketing fully with other business functions. A business plan will be required, showing how the company's objectives for the unit can be achieved within budget. This will be followed by detailed planning of the unit's functions, structure, positioning within the company, resourcing and operation, including provisions for monitoring and developing its performance.

However great the optimism of those promoting the unit, there are many hurdles to overcome before it can be up and running successfully. This chapter outlines the many decisions that have to be made during the design, planning and implementation of an in-house telephone marketing unit.

Selling the idea

Although the biggest single hurdle in getting the unit established may appear to be appropriating the necessary budget, its success will be dependent largely upon the attitude of the company's management. There are still many people who do not fully understand, or appreciate the potential of, telephone marketing; add to this the financial investment required, the possibly widespread changes in the organisation needed to accommodate it, and opposition from those who see it as a 'threat' to their own jobs, and there is obviously a major internal marketing job to be done.

Gaining the support of the board and senior management is the first step. A detailed business plan, showing how the unit can function as a profit centre, should secure their initial go-ahead. Generally, though, that will not be enough, particularly in a large organisation. The aim should be to generate enthusiasm for the project at board level. There will be many other people whose support is required to make the unit a success, and enthusiasm filtering down from above will help smooth the way. Individual lobbying of directors, explaining the key role that telephone marketing can play in achieving corporate goals, can help to inspire their advocacy. And keeping them informed and involved as planning progresses, particularly in areas which relate to their own function, will keep the project on their personal agenda. Get everyone at the top talking about the benefits and the word will soon spread.

Having overcome one major hurdle, there are still many others throughout the organisation who have to be educated to appreciate the purpose and value of the unit. Their full understanding, and continued co-operation and support, lay the foundations for successful implementation and future development. All individuals, groups and departments who will be affected by the introduction of the telephone marketing unit need to be identified and made the target of a specific plan for gaining their co-operation and support. This may include, among others, marketing services, information technology, telecommunications, personnel and training.

Telephone marketing may be new to many people and even those familiar with it may feel that it is an agency rather than a company function. Some, such as the sales force and those who spend the budgets for other marketing activities, may see it as a threat. These groups, in particular, must be targeted early before they start lobbying against the idea. The simplest and most powerful strategy is personal interest – 'What's in it for me?'. If the unit is going to handle direct sales and account servicing, for example, sales management may worry that their budget will be cut or that, by using 'inexperienced' sales people, their sales figures will plummet. In selling the idea to the sales force, who may feel devalued and that their jobs are threatened, the following points could be made:

- good people will always be needed in the field;

- the unit will provide support for their role;

- it will reduce the amount of cold calling they have to do;

- appointments will be efficiently planned and managed through direct liaison with them;

- appointments will be with contacts who are ready to buy;

- they will be provided with more detailed information on each contact before they visit;

- their efficiency and productivity will increase.

This works both ways, of course. It will have to be explained to the sales force what help the unit needs from them in order to maximise these benefits, such as close liaison and regular feedback of relevant information on customers. While the importance of selling benefits has been stressed, it is equally important to spell out what the unit needs for its success. Once the idea has been accepted, many people will be quick to lay claim to the resource and say what they want from it. Above all else, the unit must fight for the level of autonomy enjoyed by equivalent functions in the organisation.

How consultants can help

Detailed and specialist knowledge is required throughout the design, planning, implementation and development of a telephone marketing operation. Companies setting up in-house will have to buy in this expertise and the only truly reliable source in the UK, currently, are professional consultants. Their role has already been outlined in Chapter 3.

The services provided by consultants will depend on the company's specific needs, but full consultancy would typically cover the following areas.

Stage 1 – Business planning

Working closely with company management, the consultants would produce a business plan showing how the unit will achieve the corporate objectives for telephone marketing. This would cover:

- Primary and secondary objectives;

- Operational strategies;

- Work profile for the unit;

- Integration with other departments;

- Human and physical resource requirements;

- Organisation and management;

- Budgeting;

- Identification of critical success factors;

- Anticipated results.

Stage 2 – Development of working practices

The consultants would develop and recommend systems and procedures for the effective implementation and running of the unit, covering:

- Human resources and departmental structure;

- Physical resources
    - suitability of the site
    - amenities
    - telephone system and equipment
    - office layout
    - work station design
    - computerisation;

- Work planning;

- Operational systems;

- Training requirements;

- Performance measurement.

Thorough testing of key elements is generally recommended, either with an agency or in-house, to ensure that they are optimised before implementation.

Stage 3 – Ongoing support

The success of the unit will depend, ultimately, upon regular performance reviews and ongoing development. Consultants can provide support as and when required, in terms of both expert technical advice and services such as staff training. Regular review meetings and working party sessions between the consultants and relevant departments in the organisation can help to plan the short and long-term development of the unit.

Defining objectives for the unit

The objectives set for the telephone marketing unit determine most of the detail in the subsequent planning stages, including work planning, staffing, equipment, operational systems and training. They can be defined at two levels: those encapsulating overall corporate aims and direction; and those that support individual departmental or functional roles. The second level objectives are used in designing and planning the unit, but these must be defined as part of the plan for fulfilling the corporate objectives. If the company plans to boost its market share through aggressive exploitation of new markets, for example, then the unit's objectives should reflect and contribute to the achievement of this goal.

Financial objectives are necessary to show the projected return on investment and to prove the viability of the unit. One aim, for example, may be to increase monthly sales revenue by 20 per cent, from £180,000 to £216,000. Telephone marketing offers various applications that can help to generate that additional £36,000, both through direct selling and supporting the sales force. But what mix of applications will produce the best results? Should the telephone marketers concentrate on lead generation and qualification, or on servicing small and medium-sized accounts, so that the sales force can concentrate on major clients and new business? One reason for testing applications is to find out which ones are most cost-effective. Once this has been decided, specific targets can be set for the most productive activities. For example, the additional £36,000 per month might be made up as follows:

Generating 160 qualified appointments per month,
with a conversion rate of 1 in 4 and an average
order value of £750   = £30,000

Servicing small accounts, representing a saving on
sales force time of 25% — 15% of which is taken up
by the qualified appointments and the remaining
10% devoted to major customers, generating a
total additional revenue of £8,300   = £ 8,300
                                                           ———

TOTAL   £38,300

Although the initial idea for setting up in-house may have been a particular application or group of applications, the company needs to make optimum use of the resource to get the best return on its investment. *All* possible applications must be examined in the light of their potential contribution to meeting financial objectives. Because telephone marketing is continuously gathering information, applications can feed off each other and there may be complementary activities, as shown in Table 4.1, which can be added to increase cost-efficiency. Areas for future development should also be explored.

At this stage it should be possible to compile a list of clearly defined, quantified objectives, for example:

Table 4.1 Optimising the use of the in-house resource

Initial idea	Complementary applications	Future development
Lead generation and qualification	Prospecting	Customer care/ loyalty building
Appointment setting/diary management	Resource back-up for key, major and medium accounts	Integration with direct mail and media advertising
Servicing small value accounts	List building, cleaning and testing	Response handling
	Building and maintaining a database	Shareholder communications
	Market research and test marketing	Crisis management
	Invitations to events	

- to produce a minimum 800 qualified leads per month;

- to locate a minimum 100 high-revenue -potential prospects per month;

- to achieve a minimum 90 per cent attendance at each roadshow.

However, it is unlikely that all the desired objectives could be fulfilled. Careful planning of work schedules is required to analyse what can be achieved with finite resources. Some of the less cost-effective activities may have to be abandoned and some objectives amended.

Work planning

A vital ingredient in the success of the unit is planning what work it will undertake. This should take account of the variety and complexity of campaigns, their integration with other activities, and the loading on the unit. Work planning helps to identify the optimum level of resources and to ensure that they are utilised in the most efficient way. A variety of areas need to be covered, including resource levels, applications, support activities, for example list sourcing and filing, production rates (ie results per hour) and work scheduling. These are examined in the following sections.

How and where the unit will fit in

The objectives set for the unit will define how and where it fits into the organisation. It is, of course, a division of marketing, or sales and marketing, but its exact relationships with other departments will be determined by the work it undertakes. Figure 4.1 shows how a telephone marketing unit might typically fit in.

The level of understanding of telephone marketing in most organisations is low and, initially, staff in various departments are likely to be confused about the precise role and functions of the new unit. A chart like the one shown in Figure 4.1 can be a great aid in explaining the concept and showing how all the departments work together.

Physical resources

The physical resources required to meet the objectives set for the unit should be one of the earliest considerations. There can be lead times of

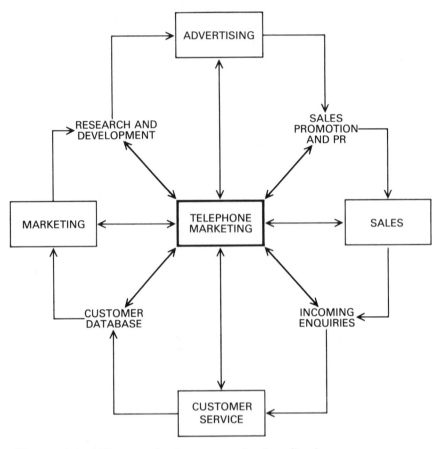

Figure 4.1 Where telephone marketing fits into an organisation.

several months for acquiring and installing the necessary equipment and orders will have to be placed at an early stage of implementation. Perhaps more urgent, however, is the selection of a site in which to house the unit. If the company does not already have a suitable site, time will be required to search for premises and to complete purchase or leasing negotiations. Some of the key factors to consider in selecting the site are:

- the amount of space required, allowing for planned growth of the unit;

- ease of communications with other functions within the organisation;

- the suitability of the physical environment;

- local labour resources, if additional staff are to be recruited now or in the future;

- efficiency of telecommunications services in the region and the availability of special inbound telephone lines, if required;

- amenities at the site and externally.

The site, equipment and other physical facilities should provide an environment which is conducive to achieving the aims of the unit as well as enabling easy expansion.

Staffing and departmental structure

Deciding the type and number of staff required for the unit, and the most effective structure, involves a number of interrelated activities:

- analysing reporting requirements, taking account of corporate policies and procedures;

- defining the tasks created;

- defining job components, roles and responsibilities, and job descriptions for all types of staff;

- setting realistic activity levels for key tasks;

- work scheduling.

Some of these activities, such as roles and responsibilities, are explained in more detail in Chapter 5, because they are directly related to staff selection. However, as well as forming the basis for the recruitment programme, drawing up job descriptions is a key step in deciding staffing levels and departmental structure. For each type of position created, the job description should include details of the tasks to be completed and the daily responsibilities, including reporting and administrative systems, that have to be maintained.

Staffing

The tasks and jobs created will depend largely on the objectives and size of the unit, and the particular applications chosen. The first step in planning the staff required, who may include callers, team leaders, a supervisor, a manager and clerical support, is to list all the tasks that will be created in achieving the objectives set for the unit. It is best to start with the callers, because their numbers and the time available for them to do things other than communicate on the telephone, such as clerical work, will determine other aspects of staffing.

Each application should be analysed to identify what tasks the caller will have to carry out. If this is making appointments for the sales force, for example, this may include:

Preparation:
    contact list preparation
    liaison with representatives on availability
The call:
    dialling/re-dialling
    number searching (if a wrong number or unobtainable)
    following the script
    noting contact responses
    call-backs
Follow-up:
    updating contact record
    informing representative of appointment details
    sending out literature
    filing

Some of these will include a subset of tasks, for example contact list preparation could include sorting according to post code (correlating with sales territories), deduplicating, carding up (putting contact details on call sheets) and number searching. In addition, there will be responsibilities for reporting results, taking part in briefing and debriefing sessions, and so on, all related to this one application.

Depending on the size of the unit, some of these tasks, such as contact list preparation and filing, may be carried out by clerical support staff, rather than callers. The viability of employing clerical support will depend on the number of callers generating clerical work and whether they could easily accommodate these duties. It is important that unnecessary jobs are not created but, at the same time, the callers' highest priority will be to generate results on the telephone and their skills should be concentrated on achieving this objective. The same is true of all jobs within the unit.

To decide the number of callers required, realistic times for the various tasks have to be calculated. The most straightforward and accurate way of doing this is by testing the application, either in-house or with an agency. The following example is for an outbound application:

Objective: qualified leads required per month	= 500
Contacts made per caller per day	= about 40
Contacts meeting the qualification criteria	= 1 in 4
Appointments made per day	= 10
Time required by one caller to generate 500 qualified leads	= 50 days
Number of callers required to generate 500 qualified leads per month (20 days)	= 2.5

These figures provide only a rough guide and do not take account of factors such as the varying quality of contact lists, seasonal variation in the availability of contacts, the provision of sickness and holiday cover for callers, and so on. In addition, some applications may require an additional time allowance, for example where special training or extensive briefing is required.

The calculations for inbound calling are more complex, but testing can once again provide guideline figures. For a new unit, this testing should be carried out by an agency because it is impractical to obtain in-house resources just for a test. In addition, an agency can provide a complete analysis of variations in call rates over time, ie call patterns. There are various factors to be taken into account, including:

- types of incoming call and the average length of conversations;

- time required between calls for completing associated tasks and preparing to take the next call;

- number of incoming calls at different times of the day;

- call patterns on different days of the week.

Other factors that may have to be taken into account include changing schedules of response-generating mechanisms, for example direct mail and media advertising, and when these are likely to prompt the first and last calls. Fairly stable patterns of calls do tend to emerge, for example call rates peaking mid-morning and early afternoon, with Monday, then Tuesday and Thursday the busiest days.

The following figures illustrate how, once detailed call patterns are available, the number of callers required can be calculated:

Average time to deal with a call, complete associated tasks and prepare for the next call	= 5 minutes
Maximum number of calls handled per hour	= 12
Peak hourly calling rate	= 120
Number of callers required at peak	= 10

The number of staff required to handled incoming calls at different times throughout the week can be calculated in the same way. Once completed, the required staffing levels enable breaks, briefing, training and so on, to be scheduled to fit in with the changing demands on the unit.

Incoming call-handling highlights the need for work scheduling. If the lowest call rate in the example above was 40 per hour, that could be serviced by 4 staff, leaving 6 free for other tasks such as data entry or mailing fulfilment. Alternatively, overlapping shifts may be used, with some staff coming in early, to handle calls from early birds, and leaving when call rates fall in late afternoon; another shift could come in later, just before the peak calling rate, and stay later to handle evening calls.

However, this is only considering one type of campaign. If several campaigns are running at once, or if they overlap, then obviously the number of staff required will rise. Detailed work planning and scheduling is therefore essential in both setting staffing levels and in making the most efficient use of those staff. Similar calculations need to be done for all the campaigns that the unit will undertake in, say, the first six months.

The greatest danger is in underestimating the number of staff required. As well as ensuring that there are sufficient people to cope with the peak workload, cover must be provided for unexpected absences and allowance should be made for growth of the unit. The efficiency of inbound call-handling, in particular, is very sensitive to staffing levels. If there are insufficient staff, money will have been wasted in generating calls that cannot be answered and every person that is unable to get through could be a customer lost for good. Even those that are answered, but only after an unreasonable wait, will be unimpressed with the company's efficiency.

If the unit is relatively large, there may be sufficient work to warrant employing clerical support staff so that more efficient use can be made of the specialised skills of callers. The number of callers will determine whether they should be divided into teams and whether team leaders will be required in addition to a supervisor.

Departmental structure and team size

Structure determines how the work of the unit will be distributed among staff, defining job functions, responsibilities and reporting relationships, so that everyone works together in the most efficient way to achieve the targets set for the unit. The best structure for a telephone marketing unit will depend upon the scale and type of work being done, the number of people involved and the flow of work. There is no ideal structure for all situations, and often it will be determined by the structure in the rest of the organisation. However, whatever structure is chosen must meet certain criteria, ie it should:

- make optimum use of human resources in meeting the objectives of the unit;

- support good communications;

- clarify the contribution expected from individuals and teams;

- clarify who is accountable to, and for, whom;

- facilitate efficient management;

- not present barriers to higher performance;

- provide opportunities for promotion;

- be flexible to meet changing needs within the unit.

The most important consideration in deciding structure is the objectives of the unit, ie the output required. Since the callers, or telephone marketers, are the basic means by which these objectives are achieved, structure is best determined from that starting point.

Telephone marketers work best in teams, enabling easier management of campaigns and acting as a source of motivation. Teams have an optimum size, which is the number of people who can be managed effectively by whoever is 'leading' the team. The basic responsibilities of leaders include:

- setting objectives for the team and planning their achievement;

- delegating tasks to make the best use of individuals' skills;
- supporting the team and individuals in achieving their targets;
- motivating team members;
- monitoring and giving feedback on individual and team performance;
- determining training needs and providing development opportunities;
- maintaining standards of performance and discipline.

If there are too many in a team the leader will not have sufficient time to fulfil all of these responsibilities effectively. In particular, there will not be enough time to involve each team member, helping them to develop and improve their performance. The symptoms of ineffective leadership include poor performance, low morale and high staff turnover, so there should be no more people in a team than the leader can manage effectively. However, having too few people in a team also has drawbacks. Three people working in a team, for example, would not have the same sharing of expertise and mutual support that would exist in a team of five or six people. There is also a temptation for the leader to become too heavily involved in doing the group's work, rather than delegating tasks to individuals to help in their development.

Telephone marketing relies heavily upon strong leadership because of the carefully planned and controlled nature of the work. The maximum team size is therefore low, compared with many other of work situations, and the practical range is from four to about eight. When there are more than eight callers it is best to divide them into smaller teams.

So what are the implications for the structure of the unit? In a unit with a single team of five callers (Figure 4.2), it may be difficult to justify a full-time supervisor if there is already a dedicated manager for the unit. The supervisory duties could be shared by the manager and a senior telephone marketer, who also makes calls to provide cover when required, to test new campaigns, and as part of quality management. On the other hand, if there is no dedicated manager, perhaps because that role has been taken on by someone in the marketing department, then a purely supervisory role may be created instead. One of the callers could act as team leader, reporting directly to the supervisor who, in turn, reports to someone outside the unit.

If 15 callers were split into three teams (Figure 4.3), a supervisor

Figure 4.2 Possible structure of a unit with five callers

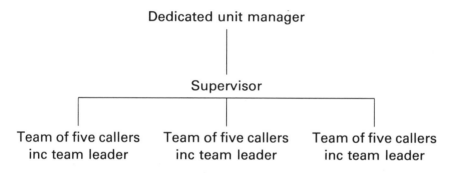

Figure 4.3 Possible structure of a unit with 15 callers

would be required, responsible for day-to-day management of the teams, in addition to a senior person within each team to act as leader. The team leaders would report to the supervisor and provide cover when the supervisor is absent. The BDMA survey found that, in agencies, the average ratio of supervisors to staff was 1 to 5.7. This is lower than that required in most in-house units, because the nature of agency work, with a large variety of campaigns, requires much closer supervision.

As the number of callers increases it will eventually become advantageous to employ clerical staff, supporting the calling teams, who report directly to the supervisor. The point at which this stage is reached will depend on the type of work being carried out by the callers. The clerical work generated by inbound calls, for example, can often be handled efficiently by the telephone marketers. However, in applications where list compilation, number searching and other repetitive jobs are involved, it would be better to assign these to someone outside the calling teams, leaving them free to make maximum use of their specialised skills.

The creation of different levels of responsibility provides a career path, with the possibility of advancement within the unit. This is an important motivating factor in individual development and provides an opportunity for the unit to grow in expertise. The precise way in which leadership responsibilities are divided and shared between these levels will depend upon the size of the unit. In smaller units the manager will be able to assume most of the duties, with the senior telephone marketer providing 'hands-on' support in areas such as results analysis, and reporting and motivation. In larger units, where more of the manager's time may be devoted to long-term planning and development, the supervisor is likely to assume higher level responsibilities, including setting objectives for the teams and delegating tasks, with the team leaders taking on more of the responsibility for things like analysis and reporting.

Reporting and accountability

The structure of the unit will define internal lines of reporting, while those with people outside the unit will depend upon how it sits within the organisation. If the unit is a major facility, then its manager may report directly to, say, the sales and marketing director, while a supervisor heading a smaller unit may report to the marketing manager. However, the actual lines of reporting are not that important, provided they are clearly defined. What has the greatest impact on the success of the unit is what is reported, and how efficiently.

Each individual will have certain responsibilities, specified in their job description, for reporting information on their activities, whether it is callers analysing and reporting on call success rates or a supervisor reporting on the success of different campaign tactics. What information is reported, and how frequently, will depend upon the nature of the particular campaign.

Overall, reporting procedures should ensure that the flow of information into, through and out of the unit fully supports the achievement of its objectives. Detailed planning of operational systems is necessary to ensure that the unit receives the information it requires, that the internal flow of information is well co-ordinated, and that people outside the unit receive the information they require.

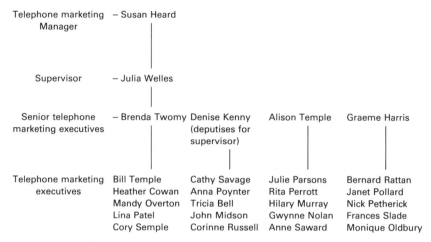

Figure 4.4 Example of an accountability chart

To work efficiently, everyone in the unit must understand fully what is expected of them and their responsibilities to and for other people. Most of this will be explicit in their individual job descriptions, but confusion can arise about levels of authority and accountability under some circumstances. If the supervisor is absent, for example, to whom do callers turn for advice and help in sorting out urgent problems? Would it be the manager, or does someone deputise, informally, for the supervisor? If there are clerical support staff, who do they turn to when problems arise with the accuracy of data received from telephone marketing executives? Confusion of this type can lead to misunderstandings, ill feeling and discontentment. One way of overcoming this problem is to create an accountability chart, like the example shown in Figure 4.4, which states explicitly where everyone stands in terms of their authority and accountability. These charts can be easily updated to reflect changes in staff members and variations in structure to accommodate different types of campaign, ensuring that everyone is always aware of their position in the unit.

Operational systems

In order to have the high degree of control and reactivity which confers on telephone marketing many of its benefits, operational systems have to be carefully designed so that the work of the unit is carried out effectively in a planned and controlled way. Systems are needed to collect, record, monitor and analyse information from calls; to monitor and measure performance and analyse results; to control the flow of work into, through and out of the unit; to define minimum standards and provide quality control procedures; and to ensure that the resources and outside support required are readily available. Many different activities may be undertaken, each requiring and generating different information which needs to be processed and acted upon in different ways. Sound procedures are therefore required for handling and co-ordinating each of these activities, and all the requirements for success of the unit should be clearly and strictly defined in the operational systems.

Manual, paper-based systems are preferable to computerisation when a unit is first established, because they are more straightforward, and can be designed and redesigned comparatively quickly. An automated unit, fully integrated with other computerised information systems in the company, can take 12 months or more to get right; a manual system can be up and running within a matter of months. During the design of manual systems, however, it is essential to take account of computerised systems with which they will have to interface, for example to conform with the format in which information may be presented from a computerised database. If manual systems are designed in this way, automating them later is comparatively straightforward. Specifications for the automation can be taken directly from the manual systems, which have been refined over a period of many months' experience to provide optimum control.

Unnecessary paperwork can be avoided by careful design of systems to make the optimum use of information, for example records of the results of calls can form the basis for performance monitoring and analysis. Simple systems which are logical and easy to use help keep errors to a minimum and ensure that they are used efficiently.

Operational systems can be divided broadly into four areas: recording; administration; procedures; and standards.

Recording systems

Accurate records of daily activities are essential in telephone marketing, providing the basis for monitoring, measuring and analysing results. All calls made or received by the unit generate information, both from the contact and through the act of making or taking the call. This data has to be recorded in a way which will show:

Call rates, breakdown of call results, quality of work and trends...	For each caller, the team and the unit...	On a daily, weekly and monthly basis...	For each strategy and campaign undertaken

Recording all of this information requires various documentation which should be designed methodically to ensure the smooth flow of information and ease of analysis. The most appropriate areas to monitor on each campaign are built into the systems to measure individual, team and unit performance, and to facilitate efficient management of staff and campaigns. Continuous monitoring and analysis of performance allows results to be constantly improved through more refined planning and control.

The recording documentation used in telephone marketing goes under various names and many different styles of design are used. Basically, however, it consists of the following types of document.

Call card   This is the first document in the recording chain and is vitally important because it details the response of individual contacts made by the caller. The design should correlate closely with the questions in the script to aid the caller in accurately recording responses. An example is shown in Figure 4.5, followed by the corresponding script, together with 'call codes' (Figure 4.6), objection sheet (Figure 4.7) and benefit sheet (Figure 4.8). Also shown is some additional documentation (*Questions and Answers* and *Caller Information*) used on the same campaign to help callers provide contacts with any information they require. (The preparation of the different types of caller documentation required for a campaign is described in Chapter 8, pages 322–34).

Call codes are simply a convenient way of categorising responses. The names used for these are not important and companies can use whatever fits in with their other systems. However, since each code represents a different type of response from the contact, the number of different responses accommodated and the way they are grouped is very important. [Text resumes, after Figures 4.5–4.8, on page 158.]

Diners Club/CUC Europe
Call card

| ORD | | SP | | NI | | AM | | NS | | UR | |

Diners to action   **CUC to action**

Address change	
Query	
Complaint	
Not received card	
Diners to call	

Membership pack	
Future potential	
Details Lit.	

Amend to:

Name: ☐ Name:

Address: ☐ Address:

Postcode: ☐ Postcode:

Home telephone: ☐ Telephone:

Calling data

1. Received Diners Card?   Y   N   Other: _____
2. Signed card?   Y   N   Other: _____
3. Particular service interest:

☐ Household goods   ☐ Garden products   ☐ Jewellery/watches
☐ Office equipment   ☐ Nearly new car   ☐ Car phone/alarm
☐ New car   ☐ Electrical goods

---

4. Questions asked (if any)

1	2	3	4	5	6	7	8	9	10
11	12	13	14	15	16	17	18	19	20
21	22	23	24	25	26	27	28	29	

Comments:

Date: _____ Time: _____
Operator: _____ Job No: _____

Reprinted with the permission of CUC Europe

Figure 4.5 Example of a call card

DINERS CLUB/CUC EUROPE
3 MONTH TRIAL £1/60-DAY FREE TRIAL SCRIPT
(use with call card illustrated)

CARD RE-ISSUES
INTRODUCTION TO HOUSEHOLD

Good evening, may I speak to Mr/Mrs ... please?

If not available: When would be the most convenient time to call back? It is in connection with his/her renewed Diners Club Card.
NOTE: DAY, DATE, TIME

THROUGH TO DECISION MAKER

Good evening, Mr/Mrs ... it is ... ringing on behalf of Diners Club. Is now a convenient time to talk to you, it is in connection with your recently renewed Diners Club Card? **(PAUSE – ALLOW CUSTOMER TO STATE IF TIME OF CALL IS INCONVENIENT – ELSE CONTINUE)**

Well Mr/Mrs ... there are two reasons for my call. Firstly I would like to confirm that you have actually received your new card to replace the current one which expires at the end of this month?

IF HAVE NOT RECEIVED CARD/CARDS

Oh, I am pleased that we have found that out. Do not be concerned, because your new card cannot be used until the beginning of March, but we <u>will</u> have to look into this for you. May I get somebody from our Member Services department to contact you regarding this?
TAKE CONTACT DAY TIME TELEPHONE NUMBER AND CONVENIENT DAY TO CALL BACK – CLOSE CALL <u>POLITELY</u>

IF RECEIVED CARD

And may I ask, have you signed the back?
IF NO : It is important that you sign the card as soon as possible, perhaps I could ask you to do that after we have finished talking. **CONTINUE TO DESCRIPTION OF SERVICE**
IF YES : CONTINUE TO DESCRIPTION OF SERVICE

DESCRIPTION OF SERVICE

Fine, the other reason for my call Mr/Mrs ... is to tell you that as a Diners Club Member you are now entitled to a special trial of our new money saving Preference Purchase Service.

"Preference" is the UK's largest Home and Motoring Service. It enables you to have telephone access to over 25,000 products all at the very best prices. For example, if you were thinking of buying something for the home, instead of actually buying it from your local retailer, all you have to do is pick up the telephone, give us a call, and we will check on our database and quote you a price on that product which you will find is generally around 5–15% less expensive than anywhere else in the UK.

Rather than go into detail about the service we offer, perhaps I could ask you Mr/Mrs ... are you thinking of buying any of the following:

* Buying anything for the kitchen – microwave, cooker, washing machine, fridge?
* Buying anything for the garden – DIY, lawnmower, greenhouse, shed, summerhouse, power tools, ladders, saws?
* Buying anything electrical – TV, video, stereo?
* Buying anything for the office – answering machine, fax, typewriter?
* Buying anything for the car – car phone, car alarm?
* Buying a new or nearly new car?
* Buying quality jewellery and watches?

REACT TO FIRST POSITIVE PROMPT WITH APPROPRIATE DESCRIPTION ON ATTACHED SHEET OF SERVICES

NOT PURCHASING ANYTHING

Well Mr/Mrs ... there is no obligation to buy, you can use the Service purely as a product information service or to compare price to make sure you are paying the lowest price locally. Also our money back guarantee states that if you do not save £50 in your first year's membership, we will refund your membership fee.

GO TO TRIAL OFFER

THE TRIAL OFFER

Well as I said earlier, as a Diners Club Cardholder, what I'd like to do is to offer you the "Preference" Service on a trial basis. The normal fee is £30 for a 12 month membership, but what we are able to do is to offer you a 3 month trial membership for £1. How does that sound?

IF YES : GO TO CONFIRMATION
IF NO : PROBE: Is there any specific reason?

AND COUNTER OBJECTION AND ONCE OVERCOME GO BACK TO ORIGINAL OFFER – IF NECESSARY THEN GO TO STEPDOWN

STEPDOWN

I'm sure you would agree that this is an opportunity that can't be missed. We really think you would get great benefit from the Service. Instead of a three-month trial for £1 let's put you down for a 60 day trial for free instead, that way you can use the Service, see the benefits and it's not actually costing you anything. How does that sound?

IF YES : GO TO CONFIRMATION
IF NO : PROBE: Is there any particular reason? **COUNTER SPECIFIC OBJECTION – IF STILL NO, THANK AND CLOSE**

THE CONFIRMATION

Fine, just to confirm everything with you – to encourage you to try the Service, you are being offered ... of the Service at ... Once you have had a chance to use the Service, we are hoping that you will accept a full year of membership for only £30. If you do, we will automatically charge you after your ... are up, and this £30 will appear on your Diners Club Statement. If you decide that the Service is not for you, please call the Service during your trial and your account will not be charged.

May I just check your address, I have ... is this correct?
NOTE ANY CORRECTIONS, CHECK SPELLING

IF ADDRESS CHANGE

I have made a note of your new address Mr/Mrs ... As a matter of precaution someone from our Member Services Department will have to contact you for a security validation before we actually change your record details.
TAKE DAY TIME TELEPHONE NUMBER

Fine Mr/Mrs ... we will send you your Membership Pack which will include details of our written promise of the lowest price guarantee, in the next few days. You will also receive on a regular basis our Advantage Magazine giving you details on the latest services.

Thank you again for your time. I am sure you will be pleased with the Service provided. Goodbye.

IF UNCLEAR : **REPEAT SLOWLY AND CAREFULLY THE TERMS OF THE OFFER ABOVE**

IF UNHAPPY TO PROCEED : **GO TO SPECIFIC OBJECTION AND COUNTER**

ALWAYS
CLOSE POLITELY THANKING CUSTOMER FOR THEIR TIME

* * * * *

Diners Club/CUC Europe
CALL CODES

Ord 1: Accept 3 month trial for £1.
Ord 2: Full membership – £30.
Ord 3: Offered 3 month for £1/accepted 60 day free trial.
Ord 4: Offered full membership/accepted 60 day free trial.

Special: **(SP)**	a. Want to pay by another card or cheque. b. Query on specific product. c. Query about Diners Club. d. Not received Diners Club Card. e. Want to think about it. f. Insist on being sent more detailed literature. g. Complaint about Diners Club. h. Other.
Not interested: **(NI)**	a. Membership too expensive. b. Not planning any purchases. c. Would not discuss. d. Does not buy over the telephone. e. Prefer to shop locally. f. Other.
Already a member: **(AM)**	Already a member through another card.
Number search: **(NS)**	a. Wrong number. b. BT message/fault on line. c. Dead line. d. Continuous tone. e. Fax number.

     f. Office number.
     g. Other.

Unreachable: a. Decision maker no longer at that address.
(UR)   b. Duplicate.
                 c. Tried three times.
                 d. Decision maker unavailable during call period.
                 e. Other.

Reprinted with the permission of CUC Europe.

Figure 4.6   Example of a script, together with call codes

∗   ∗   ∗   ∗   ∗

Diners club/CUC Europe
OBJECTIONS
(use with script illustrated)

1. **No/Not interested**.

I can appreciate that Mr/Mrs ... , may I please ask is there any
particular reason?
IF REASON IS GIVEN – GO TO APPROPRIATE OBJECTIONS
IF NO REASON IS GIVEN – CONTINUE ...

Other people have told me exactly the same thing until they had a
chance to try "Preference". They found it easy and convenient to
use and it saves money at the same time. We really think that you
will have the same experience, that is why we are offering you the
first ... months of Service for ... That way, you can use the Service
experiencing the benefits first hand. If you decide the Service is not
for you, simply call the Service within the ... trial and the £30 will
not be charged to your Credit Card Account. Perhaps we could start
your membership tonight Mr/Mrs ... , how does that sound?
PAUSE – WAIT FOR ACCEPTANCE OF OFFER

IF YES : GO TO CONFIRMATION
IF NO : AND ANOTHER REASON IS GIVEN GO TO OBJECTION
          IF NO REASON IS GIVEN POLITELY EXIT CALL

2. **Send information**.

Well Mr/Mrs ... I can do better than that for you! I would like to
enrol you tonight so you can try "Preference" for a ... month trial at

a cost of ... The actual membership material includes information and complete instructions on how to use the Service. That way you can see for yourself how much time and money the Service can save you. If you decide not to continue within the ... trial, call the Service and the £30 will not be charged to you. So Mr/Mrs ..., with your permission, I would like to start your membership tonight, Okay?

PAUSE – WAIT FOR ACCEPTANCE OF OFFER

IF YES : GO TO CONFIRMATION
IF NO : AND ANOTHER REASON IS GIVEN GO TO OBJECTION
IF NO REASON IS GIVEN POLITELY EXIT CALL

3. **I do not buy over the telephone**.

I can appreciate that Mr/Mrs ... , but the good thing about "Preference" is that it's not just for ordering goods over the telephone. You can use it just to check prices whenever you buy something from the shops, and for products like jewellery and watches you actually deal direct with the suppliers. We just put you in touch with them. "Preference" can provide you with unbiased information, help you draw-up a short list of models that meet your requirements, and it gives you details on the features of specific models. With this in mind Mr/Mrs ... perhaps we could start your membership tonight. How does that sound?

PAUSE – WAIT FOR ACCEPTANCE OF OFFER

IF YES : GO TO CONFIRMATION
IF NO : AND ANOTHER REASON IS GIVEN GO TO OBJECTION
IF NO REASON IS GIVEN POLITELY EXIT CALL

4. **I'm an impulse buyer/I don't want to wait for delivery**.

I can understand that. However, the information and savings on over 25,000 household products and all makes of new cars available through the Service would make the short time it takes for delivery worth the wait. Or if you prefer, use the Service to obtain price quotes, to make sure you are paying the lowest price possible when you shop locally. Please remember if you don't save £50 in your first year's membership, we will refund your fee in full, so why not try out "Preference" for ... for ... How does that sound?

PAUSE – WAIT FOR ACCEPTANCE OF OFFER

IF YES : GO TO CONFIRMATION
IF NO : AND ANOTHER REASON IS GIVEN GO TO OBJECTION
IF NO REASON IS GIVEN POLITELY EXIT CALL

5. **I'll never use it/I'm not going to buy anything.**

Mr/Mrs ... most people don't plan all of their purchases one year in advance. Unexpected purchases do arise. So, if your washing machine breaks down, or you need to buy gifts for holidays, birthdays, anniversaries, or if you see that video or microwave you have always wanted, "Preference" will be there to save you money. So why not take advantage of this guaranteed offer and see how much money you can save. How does that sound?
PAUSE – WAIT FOR ACCEPTANCE OF OFFER

IF YES : GO TO CONFIRMATION
IF NO : AND ANOTHER REASON IS GIVEN GO TO OBJECTION
IF NO REASON IS GIVEN POLITELY EXIT CALL

6. **Do not call/Too many calls/Consumer annoyance.**

   i) Mr/Mrs ... please accept my apology on behalf of Diners Club. We are sorry that this has happened.
   ii) Thank you for bringing this situation to our attention and again Mr/Mrs ... my apologies for any inconvenience you may have had.

7. **I can't afford it.**

(If consumer is unemployed, retired or no longer has the card, terminate the call)

I can understand that, Mr/Mrs ... however, what you may want to consider is that "Preference" can save you hundreds of pounds on many of your purchases. That way, you will have more available cash to use elsewhere. With a ... trial for ... you will be able to use the Service to see how much time and money you will be able to save. If you do not save £50 in your first year, we will refund your membership in full. How does that sound?
PAUSE – WAIT FOR ACCEPTANCE OF OFFER

IF YES : GO TO CONFIRMATION
IF NO : AND ANOTHER REASON IS GIVEN GO TO OBJECTION
IF NO REASON IS GIVEN POLITELY EXIT CALL

8. **CATCH-ALL OBJECTION.**
No/Not interested, I can't afford it, I'll never use it, no funds available

Mr/Mrs ... keep in mind that Members save around 5 to 15% on purchases they make throughout the year anyway. In addition you will receive:

* A ... trial for <u>only</u> ...
* Unbiased information on over 25,000 household products and every make of new car.
* The Advantage Magazine reminding you of our extensive range of products and services — and our valuable Auto Action pack.
* A refund of your first year's membership if you do not save £50 in your first year.

As you can see you have absolutely nothing to lose, so why not give the Service a try and see how much you can save, perhaps I could start your membership now, how does that sound?
PAUSE – WAIT FOR ACCEPTANCE OF OFFER

IF YES : GO TO APPROPRIATE PART OF SCRIPT
IF NO : AND ANOTHER REASON IS GIVEN GO TO OBJECTION
           IF NO REASON IS GIVEN POLITELY EXIT CALL

9. **Hesitant.**

Well Mr/Mrs ... I can understand that you might be slightly doubtful about "Preference", but what we're offering you is ... access to products at the lowest prices in the UK, with no obligation for ... What we are saying is — here is a service we really think you will benefit from and because it is new we would like you to have the chance to try it before you pay the full fee. If, at the end of your ... trial, you decide it is not something for you, just let us know and we <u>will not</u> bill the £30 to your account. How does that sound Mr/Mrs ... ?
PAUSE – WAIT FOR ACCEPTANCE OF OFFER

IF YES : GO TO APPROPRIATE PART OF SCRIPT
IF NO : AND ANOTHER REASON IS GIVEN GO TO OBJECTION
           IF NO REASON IS GIVEN POLITELY EXIT CALL

10.   <u>I want to think about it/speak to spouse</u>.

Well Mr/Mrs ... I can understand that, but the only way of making a fair decision is to join on a trial basis. That way you will receive full information and benefits offered. If you decide within your trial that it is not for you just call the Service and cancel without owing a penny. So why not take advantage of this guaranteed offer and see how much money you can save, perhaps we could start your membership tonight?
PAUSE – WAIT FOR ACCEPTANCE OF OFFER

IF YES : GO TO APPROPRIATE PART OF SCRIPT
IF NO : AND ANOTHER REASON IS GIVEN GO TO OBJECTION
    IF NO REASON IS GIVEN POLITELY EXIT CALL

11.   <u>Require goods of less than £50</u>.

The reason we supply goods over £50 only is because it's on these products that we are able to offer the best discounts. And even if you are not planning on purchasing goods over £50, "crisis purchases" often crop up throughout the year (ie broken washing machine etc). Bearing this in mind perhaps we could start your membership tonight, how does that sound Mr/Mrs ... ?
PAUSE – WAIT FOR ACCEPTANCE OF OFFER

IF YES : GO TO APPROPRIATE PART OF SCRIPT
IF NO : AND ANOTHER REASON IS GIVEN GO TO OBJECTION
    IF NO REASON IS GIVEN POLITELY EXIT CALL

12.   <u>Don't like cost of joining fee</u>.

i) (3 months for £1)
I am sorry to hear that Mr/Mrs ... but it is only a nominal charge to cover part of our administrative costs. If it's a problem we can reduce the joining fee, but that would mean reducing your trial period to 60/30 days instead of 1 year/3 months. Which of those would you prefer?
ii) (No trial)
If you enrol tonight I can offer you a special 60 day free trial of "Preference", so that you can try the Service out. How does that sound?
PAUSE – WAIT FOR ACCEPTANCE OF OFFER

IF YES : GO TO APPROPRIATE PART OF SCRIPT
IF NO : AND ANOTHER REASON IS GIVEN GO TO OBJECTION
           IF NO REASON IS GIVEN POLITELY EXIT CALL

13. **How do I know your goods are competitively priced?**

We guarantee our prices are the lowest you will find available to the public in Great Britain. If you do find goods cheaper than ours, and provide us with proof of this (ie advertisement) we will refund you the difference plus 20% of that difference. With this in mind Mr/Mrs ... may we put you down for a ... trial for ... ?
PAUSE – WAIT FOR ACCEPTANCE OF OFFER

IF YES : GO TO APPROPRIATE PART OF SCRIPT
IF NO : AND ANOTHER REASON IS GIVEN GO TO OBJECTION
           IF NO REASON IS GIVEN POLITELY EXIT CALL

14. **No interest in shopping this way**.

I understand what you are saying Mr/Mrs ... however, I am sure you would agree that the concept of 'Preference' is a quick, easy and convenient way to shop. We have upwards of 25,000 products (stereos, TVs, Hi-Fi, videos, washing machines, dishwashers etc) and all well-known manufacturers' brands – Sony, JVC, Panasonic, Canon, Zanussi, etc. With this is mind Mr/Mrs ... perhaps we could put you down for ... trial for ... ?
PAUSE – WAIT FOR ACCEPTANCE OF OFFER

IF YES : GO TO APPROPRIATE PART OF SCRIPT
IF NO : AND ANOTHER REASON IS GIVEN GO TO OBJECTION
           IF NO REASON IS GIVEN POLITELY EXIT CALL

15. **Prefer to view goods prior to purchase**.

I agree Mr/Mrs ... however you can still do that. We can provide you with a short list of models which fit your exact requirements then all you have to do is go to your local retailer, view the goods, have them demonstrated and use our Service to provide you with price comparisons. With this in mind Mr/Mrs ... may I put you down for a ... trial for ... , how does that sound?
PAUSE – WAIT FOR ACCEPTANCE OF OFFER

IF YES : GO TO APPROPRIATE PART OF SCRIPT

**IF NO : AND ANOTHER REASON IS GIVEN GO TO OBJECTION
IF NO REASON IS GIVEN POLITELY EXIT CALL**

16. What if items arrive broken?

We do everything in our power to ensure that damage to goods is not incurred. We also provide an After Sales Service should you have any problems. With this in mind Mr/Mrs ... may I put you down for a ... trial for ... , how does that sound?
PAUSE – WAIT FOR ACCEPTANCE OF OFFER

**IF YES : GO TO APPROPRIATE PART OF SCRIPT
IF NO : AND ANOTHER REASON IS GIVEN GO TO OBJECTION
IF NO REASON IS GIVEN POLITELY EXIT CALL**

Reprinted with the permission of CUC Europe

Figure 4.7 Example of possible objections

* * * * *

DINERS CLUB/CUC EUROPE
SERVICES (benefit sheet)
(use with script illustrated)

ELECTRICAL PRODUCTS/HOUSEHOLD ITEMS

Well Mr/Mrs ... We have over 25,000 top brand name products that are worth shopping around for, generally valued at over £50. Our range of products cover everything from **(MENTION PRODUCT RELEVANT TO PROMPTED RESPONSE)**. All of which are well-known manufacturers brands – Sony, JVC, Philips, Panasonic, Zanussi and many more, but all at special, low "members only" prices.
(GO TO TRIAL OFFER)

JEWELLERY/WATCHES

Well Mr/Mrs ... We would offer you an exclusive jewellery and watch service with savings of 25% against the normal selling price of quality rings, bracelets, necklaces and you can save 15% on quality watches valued at £200. Also, all jewellery is sent on seven days home approval, to make sure it is exactly what you want.
(GO TO TRIAL OFFER)

NEW CARS

Well Mr/Mrs ... We have facts, figures and advice on all makes and models of new car. You can save a guaranteed £500 off the manufacturer's list price and usually much more buying this way, or perhaps as importantly get a higher specification model for the same money. Also if you prefer to buy locally you can use our prices to get the best possible deal.
(GO TO TRIAL OFFER)

NEARLY NEW CAR SERVICE

Not only does this service provide members with valuable and unbiased advice on all aspects of buying nearly new cars, but we are now also able to offer you the opportunity to purchase ex-daily rental cars through our Service. All the cars on offer are of a guaranteed standard, less than six months old with no more than 8,000 miles driven. The models on offer range from Escorts to Sierras, Astras to Carltons.
(GO TO TRIAL OFFER)

USED CAR ADVICE AND INFORMATION SERVICE

We also offer unbiased advice on buying and selling used cars, helping you to avoid the many pitfalls. We are also able to provide you with our Auto Action Pack.
(GO TO TRIAL OFFER)

CAR ALARMS/CAR PHONES

Our consultants are instantly able to offer you the best prices and advice on many makes of car alarms and car phones. Not only that, we are also able to arrange installation.
(GO TO TRIAL OFFER)

Reprinted with the permission of CUC Europe

Figure 4.8 Example of a benefit sheet

DINERS CLUB/CUC EUROPE
QUESTIONS AND ANSWERS

1. How does the Service obtain low prices and the selection of merchandise?

"Preference" has a computer database containing price and product information on over 25,000 top brand name products and on every make of car from suppliers and wholesalers around the country. Because "Preference" deals directly with the supplier, most over-head costs are eliminated and members are able to shop at near wholesale prices.

2. If I order something, how do I pick it up?

All goods ordered are delivered to any specified destination within mainland Britain at no extra cost. In the case of cars, in some circumstances, a nominal amount may be charged. There are no hidden extras!

3. How long does it take to get a price quote?

The consultant will quote you the total price (including VAT and delivery) within seconds.

4. How much can I order? How often can I call?

You can call as often as you like, and order as many products as you like, but we do limit the number of any one model to six per order.

5. When I call the Service, how will the operator know I'm a member?

The operator will ask you for your membership number.

6. Am I under obligation to make purchases?

No. You're under no obligation to purchase. You can use 'Preference' to obtain product information and price quotes which can aid you in shopping for the best value.

7. Can I get a refund of my membership fee?

If you don't save £50 in your first membership year, then on request, your membership fee will be refunded in full.

8. How long does it take to receive an order?

Most purchases are delivered within three weeks. The average is about 14 days.

9. Can I cancel an order?

You can cancel your order as long as the merchandise has not been despatched. After the merchandise has been despatched, your request for cancellation would be handled on a case by case basis. Our experienced After Sales Department will assist you.

10. Product/brand name examples.

All makes and models of new car are available through "Preference".

The Home & Motoring Service aims to offer the very widest range of top brand name models currently available in the UK. Household names available include Hotpoint, Sony, Flymo, Omega, Amstrad and Zanussi.

11. Do I have to pay by my Diners Club Card?

We recommend that you use your Diners Club Card because it's the fastest, and most convenient way, to process your order. However, we do accept other methods of payment.

12. Are there any additional/hidden charges?

There are absolutely no additional charges or fees, and you're under no obligation to make a purchase. The price quoted by your Consultant is always the fully delivered price.

13. Do I receive a warranty/what if my product needs servicing?

All warranteed merchandise you purchase comes with all the manufacturers' guarantees and warranties in full effect if applicable. If it needs service under warranty, the manufacturers' authorised service outlet will repair it. However, if you fail to get satisfaction from the manufacturer or have any queries, our After Sales Actionline will be happy to assist you. "Preference" will do everything it can to make sure you're a satisfied customer.

14. When can I phone/use the Service?

All services are available 9 am to 5.00 pm Monday to Friday. The Household and Leisure Service is additionally available Monday – Friday evenings, 5.00 pm to 9.00 pm and Saturday 9.00 am– 5.00 pm The Motoring Service is additionally available Monday to Friday 5.00 pm–5.30 pm and 9.00 am–12.30 pm on Saturday.

15. What's in the Membership Pack?

Your Membership Pack will include full instructions on how to use the Service, along with your personal membership card and our written lowest price promise.

16. Sounds like too much trouble.

Actually shopping through "Preference" could not be easier. All you have to do is 'phone the Service and give the name and model of the product you're interested in to the consultant. They will quote you the fully delivered price. Then if you decide to purchase through the Service your order will be delivered to any specified destination in mainland Britain. Using "Preference" is as simple as picking up your telephone.

17. Can you send me/do you have a catalogue?

No, Mr/Mrs ... we would need around 70 large mail order type catalogues and they would be out of date before they went to print. But once you're a member, you will receive our Buyers Advantage Magazine featuring articles on certain products, which is available quarterly. If you're thinking of buying something we would recommend that you ring the service first.

18. How/when will my membership be renewed? What happens at the end of 12 months?

Mr/Mrs ... to ensure you receive uninterrupted service your membership will automatically be renewed in your twelfth month of paid membership and the £30 membership fee will appear on your following statement.

19. I have a problem with my account, who should I call?

Mr/Mrs ... Diners Club Membership Service handles all enquiries regarding account information. You may contact them on 0252 513500 or alternatively, if I can take your day time telephone number, I will get them to give you a call.

20. How was I selected for this offer/why did Diners Club give you my number to call?

You were selected because you are a valued Diners Club customer and would most likely appreciate this special convenient time and money saving service.

21. £50 savings guarantee/membership guarantee.

We are so confident that we can save you money, that if you haven't saved £50 through using the Service in your first year, we will on request refund your membership in full. (Any application of this guarantee must be made no later than thirty days from the end of your first year's membership.)

22. Best price guarantee/Home Service guarantee.

We guarantee that if you find the same item for immediate sale to the public at a lower price elsewhere, in the UK, and notify the Service within 15 days of purchasing the product through the Home Service, we will not only refund the difference but also refund another 20 per cent of that difference. (Just send in verifiable proof, such as a copy of the advertisement.)

23. £500 savings guarantee – Motoring Service.

We guarantee to save you at least £500 off the manufacturer's list price, plus 'on the road charges', on any make or model of new car bought through the Motoring Service.

24. More information on jewellery service.

Well it's very simple really. All you do is give us a call. We then pass your details to our jewellery supplier who, after giving you a call to find out what you have in mind, will send you the items after payment on seven days home approval. The items are only of the highest quality but if they aren't suitable they can be returned and all your money refunded. There's no obligation to buy, and savings would be up to 25 per cent against high street selling prices.

25. More information on new and nearly new cars.

You can have advice and information on all makes and models of new car, with a guaranteed saving of at least £500 off the list price.

Also, you have an opportunity to buy ex-rental cars which will be of a guaranteed standard, less than six months old and with no more than 8,000 miles driven. But more significantly we offer some dramatic savings on the book price.

26. More information on used car advice and information service.

What the Service offers is an impartial guide to members on the various ways of selling a used car, independent advice on prices and how to avoid pitfalls. We also offer a 'collect and sell' service, so that if a member doesn't want to deal direct with the buyer, we can arrange to have the car sold at auction. We also offer independent prices and advice on buying a used car.

27. More information on the Home Service.

'Preference' holds over 25,000 top brand household and leisure items which generally cost over £50 and which are worth shopping around for. We provide information which helps our members when shopping around and, as well as providing a very convenient means of purchasing items, we guarantee the lowest prices in the country. So really it is a very worthwhile service.

28. How does the . . . trial work?

Mr/Mrs . . . the offer works like this; to enable you to try the service, you are being offered . . . of the Home and Motoring Service at . . . Once you've had a chance to use the Service, we're hoping that you'll accept a full year of membership for only £30. If you do, we will automatically charge you after your . . . is up. If you decide that the Service is not for you, please call the Service during your trial and your account won't be charged. That number will be in your membership kit.

29. Will I still get my dividend points using this Service?

Yes Mr/Mrs ... any of the products purchased via "Preference" will still entitle you to get your dividend points.

* * * * *

Diners Club/CUC Europe
caller information

What company are you calling from?

We are calling from The Decisions Group, a telephone marketing agency commissioned by Diners Club to conduct a customer services programme to members.

IF NECESSARY : Our aims being to check that you have received your re-issued card and to notify you of an exciting new service.

Where did you get my name and address from?

We are calling from The Decisions Group, a telephone marketing agency commissioned by Diners Club to conduct a customer services programme to members, ensuring that, for fraud and security reasons, charge cards have been received and signed.

POINTS TO NOTE

SPEAK TO NAMED CONTACT ONLY – NOT SPOUSE
NOTIFY MEMBER OF SECURITY VALIDATION PROCESS

ALWAYS REFER TO DINERS CLUB CARDHOLDERS AS MEMBERS

IF NOT RECEIVED ALL CARDS
TERMINATE CALL (NOTE ON CALL CARD)

PRODUCT QUERY/ACCOUNT QUERY
REFER TO MEMBER SERVICES DEPARTMENT 0252 513500/OR NOTE
CONVENIENT DAY FOR MEMBER SERVICES TO CALL BACK

* * * * *

They help to ensure that appropriate follow-up action is taken and determine what information about the market will be obtained from the campaign, which helps in planning future activities. In the Diners Club/CUC Europe campaign, for example, callers were not only recording four different types of 'order' (ORD) for the

'Preference' service, but also specific reasons why certain contacts were 'not interested' (NI) and the accuracy of the telephone numbers being called (NS).

The call card, once completed, contains a great deal of valuable information, according to what has been incorporated in the design, for example:

- who made the call – for checking individuals' accuracy and ensuring that the same person can call back if necessary;

- confirmed details of the contact – so that the database can be updated;

- the type of 'order' placed, perhaps a literature request, so that the appropriate action can be taken;

- reasons for negative responses, which can be useful in refining the campaign, planning new marketing strategies etc;

- special problems – so that appropriate action can be taken;

- details of new leads;

- feedback on products or services, for example usage;

- which advertisement generated an incoming call.

The use of call codes enables information from individual telephone marketers, and the team as a whole, to be collated quickly without having to read through every call card. Responsibilities for reporting information, and the frequency, will depend on the nature of the campaign. Where swift action is required, such as sending out a brochure, call cards may be sorted periodically throughout the day and passed to whoever is handling brochure fulfilment. On the first day of a campaign, unexpected results or the failure to gain the expected level of positive responses, will generally be reported immediately to the supervisor or team leaders. Call cards provide the basis for this type of detailed, organised reporting.

Accuracy and legibility of recorded information are critical and it is essential that the need for accuracy and clear handwriting are stressed and that standards of quality are closely monitored and rigidly maintained. Call cards enable supervisors periodically to 'quality check' individuals' work, by telephoning a proportion of the contacts to gauge the accuracy of the data recorded.

Caller's Log

Name: ....   **Date:** ....

COMPANY NAME	POSTCODE	CALL CODE	TIME OF CALL	COMMENTS	CHECKED BY

Figure 4.9 Example of a caller's log

Caller's log Telephone staff use this form to record brief details of each call they make. An example is given in Figure 4.9. The form serves a number of important functions:

- it shows, at a glance, how many calls each person has made/received, including the number of calls made per hour (call rate), and the outcome of each one;

- it provides information on the timing of each call (which can influence results) and the time between calls (a combined indication of call length and the time the telephone marketer takes to prepare for the next call);

- it shows how each contact has reacted to a call, for example pleased, indifferent, unhappy;

- a supervisor uses the form to cross-check every call card.

This document provides further information for monitoring and controlling telephone activities. A sizeable fluctuation in the call rate at different times of the day, for example, could indicate that callers need motivating during the troughs. A disproportionate number of negative responses at particular times of the day could suggest that the target audience is not very receptive to this type of call at that time of the day.

Call breakdown sheet   Telephone marketers use this sheet to provide a breakdown of each day's calls, recording the number of each category of response they have received (taken from their completed call cards). Supervisors use the same sheet to collate this information from all telephone marketers and, if there is more than one team working on the campaign, from each team. A completed example is shown in Figure 4.10.

The breakdown sheet is a very simple mechanism which provides a wealth of information for managing, controlling and improving a campaign. It monitors precisely what is happening on the campaign, by individual, by team and overall, on a daily and cumulative basis. For example, it shows:

- call rate (total calls divided by call hours);

- conversion rate (positive responses divided by total calls);

- daily trends in type of response;

- daily trends in call rate and conversion rate;

- total number of calls and positive responses to date;

- number of calls still to be made (total leads minus total calls made);

- number of positive responses still required (target minus number achieved so far).

Call breakdown sheet

Operator name: ..Douglas............   Targeted call rate: ..3–4.........
Client name: ....   Targeted conv. rate: ..15%......
Job no: ..D..178....................   Project: ..Test Drive...........

| | | Effective calls | | | | | | | | Objectives | | Non-effective dials | |
DATE	CALL HRS.	TD1	TD2	AS	LIT	N11	N12	SP	TOT. EFF. CALL	CALL RATE	CONV RATE	UR	N/S
21/5	5	2	6		4		2	4	18	3.6	44%		3
TOTAL	5	2	6		4		2	4	18	3.6	44%		3
22/5	6½	5	7	3	6		3		24	3.7	50%	3	5
TOTAL	11½	7	13	3	10		5	4	42	3.7	48%	3	8
23/5	6	4	12		4	2	2		24	4	67%		5
TOTAL	17½	11	25	3	14	2	7	4	66	3.8	55%	3	13
TOTAL													
TOTAL													
TOTAL													

Call Codes
TD1 – Test drive model A.
TD2 – Test drive model B.
AS   – Already supplied.
LIT   – Information requested.
NI1   – Not interested in test drive.
NI2   – Interested in test drive but not now.
SP   – Special interest for the future.
UR   – Unreachable.
N/S – Number search.

Figure 4.10 Example of a completed call breakdown sheet.

A supervisor can use this information to decide what action is required, if any, to optimise campaign results. Here are some examples of questions to ask.

- If an individual or team call rate is lower than average or falling, what is the reason and what can be done to improve things? Is it poor technique, lack of confidence, low morale? Does the caller or team need re-briefing?

- Similarly, if the conversion rate is falling, what is the cause and what can be done about it?

- If the number of responses in one category is unexpectedly low, what is the reason? Could it be the script, the approach, the target market? What can be done about it?

- If the number of positive responses, perhaps orders or literature requests, is unexpectedly high, are the resources available to meet these needs?

- If half the campaign calling time has been used up and only a quarter of the leads have been contacted, can the calling rate be stepped up or should additional staff be briefed?

The information on this document is obviously invaluable for monitoring and controlling a campaign – provided that it is used effectively. Some people advocate doing an hourly analysis of calls, although this is rather cumbersome and time-consuming, and the information is rarely used. On occasion, however, it can be useful. If the best time for calling a particular target market is not known, for example, then hourly analysis of call results will quickly show when contacts are most readily available. Similarly, it can be used to show at which times telephone marketers are generally flagging and need a break (although this information can also be identified from the caller's log).

A skilled supervisor will have no trouble using a manual system for this type of analysis, and acting upon it, but computerisation offers greater speed and flexibility where a large amount of interrelated information is gathered. Comparing regional variations in response combined with variations in different target markets, for example, requires considerable cross-correlation and extensive work if done manually. Using a computerised system, it is simply a matter of keying in the parameters and reading the printout.

Other documentation   Some types of application may require other documentation. In making appointments for a sales force, for example, some kind of diary would have to maintained for each representative. When booking people on to company events, a running total of acceptances has to be maintained to ensure that an event is not overbooked.

Management reports   Campaigns result in a diverse range of information of value both to the management of the unit and to internal users of the resource. Users will have specified at the briefing stage what information they require, according to the objectives of the campaign. Apart from the number or value of orders achieved, for example, they may have wanted specific information on why people were or were not buying, what size of company was placing orders most frequently and so on. The telephone marketing manager, on the other hand, will be especially interested in how efficiently the campaign was run and perhaps how it compares with other campaigns targeted at similar target audiences or those run in similar vertical markets. Lessons can be learned to help improve the general efficiency of operations, and the design and running of future campaigns.

Administrative systems

Telephone marketing involves a considerable amount of administrative work, because of the detailed planning, the use and generation of large volumes of data, and the close monitoring and control of activities. Departmental structure, examined earlier, plays a major role in effective administration. Roles and responsibilities for each member of staff will have been clearly defined to meet the specified objectives of the unit, and the administrative systems should be designed to formalise the execution, monitoring and control of these activities. Recording systems obviously play a key role in administration, as do procedures.

Procedures

Procedures for all aspects of the unit's operation should be clearly defined at the outset, covering areas such as:

- staffing matters, for example selection and recruitment, disciplinary procedures, appraisal, performance and salary reviews, training;

- liaison with users – who, when, where, how often?

- development of campaign strategies, briefs, call content and scripts;

- call cycling, for example how many times will unavailable contacts be recalled and how will callers keep track of this, and how will call-backs be organised?

- lead sourcing and preparation;

- callers briefing and de-briefing – when, where, how, and by whom?

- data recording and collation;

- data entry;

- filing.

Procedures need to be regularly updated and refined to accommodate changing needs, for example if and when the unit begins to handle mailing fulfilment or if it is computerised.

Standards

Clearly defined standards of performance are a key feature of the way in which telephone marketers are managed efficiently through monitoring and control of their activities. Everyone, no matter what their job, needs to know exactly what is expected of them, in terms of both quality and quantity of work, if they are to work to the best of their abilities. Having standards of performance defined for all aspects of a job helps both telephone marketers and management as follows.

- For **telephone marketers** they:
  - set clear targets to aim for in each of their activities;
  - encourage them to stretch themselves to achieve higher performance;
  - provide a yardstick against which to measure their abilities and their contribution to the success of their team;
  - add to job satisfaction when targets are achieved.

- For **management** they:
  - provide a way to motivate staff;

- provide a yardstick against which to monitor and measure individual and team performance;
- help to identify areas of individual and team weakness and strength;
- help to plan development activities to improve performance.

There are different kinds of standards and some are easier to define than others. The number of calls that should be made in an hour, for example, is easily defined and it is equally straightforward to measure what individuals achieve. When it comes to more qualitative issues, however, such as telephone manner or handling objections, standards of performance are more subjective. The way around this problem is to ensure thorough initial and ongoing training. People should be shown regularly, by example, what standards they should be achieving. Careful monitoring of call results will generally indicate if there is a problem, which the supervisor can then identify by listening in to calls.

Specific activities for which standards have to be set will vary, depending on the campaign, but the main areas to cover include:

- call handling, for example use of script, objection handling, application of background knowledge;

- objectives of the call, for example identifying needs, grading prospect potential, setting appointments;

- calling statistics, for example call rate, decision-maker contact rate, conversion rate;

- recording of responses;

- associated tasks, for example diary maintenance, mailing fulfilment, liaison with users.

The process of setting, monitoring and maintaining standards has to be built into the operational systems, for example the use of call records to monitor and measure performance. Standards are maintained through a variety of measures, such as training and motivation, for which there should also be clear procedures. Expected standards of performance will obviously change as staff become more experienced and skilled. Many of them will also change from campaign to campaign, and during a campaign. Setting objectives and targets for different campaigns, and upgrading them as campaigns progress, is an ongoing process which is a part of campaign planning and management described in Chapter 8.

Designing and developing operational systems is clearly a complicated and time-consuming process. However, it provides the framework through which activities are co-ordinated and integrated to ensure success of the unit. As such, it is the key to successful implementation of in-house telephone marketing and, wherever possible, all systems should be tested, benchmarked and fine-tuned prior to the launch of the unit.

The database and information management

A database is essential for the efficient running of an in-house telephone marketing unit, and its value is greatly enhanced when it forms a shared resource for all sales and marketing activities. Establishing a successful database starts with thorough planning, which should cover the following areas.

Will the database be computerised?   Although the telephone marketing unit is best run on manual systems initially, the benefits of computerising the database greatly outweigh any disadvantages. Without the storage and analytical capabilities of a computer system, the volume and variety of data that can be held, and the sophistication of analysis, is severely limited.

There is a growing choice of relatively inexpensive software applications packages which offer sophisticated information management to support sales and marketing activities. The application areas of one such product, *Pro.File* from CCS Pippbrook, are shown in Table 4.2. Many of these software products provide the capability to export data to other systems, which means that integration with other systems, perhaps when the telephone marketing operation is automated, for example, is relatively straightforward.

An increasingly popular way of justifying the investment required to establish and maintain a sophisticated computerised database is by employing a telephone marketing agency or other specialist to test its viability. They can provide consultancy to help the company design, build and maintain the database, or carry out the work on their own premises. In the latter case, once it is up and running and has proved cost-effective, the database can either be transferred in-house or

Table 4.2 Example of the features offered by modern sales and marketing support systems

Pro.File – Application areas	
Marketing database:	*Telephone marketing:*
• Data collection • Customer/Prospect profiles • Lead generation and tracking • Response analysis • Competitive products • Management reports • Statistics • Letters and labels • Major account management • Commercial database	• Customer/Prospect Records • Prompted re-calls • Re-order cycles • On-line telesales – inbound/outbound • Call summaries • Management reports • Action lists
Field sales management:	*Customer care:*
• Sales records • Lead generation • Appointments diary • Pre-call briefing reports • Post-call reporting • Journey/territory planning • Account monitoring • Sales force monitoring • Reports and analyses • Bonus calculations • Quotation tracking • Management reports	• Customer histories • Contract renewals • After sales servicing • Maintenance and support contracts • Consumables promotion • Repeat purchase promotion • Customer loyalty programmes • Customer correspondence generation • New products into client base

Source: CCS Pippbrook Limited, reprinted with permission.

managed long term by the agency. If there is a prospect of the database being brought in-house, it is vital that the system used by the agency will allow data to be easily transferred to the company's computer system and that the format of data is compatible with any other systems, such as accounts, that will link with the database. Specialists will also often be able to provide training for company staff responsible for the management and development of the database.

What are realistic objectives for the database? The company's short and long-term business objectives need to be analysed to identify what support the database must provide, for example what sales and marketing management information is, and will be, required. The first step is to decide who will use, and contribute information for, the database. Their individual needs will determine the information to be stored and help ensure that the full potential of the database is exploited. Above all, the database should provide all the information management support required to meet the objectives of the telephone marketing unit. Financial objectives for the database should also be set to act as a benchmark for ongoing evaluation of its performance and productivity.

There is a significant danger, when planning and using a large computerised database, that it will come to dominate all other company systems. The infomation it provides is of such value that it can be seen, mistakenly, as the core resource in managing the company. As such, it can have a stifling effect by dictating and restricting business strategies and tactics. The database has only a support role, like any other management system, and it must be set realistic objectives.

Who will bear the cost?   This issue becomes increasingly important the larger and more costly the database. Ideally, in the long term, it should be shared proportionately between all departments who benefit from the database. This will entail selling the benefits to all prospective users.

A database can be highly cost-effective, but setting one up is a complex and costly exercise. Maintaining it is even more costly. If dedicated outbound calling is used, for example, it could cost in the region of £300,000 a year to maintain a database of 100,000 names. However, this can be reduced considerably if outbound and inbound campaigns include database cleaning as a secondary objective, and if the database is a shared resource with different departments contributing to the database.

In recent years there has been a trend towards co-operative usage of databases, where several companies, each with a different interest in particular target markets, share the costs of establishing and maintaining a large database. In a similar vein, Connections in Business, British Telecom's telephone marketing division, maintains a massive business database which is continuously developed with major customers. These customers have the sole use of the information relevant to their needs at a fraction of what it would cost to maintain a similar database themselves.

How will the database objectives be achieved? The contribution the database should make to different corporate activities will have been defined when setting its objectives. Achievement of those objectives should be carefully planned, detailing the flow of information in and out of the database to and from all the relevant functional and operational departments. This should include specification of what information will be required and in what format.

Who will maintain and manage the database? At an early stage it should be decided who will be responsible for entering information on to the database, both at the beginning and once the database is established. If the database is computerised and integrated with other systems, such as accounts, some of the updating will eventually be automatic. However, for a new database, the major proportion, if not all, of the initial data entry will probably be manual. Management of a large database, with responsibility for its usage and long-term development, is a specialised job and the person appointed may require training.

What information will the database hold? Information is what gives the database its value but it is all too easy to get it wrong, by over-burdening it with irrelevant, useless information, or not including information essential to meet its objectives. The information required by all users of the database, on each type of contact, should be clearly defined so that all their needs are accommodated. However, the amount of information that can be held on each contact and used effectively will obviously be determined by the sophistication of the system being used. On an existing business customer it might contain the following details:

- company name, address, phone number and post code;
- type of business;
- number of employees;
- number and location of sites;
- turnover;
- types of products/services used;
- total amount/breakdown of annual spend on these;

- current supplier/usage of competitors;

- decision-maker name(s) and job title(s);

- personal details, for example hobbies and interests;

- original lead source;

- contact history – activities (such as appointment, seminar attendance, telephone marketing campaigns, direct mail, service requests), with date and outcome (including contact comments, preferences etc);

- sales of products/services, with dates and details of price, discounts, special offers etc;

- total value of sales;

- credit status and payment performance.

A consumer database will cover some of these areas (for example usage of competitors and contact history), as well as information such as sex, age, profession, salary, family status, number and age of children, hobbies and interests, type of property and whether it is owned or rented.

This type of information enables the relative value or potential value of contacts to be calculated so that the database can be segmented and marketing activities planned accordingly (segmentation will be examined in more detail in Chapter 9). Maximum benefit is obtained when information can be analysed quickly and flexibly, for example in using the profiles of existing high-value customers to identify potential high-value prospects.

Note that, in the UK, the collection, storage and use of personal data is covered by the Data Protection Act 1984, the implications of which are examined in Chapter 10.

Where will the information be obtained? One of the biggest tasks in establishing a database is collating the vast amount of information which already exists in different parts of the organisation, such as accounts, the sales force and the service department. Unfortunately, this information is often found in different formats. A big headache for the banks, for example, when they began establishing marketing databases, was that their records were all based on account numbers rather than account holder/customer names. The first task is therefore to sift through the available information, including lapsed customers, prospects and other leads, and merge it into individual records. In the long term, when a fully-fledged marketing database is established, all departments should operate compatible systems.

The next immediate source is likely to be new data coming into the organisation. Every department and individual responsible for providing information for the database should be set a minimum standard of information for each type of contact and contact activity. An important source is the sales force, who must be encouraged to pass on relevant information from and about customers. Procedures must be developed to ensure the smooth flow of information in and out of the database and all staff affected should receive appropriate training, for example to ensure that information is accurately collected and recorded.

It makes sense to gather information when it is most readily available and this should be taken into account when setting minimum standards of information for each contact activity. Application forms for AA membership, for example, ask for the applicant's motor insurance renewal date (ie when to approach them to sell motor insurance) and date of birth (for selling life policies).

Information on new prospects and suspects may come from direct mail coupon responses and telephone marketing, or it can be researched or bought in. Sources of data include list brokers, trade directories and trade organisations, local chambers of commerce and business telephone directories. All information obtained should be added to the database as soon as possible to avoid duplication.

Establishing, maintaining and developing a marketing database, examined in more detail in Chapter 9, is a highly complex and costly exercise which is likely to require changes in many areas of company operations. Total management commitment is therefore required if the database is to achieve its full potential.

Telephone equipment and lines

The requirements for telephone equipment and lines will have been partly defined by the choice of applications for telephone marketing, either inbound or outbound, and their scale. A small unit of 5 callers making outbound calls, for example, will require a different scale of investment and planning than a unit with 50 callers handling inbound as well as outbound calls. In either case, however, careful analysis of likely telephone traffic flow is necessary to ensure that the optimum level of resources are provided. Inbound and outbound call-handling should be considered separately.

Outbound calls

The number of outbound lines required is determined by the expected peak activity levels within the unit, ie the number of callers who will be making calls at the same time. This figure will have been determined when planning staffing levels and work schedules. However, it is important to make allowance for unexpected demands and growth of the unit by providing an additional line or lines, according to the scale of the operation. Lines will also be required by the supervisor(s) and manager, and provision must be made for internal communications.

Inbound calls

Deciding on the inbound call-handling requirements is generally more complex. The number and type of lines required are determined by the applications and the expected peak call rates. But, unlike outbound calls, it is not necessary to have a one-to-one ratio of lines per call. Call-queuing systems are available which hold incoming calls when all lines are engaged and release them once someone is available to answer. The type and sophistication of the system chosen should provide optimum efficiency of call handling. If special services are required, such as 0800 or FreeFone, a choice has to be made based on which will be the most cost-effective for particular applications (*see* pages 179–80).

Mistakes in planning inbound call-handling can be costly, through choosing the wrong type of lines, not providing sufficient capacity, or in paying for capacity that does not get used.

Automatic call distributors (ACDs)

ACDs, which are call-queuing systems, are becoming increasingly sophisticated. At the basic level they act like an automatic switchboard. When all lines associated with a particular telephone number are engaged, someone dialling that number will hear the ringing tone, rather than the engaged tone, and will be held in a queue until someone is available to answer it. Calls are released in the order they come in, so that they are answered on a first-come, first-served basis. The major drawback is that callers may think that, when they hear the ringing tone but no one answers, the telephones are unattended.

At the next level are ACDs which use digital technology to answer calls as they come in, with a message such as 'You are held in a queue and your call will be answered as soon as possible'. Some systems also provide the facility for callers to leave their personal details, so that they can be called back as soon as someone is available to talk to them.

Another facility provided by some ACDs is Direct Dial In (DDI). This enables a range of telephone numbers to use the same group of telephone lines, with the ACD identifying which number was dialled. The main advantage is greater flexibility and efficiency, utilising the same lines for several numbers. So the number range 0800 200 200–210 could have each of the 11 numbers dedicated to a different application, for example, or different geographical regions. When one of these numbers is dialled, for example 0800 200 205, the ACD identifies the number dialled and displays it to the telephone marketer who can then answer the call appropriately. This is how some large agencies, with many campaigns running concurrently, are able to answer incoming calls with the client name. Some ACDs can be linked to computers. As a call comes in the ACD identifies the number dialled, tells the computer, and when the call is released to a telephone marketer the computer sends information relevant to the campaign assigned to that telephone number. If four inbound campaigns were being run concurrently, for example, this could be used to call up automatically the relevant script according to which number has been dialled.

There are several benefits in using automatic call distributors. Call-queuing means that, provided the company does not mind callers having to wait, calls can be serviced efficiently with a smaller number of staff. They make more efficient use of staff by distributing calls evenly, and also provide statistics on calling patterns which is invaluable for monitoring campaigns and organising staffing schedules. DDI enables more efficient use of lines with corresponding cost savings.

The choice of the number of lines and switching equipment depends on the applications, and the expected volume and peak levels of calls. Testing an application with an agency will provide details of calling patterns and British Telecom will use this to analyse traffic flows and recommend the optimum number of lines. Getting the correct level of switching capacity is essential for efficient call-handling. If it is too low, the unit will not be able to cope with incoming calls and money will have been wasted in generating those calls. If it is too high, money will have been spent providing capacity that is not needed.

Call monitoring and taping equipment

Call monitoring, by a supervisor or senior telephone marketer, is an essential element in the training and development of callers. A variety of silent monitoring equipment is available which enables someone to listen in to a call without either party in the conversation being disturbed. This is far more effective than the supervisor sitting next to the caller, because the caller is unaware of the monitoring and the supervisor can hear clearly both sides of the conversation.

Equipment for taping calls can serve a similar purpose, regularly taping a proportion of calls for monitoring purposes, although it may also be used where all calls must be monitored, perhaps for legal reasons. It is not illegal in the UK for one party in a telephone conversation to record it without informing the other party(ies). However, under the Interception of Communications Act 1985, 'a person who intentionally intercepts a communication in the course of its transmission by post or by means of a public telecommunicaitons system shall be guilty of an offence'. It is illegal, therefore, to record or listen in to the calls of third parties, ie when the person recording or eavesdropping on the conversation is not participating in it. Technically, therefore, a call can only be recorded, or monitored live, at the instigation of the telephone marketer participating in the conversation.

Special inbound services

The facilities provided by special telephone services, such as LinkLine and Callstream have been described in Chapter 2. Numbers provided under these services carry only incoming calls, which is why they must be planned independently of outbound requirements.

Waiting times for provision of the different services range from around ten days, up to possibly four months (although sometimes much less), so a decision on which service is required, how many lines and when, must be made early in the planning process. Each service has a different charging structure, which means that one may prove more cost-effective than another according to the number of calls generated by the particular application. The cost of alternative services should therefore be evaluated for each application. The following details, correct in December 1990, are provided only to illustrate how the various services are more suited to some applications than others. All costs are exclusive of VAT and lead times are approximate.

LinkLine 0800 and 0345   Both these services are offered under three different price options. The connection charges and quarterly rental are the same, but the call charge structure is slightly different, reflecting the cost of a local call borne by callers using 0345 numbers.

Table 4.3   British Telecom LinkLine price options

LinkLine (0800 & 0345) Options		
	Option 1	*Option 2*	*Option 3*
Connection charge (per number)	£250	£250	£250
Quarterly rental (per number)	£50	£300	£87.50
Call Charges (per minute or part thereof)			
0800 rate – peak	17.6p	16p	16p
standard	13.2p	12p	12p
cheap	9.9p	9p	9p
0345 rate – peak	14.6p	13p	13p
standard	11.2p	10p	10p
cheap	7.9p	7p	7p

The options are shown in Table 4.3. With options 1 and 2, calls come through on the company's normal telephone lines, so that they can also be used for normal incoming and outgoing calls. Normal charges therefore apply for this usage, in addition to the LinkLine charges. Option 3 provides customers with dedicated LinkLine exchange lines, which can only be used for incoming LinkLine calls. There are also volume reductions on call charges under options 2 and 3 for both services. In each calendar month the number of minutes charged for all calls (excluding those from Telecom Eireann) to a single telephone billing number is accumulated; this determines the price applicable to the next call. Discounts vary from 10 to 48 per cent, depending on the service and the price option.

Option 1 is aimed at companies who want to take advantage of the service, but who do not expect a large volume of calls. The second option is aimed at those who expect a larger volume of calls and at those who want the flexibility of a choice of number(s) from those available. Option 3 is aimed at companies who also expect larger volumes of call, and want a choice of number(s) (when ordering 11 or more lines), but who also want to be able to segregate their LinkLine calls from ordinary telephone traffic.

Both LinkLine 0800 and 0345 services can be obtained in about ten days.

Advanced LinkLine   To obtain Advanced LinkLine, companies first subscribe to a LinkLine option appropriate to their needs, paying the connection charge, quarterly rental and call charges applying to that option. Then there is a one-off connection charge of £2,000 for Advanced LinkLine services, plus a call charge, in addition to the LinkLine costs, of 1p per minute or part thereof. Each change to the call-handling requirements at the customer's request is charged at £300, and activation of a pre-set emergency plan costs £75 on each occasion. There is also a connection and rental charge for any customised messages the customer may require. Lead times for the provision of the Advanced LinkLine service depend partly on the amount of work required to analyse a company's call-handling requirements.

Callstream   Charges for the Callstream (0898) service are shown in Table 4.4. There is a minimum rental period of 12 months for the basic facility, and 12 months for the managed service, unless 30 lines

Table 4.4 British Telecom Callstream (0898) service charges

BT Callstream (0898)	
Basic facility (minimum 10 lines per location)	
Connection charge (per exchange line)	
Within a Callstream home exchange area	£126.74
Outside a Callstream home exchange area	£315.00
Rental Charges (per line per quarter)	
Varies depending upon proximity of	from £24.83
premises to the Callstream exchange	
Managed service (minimum 10 lines)	
Connection charge	nil
Charge per line per quarter	£250.00
Charge per 3 minutes memory (per quarter)	
For messages changed:	
no more than once per week	£75.00
no more than once per working day	£200.00
Mass Access Service* (up to 500 lines available)	
For 1 quarter	£120,000–£148,000
For 1 week	£12,000–£14,000
For 1 day	£2,400–£2,800
For 1 evening (8pm–midnight)	£800
* Prices vary according to precise requirements; typically they would be as shown	

or more are being rented, in which case it is only 3 months. Some or all of the cost of using Callstream lines can be recouped, depending on the volume of calls generated. The renter receives 22.5p per minute of usage, paid monthly, which comes from the charges made to callers.

The demand for Callstream lines at December 1990 was high and service provision could take around three to four months. Set-up of a managed service takes about ten days.

International 0800   This service is charged at £82.50 per quarter per number, plus the cost of calls which are charged per second or part second of connected time at the prevailing international rates. The minimum rental period is three months. Chargeable time over 2,000 minutes per number per quarter attracts a discount of approximately 10 per cent. An archiving service is available which enables customers to retain their International 0800 numbers while barring any calls; this has a reduced rental of £45 per number per quarter. Service can be provided within about three weeks.

FreeFone   There is a one-off set-up charge of £250 per FreeFone name, plus a quarterly rental of £50. Calls are charged to the renter at the operator-assisted rate, varying according to the time of day and where calls originate, and there is a minimum three-minute charge. Calls made from private telephones are charged by the minute thereafter, and from payphones in three-minute steps. In addition, there is a surcharge of £1.00 per call (effective from April 1991). Service can be provided within about four weeks.

Deciding which type of service is required involves evaluating the facilities offered by each against the intended application, and calculating the overall cost. In choosing between LinkLine 0800 and 0345, for example, the principal criterion will be what proportion of prospective callers will be deterred, if any, by having to pay for their call, albeit at the local call rate. Choosing between the three LinkLine price options depends upon the expected volume of calls, whether the company wants a choice of number and/or a dedicated line. British Telecom estimates that a company receiving around 40 calls per day, for example, would find option 2 more cost-effective than option 1, because the lower call charges more than offset the higher quarterly rental.

The cost of using Callstream can be calculated by comparing the revenue that would be generated by the expected volume of calls, and the charge period during which they are likely to be made, with the set-up, rental and running costs. The volume of calls will obviously depend on the appeal of the offer being made, for example providing valuable or interesting information, the opportunity to obtain a free sample or the chance of winning a prize. A test by a managed service provider will provide an approximate figure for the cost of, or the revenue generated by, providing a long-term telephone-based information service.

FreeFone offers the added value of branding, callers do not need to remember a string of numbers, and the service renter receives a report on the time calls were made and where they originated. Despite its high cost per call, it can be more cost-effective than LinkLine when a comparatively small number of high-value responses are generated, and for short-duration/low-volume campaigns.

Deciding whether the additional cost of using Advanced LinkLine can be justified involves evaluating the sophisticated facilities it offers. In a national campaign using a single telephone number, for example, what advantage will be gained from having incoming calls automatically routed to local offices? When using different regional numbers, what will be the cost benefit of having all calls made outside business hours routed automatically to one office? Some companies using the service have arranged to have calls which cannot be answered in-house, because of the momentary load of calls, to be diverted to a telephone marketing agency. The sophistication of the service, which is under continuous development, is such that expert analysis of call-handling requirements is required to exploit it fully. British Telecom will advise companies on this and all their other services to ensure that their requirements are met cost-effectively.

The selection of telephones and headsets is covered towards the end of the next section.

The working environment

To get the best out of skilled staff they need to be encouraged and stimulated to achieve high standards of performance; they need to feel that their contribution is valued and that the company is doing everything possible to support their efforts. Providing the right type of working environment plays a key role in creating this type of atmosphere and it is particularly important in telephone marketing, where the work is often tedious and monotonous. This extends beyond the physical environment, of course, and includes the style of management and corporate policies, systems and procedures. The latter two elements are described in Chapter 7 in connection with motivation.

The physical environment

The physical environment should be conducive to, and supportive of, efficient working on both physical and psychological levels. Visiting a variety of telephone marketing agencies will provide tips on the type of environment that would work best for a particular in-house unit. There are two main elements to consider – the workspace and physical resources.

The workspace This should be light and airy, with a good level of natural light throughout the day, a comfortable, even temperature (ie good ventilation and heating), low levels of noise and minimum through traffic. Artificial lighting should provide a diffuse rather than patchy light and not be too bright.

Although the background noise of others working provides a stimulating environment, several people talking at once, particularly if some of them have bad lines, can create a distracting level of noise. A thick, good quality carpet and soundproofed walls and ceilings help to keep noise to acceptable levels.

Open-plan offices work best, allowing easy communication and creating a buzz of activity. In smaller units the supervisor and manager are best situated in the same room. In a large unit it is often more practical to have the manager situated in a separate office off the main calling area. If the telephone marketers are going to be divided into teams, members of each team are best grouped together and physically separated from other teams. This helps to build working relationships, facilitates the flow of work and consolidates team identity. There should also be some form of demarcation between different teams, for example at groups of work stations rather than all lumped together. Again, this helps to create a sense of team identity. Overcrowding must be avoided at all costs.

In addition to the workspace, there should be somewhere for staff to get away and relax during their break times. This may be where staff lockers, facilities to hang coats, and so on, are provided. Since smoking in the work area should be banned, this room can serve as a smoking area, although it may be necessary to provide separate smoking and no-smoking rooms. These areas should provide a level of comfort, for example with armchairs, conducive to relaxation.

Physical resources It is obviously essential to provide all the resources essential for people to carry out their work. However, when planning what is required, the aim should be to ensure that resources place no constraints on individuals' performance. So, for example, a photo-copier for which there is often a queue, or which is unreliable, is inadequate. Unnecessary frustrations must be avoided.

Opinions are divided on whether it is best to provide callers with tables or desks, although the manager and supervisor will require desks. Whichever is used, adequate provision must be made for storage of paperwork, pens and anything else that is in regular use. The work surface should be large enough to accommodate any reference materials being used and enable easy organisation of work, and it should be of a height which is comfortable for working.

Comfortable, practical chairs are essential. They should be on castors, adjustable for height and the angle of the back, cloth-covered and without arms.

Ample storage space and filing facilities are essential, since a great deal of paperwork will be generated which can quickly create clutter and make organised work difficult. Shelf space will be needed for telephone, trade and other directories. This should be organised in such a way that location of a specific type of directory is easy, and the shelves must be easily accessible, ie not too high or too near the ground.

A notice board is required for posting general information, as well as a board (or boards) for displaying details of current campaigns, individual and team results, incentives and so on. Any type of board which can be written on is suitable, provided it is large enough to be seen easily by staff, for example a flipchart or whiteboard.

The decision on what type of telephones callers will use may have been determined by the selection of an automatic call distributor (ACD). Some of these come with special terminals instead of the standard handset, while others allow connection of a handset. If a choice is possible, telephone handsets should be chosen for ease of use, comfort and efficiency. Multi-frequency dial tone phones are the most efficient for outbound calling, since these tive almost immediate connection provided the company, and the person called, are connected to a digital exchange. This, combined with the speed of push-button dialling, can have a considerable impact on call rates. Telephones will get a lot of use and need to be robust. The grip and the earpiece also need to be tested for comfort in constant use.

Whether it is best to use headsets or not will depend partly on the applications. For high-volume inbound call-handling they are essential if maximum efficiency is to be achieved. However, although modern headsets are comfortable and provide clear communication, not everyone likes using them and some companies offer staff a choice between a headset and handset. There are many different styles of headset and, again, comfort and efficiency should be the main selection criteria. However, since some ACDs only accept their own headsets, there may be no choice.

Everything which can be done to show staff that the company cares about them should be done. This includes ensuring that the workspace is cleaned efficiently every day, maintenance is carried out quickly and with minimum disruption and, if possible, on-site facilities are available to provide drinks and snacks at break times.

Automation

There are a number of opportunities for automating telephone marketing operations. Computerisation of a database is described earlier in this chapter, while Computer Assisted Telephone Interviewing (CATI) and voice recognition systems are outlined in Chapter 2.

Telephone marketing technology is already highly sophisticated in some areas, but it is still in its infancy. Even the next few years are likely to see a revolution in the ways in which technology can be applied, both to increase efficiency and broaden the applications of telephone marketing. The rate of technological advancement makes it impossible to do anything more than examine the pros and cons of automation using current technology, and to highlight the factors that need to be considered in selecting equipment.

Computer Assisted Telephone Interviewing (CATI)

It is stressed earlier in this chapter that, when first setting up in-house, it is best to use manual systems. Telephone marketing needs continuous tweaking to achieve the best results and this is very difficult if systems have been rigidly specified by computerising the whole operation at the start. The only exception to this may be where a very large inbound call-handling unit is being established. Even here, however, careful development of systems, probably using the expertise of an agency, is essential. For smaller units, the time may come when computerisation is either advantageous or the only way to manage the volume of work being undertaken.

Whether or not to implement CATI is ultimately a commercial decision based on an evaluation of the costs versus benefits of the particular system being considered. It will not help to create strategies for successful campaigns, but it will improve operational efficiency if the right system has been chosen. The features offered by one applications software package, TOPCAT, are listed on page 70. The benefits, depending on the software chosen, can be summarised broadly as:

- improved speed and efficiency of call-handling;
- improved customer service;
- ease of use for operators;
- real-time monitoring and immediate access to cumulative results;
- more efficient supervision and management;
- statistical information and management reports, on demand;
- transfer of data to and from other systems;
- integration with other systems, for example order processing;
- cost savings, for example on administration;
- revenue from more flexible and new applications.

These benefits are impressive, but they must be weighed against the disadvantages, of which there may be three major ones. First, although costs of both hardware and CATI software have fallen in recent years, it can still represent a major investment. While small PC-based systems can work out at under £500 per work station, this can rise to several thousands with top-of-the-range systems.

Secondly, staff will have to use the system. Obviously it must meet their specific needs in relation to the work they have to do, but the idea of automation should be introduced to them carefully. Even if a manual system has been in use for only three months or so, there may be considerable resistance to change. To encourage acceptance of, and even eagerness to use, the system, those who will have to use it should be involved at an early stage of discussions about its specification.

Finally, a sophisticated system, integrated with other systems in the organisation, can take more than a year to get up and running. Total commitment and co-operation of all those involved is required to ensure successful implementation and minimise disruption to existing operations.

These latter two points are more obstacles than disadvantages; they can be overcome by careful planning and management. The final decision, then, comes down to whether or not automation will generate more money than it costs. This is difficult to calculate without some measure of the increased efficiency that can be achieved, and knowledge of what additional opportunities automation can create. An agency can often provide a solution. If automation is not going to extend outside the unit, ie not being integrated with other company systems, then an agency can test in-house applications on their own automated systems. This will provide comparative figures for manual (in-house) and automated (agency) systems. If the system is going to be fully integrated the problem is more complex, because an agency obviously cannot simulate all the client's business systems. However, some agencies have considerable consultancy experience in this area and can provide costings to show the viability, or otherwise, of this high level of automation.

The prospect of automation can be very seductive, particularly in situations where the workload is becoming unmanageable. However, there may be other ways around this type of problem. More efficient use of human resources, perhaps introducing a clerical function to handle processing of information or rescheduling campaigns to make better use of telephone marketers, may provide a more cost-effective solution. All avenues should be explored before deciding on auto-mation and setting about choosing a system.

Choosing a system

The range and sophistication of software applications packages for telephone marketing is growing constantly. It includes, for example, products such as TOPCAT from Norsk Data, Edge from Datapoint, and TeleMagic from Prospects For Business, each with a different mix of features of varying sophistication. Packages are available to accom-modate almost any number of users, running on hardware ranging from IBM-compatible PCs up to UNIX minicomputers.

The first step in choosing a system is to write out a specification of what it must be able to do. This may involve consultation with people from the company's information technology (IT) or data processing department, as well as staff of the telephone marketing unit, and should cover the following areas:

- If the company has an IT strategy, what implications does this have for the automation of telephone marketing operations?

- What other hardware and software, if any, must the system be compatible with, ie other systems with which it will be linked, such as a database?

- What switching equipment, such as an automatic call distributor, must the system be compatible with?

- What features must the system provide to accommodate all the envisaged applications, for example in the areas of outbound and/ or inbound calls, script management, database management and updating, call monitoring, results analysis and style and content of reporting?

- What degree of flexibility is required to enable the development of creative campaigns, ie not restricted by the system?

- What volume of calls will the system be required to handle?

- What volume and variety of information will have to be accessed and recorded, and what is an acceptable response time for these processes?

- Who will be developing applications on the system and what level of expertise do they possess, ie how easy must the system be to programme, or learn to programme?

- Who will be using the system (callers, supervisor, manager) and what level of expertise do they possess, ie how easy must the system be to use, or to learn to use, and what extent of training will be required?

- What degree and ease of expansion must the system provide, and at what level of cost?

- What software, and perhaps hardware, support is available in-house, ie what level of support will be required from the supplier?

The answers to questions like these will provide a detailed specification of the system required to meet the company's needs, which can be used as selection criteria for evaluating those available. With the growing range of CATI software available, it is increasingly likely that the company will already have compatible hardware, even though additional processing and/or storage capacity may be required.

Two particularly important criteria are system flexibility and options for expansion. Telephone marketing is a highly creative medium and any system which is not flexible enough to accommodate continuously changing needs should be avoided. Similarly, any system which does not allow easy expansion (often available on a modular basis) to accommodate growth, could lead to early redundancy and the need for major reinvestment.

The choice of systems currently available is sufficiently wide to meet most needs. If there is any doubt, however, the rate of technological development is such that it may be worthwhile postponing a decision about automation for 6–12 months. Alternatively, some suppliers offer a bespoke service where they can tailor a system to the client's needs. If this route is chosen, it is vital to beware of the trap of creating a need for the supplier's expertise whenever the system has to be reconfigured.

Automation in the context of marketing databases is examined in Chapter 9, pages 356–76.

Voice recognition systems

The features and use of systems capable of recognising and processing the human voice are outlined in Chapter 2. Although early systems have been primitive, rapid development is yielding more efficient and useful systems. The investment required to enter this area can be very high, however, and it is currently proving difficult to justify, even for some telephone marketing agencies.

Certainly the future of voice recognition, with increasing reliability and sophistication, and falling costs, is an area that will interest many in-house telephone marketing operators. Using dedicated inbound telephone lines it will enable companies to offer a wide range of attractive services to customers, around the clock, while avoiding high staffing costs. With premium rate services, such as British Telecom's Callstream, revenue can be generated while serving market needs.

The equipment available at the moment is limited in range and capability, although many new products are coming on to the market as manufacturers solve earlier problems, particularly with reliability. The names and addresses of some manufacturers of these systems are given in Appendix B.

Because the technology involved is advancing so rapidly it is difficult to give an adequate guide to factors that may be relevant when selecting a voice recognition system, but this could include the following:

- How many line connections, digital and analogue, does the system provide?

- Does it provide a live feed facility, ie a dedicated line(s) for feeding live information into the system?

- Does it have a direct exchange line facility, ie non-premium rate (used, for example, to update and manage the system remotely)?

- How much memory is there for outgoing messages or 'programmes' (usually quoted in hours)?

- Does the system provide call statistics?

- Can it recognise multi-frequency dial tones?

- What type of voice recognition is available – speaker-independent (recognises words), speaker-dependent (caller has to 'train' system to recognise words), voice detection (responds to noise rather than specific words)?

- What is the degree of reliability in voice recognition?

- Can the system record callers' messages, such as name and address, what is the capacity (in hours), and how is this information downloaded?

- How easy is the system to programme?

- Can the system be connected to databases or other computer systems?

- Does it have BABT approval, ie for connection to the telecommunications network?

- Can the system be upgraded?

- What does it cost, including any ancillary equipment essential for the intended applications?

This list does not cover all the facilities currently available. There are systems, for example, which provide a voice mail facility where callers can leave messages for mailbox owners; a dial-out facility so that the system can transfer an incoming call, for example to a live operator; and a fax facility whereby callers can request additional information which is then automatically faxed to them, either back down the same line or to a number specified by the caller using a multi-frequency dial tone phone.

Setting up a voice recognition facility for handling inbound calls is a very complex and costly exercise. Systems vary in price from around £10,000 to well over £100,000. In addition, there are the costs of telephone lines, programmers, maintenance staff and any ancillary equipment, such as call loggers, which may not be included in the system. Not many systems currently offer the possibility of upgrading, and therefore smaller systems could be quickly outgrown in terms of capacity and features. Unless a company is committed to making a major long-term investment, the best way currently to use voice recognition technology for telephone marketing purposes is to employ the resources of a specialist, either a telephone marketing agency or a dedicated service provider (addresses for some of the latter will be found in Appendix C).

Other automated systems

Apart from automatic call distributors (ACDs), which have been described already, there are an increasing number of opportunities for automating other systems in a telephone marketing operation. Management of telephone traffic, for example, is aided by software applications packages such as RAII from Callscan. This runs on a PC and is designed to work with a wide range of telephone systems to provide real-time reporting, on screen, of current call activity. Information provided includes the number of calls being handled, how many incoming calls are in conversation or still waiting to be answered, average call duration, average time being taken to answer calls, and how long it will take to clear the queue of calls at the current rate of call handling. A key advantage of this type of software is that it helps to ensure optimum staffing levels to minimise caller waiting times and the number of lost calls; it thus serves some of the functions of an ACD, but at a much reduced cost. Callscan also provides software to enhance the reporting capabilities of ACDs.

Automation of field sales tasks is another important area of development. The results of central telephone activity, for example, such as appointments or customer enquiries which require personal attention, can be communicated via modem to sales representatives' laptop or home-based computers for appropriate action. In the same way, sales reps can keep their office support staff and management up to date on the outcome of their field activities, as well as having documentation such as letters, quotations and order confirmations generated centrally.

Some products have specific applications in the telephone marketing environment. Phone Disc, for example, launched by British Telecom in March 1991 (and described on page 378), helps to automate number searching. There are also opportunities for improving strategic and tactical planning. Software for geodemographic profiling (*see* page 365), for example, can be used to identify geographical areas where the population meets certain criteria or to identify the characteristics of a defined area, thus enabling more accurate targeting of marketing communications.

Many new opportunities will arise as technology advances, and companies wishing to take full advantage of these will need to dedicate a member of staff to monitor applications of the relevant technologies.

The Association for Information Systems in Marketing and Sales (AIMS) maintains and publishes a register of IT-related products and services supplied by member companies. Anyone wishing to obtain further details can contact them at the address given in Appendix B, page 479.

Support services

The need for many different types of support service will have been identified during the design and planning of the telephone marketing unit. These are essential to the smooth and efficient operation of the unit, and should cover areas such as:

- personnel;
- induction, training and development;
- purchasing and supply; and
- equipment and office maintenance.

Sound systems and procedures are required to ensure that the necessary support is available as and when required. If the unit is housed on the same site as other company operations, then the provisions made for those can often be extended. Otherwise, new arrangements will have to be implemented.

So what will it cost to set up and run?

The cost of running an in-house unit with six callers was shown in Chapter 3 (page 90) to be around £300,000 a year, with additional

Table 4.5 Possible timescales for setting up an in-house telephone marketing unit

Implementation schedule	
Weeks 1–2:	Prepare the business plan.
Week 3:	Agency presents plan.
Week 4:	Set implementation objectives.
Weeks 5–10:	Develop operational plans and systems.
Week 11:	Agency presents recommendations.
Weeks 12–13:	Agency produces deliverables.
Weeks 13–15:	Select site, specify and order equipment.
Weeks 17–18:	Test and benchmark.
Weeks 18–20:	Design selection process.
Weeks 22–25:	Design training courses.
Weeks 31–37:	Staff selection.
Weeks 34–launch:	Internal and external PR.
Weeks 38–42:	Staff induction and skills training.
	Test and fine-tune systems.
Week 43:	Launch unit.

first year costs of up to around £80,000. This is a basic, no frills operation and costs can escalate dramatically as the number of callers increases. A much larger unit may require an Automatic Call Distributor, for example, which could add significantly to expenditure on equipment, depending on the capacity and sophistication of the system chosen. Staffing and telephone line and call costs would also be of a different magnitude.

While telephone marketing offers the prospect of a healthy increase in profitability, the level of investment, even for a modest operation, is such that extreme care must be taken to ensure that the full potential of the resource is realised.

Implementation

All the work that goes into the design and planning of the unit should culminate in smooth, trouble free implementation. Precise timescales for implementation will depend on many factors, particularly the lead times for delivery and installation of equipment, the size of the unit, the complexity of initial telephone marketing applications and the management approval structure of the organisation. However, an example of realistic timescales for setting up in-house, using the consultancy services of a telephone marketing agency, is shown in Table 4.5.

Many of the activities involved in setting up in-house, such as staff selection and recruitment, and training and development, are examined in more detail in subsequent chapters.

5

Staff Selection and Recruitment

The quality of staff in a telephone marketing unit is probably the single most important factor in determining its success. A telephone call may be the first, and sometimes the only, contact a customer has with the company. Every contact represents a lifetime of opportunities for the company and this can be lost on a single call. Every call therefore has to be handled with the highest degree of professionalism in order to build and maintain long-term relationships with customers.

Staffing strategies have changed considerably as the telephone marketing industry has grown and matured. The importance placed on customer service now requires a very high degree of professionalism, with better communication skills and product or service knowledge, as well as high levels of commitment. Telephone marketing has become a career, rather than a job, and companies need to recruit staff who are looking for that opportunity. Only by employing the right staff, developing their skills, and keeping them, can the unit truly thrive. Staff must individually be capable of achieving the standards set for them, have the commitment continually to strive to improve their performance, and be able to project the professional image required by the company. They must also be able to work together as a team to achieve their common objectives.

The type of staff required depends on the structure and organisation of the unit, which determines individual roles and responsibilities. The development of job descriptions identifies the skills and personal qualities required for each position. In turn, these define the criteria for selecting staff and the best type of selection procedure to use for each position.

The skills shortage

The shortage of skilled staff is being felt in many sectors of European business, and telephone marketing, where skilled people are the key resource, is probably being hit as hard as any.

According to a CBI report, *The Road Ahead: the CBI Pay and Performance Presentation 1988–89*, the number of 16–19–year-olds entering the labour force in the UK is expected to have fallen by just over a quarter, from 2.6 million to 2 million, between 1987 and 1994. The report stresses that this will be a recurring problem well into the 21st century and that companies should formulate long-term strategies to minimise the impact. Similar trends exist throughout Europe.

There are many other factors adding to the pressure on corporate staffing and recruitment policies, for example:

- the growth of a marketing culture where the needs of individual customers are given priority;

- more demanding customers, in terms of price, quality, design and standards of service;

- higher expectations among employees;

- increased competitive pressures within the Single European Market;

- the removal of barriers to the movement of staff throughout Europe, increasing the competition for already scarce human resources.

The CBI report goes on to say:

> The significance of all such pressure will vary from company to company. What is important is that each firm should identify and take action to reduce the pressure. For many, this action will involve increased training, greater flexibility, better communication with employees and the development of suitable pay systems. Greater flexibility to raise performance and to overcome shortages may involve changes in work organisation, new approaches to recruitment, and the better use of people.

One-third of the UK telephone marketing agencies responding in the BDMA survey felt that a shortage of skilled staff was the biggest problem facing the industry. They highlighted difficulties in recruiting staff, training them to the level required and keeping them. The problem in London and the South East is further aggravated by high demand and the high cost of living, although the shortage is largely confined to telephone marketing executives, rather than experienced management staff.

The telephone marketing industry is still young and evolving rapidly. Many companies are investing heavily in growing their own experts and, as more companies set up in-house units, competition for these skilled personnel will escalate rapidly. Protecting this investment is crucial and the issues of recruitment, retention and training of staff have become a key element in planning for long-term growth. There are many ways in which these issues can be addressed, as follows.

Widening the recruitment net, for example:

- more recruitment of women returners, with more part-time opportunities;

- more recruitment of the disabled;

- increased liaison with schools, colleges etc;

- flexible working opportunities;

- relocation of certain functions to areas of higher unemployment.

Attracting more applicants, for example:

- better targeting of the labour market;

- exploiting the means available (press, consultants etc);

- providing guaranteed jobs for school leavers;

- enhancing the image of the company within the relevant sectors of the labour market;

- providing better terms and conditions, and remuneration packages;

- improving strategies to 'sell' the company.

Keeping employees, for example:

- improving selection and recruitment procedures to ensure the right people are employed;

- restructuring 'reward' systems to encourage active long-term involvement in the company –

- flexible hours
- more attractive remuneration packages (profit share, share options)
- special paid leave
- better training and development opportunities
- attention to motivation and job satisfaction.

Making better use of employees, for example:

- using more temporary, though skilled, employees to maintain an optimal workforce under varying workloads;

- moving towards multi-skilling of employees so that they can carry out a wider variety of tasks;

- more active involvement of employees in their work and that of the company;

- more efficient management.

The practicalities of implementing these measures varies from company to company, and any action taken for a telephone marketing unit would generally have to conform to corporate policies and culture. However, the recruitment, training and retention of staff is assuming critical importance and establishing a new operation is an ideal opportunity to review corporate policies in these areas.

Full-time or temporary staff?

It is traditional for agencies to employ a mixture of full-time and temporary staff. Extreme variations in workload, particularly with outbound calling, mean that it is generally more practical for them to maintain a smaller core of permanent staff and to employ fully trained, non-permanent callers to cope with peak workloads. Agencies, because they can offer a fairly regular supply of work, are able to maintain a register of available skilled people. The situation is generally different for an in-house unit, particularly a small one, although there are some advantages, as well as disadvantages, in employing temporary staff.

- The **advantages** can include:
  - a larger pool of available staff by offering interesting work, possibly part time, for example to housewives and single parents;

- greater commitment to what may be perceived as a valuable opportunity;
- more concentrated effort if staff are working short shifts;
- greater flexibility in dealing with changing demands on the unit.

- The **disadvantages** can include:
  - lack of continuity;
  - less opportunity to develop staff;
  - attracting perhaps less career-minded people, who may not be fully committed to the company.

The attractiveness and practicality of employing temporary staff may depend on the type of work being undertaken in the unit. Consumer calling in the evenings, for example, may provide a very attractive part-time job for married women with children. On the other hand, it would be impractical to employ part-timers to service business accounts by telephone, because it is preferable to have one person servicing a group of customers and they may ask to be called back when that person is not working. Nine out of ten companies responding in the BDMA survey employed their telephone marketers on a permanent contract, while 8 per cent had them on temporary contracts and 2 per cent used both methods. Ultimately, however, the decision should be based on what is best for the long term success of the unit.

Terms and conditions of employment

The terms and conditions of employment for staff of the unit should be considered before starting the selection and recruitment process, because it can have implications for the quality of staff that can be attracted and recruited. If the company's pay structure dictates that it has to pay less than the going rate for telephone marketers in the region, for example, it may have to settle for less skilled staff and rely more heavily on initial training. Similarly, if the company can pay above the going rate, it should be possible to attract more highly skilled people and the selection process should be tailored accordingly.

The grades of the positions created in a telephone marketing unit, and the corresponding salary range and benefits, will usually be equivalent to similar positions in the company. However, because of the nature of telephone marketing work, several different methods of payment are used to help motivate staff. Among the companies responding in the BDMA survey, 54 per cent paid telephone marketers just a basic salary, while 24 per cent also paid a commission, 12 per cent paid an incentive, and 8 per cent paid both commission and an incentive on top of the basic salary. Only 1 per cent paid solely on a commission basis. The most popular form of additional payment was a commission based on the number of orders achieved, with other incentives including holidays and profit-related bonuses.

If the payment structure is not dictated by corporate policy, there are pros and cons which must be weighed up before deciding which method of payment will be used. Here are some of them.

Basic salary When paying a fixed salary it is far easier to manage and control costs, by ensuring that predetermined targets are achieved. Staff also like the 'security' and it avoids creating a hard-sell environment which is undesirable for many telephone marketing applications. However, without the opportunity to increase their earnings there is little motivation for staff to improve their productivity, and standards can fall.

Commission Paying a commission, for example per order or appointment achieved, acts as motivator for staff and has been found to produce better results than if they are paid just a basic wage. However, it can create an aggressive, high-pressure environment which customers find unpleasant. The result can be a higher proportion of cancelled orders or appointments, thus reducing the effectiveness of the strategy. There is also a temptation for telephone marketers to bend the rules, for example lowering the standards of lead qualification criteria, in order to earn commission.

Paying commission becomes very complex where staff are carrying out a wide variety of tasks on which the value to the company of positive results are different. It is also difficult to ensure that all staff have an equal opportunity to earn commission, unless it is done on a team basis. This, too, can cause problems if some team members do not 'pull their weight'.

Bonuses A bonus is generally a payment made, in addition to the basic salary, for productivity above an agreed level. Provided the basic salary is reasonable, and the possible bonus earnings are not too high, it can encourage higher productivity without the risk of creating a hard-sell environment. Fifteen per cent of agencies responding in the BDMA survey operate a bonus scheme linked to productivity.

Incentives A wide variety of incentives can be offered to encourage higher productivity, and the only major drawbacks with these schemes are that they have to be well planned and carefully managed. While only 5 per cent of the agencies responding in the BDMA survey pay commission, 35 per cent use incentives ranging from cash and gift vouchers to alcohol and other prizes.

The work of telephone marketing supervisors and managers does not directly involve the generation of results on the telephone, and therefore their pay structure may be simpler. However, it is still desirable to have some form of productivity-related reward to act as a motivator. The use of different types of 'payment' in relation to staff motivation is examined in more detail in Chapter 7.

Factors other than pay which must be considered include the hours of work, the amount of leave, probationary period, and what benefits can be offered, such as a pension scheme, subsidised restaurant and travel loans, sports and recreational facilities, and other benefits of the type mentioned above in relation to the skills shortage. Offering an attractive package can help to attract, and make it easier to recruit, higher quality staff. In the long term, it will also help to reduce staff turnover. Consultants employed to help set up an in-house unit will often offer advice in this area, although corporate policy may allow little leeway. However, the increasingly severe shortage of skilled telephone marketers may mean that some companies will have to reconsider their personnel policies.

Rules and regulations for telephone marketing staff should also be formulated at this stage; the company may want to mention some of these in job advertisements and applicants will need to be told about them during their interview. These rules and regulations will often be determined by existing company policies, although some are required which may not apply to staff elsewhere in the organisation.

Scheduled breaks, for example, are particularly important because the job requires sustained effort and concentration. A break of 20 minutes in a 3-hour session is fairly common, although some companies allow staff to take a short break at any time they feel they need one, provided someone is covering for them. Regular breaks provide an opportunity to relax and have refreshments and a cigarette.

A no-smoking rule should be strictly enforced in the calling area. Apart from a smoky atmosphere encouraging dry throats and coughs, the sound of someone smoking on the other end of the line can be very irritating to customers. It also makes it very difficult for the telephone marketers to communicate properly. This applies equally to eating and drinking while working on the telephone.

Punctuality is also something that should be strictly enforced because it can be extremely important under some circumstances, for example ensuring sufficient staff are available to handle incoming calls.

Job descriptions and personal profiles

The process of defining the tasks and job positions created within a telephone marketing unit, as a preliminary to deciding staffing levels and departmental structure, is outlined in Chapter 4. Creating job descriptions, or job specifications, for each of these positions is an essential preliminary to identifying the type of people required to fill them.

The format in which companies lay out job descriptions, and the information included in them, varies considerably. However, they generally include most, if not all, of the following information:

- job title, location and department;
- brief description of the job function and its overall objectives;
- reporting relationships, ie to whom the job holder is responsible;
- who the job holder will work with;
- main duties of the job, both regular and occasional, with an indication of the proportion of time spent on them, their relative priority, volume of work etc;
- resources and support available, where relevant, for the completion of these duties;
- main responsibilities, for example for completion of work, administration, reporting, staff, equipment, decision-making etc, with examples of the standards to be maintained if these are not obvious;
- terms and conditions, such as hours, pay, shifts, leave, bonuses and other benefits;
- the training provided, whether internal or external;

- career prospects for the job holder within the organisation.

Examples of job descriptions are given in Figures 5.1 (telephone marketing executive), 5.2 (team leader), 5.3 (supervisor) and 5.4 (manager).

A job description serves a number of purposes. First, it helps to identify the skills, qualities and experience a person requires to do the job effectively. Then, when staff have been recruited, it provides job holders with a clear breakdown of what they are expected to do and serves as a reference point for the contribution they are making. It also forms the foundation for training and development, by showing what individuals should be able to do, and providing a framework for identifying their strengths and weaknesses. Job descriptions therefore play a fundamental role in recruiting the right staff and getting the best out of them. Meticulous attention should be paid to ensure that individual jobs are defined clearly and accurately, and that collectively, ie for all the jobs created, they provide a sound basis for achieving the objectives of the telephone marketing unit.

Job descriptions should be reviewed regularly to ensure that the allocation of tasks is making the best possible use of staff resources. Growth and development of the unit is obviously likely to lead to changes. Apart from the addition of new tasks, there may be changes in task priorities, reporting procedures, administrative systems and so on. When the job descriptions of existing staff are being amended, it is vital that the proposed changes are discussed with them, explaining the reasons for the changes and how it will affect their role. What help will be provided in acquiring any additional skills required should also be explained.

After creating job specifications, the next step in the selection and recruitment process is to create a personal profile of the ideal candidate for each of the different positions. A personal profile is simply a list of the skills, qualities, experience and qualifications required to do a particular job effectively, and is used to help assess the suitability of individual applicants. Although personal profiles can take many forms, they generally classify this information under a number of headings. The headings are not important provided that the information is presented in a way which will help the interviewer assess applicants. One format, for example, uses seven headings: knowledge, skills and experience; intellectual factors; personality; motivation; physical qualities; disposition; and circumstances. However, most organisations, if they regularly use personal profiles, will have a preferred format.

Title:	Trainee telephone marketing executive
	Telephone marketing executive
	Senior telephone marketing executive
Department:	Telephone marketing unit
Reporting to:	Telephone marketing supervisor
	Telephone marketing manager
Position in company:	Telephone marketing executives (TMEs) are directly responsible to the telephone marketing manager and work alongside a team of other TMEs

Main purpose of job:

To make or take telephone calls, according to a specified brief, with the purpose of promoting, selling, researching a product or service, educating the market or servicing accounts.

Duties and responsibilities:

To work on a variety of campaigns whose timescales depend on workloads, skill areas and experience.

To participate in briefing sessions before each project, to include an explanation of the objectives, targets, scripts and other relevant information, and role playing.

To fulfil and adhere to the aims and objectives outlined in the campaign brief.

To make a targeted number of calls per day as specified by the telephone marketing supervisor.

The content and purpose of the calls will vary according to the project, but could include [according to the applications undertaken by the Unit]

To carry out daily administrative duties, such as recording comments from calls on data capture documents and providing a daily analysis of the calls by using the appropriate coding.

To produce and communicate to the telephone marketing supervisor any information relevant to a campaign's success, eg results, feedback, ideas for improvement.

To participate in de-briefing sessions, to discuss the current project, as and when required by the telephone marketing supervisor.

To aid the telephone marketing supervisor, according to experience [Trainee TMEs, 10% of the time; TMEs, 15% of the time; Senior TMEs, 30–100%], by doing the following duties:

The fulfilment of these tasks and responsibilities may involve overtime (ie evening or weekend work), which may be requested according to the demands of the project.

TMEs and Senior TMEs

Motivate calling team skills to improve and maintain standards by example.
Motivate and incentivise callers.
Produce daily call results, including a breakdown of all calls completed, call rates, and call conversion rates.

Senior TMEs

Check — all data capture documents to ensure the information matches the brief requirements
  — the quality of data capture, by re-phoning at least 10% of people called to confirm accuracy
  — tapes of calls made to ensure that callers are achieving the results required by the brief and give feedback to the telephone marketing supervisor on standards of performance.
Check overall performance and attitude of callers and keep the telephone marketing supervisor informed of daily changes.
Supply the telephone marketing supervisor with an overall analysis of results by producing a basic report containing only key points of interest in relation to the full campaign.
Stand in for the telephone marketing supervisor, as and when required.

Figure 5.1   Job description for a telephone marketing executive

* * * * *

Title: Team leader
Department: Telephone marketing unit (TMU)
Reporting to: Telephone marketing supervisor
                               Telephone marketing manager
Position in company: Reports to telephone marketing supervisor, co-ordinates telephone marketing executives (TMEs)

Main purpose of job:

To make or take telephone calls, according to a specified brief, with the purpose of promoting, selling, researching a product or service, [0% — 100% of the time].
To co-ordinate a team of TMEs on a daily basis, check the quality of their work, produce a daily results sheet and liaise with the telephone marketing manager [0% — 100% of the time].

Duties and responsibilities:

Team leaders are assigned to a variety of campaigns for varying timescales depending on workloads, skill areas and experience. They are required to fulfil and adhere to the aims and objectives as outlined in the campaign brief and to make a targeted number of calls per day as specified by the telephone marketing manager.

A brief takes place prior to each project which includes an explanation of the objectives, targets, scripts and other relevant information for the job. It also includes role playing.

The content and purpose of the calls varies according to the brief, but will usually involve areas such as [according to the applications undertaken by the unit].

To carry out daily administration duties eg:

- recording comments from calls on data capture documents;
- providing daily analysis of the calls by using appropriate coding.

To participate in de-briefing meetings.

To check all data capture documents to make sure information captured matches that defined in the brief; then to report to the telephone marketing manager with details of the standard of performance.

To quality check all data capture documents, ie re-phone at least 10% of the TMEs' data capture documents to make sure that the information captured is accurate; then to report to the telephone marketing manager with details of the standard of performance.

To produce daily call results, including a breakdown of all calls completed, call rates, conversion rates etc.

To check overall performance and attitude of TMEs and keep the telephone marketing manager informed of daily changes.

To produce and communicate any relevant information for a campaign's success to the telephone marketing manager, ie feedback, ideas for improvements, results etc.

To improve and maintain standards by example.

Figure 5.2 Job description for a telephone marketing team leader

* * * * *

Title: Telephone marketing supervisor
Department: Telephone marketing unit (TMU)
Reporting to: Telephone marketing manager
Position in company: Liaises with telephone marketing manager and has responsibility for team leaders and telephone marketing executives (TMEs)

Main purpose of job:

To have responsibility for quality and performance within the department.

To train and develop the team leaders and TMEs, as and when needed, by the most appropriate method.

To run a staffing schedule and allocate staff to the most appropriate project.

To work within pre-set and defined budgets.

To take action to ensure that any problems arising within projects are resolved to the satisfaction of the telephone marketing manager.

To ensure a satisfactory and professional TMU user service.

To produce ideas and participate in the company's overall strategy for the unit.

Duties and responsibilities

Operations

Scheduling and monitoring calls and reporting to the telephone marketing manager.

Staff scheduling, monitoring and reporting

Ensuring the calling area provides the optimum environment for the efficiency and success of the Unit.

Monitoring and reporting on campaign performance.

Monitoring and reporting on integration of telephone marketing with other direct marketing methods being used.

Personnel

Train the team leaders and TMEs, as and when required, with the necessary telephone marketing communication skills and administrative skills.

Ensure the calling team are motivated and maintain the enthusiasm and buzz needed to ensure a successful team.

Monitor and report on the morale of the calling teams.

Line management of team leaders and TMEs.

Figure 5.3 Job description for a telephone marketing supervisor

* * * * *

Title: Telephone marketing manager
Department: Telephone marketing unit (TMU)
Reporting to: Sales and marketing director
Position in company: Liaises with telephone marketing supervisor and team leaders; has overall responsibility for TMU staff and operations

Main purpose of job:

To provide telephone marketing knowledge and skill to run the telephone marketing teams within the company and provide a professional and effective telephone marketing service to TMU users.

Duties and responsibilities

Operational

Schedule high potential and confirmed telephone marketing work and plan the resources needed to hit performance and deadlines.
Monitor and be responsible for the performance of all telephone marketing campaigns in training, resources, telephone skills and results.
Monitor and be responsible for the quality of all telephone marketing campaigns.
Monitor the briefs and de-briefs to team leaders and telephone marketing executives (TMEs) of each telephone marketing campaign.
Be responsible for the technical development of the telephone marketing unit and keep up to date with developments relating to communication equipment and computerised telephone marketing.
Develop telephone marketing techniques to constantly improve the results and performance of the calling teams.
Report daily on performance and the quality of results to the sales and marketing director, and weekly at a senior management meeting.

Personnel

Monitor the recruitment of calling staff and liaise with personnel on the staffing requirements, calibre of staff and timings.
Train the team leaders and TMEs, as and when required, with the necessary telephone marketing communication skills.
Manage, motivate and develop the team leaders, increase their skills and upgrade their professional approach to their job.
Ensure that all pay, bonus and incentive schemes are fair and have a positive effect on performance and quality.
Ensure the calling teams are motivated and maintain the enthusiasm, and buzz needed to ensure and secure successful teams.

Finance

Monitor and be responsible for the direct cost versus the set budget for all telephone marketing campaigns. Take appropriate action to maintain the direct cost at or below the target.
Be aware of the individual targets, revenue, direct cost and financial targets set for the unit.
Monitor all the unit's fixed costs.

Report weekly to the sales and marketing director on the unit's direct cost versus budget.

Sales and marketing

Advise the team leaders on potential call rates and conversion rates. Liaise with the sales and marketing director on campaigns' procedures, results and timings.
Publish a monthly management report.

Figure 5.4 Job description for a telephone marketing manager

* * * * *

The priority of tasks comprising the job should determine which are the most important skills, qualities and the type and level of experience to look for in applicants. It is increasingly difficult to recruit good telephone marketers and it is highly unlikely that any applicants will be the 'ideal'. So, bearing in mind that training will be provided, it is desirable to keep the profile as broad as possible. When looking at the type and level of experience required, for example, the company should decide what areas of experience other than telephone marketing would help equip someone for the job, for example sales, customer service and experience of similar products or services. In terms of education, while it is desirable to state what formal qualifications are required, it has to be decided whether this requirement will be waived if an individual has a certain amount of relevant experience or different qualifications of equivalent grades.

The result of profiling is a list of criteria against which applicants for each job can be assessed. An example for telephone marketing executives is shown in Table 5.1. These criteria should be quantified wherever possible, for example a minimum acceptable level of education and experience. Sometimes criteria are classified as being essential, preferred or advantageous, and some may have to be broken down into separate elements to aid assessment. The criteria relating to the voice, for example, may include clarity, good pace, confidence, friendly tone and so on. If candidates are going to be given tests as part of the selection process, for example to measure numeracy or aptitude, then minimum acceptable scores should be stated for each of these. Similarly, if personality profiling questionnaires are going to be used then the selection criteria should refer to an acceptable result.

Table 5.1 Selection and assessment criteria for a telephone marketing executive

---

Telephone marketing executive – selection and assessment criteria

Personal qualities/abilities

Self-disciplined	Professional telephone manner
Self-motivated	Able to overcome objections
Able to deal with rejection	Able to identify and sell benefits
A positive attitude	Outgoing
Ability to identify a sales opportunity through conversation	Confident
	Able to work under pressure
Able to adopt a soft-sell approach	Functions well in a team environment

Assessment criteria

1. Communication

   (interpersonal)
   - Listening skills
   - Articulate
   - Assimilation
   - Interpretation
   - Empathy
   - Voice
   - Creative

   (group)
   - Able to work within a team
   - Constructive contribution
   - Flexibility
   - Consideration for others

2. Conscientiousness
   - Work well, diligently
   - Achieve targets
   - Attention to detail
   - Willing to learn
   - Determined

3. Technical ability
   - Education level
   - Experience to date
   - Handwriting
   - Computer experience
   - Circumstances eg. location
   - Analytical
   - Numerate
   - Aptitude

4. Personal qualities
   - Humour
   - Self-discipline
   - Tenacity
   - Level of ambition
   - Ability to control pressure to achieve positive result
   - Smart appearance
   - Motivated/positive attitude

Selection criteria

This section is devoted largely to what makes a good telephone marketing executive, since there is generally less material published on this, than the qualities of a good supervisor or manager.

Telephone marketing executives

The selection criteria for telephone marketing executives (TMEs) depend partly on the type of work that will be undertaken by the unit. The skills and attitude required to make outbound sales calls, for example, are quite different to those required in handling inbound enquiries. The criteria summarised in Table 5.1 relate to TMEs whose duties and responsibilities include upselling, downselling, cross-selling, selling benefits and establishing customer needs. The following descriptions relate to skills and qualities required for a broad range of telephone marketing applications, and therefore may not all be relevant in the selection of staff for a particular unit. The criteria are grouped under the headings used in Table 5.1 – communication skills, conscientiousness, technical ability and personal qualities.

Communication   Above all else, TMEs must be good communicators when dealing with both outside contacts and colleagues. The ability to listen, understand and quickly interpret and assimilate what someone is saying is particularly important. Being able to show that they are listening and understand is also essential, as this inspires confidence and creates a more personal bond, both of which are conducive to a successful call. Empathy (the ability to understand others' feelings and identify the true meaning behind what they are saying) is another important quality.

TMEs need to be articulate, drawing on their knowledge and communication skills to express themselves clearly, accurately and succinctly, as well as being able to use questions to clarify information. They should be fluent in their use of language and able to respond quickly to steer a conversation in the desired direction, while fully meeting the other person's immediate needs. The use of their voice should be equally fluent and reflect both the meaning of what they are saying, and the image required by the company. In general, the voice should be clear, confident and easy to understand, with good use of pace and tone for emphasis. Anyone with a strong regional accent should be able to demonstrate good articulation. Good use of the voice can have a strong positive impact, which is obviously essential in telephone marketing. Since this is an area in which people cannot be easily trained, particular attention must be paid to the voice during selection.

TMEs will be required to report their results and give other information, such as feedback and ideas on campaigns, on a regular basis. They should therefore be open and forthright and not of a type to withhold information or be reticent about expressing their ideas for fear of criticism.

Good communication is what binds a group of individuals together to form a cohesive, productive team and TMEs must be able to work effectively as team members. They should enjoy team working and be able to make a constructive contribution, displaying the ability to listen and a willingness to co-operate and share for the benefit of others, rather than being consumed with their own achievement. An ability to trust and inspire trust are highly desirable because they help to build team spirit.

Conscientiousness   Many telephone marketing tasks are repetitive, and sometimes boring, and every call can present barriers to successful completion. TMEs need to be hardworking and show determination to maintain high levels of effort in order to achieve their targets. They should appreciate the purpose and importance of targets, and not see them as a method of policing their work, but rather as an opportunity to show what they can do, and a means of monitoring through which they can improve their skills and performance. A willingness to learn is essential.

Even in laborious tasks TMEs must have a high regard for detail and the accuracy of their work, and be willing to accept responsibility for results, reporting and so on. An ability and willingness continuously to review their work against targets and required standards, and take appropriate corrective action when these are not being achieved, are also essential.

Technical ability   TMEs obviously need to be literate and numerate, and they should have achieved a certain level of education. Formal qualifications are not as important as experience in the industry, or related areas, which in turn is not as important as good communication skills, eagerness, and the ability and willingness to learn.

Experience which is relevant to telephone marketing can cover many areas, depending on the work being undertaken, and it should demonstrate technical ability as well as the other qualities required in the TME. Some computer experience, such as a familiarity with the basic principles of computerised databases, may be required for the job, although lack of experience in this area should not rule out otherwise good candidates.

Administrative skills, including the ability to organise and co-ordinate their personal workload, are important. Their handwriting should be legible and show no characteristics which might lead to errors in transcription, for example confusion in distinguishing two numbers. TMEs need an aptitude for applying their skills flexibly, so that they can quickly adapt to new situations and deal with problems efficiently.

Finally, individuals' circumstances, such as where they live and their domestic commitments, should not be likely to be of any hindrance in performing their work efficiently, for example being able to work evenings, if this is required.

Personal qualities   The single most important characteristic of a good TME is enthusiasm and a positive attitude towards the work. They need to be able to approach every call as a new opportunity and not be discouraged by rejection or the repetitive nature of the work. Self-motivated and self-disciplined people who are ambitious to succeed through diligent hard work, and who continually strive to exceed their personal best, are ideal. They need to be tenacious and willing to persevere with difficult calls, without becoming obstinate or unreasonable, to achieve a positive result.

TMEs should be confident, outgoing, cheerful, helpful and have a good sense of humour. Overall, they should be able to reflect the image of the company and 'sell' themselves. A smart appearance, though not always essential, for example where there is no contact with people outside the company, reflects their personal attitudes.

These are the characteristics to look for in applicants for the position of telephone marketing executive. It is highly unlikely that any applicant will have all of these qualities and the selection process consists of deciding which individuals have the mix of qualities of the highest 'value'. In addition, the aim should be to create a team there individuals complement one another in terms of both skills and personality. These issues will be examined later under 'selection'.

Team leaders

Team leaders are basically telephone marketing executives with extra tasks and responsibilities. Therefore, they should meet all of the criteria for selection of TMEs and possess certain additional characteristics. The precise role of team leaders will vary according to the structure of the department but, as the job title implies, they are leaders. They may have responsibilities in areas such as supervision of their team's work and motivation of team members, and will therefore require appropriate leadership skills and qualities. Each of their tasks beyond those of a TME, for example if they brief their teams or help to design and test campaigns, should be examined carefully to identify what characteristics are required to do the job effectively.

Supervisors

The precise role of supervisors will depend on the unit's structure and how leadership responsibilities are to be shared, for example between a manager, the supervisor and team leaders. However, they must have highly developed 'people' skills as they are basically the first-line manager of the team(s) of telephone marketers. They should have excellent interpersonal and group communication skills, be diligent in monitoring individuals' performances, provide motivation when needed, and be able to identify training needs and deliver, or arrange, appropriate training. Supervisors should always be perceptive to the needs of others.

Good organisational skills are essential, including the ability to plan and schedule workloads. Flexibility, and an aptitude for identifying opportunities for improving performance and taking the appropriate action, are qualities needed to make optimum use of resources.

To fulfil their role effectively, supervisors should ideally have first-hand knowledge of a TME's work so that they fully understand their needs and the functioning of operational systems.

Managers

The role of the telephone marketing manager will depend largely on the size and structure of the unit, and how it is integrated into company operations. In a large unit, for example, the supervisor may assume day-to-day leadership responsibilities while the manager concentrates on campaign planning and development in liaison with the heads of other departments. A small unit probably would not even have a dedicated manager, responsibility for the unit being assumed by, say, the marketing manager.

Whoever has this responsibility will require the traditional qualities of a good manager, such as good communication, administrative and leadership skills. A sound understanding and experience of telephone marketing is obviously essential, but the depth of knowledge and skills required will vary, depending on the precise role. An understanding and experience of direct marketing, especially direct mail and marketing databases, is also required, as the job will include integrating these areas of activity. The manager's role will generally include:

- recruitment and selection;

- identifying and meeting training needs for specific campaigns;

- strategic planning;

- work profiling, scheduling and staffing;

- preparing, planning and setting up a campaign;

- analysing and reporting on campaign results.

The manager, ideally, should have a couple of years' experience in telephone marketing/direct marketing at supervisory level or above. However, commitment to the successful growth and development of the unit, combined with intelligence and the ability to learn, are generally more important, particularly given the increasing demand for skilled people.

Selection criteria for each position in the unit should be clearly laid out, ideally in the form of a checklist, for the interviewer(s) to use. It is recommended that three different types of interview are used – telephone, group and one-to-one – and different mixes of criteria will be relevant at each of these.

Attracting applicants

There are many different sources of telephone marketing staff, but whether these will yield the personnel required will depend on a variety of factors, including the attractiveness of the package on offer, the number, type and calibre of staff required, and prevailing labour market conditions.

Existing staff

People already working within the organisation have the advantage of knowing the company, its culture, markets and so on, and can be a good source of telephone marketing executives. However, this should not be seen as a 'cheap' option and the same rigorous selection process should be followed as for any other method of finding staff. A supervisor may also be found internally, although the requirement for experience of working as a TME may be a stumbling block. The likelihood of finding a suitable manager is more remote, particularly for a large unit. A very heavy investment in training, and sufficient time, would be required to equip an inexperienced person to manage a telephone marketing unit effectively from day one.

If an existing telephone marketing operation is being expanded, there is the possibility of internal promotion as a source of the supervisor and manager. Friends of existing staff can be a good source of TMEs, since they are often like-minded people and will already know broadly what the job entails. However, care should be taken to ensure that groups of friends do not form factions which could create an unwanted source of rivalry.

Advertisements

Some methods of attracting applicants are more suitable than others for the different positions that may be on offer and any advertising should be carefully targeted according to the circumstances. The main options are as follows.

Newspapers Advertising in national newspapers is best limited to recruitment for senior positions, partly because of cost but also because few people are likely to think it worthwhile relocating for the salary offered to a telephone marketing executive. Using newspapers with specialist sections will probably achieve the best response. Local and regional newspapers can be a useful source of TMEs, although the response rate may be disappointing, particularly if there is low unemployment in the area.

Trade press Advertisements placed in the relevant trade press, such as marketing and direct marketing publications, are probably the best source of experienced and career-minded people, especially for management positions.

Magazines The increasingly popular giveaway magazines generally have a large readership, particularly those who are unemployed or considering a job change. Provided applicants are screened effectively, this may be a good source of TMEs and possibly supervisors.

Two other places to advertise the post of TME are on local radio and at job centres, although these are generally unlikely to generate a large, high-quality response. Careers centres at business schools and other places of relevant professional training are a good source of management material. This is perhaps most relevant where a unit has already been established and the company is always on the look-out for potential 'star' material to fuel organic growth. Maintaining links with educational establishments has become increasingly mportant as the supply of skilled people has fallen and potential applicants have become more discerning.

Wherever a vacancy is advertised, the advertisement itself should be prepared carefully. Notwithstanding cost and any limitations imposed by the medium being used, the ad should grab the attention of the type of people the company wants to attract and encourage them to make contact. The amount of detail given in job advertisements varies tremendously – some contain infuriatingly little and others give too involved a story. Both types can have advantages, although care has to be taken if they are going to succeed. A basic minimum of information would include:

- a brief description of the company;
- job location, duties, responsibilities and opportunities;
- experience and/or qualifications required;
- an indication of the value of the remuneration package;
- a contact name and telephone number.

The amount of detail given about the remuneration package is a matter for the company to decide, according to what it is prepared to offer, what calibre of people are required, what the competition is offering and the prevailing state of the targeted labour market. The most important part of the advertisement is the telephone number. Whether recruiting TMEs, a supervisor or manager, successful applicants require good telephone communication skills and a telephone response is the ideal way to screen applicants early, thus minimising the overall cost of recruitment and selection. Some advertisers deliberately omit their address in order to discourage postal applications.

Recruitment consultants

There are broadly three types of consultant who help with recruitment: general recruitment agencies, specialist recruitment consultants; and telephone marketing agencies. General agencies can often provide a fairly large number of candidates, although they are usually not comprehensively screened and consequently there is a large fall-out at the interviewing stage. Although no charge is usually made unless a candidate is employed, this can still be an expensive, as well as a time-consuming, option because the interviewing has to be done by the client. The specialist recruitment consultants, of which there are an increasing number specialising in marketing services, tend to do more screening before the client becomes involved and therefore provide a higher calibre of staff for interview. Many also provide advice on, or draw up and place, job advertisements for their clients. Some telephone marketing agencies offer a full consultancy service which includes every step of selection and recruitment, from drawing up job descriptions and selection criteria, to placing advertisements and helping to interview applicants. The cost of this type of service, or any part of it, is generally recouped by the benefit of having expert help in recruiting the highest calibre of candidate under the circumstances. Whatever the extent of consultants' involvement in the selection and recruitment process, thorough briefing by the client is obviously essential if they are going to provide the best possible service.

Finding staff at short notice

Recruitment can take a considerable time, particularly when placing ads in monthly trade journals, and be costly. It may be that circumstances mitigate against using the methods described – perhaps staff are required immediately or on a short-term basis where the cost of advertising or hiring a recruitment consultant cannot be justified.

Some telephone marketing agencies can help in these situations, providing skilled staff from their own pool who can either operate as an independent unit or join an existing team. The staff, who can include telephone marketing executives, supervisors and experienced management, are fully briefed on the company, its markets, products and services. The service has been found particularly useful in situations such as crisis management, credit control, recruitment shortfall, seasonal workloads and large, unanticipated numbers of inbound calls.

Before any action is taken on attracting applicants from outside the organisation, it is vital that plans have already been made for interviewing candidates.

Interviewing

There are three types of interview in general use for telephone marketing recruitment: 1 telephone; 2 group; and 3 face-to-face personal interviews. The main purpose of the first is to assess telephone communication skills, the second to assess interpersonal skills and leadership potential, and the purpose of the third type is self-evident. Each type of interview is particularly good for assessing a particular group of characteristics, as is shown in Table 5.2. However, the type of interview(s) used will vary according to the number and seniority of staff being recruited, for example:

$$\begin{matrix} 1 \\ 2 \\ 3 \end{matrix} = \begin{matrix} \text{a team(s) of telephone marketing executives, } or \\ \text{a team(s) of TMEs and a supervisor(s)} \end{matrix}$$

1 – individual TMEs (up to about three), *or*
3 – a supervisor

3 – management staff

These strategies can vary according to how responsibilities are shared within the unit. A supervisor in a large unit, for example, may require a similar level of experience and know-how to the manager of a small unit, and the strategy is likely to be just a face-to-face interview. The purpose and method of using telephone and group interviews will become clear in the following sections.

Table 5.2 Criteria measurement at interviews for telephone
marketing executives

	Telephone interview	Group interview	One-to-One interview
Communication skills (interpersonal)	* *	*	* *
Communication skills (group)	–	* *	–
Conscientiousness	*	* *	*
Technical ability	* *	*	* *
Personal qualities	*	* *	*

Many organisations, especially the larger ones, have well-established
interviewing procedures which may differ from those outlined here,
which are provided simply to illustrate how some companies recruit
telephone marketing staff.

The telephone interview

Good telephone skills are essential in TMEs and supervisors, and it
would be a waste of time and money to interview people who do not
have this basic prerequisite. There is an ideal opportunity to assess
telephone skills when applicants first telephone about a vacancy.

Ideally, telephone responses to advertisements should come in on a
line dedicated for the purpose, with a skilled interviewer always
available to answer calls. Apart from avoiding overloading the switchboard, it creates a far better impression with applicants if their call is
answered directly. The telephone interview can be used in one of two
basic ways: either simply to gauge the telephone skills and manner of
the applicant, prior to sending out an application form, or to obtain
some of the information that would normally be given on an
application form. It is advisable to use the latter, which is a far more
effective screening method.

The interview should be conversational and aim to elicit the
following type of basic information:

- name, address and telephone number(s);

- age;

- basic details of education;

- work experience, for example telephone/sales, customer service, market research, with details of duration and specific areas of interest/enjoyment;

- reason for interest in the job, and why they think they would be good at it;

- if currently in a job, reason for wanting to leave;

- when available;

- availability for evening/weekend work, if applicable.

Some companies ask for other details, such as distance or travelling time to the job and previous or current salary. However, the main purpose of this interview is to gauge the telephone skills and manner of applicants, listening for things such as:

- a clear, easily-understood voice which creates a 'positive' impression;

- interest in the job and enthusiasm for the work;

- listening skills, for example without interrupting, acknowledging what has been said, asking pertinent questions to clarify information or give feedback;

- signs of having prepared for the call, for example the ability quickly to recall relevant experience;

- order of priorities, ie what they ask about first or seem most concerned about;

- the relevance and quality of questions asked, for example about the nature of the work, the company, pay and other benefits, training given;

- degree of control of the call;

- confidence and enthusiasm throughout the conversation;

- level of contribution to the conversation;

- positive end to the call, for example asking what happens next.

Most of the interviewing skills used in the face-to-face situation come into play during a telephone interview. However, it differs in that, ideally, the interviewer should be able to say at the end of the conversation whether or not they want the applicant to attend an interview. This means that they have to assess individuals during the conversation and respond quickly. This is aided by having a telephone interview form – a script or list of questions – which incorporates a simple mechanism for recording applicants' responses and enables the interviewer to come to a decision at a glance. The aim is not to record details, which can be done later, but to determine whether or not it is worthwhile interviewing an individual. A simple three-level grading system will suffice at this stage, for example good/average/poor, or interview/standby/reject.

Only the key selection criteria should be listed on the interview form and these should be stated as succinctly as possible, for example voice, listening skills, confidence, call control. To use this method it is obviously important that the interviewer is able to recognise the qualities required easily and to grade them against an ideal. Consistent grading is essential and it is best if one person conducts all the telephone interviews for a particular position.

When it is obvious, during the conversation, that someone is unsuitable, the interviewer should end the conversation politely at a convenient point. Those who are suitable should be told when, where and what type of interviews are being held, and asked if they can attend, with acceptances being logged on a timetable. Interviews should be held within a week of the telephone screening and written confirmation sent within 24 hours, together with any documentation, such as an application form, to be completed by the candidate and returned either prior to, or at, the interview.

The number of candidates required for interview should be determined before calls start coming in. The ratio of candidates required to the number of TME placings will depend upon the effectiveness of the screening. For example:

- there is generally a high fall-out rate when using recruitment agencies, for example because of lack of detail provided to the client or lack of commitment from the applicant – it is therefore wise to allow a candidate/placing ratio of around 8 to 1;

- following press advertising without effective telephone screening it is best to allow a ratio of about 6 to 1;

- effective telephone screening means, hypothetically, that every candidate should be suitable – however there is a risk factor, for example the possibility of personality clashes or bad visual presentation, and it is wise to allow a ratio of 4 to 1.

These ratios also allow for candidates not turning up for interview. The ratio for supervisors will depend on the degree of experience required, but 3 to 1 should be sufficient.

Once the required quota has been booked for interview, subsequent callers can be told that the vacancies have been filled and/or asked for their details in order to be contacted later. If, after the interviews, insufficient recruits have been found, these people can be interviewed by telephone and compared with those marked 'standby' during the original telephone interviews – the best being selected for another round of interviewing.

If a team of TMEs is being selected, or a team and supervisor, the next stage is the group interview.

Group interviews

The importance of working in a team in telephone marketing has been stressed already, and group interviews help to assess this aspect. They are used to select a team of people together, looking for characteristics such as good interpersonal skills, outgoing personality, a co-operative and sharing attitude, and a willingness to put ideas forward; in addition, they provide the opportunity to compare individuals under the same circumstances. Because of the way group interviews are structured, they can also help to identify a team leader or supervisor among the candidates.

Group interviews can be arranged to precede one-to-one interviews on the same day and generally take around three to four hours. Ideally, there should be two 'interviewers' or observers to run the session – perhaps one from personnel and one from the marketing or other appropriate department. The same observers should run all the sessions held to interview for the same position(s). Twelve people is about the maximum that can be assessed effectively in one session, and the agenda might be as follows.

Introduction to the company (20 minutes) This would cover the company, its markets, objectives, competitors etc.

The unit's role and TME's/supervisor's role (20 minutes)   This would describe the function of the unit, how it fits into the company and what the work entails.

Tests/questionnaires/inventories (1 hour)   Some companies use this type of assessment tool routinely and they can cover many topics, from numerical reasoning skills to personality factors. Their main value lies in the fact that they can – if well designed – provide objective measurement of characteristics that may not be available from other sources.

Group exercise (40 minutes)   This operates in much the same way as syndicate training groups, where the group is given a discussion topic or problem to tackle and then subdivided into 'teams'. However, it differs in the respect that, for this purpose, a leader is not appointed in each team. Dividing the session group in two, with team sizes of four to six, gives each member an opportunity to contribute fully within their team. The discussion topic or problem should be designed to elicit the type of characteristics the company wants in its recruits, and it is useful to have special forms designed to capture the relevant information about individuals. While the teams work on the problem, the observers should be looking at things such as how individuals work together, who contributes ideas, how good their interpersonal skills are, and whether anyone naturally assumes the role of team leader.

Questions and answers (10 minutes)   This is an opportunity for the candidates to ask questions, both on what they have been told earlier in the session and on any other relevant topics which interest or concern them.

Refreshments (20 minutes)   A group interview can be quite an ordeal and providing refreshments, such as cheese and wine if it runs into the evening, is a way of thanking people for being there, as well as providing an opportunity to talk to them in a more informal atmosphere. Any further questions that arise can be answered during this period.

The observers should assess individuals throughout the session, even during the Q&A and refreshment periods, in order to gain as full a picture of candidates as possible. If the company is seeking a supervisor from among the candidates, individuals who have shown this potential should be identified at this stage. This will enable their next interview to be conducted accordingly. However, no final selections are made until after the one-to-one interviews.

Personal face-to-face interviews

There are too many good books on interviewing skills and techniques to make it necessary to cover the subject in depth here, although there are some points worth highlighting.

The purpose of this interview is to gain a more thorough knowledge of candidates – their background, experience, skills, personality and ambitions – and to provide them with more information about what it would be like to work for the company. It is also an opportunity for them to reveal qualities which may not have come across in the telephone or group interviews. Once again, it is a good idea to use a checklist of characteristics sought in the ideal candidate, concentrating on those aspects which are best revealed in this type of interview (Table 5.2).

If a supervisor is being recruited from amongst the candidates, the interview of the appropriate people identified during the group session should obviously concentrate on discovering whether they have supervisory skills and/or potential.

An important area to explore is candidates' aspirations and level of drive. Apart from reducing staff turnover and the associated costs, career-minded people will help to ensure the future growth and development of the telephone marketing unit. At the same time, the opportunities for training, development and progress within the company should be emphasised.

Some companies use telephone role-plays or ask candidates to read a simple script with the interviewer taking the role of the customer. This can help to reveal how well candidates would be able to handle real telephone presentations. Although their telephone skills and manner will have been assessed already, having to conform to a script or campaign objectives is very different to normal conversation. Apart from assessing how well individuals can present themselves under these constraints, this method can also be used to find out how easily and accurately they can follow directions. This is done by asking candidates to read the script a second time after giving them pointers on the way to present it, perhaps to a particular type of customer or to give greater emphasis in certain areas. This whole exercise can also be used to assess how well they understand what they are doing in following the script, simply by asking some questions, such as: 'Why do you think we said . . . at that stage?'; or 'What do you think was the purpose of including . . . ?'.

Handwriting can be assessed from the application form and written tests used in the group interview. The company may wish to test keyboard skills, if these are required, particularly if candidates have little experience in this area.

Finally, it is vital to remember that a primary criterion in selecting TMEs is their aural presence. This is what will create impact over the telephone. Appearance and mannerisms, for example, should come low on the list of selection criteria, if they are included at all.

Once the interviews have been completed, what is sometimes called a 'wash-up' session is held. This is where all the interviewers involved in screening applicants gather to compare their assessments. One reason for doing this is to check that, as a group, they have graded people consistently. In the group session, for example, if one observer rated someone highly on a particular characteristic and the other graded that person poorly, the reasons for the discrepancy must be explored. Was it a personality clash, for example? Or perhaps the one observer missed or misinterpreted what the individual had said or done. Agreement must be reached on what is a fair rating for each candidate on all of the selection criteria before the group starts the selection process.

Interviewing for supervisors and managers

Interviews for supervisors and managers are obviously conducted differently, along the lines of normal interview procedures. However, given the shortage of experienced personnel, candidates may have little or no experience of telephone marketing supervision or management. If this is the case, the importance of exploring how well they will be able to transfer their skills cannot be overestimated. This can be done through normal interviewing techniques, such as discussing hypothetical situations and gauging candidates' understanding of different aspects of telephone marketing.

Selection

The selection process consists of comparing the rating of individuals on different selection criteria to find those who have the best mix of skills, qualities and experience. All candidates will be stronger in some areas than others, and the overall value of their mix of strengths and comparative weaknesses have to be compared. This can only be done effectively if the selection criteria have been rated according to their relative importance.

Although candidates' ability to do the work is the primary consideration, there may be other factors to consider. Early growth of the unit, for example, would require some people who have good potential for development or perhaps a slightly different type of background experience than is laid down in the personal profile. If there is the prospect of early growth, the priority of the selection criteria would be slightly different for a select number of candidates.

Some candidates may be very strong in most of the desired characteristics, but weak in one or two areas. It may be advantageous to recruit these people and provide special training to overcome their weaknesses, provided that they have the vital skills required to do their work in the interim.

If there is some variation in the work that different members of the team will do, the aim should be to select individuals who are able to do another person's work in addition to their own. This provides cover, for example in the event of absences, as well as the opportunity for the rotation of tasks (for cross-training and to help relieve boredom), and helps to create a more cohesive team where individuals come to understand the demands placed on one another.

Some candidates may appear over-skilled and perhaps be asking a higher salary than the company had expected to pay. If the job has not been underestimated and the personal profile of the ideal candidate is accurate, the company has to decide whether it is prepared to pay for this greater level of expertise which is not essential for the job. Recruiting such people has advantages as well as some major drawbacks, for example:

- their expertise
    - may be a valuable resource for training other staff
    - may help to provide a better quality and/or more efficient service

  – may be required as the unit grows;

- it is useful to have a high achiever, within a team of TMEs, to act as a pace setter;

- their skills would be under-employed, at least initially, and they easily may become dissatisfied with the job;

- they can disrupt other team members;

- disparity of salaries, either within the unit or across departments, can cause damaging resentment;

- any additional salary costs would impinge on the cost studies done for the unit.

All these factors, as well as any relating to the organisation's specific needs and policies, should be considered in reaching a consensus on which candidates to select. Before an offer is made, however, references may be taken up and, if the offer is made, it may be conditional upon the outcome of a medical examination.

Selection and recruitment for 1992

Whether or not the company plans to use telephone marketing immediately for developing its markets in other European countries, the many issues it raises should be considered before recruiting new staff.

Language skills and knowledge of how to deal with cultural barriers will become increasingly important across many areas of operation for companies selling abroad. People with these skills are currently at a premium and command appropriately high salaries. Even if recruits already possess the appropriate language skills, additional training is likely to be required on the company's markets in the target countries. Many companies are already providing language training for staff in selected positions and some are targeting their recruitment programme at people who are most able to take advantage of this training.

Job mobility between European countries will steadily increase the competition for other countries' bilingual or multilingual nationals. In the UK, for example, it would be preferable for a company selling into Germany to employ a native German with less fluent English, than employing a British person who may be fluent in German, but who does not understand the relevant cultural aspects of selling in Germany.

Although the new Europe provides a wider catchment area for recruitment, employers will have to develop contacts and strategies for attracting overseas applicants. Remuneration packages, for example, will have to be at least comparable to those of European counterparts if people are going to be enticed to move. Companies will also have to come to terms with differences in the education and training systems and personnel policies in different countries.

Many telephone marketing agencies have been gearing up to provide a multilingual service, either directly or through overseas branches or networks, which enables clients to buy in expertise to take advantage of international opportunities. However, this is unlikely to provide the best solution for companies needing a permanent resource. Since it is not only the telephone marketing operation which is affected, all companies should be re-evaluating their recruitment and training programmes to ensure that their prospects in Europe are not severely restricted by a lack of appropriately qualified staff.

Efficient selection and recruitment plays a fundamental role in creating a team with high morale who are likely to stay with the company and strive continually to achieve the highest possible levels of performance. If this process has been carried out effectively, new recruits will be fired with enthusiasm. That valuable commodity must be supported and nurtured from day one, which is why the training and development programme must be in place when staff are recruited.

6

Staff Training and Development

Employee training and development is increasingly accepted as the most important element in corporate human resource policy for the 1990s. As skills shortages bite, companies have to invest more and more in building up the knowledge, skills and attitudes of employees to enable them to achieve corporate objectives. Nowhere is this more true than in the highly people-intensive telephone marketing industry. Rapid, sustained growth over the past ten years has meant an increasingly severe shortage of skilled personnel which shows no signs of abating.

Telephone marketing is an expensive form of communication and companies can ill afford to allow margins to be eroded further by paying the upward spiralling salaries commanded by experienced staff. Even when skilled staff are recruited, their mix of skills and ability to work together as a team rarely leads automatically to optimum performance. The nature of telephone marketing, where every call must be made to count day in, day out, also means that regular refresher training must be provided to help sustain individuals' motivation and performance. A good training programme is therefore essential in establishing and maintaining a successful telephone marketing unit. However, there are many diverse benefits, for example:

- the opportunity for self-development attracts more staff of a better calibre;

- optimum results can only be sustained through continuous development of staff expertise;

- job satisfaction, motivation and commitment increase;

- staff turnover is reduced;

- equipping individuals to take on more demanding roles builds a resource to meet expansion needs and cushions the effects of promotion or departure of experienced personnel;

- individuals can cope with changes in objectives, work tasks, working practices and organisational culture without a reduction in their effectiveness;

- a broader skills base provides greater flexibility in resource deployment, enabling more efficient planning and management;

- showing care for individuals' development and future success helps to improve employee relations.

The findings of the BDMA survey suggest that not all companies using telephone marketing in-house are fully aware of the importance of training. Nearly one-quarter (22 per cent) reported giving telephone operators 5 or less hours of training before starting live calling, compared with an average of 28 hours and 18 per cent who claimed to provide 40 hours or more. Similarly, only 28 per cent of companies provided additional supervisory training, compared with 87 per cent of agencies.

Establishing a rolling programme of staff training and development should be a major priority for all companies who use telephone marketing. Without this key investment there is little chance of the telephone ever being used to its full potential as a marketing tool. Whether training is provided by company staff, external specialists or both, the first step in establishing such a programme is to identify the training needs.

Identifying training needs

This section is relatively detailed because the training needs created when a telephone marketing unit is first established are not always clear cut. In addition, there must be a methodology for ongoing identification of training needs to ensure the continued success and development of the unit.

There are two elements to identifying training needs – deciding who needs to be trained and what they need to learn through training – which are the same whether a company is revitalising an existing in-house telephone marketing operation or establishing a new unit. The two activities are inseparable from wider personnel issues and their effectiveness, together with that of subsequent training, relies upon having sound operational systems and procedures covering areas such as:

- job descriptions;

- staffing and work scheduling;

- performance monitoring and appraisal;

- training provision and allocation;

- career development.

Identifying training needs must be a methodical, continuous process. To understand its importance fully we need to go back to basics. When a unit is being planned, the objectives set for the unit determine its relationship with other company operations, its structure, the tasks and jobs created (defined in job descriptions) and the knowledge, skills and attitudes required to carry out those jobs effectively (defined in personal profiles). The achievement of the unit's objectives therefore depends, ultimately, on how well the knowledge, skills and attitudes of staff equip them to do their jobs effectively. Any gap between what they can do and what they need to be able to do must be bridged by training. This is sometimes called 'the training gap'. In addition, however, it is also desirable to help staff develop as individuals, for the reasons given above. So there are two sets of training needs.

- *Departmental training needs*, which is the training required to ensure that, collectively, staff have the knowledge, skills and attitudes required to achieve the objectives of the unit.

- *Individual training needs*, which is the training required by members of staff to meet their personal targets and to help them develop as individuals.

There are many factors which can influence this system. It is unlikely that staff, for example when first recruited, will accurately match the personal profile for their job, or work with complete efficiency with other members of their department. Hence, there will be an initial training need. Subsequently, there will be an ongoing training need arising from constantly striving to improve performance and maintain staff motivation, for example through refresher or follow-up training. Any change in the unit's objectives, in terms of the nature of tasks and/

or targets (qualitative and quantitative), can obviously give rise to additional training needs.

In addition, a telephone marketing unit does not operate in isolation. Personnel outside the unit contribute to achieving its objectives according to the degree of integration with other company operations. So they, too, will have training needs in terms of their interaction with the unit. And, of course, any change in their departmental objectives may have a feedback effect on the role of the unit's staff and their training needs.

Consequently, the knowledge, skills and attitudes required by staff, individually and collectively, both within and outside the unit, for the unit to achieve and maintain optimum efficiency and productivity are in a state of constant flux. Hence, identifying training needs must be a continuous and accurate (ie methodical) process, dealing first with departmental and then individual needs.

Departmental training needs

Deciding the overall training needs for the unit to achieve optimum performance can be divided into three stages:

1. establishing what tasks need to be done to achieve the objectives of the unit;

2. analysing what knowledge, skills and attitudes are required to do those tasks effectively;

3. comparing that with the knowledge, skills and attitudes already possessed by staff (any gap is a training need, ie learning that is required).

Note that stage 1 will generally encompass staff outside the unit, and will definitely do so if telephone marketing is well integrated into company operations.

Identifying training needs in this way can be fairly complex and it is helpful to use some form of diagram, such as the matrix shown in Table 6.1. This can be used to chart the level of performance of individuals in the various activities involved in a particular application and, ultimately, those required to achieve the objectives of the unit. The example shows the training needs relating to general call handling and could be extended to include other performance criteria relating to specific applications. If the application was direct sales, for example,

Table 6.1 Matrix for identifying and recording training needs

Names	Work activity	Voice	Call structure	Getting through	Opening call	Questioning	Listening	Sales presentation	Closing	Overcoming objections	Dealing with awkward situations	Product/service knowledge
Judith Spence		4	4	5	4	5	5	4	3^T	4	3^T	4
Mary Williams		3^T	4	4	4	4	4	3^T	4	5	4	5
Beth Jamieson		4	2^T	4	4	2^T	3^T	2^T	3^T	3^T	2^T	2^T
Andrew Davies		4	4	4	5	4	3^T	4	3^T	4	4	4
Billie Walters		4	4	5	4	5	5	4	4	3^T	3^T	4
Mary Jamieson (*team leader*)		4	4	5	4	5	4	5	5	4	4	5
Eileen Jackson (*supervisor*)		5	4	4	4	5	5	5	4	4	5	5
Current capacity		6	6	7	7	6	5	5	4	5	4	6
Ideal capacity		7	7	7	7	7	7	7	7	7	7	7
Shortfall		1	1	–	–	1	2	2	3	2	3	1

Key: 1 – very poor
2 – fail
3 – adequate
4 – good
5 – excellent
T – training indicated

then order form completion or order processing could have been included. Note that the supervisor and sometimes the manager may be included, even if these people are not involved directly in carrying out the various activities.

This is done for a number of reasons. First, they can be involved in some aspects of the application (for example identifying and deciding how to overcome possible objections), and their performance and training needs therefore impinge upon the success of others. Also, in the absence of the supervisor and/or manager, there should be individuals who are able to fulfil the essential aspects of their roles. Finally, the supervisor and/or manager will be at least partly responsible for training team members and can only do so effectively if they possess the appropriate knowledge and skills. The matrix may also include people from outside the unit. If it was based on an appointment booking application, for example, then the members of the sales team could be included, for example to cover activities like liaison/providing feedback.

The performance of each individual in each area is recorded using the graded scale. The current capacity is the sum of all those whose performance is acceptable or above. In the example given, an 'adequate' performance is not acceptable and has been taken as an indication of a training need. The ideal capacity is that required to meet all the development needs of the unit, for example:

- to improve performance through an improvement in knowledge, skills and attitudes;

- to accommodate an increase in the volume of work;

- to improve cover for absences;

- to accommodate the introduction of a new task.

The shortfall is the number of people who need to be trained to achieve these development needs and the grading system helps to decide who it is best to train to overcome this shortfall. This decision will be based largely on the development needs (for example improving performance by training those whose current ability is poor in certain areas, or training someone with little or no experience in the application to accommodate an increase in the volume of work or to improve cover for absences), but also taking into account individual training needs (*see* next page). A 'T' placed in a box indicates an individual selected for training to acquire learning in a particular area. Deciding what has to be learned is examined later under 'Setting training objectives'.

Individual training needs

Some individuals will be identified for training when the needs of the unit are assessed. In addition, however, they will also require training to take them to the next stage of their personal development plan. Personal development plans are drawn up during performance appraisal interviews, the first of which should be held after the successful completion of each individual's probationary period (these plans are described later under 'Performance review and appraisal'). The choice of who will be trained to meet departmental needs can often take account of personal development needs. If someone's plan includes the acquisition of wider experience, for example, this may coincide with the need to provide an additional person to work on a particular application. Training is often concentrated on overcoming weaknesses and reinforcing strengths (although the latter is not marked on Table 6.1), but there should always be provision for wider personal development. Once decided upon, individual training needs can be marked on the same matrix as departmental needs.

Although training can help to create or improve an attitude and engender commitment, an attitude problem is the wrong reason to train. It can have a detrimental effect on other delegates and may make the individual problem worse. If people feel that they have outgrown their job or they have become bored, for example, and their level of commitment has fallen, sending them on a training course, covering familiar ground, will simply compound the problem. An attitude problem of this type should be dealt with before training.

Training needs must be identified precisely in order to decide what training will help individuals acquire the appropriate learning, which is the difference between the knowledge, skills and attitudes (KSA) required and those already possessed by the individual. The next section examines how this is done.

Setting training objectives

A training objective is a precise statement of what an individual will be able to do as a result of training. It helps to identify what training is appropriate and acts as a yardstick to measure learning and the effectiveness of training. To be effective, the statement of a training objective should include an exact description of what the individual will be able to do as a result of training, the standards required and the circumstances under which these should be achieved. One of the training objectives derived from the matrix shown earlier, for example, might read:

> At the end of her training Beth Jamieson will show an average 30 per cent improvement in her successful call rate, from 15 per cent to 20 per cent, arising from improvement in the following areas: call structure; questioning and listening; closing a call; overcoming objections; and product knowledge.

This is the task objective for training. To identify precisely what needs to be learned it has to be analysed in terms of the KSA required. Task analysis can be a fairly complex and daunting exercise; written communication, for example, can be broken down into about 30 elements. However, once completed it is invaluable because it shows precisely what KSA are required to complete a particular task. Table 6.2 shows those required in making a sales presentation. By comparing the KSA Beth Jamieson possesses with those on this chart it is possible to identify where she needs to improve (shown in italics). Now it is much easier to identify the type of training which will help her to improve her ability to make sales presentations. In this case,

Table 6.2 Partial task analysis for Beth Jamieson's training objective (KSA in italics are those where improvement is required)

Knowledge	Skills	Attitudes
Sequence of a sale	Effective use of language	*Confidence*
		Perseverance
Why people buy	*Listening*	
Target audience needs	*Questioning*	
	Clarification	
	Interpreting/ paraphrasing	

for example, a refresher course in telephone sales skills, either incorporating or as well as product training, may be the most effective
option, because it would also encompass other areas where she needs
to improve, ie call structure, closing, overcoming objections and
dealing with awkward situations. If there had been an isolated
weakness, such as opening a call, coaching may have been the
preferred option.

Detailed knowledge of individuals' KSA comes from monitoring
and appraising their work, which is examined in more detail later in
this chapter. However, when a unit is first established, with either
existing or newly recruited staff, training needs are likely to be very
broad and may involve people from many departments.

Who needs to be trained?

Training is required whenever individuals' knowledge, skills and
attitudes do not meet those required for the tasks they have to do. It
should be obvious, therefore, that many people throughout the
organisation may require training when a telephone marketing unit is
established. Anyone whose job interfaces with the work of the unit
will require knowledge of telephone marketing and the unit's role, the
appropriate skills to meet this new aspect of their job, and the correct
attitude to telephone marketing and their role in it. This could
encompass anyone from the receptionist to the financial director, and
is above and beyond the training required by telephone marketing
executives, team leaders, supervisors and managers working in the
unit. Even if experienced personnel are recruited for the unit, there
will be a training need in terms of the company, its products, services,
markets and so on.

Many companies restrict telephone skills training to those who
generate revenue directly on the telephone, such as telephone sales
personnel. However, this type of training is invaluable for anyone who has regular telephone contact with people outside the
company, such as reception staff, administrative and secretarial staff,
and customer service and accounts departments.

What topics should training cover?

The aim of initial training is to equip everyone involved with adequate
knowledge, skills and attitudes to achieve the targets set for the unit,

and to provide a foundation for future development. Subsequent training will concentrate on improving performance, meeting the demands placed on staff by development of the unit, for example into new applications or database marketing, and providing development opportunities for individuals.

A comprehensive training plan should be drawn up detailing the training that will be provided for staff within and outside the unit. For those working in the unit this should include details of opportunities for promotion, since a clearly defined career path helps to encourage long-term commitment. The plan, which should be updated regularly to accommodate changing circumstances, will ensure that training equips staff to meet the unit's current objectives, as well as catering for its growth and the development of individuals.

The topics that training should cover, and the timescales over which it is carried out, will depend upon various factors, including existing skill levels, the type of work undertaken by the unit, its structure and how it is integrated with other company operations. However, there are a number of generic headings which indicate the range of training that may be provided:

- induction;

- administrative and clerical skills;

- telephone techniques;

- telephone sales skills;

- management training;

- refresher training;

- specialist training, such as database management.

A three-stage training course is often recommended for newly re-cruited telephone marketing executives, covering induction, telephone marketing techniques and on-the-job training. Details of the content of this type of training, and some of the other types listed above, will be given later in this chapter. The subsequent training needs will be unique to the unit and may cover anything from team working to language skills. These will be determined, on an ongoing basis, by the knowledge, skills and attitudes required to meet the needs of the unit and individual members of staff.

Training providers

Telephone marketing is a highly skilled activity requiring specialised training. Few companies have yet acquired the industry knowledge and expertise necessary to design and run effective telephone marketing courses themselves. Some utilise the expertise of the larger telephone marketing agencies, who offer full training consultancy and/or public courses, or one of the general training organisations offering courses in this area. In the BDMA survey, however, 82 per cent of companies claimed to train their own telephone marketing executives, with only 8 per cent using outside consultants as well as their own staff. Given the specialised nature of telephone marketing, and the general lack of expertise in using the medium, the soundness of taking this route is questionable. The situation will hopefully change, however, as the marketplace becomes more educated and awareness of the importance of professional training increases. This can be achieved through the efforts of professional trade bodies, such as the BDMA, the introduction of courses at professional training establishments, such as business schools, and the continued efforts of agencies in providing centres of excellence in the use of the medium.

Training needs are not only met by trainers, of course. Managers and supervisors also play a key role in training, sharing responsibility with the personnel and/or training department to ensure that the training needs of their staff are met. They are ideally placed, working at the sharp end, to identify training needs on a day-to-day basis and help to meet them through activities like coaching. All managers should be able to provide *ad hoc* on-the-job training in areas such as interpersonal skills, to help staff work together more effectively as a team, but they may not have the knowledge and experience to provide training in telephone marketing-related skills. Management training courses are now available which cover these areas and some courses can be tailored for trainers to equip them to give managers the training support they require.

The more experienced staff in a telephone marketing unit can also help with training. Encouraging them to pass on their knowledge and expertise to their less experienced colleagues has benefits for both parties. It gives instructors a sense of achievement and an opportunity to review their working methods, while the less experienced person is obviously helped to acquire new knowledge, skills and attitudes, and can be confident in the knowledge that someone is on hand if any problems or difficulties arise. For both, it can help to develop a closer working relationship. These benefits only accrue, however, if instructors are chosen carefully. The best people to instruct others are not necessarily those with the greatest understanding, skill or time in the job. They need to be able to explain things clearly, step-by-step, giving neither too much nor too little information, and at a pace determined by the individual learner. Empathy with the needs of the learner, together with good working practices and attitudes, are essential.

Experts from other departments in the organisation may also be involved in training, in its broadest sense, particularly where the telephone marketing unit is integrated with other operations. The reverse situation is also true. Telephone marketing staff, once they have gained sufficient knowledge and experience, can help to explain what they do and how their department operates. Mutual knowledge of what different departments do, how they operate, and what use is made of the information they provide each other with, can be of great benefit as follows:

- it increases understanding of other departments' roles and responsibilities, how they interact and the support they need to provide each other;

- it places telephone marketing in the wider context of company operations and increases commitment to the success of the unit throughout the departments involved;

- it helps to develop a good working relationship and increases commitment to ensuring each other's needs are met.

Experts from the relevant departments are not necessarily the best people to present this information, but they can be involved in the preparation of course materials and the briefing of trainers.

Training methods

A variety of methods are employed in providing effective training in telephone marketing-related skills. These include the following.

Formal courses These may be designed and run by company trainers, perhaps incorporating training materials bought in from outside, or by external trainers. They may include the use of workshops, role-plays, live calling, case studies, workbooks and video. All courses for telephone marketing executives should utilise role play, which can be taped and constructively critiqued during playback. Delegates are in a 'safe' environment and they are therefore much more open to learning from their 'mistakes'. Ideally, the role-play should be centred around applications and markets relevant to the delegates' own work situation. Video for telephone marketing training was being produced in the UK for the first time in 1990.

The types of courses available are described in more detail later in this chapter.

Hands-on training   Practical work, where trainees can practise, refine and develop the skills they need in their work, should form a significant proportion of telephone marketing executives' training, and begin as early as possible. During initial training, at the induction stage, it is common to give trainees increasingly sophisticated tasks, perhaps starting with number searching and ultimately progressing to live customer calling, so that they can put into practice the theory they have been learning. Individuals are supported and helped to learn while doing this work through coaching. However, the greatest amount of hands-on training takes place on the job, starting where induction ends and continuing for as long as a person is employed by the company.

Telephone systems are available which help with hands-on tele-phone training by providing facilities for live monitoring as well as recording and playback of calls. These can be used during induction, when trainees make their first live calls, and for subsequent call monitoring and on-the-job coaching. Playing back recorded calls enables both the trainer, or coach, and the telephone marketing executives to analyse their calls, identify strengths and weaknesses, and take appropriate action to help them improve their performance.

Coaching   This has been described as, 'Systematically increasing the ability, experience and work performance of people by giving them tasks designed to provide learning opportunities, and giving guidance and feedback to help them learn from them'. It is generally conducted by the manager and/or supervisor and requires someone with coach-ing skills to do it effectively.

Any task through which a person can learn something, with guidance and feedback from the coach, provides an opportunity for coaching, for example:

- giving tasks to those with least experience in doing them;

- helping people analyse and rectify mistakes or difficulties;

- helping people analyse the reasons for their successes;

- planned delegation for the purpose of coaching;

- after a change in job content, perhaps following promotion or departmental restructuring;

- providing cover for more senior staff;

- carrying out the development plan agreed at performance appraisal.

The nature of telephone marketing, where a single telephone call constitutes a complete task, makes it ideal for coaching. However, there are drawbacks as well as benefits to coaching. Giving a task to a less experienced person, for example, involves the manager spending time briefing and coaching the individual. It also introduces an element of risk because the task may not be completed as effectively or as quickly as when it is given to an experienced person. On the other hand, it helps the individual to develop, it broadens the skills base in the unit, improving flexibility and cover for absences, and helps to improve overall performance. Every coaching opportunity should be viewed in the light of the balance between the development needs of individuals, task priorities, and the overall needs of the unit.

Self-study This can take several forms, including reading, computer-based training (CBT) and interactive video (IV). A great deal of valuable information can be gained from reading about the company and its products or services (in brochures and newsletters), about its markets (through company information and pertinent trade press coverage) and about telephone marketing, particularly as it applies to the applications used within the company (in the trade press and books). CBT and IV packages pertinent to telephone marketing are currently very rare but, as the industry expands and demand for more cost-effective training increases, more technology-based training materials are likely to become available.

Self-study should be stimulating and create enthusiasm among trainees. It is important to ensure that maximum encouragement and opportunity is given to trainees to apply their learning in their work as soon as possible. Creatively-used interactive media like CBT and IV often include work-based tasks to help trainees put theory into practice. Any form of self-study, including reading, special projects and visits to other departments or company sites, should be supported by practical elements to help trainees apply their learning in their work. These can cover any topic of which they have gained knowledge or understanding, for example asking them to identify what features of a product are most likely to appeal to different target markets, or outlining all the ways in which the information obtained from a telephone call could be used within the company.

The choice of which mix of methods to use, and when, depends upon the situation. When the aim is to equip recruits to become productive as soon as possible, for example, there is likely to be a strong emphasis on formal courses combined with hands-on training and self-study. Subsequently, the emphasis will shift to include on-the-job coaching, together with a continuing programme of formal courses – both to upgrade or provide new skills, and as refresher training, when appropriate.

Externally-provided training

There are basically two types of training course available from external sources – public and tailored. Public courses cover a fixed range of topics and training objectives, while the tailored courses are designed to meet the precise needs of a particular company. Both may be conducted on a company site or externally, depending on the provider and the client's needs, and either can be used for initial or refresher training.

The objectives and content of some of the public courses available, on topics such as telephone techniques and telephone marketing management, are described later in this chapter. The degree to which these can be tailored, for example by the inclusion of company-specific case studies and role-plays, is usually fairly limited, and depends on the willingness of the provider and the number of different companies sending delegates on the course. Although training is more effective using tailored courses, there are situations where public courses are more practical for reasons of cost, for example where only a couple of new recruits are being trained, or where a delegate is likely to benefit from mixing with people from other companies – as in management training.

Using a good consultancy, tailored courses are designed to take account of all relevant aspects of the client company, including its

Table 6.3 Questions to ask when choosing telephone marketing training

Choosing a training provider
General questions
<ul><li>What knowledge of the industry and training experience does the provider have?</li><li>Does the provider also offer follow-up and refresher training? It is preferable to use one provider.</li><li>Where is the training conducted, eg is it convenient; is it in a real telephone marketing environment with opportunities to experience the work first-hand?</li><li>What will the training cover?</li><li>What is the duration of the training? Is this practical in terms of the knowledge, skills and attitudes to be acquired by delegates?</li><li>What methods are used, eg case studies, workshops, role play and live calling with taping and analysis of calls?</li><li>How are delegates actively involved and what methods are used to achieve this?</li><li>What level of participation is achieved?</li><li>What is the cost and what does it include, eg is all documentation, like handouts and delegate manuals, included?</li><li>Overall, will the course meet the company's training needs/objectives?</li><li>How do the costs of equivalent courses from different providers compare?</li><li>How is training effectiveness evaluated and validated?</li></ul>

Public courses	Tailored courses
<ul><li>How many delegates will there be on the course? The smaller the number, the more attention each will receive and the greater their opportunity to participate (a recommended optimum is 6 delegates, with a maximum of 8).</li><li>What does the course cover?</li><li>How relevant is the content of the course to the training needs of staff eg. applications, company markets, products and services?</li><li>Can company-specific information be incorporated into the course, eg case studies and market information?</li></ul>	<ul><li>Can they provide courses for all levels of staff that require training? If not, try elsewhere.</li><li>What experience does the provider have in delivering tailored training for telephone marketing staff?</li><li>For what clients have they carried out similar work, and can they be contacted for references?</li><li>If required, how will training needs be identified?</li><li>Will they present training objectives and criteria for measuring training effectiveness for agreement?</li><li>What elements will be company–specific?</li></ul>

products and services, its markets and the nature of its telephone marketing operation. The consultants will agree with the company the training objectives and criteria for measuring their success in achieving them. Full training consultancy would also include identification of training needs through a training needs analysis. Courses include activities specific to the company, including role-plays and 'live' calling on a real telephone marketing campaign. These courses are valuable when the company wants to train a group of people because they simulate the team's interaction in the real work situation. Although it is more expensive, it is highly effective and can even produce revenue-earning results with the live calling. The precise content of tailored courses can vary tremendously because they are company-specific. However, when they are used for initial training they will generally cover the same objectives and range of topics as the public courses.

External training providers should be chosen with great care, ideally by an experienced trainer and someone with experience of telephone marketing. A good agency, with appropriate training resources, has the industry expertise to provide what is probably the more thorough and effective training. General training organisations, although often more experienced as trainers, do not have the required depth of experience of telephone marketing. The key questions to consider are summarised in Table 6.3.

The cost of both public and tailored training courses varies considerably, but the following figures provide a rough guide to the range of charges, exclusive of VAT, made in the UK in 1990.

Public courses:

Telephone techniques (1 day)	£150–175 per delegate
Telephone sales skills (2 days)	£275–350 per delegate
Telephone marketing management (5 days)	£1,200–1,450 per delegate
Training skills (2 days)	£380–425 per delegate

Tailored training:
1–3 days' training needs analysis
2–4 days' preparation
2–5 days' course delivery @ £500–1,000 per day

It should be remembered that, while cost is an important consideration, good quality training will result in a much higher return on investment than that which is poorly designed and delivered. Good training, even if it appears expensive, is therefore more cost-effective and will help to guarantee the success of the unit.

Whether public or tailored training is used, its effectiveness should be assessed continually to aid in future training selection. Apart from asking delegates to report on their training, whether provided by internal or external trainers, continuous monitoring of performance will help to identify strengths and weaknesses in the training, together with opportunities for developing it.

The following descriptions of the types of training that may be provided are intended as a guide only. The types of courses used and the mix of topics covered should always be tailored as closely as possible to meet the training needs of the telephone marketing staff.

Induction

New recruits, perhaps with little or no experience of their new role, will arrive on their first day at work experiencing mixed emotions. They will often be excited at the prospect of new challenges and new prospects, but probably also nervous about working with strangers and in a new environment, and perhaps anxious about their ability to do the job well. Induction should aim first to capitalise on the recruits' positive emotions and to ensure that any worries or concerns they may have are dispelled. Then it should provide comprehensive training to enable them to become efficient and productive as soon as possible.

Most organisations have set induction procedures and the content of initial training varies widely. Apart from providing background information on the company, its structure, products and services, markets and so on, it should cover all aspects of the job, from telephone techniques to systems that have to be maintained.

Planning induction

An induction plan should be drawn up, bearing in mind its two main objectives – to make the new recruits feel welcome, allay their fears and help them fit in, and to enable them to do their new job effectively. The first of these objectives dictates the atmosphere that must be created by induction. It should be enjoyable, exciting and rewarding. This is achieved by ensuring that induction is carefully planned to meet all the needs of the recruits and actively involves them in the work of the company from day one.

The plan should set out what topics are going to be covered, how, by whom and the timing of the different elements. It forms the basis for organising induction training and provides a guide to the recruits. Any changes which occur in the company should be reviewed to see if they should be accommodated in the plan, and all documentation, for both trainers and recruits, should be available on the first day of induction.

Induction topics

The content of induction training varies widely across companies and for different jobs, but there are general areas that should be covered. Some of the topics that have to be covered are determined by employment law, for example applicable disciplinary procedures. Other induction topics are determined by answering the following question. 'What do recruits need to know to allay their fears, help them fit in and feel a welcome addition to the organisation, and to enable them to do their new job effectively?'. The answer, in terms of telephone marketing executives, may give rise to the following range of induction topics.

The company:

- background and growth;
- structure and function of departments;
- corporate culture and style;
- corporate objectives;
- company rules and disciplinary procedure.

The department:

- role and responsibilities of the department;
- relationship to other departments

Company products/services:

- detailed product/service descriptions;
- applications;

- current and future markets;
- position in the market;
- customer profiles;
- unique selling points (in terms of customer benefit rather than technical features);
- likely objections to products/services;
- competitors and their products/services.

Telephone marketing techniques:

- an introduction to telephone marketing;
- communication skills;
- preparation and planning;
- call structure;
- reaching the decision-maker;
- controlling the call;
- expressive and descriptive techniques;
- the presentation;
- closing the call;
- objection handling/difficult questions and customers;
- customer relations.

Systems and procedures:

- recording systems;
- reporting;
- administrative systems, such as order processing;
- computerised systems and system operation;
- procedures, such as briefing and de-briefing, lead sourcing and preparation;
- standards;

- performance monitoring and appraisal.

Roles and responsibilities:

- job function and objectives;

- reporting relationships;

- main duties;

- main responsibilities, including targets and standards, call analysis and reporting;

- level of authority;

- resources and support available.

A similar range of topics would be covered for supermisory and management recruits, except that, obviously, the elements relating to the job would change. The order in which these topics are covered would vary according to normal company procedures and the training methods being used. However, they should not be viewed as distinctly separate areas for training. There is a considerable amount of overlap and an integrated approach is far more effective. Reintroducing topics that have been covered earlier, but approaching them from a different viewpoint, also helps to reinforce learning. The unique selling points of the company's products or services, for example, can be highlighted again during training in telephone marketing techniques.

The objectives and contents of some of the courses that may be used for induction, and for refresher training, are examined later in this chapter.

Induction personnel

It is preferable to involve a variety of personnel in induction training because it makes specialist skills available, helps to keep the training interesting, and introduces recruits to a wider range of staff. However, it is vital that the personnel chosen are excellent communicators and able trainers. It is pointless involving technical experts if they do not have the ability to train the recruits. It may be preferable, therefore, to have product experts, for example, briefing a professional trainer and helping to prepare course materials.

When specialists are chosen to conduct training they must be committed to helping the recruits learn and ensure that they are available on the dates marked down in the induction plan.

Induction methods

All the training methods described earlier in this chapter may be employed during induction. However, a large proportion of it, particularly in the early days, will consist of formal courses with a high practical content.

Thorough and well-designed documentation is an essential part of induction. This should be prepared well in advance, so that it can be handed out to recruits at the appropriate time, and may include:

- a detailed induction plan and timetable;

- corporate brochures;

- product or service literature;

- newsletters and house journals;

- administration documentation;

- course handouts;

- computer manuals;

- system documentation and guides;

- practical exercises.

Any explanation which may be required, such as the purpose of particular records and how they have to be completed, should either be written on the documents or firmly attached to them. It should be stressed to recruits whether materials supplied to them are their personal property, on which they can write or attach notes as they wish, or simply on loan.

Plenty of practical exercises, of the type described earlier under 'self-study', should be incorporated into the induction training from day one. These help to consolidate and build on learning, and to monitor the amount of knowledge and understanding gained by individuals. One of the main objectives of induction is to help recruits become productive as soon as possible and it is therefore important to ensure that there are plenty of opportunities for them to put theory into practice. Apart from playing a vital role in the learning process, working on practical tasks gives recruits a sense of achievement and helps to maintain their motivation.

These tasks should be designed to test individuals' learning and also to stretch them slightly, to provide a challenge and to prime them for further learning. Tasks could start with things like number searching, progressing to handling straightforward incoming calls and filling in record cards, and then on to more complex outbound calls. Should there be unforeseen circumstances which delay a part of the induction plan, practical exercises can also be used to fill the recruits' time productively and ensure that they do not become bored.

Regular breaks are also extremely important because new recruits will have to assimilate a lot of information. If sessions are too long there is a great risk that they will become inattentive.

Recruits will accumulate a great deal of documentation during their induction and it is useful for them to be supplied with some form of folder to keep everything together.

Induction timing

The overall time allowed for induction is a somewhat arbitrary period, depending largely on how long the company believes it will take for recruits to become 'productive'. There is no distinct line between the induction training required to help someone become productive, which is a subjective decision, and the continuous, ongoing training that should be provided to help individuals develop and improve their performance.

The calibre of recruits will also have an influence. If they all have experience in telephone marketing, for example, their induction may be biased more towards topics such as corporate style, products and services, and systems and procedures, with less time spent on telephone techniques *per se*. The amount of time to be spent on different topics, and overall, should therefore be viewed flexibly, considering factors such as:

- the amount recruits have to learn on each topic to make them 'productive';

- the rate at which they can reasonably be expected to learn;

- the importance of incorporating regular practical exercises to consolidate and reinforce learning;

- the need to ensure that recruits are not left to 'find their own way around' or 'get bored';

- the availability of induction personnel.

These factors give rise to a number of important points. First, recruits should not be overloaded with unnecessary new information, particularly if it is highly detailed and may lead to confusion about even basic facts. For example, is it essential for recruits to gain a thorough knowledge of products, services, systems and procedures, or could some of this be deferred until later? Similarly, recruits cannot be expected to assimilate a large number of new names and faces in the first few days, so they should be introduced to company personnel step-by-step in a logical fashion, according to their immediate needs and the content of their training.

The sequence of training should be planned to achieve the objectives of induction in the most efficient way. Practical tasks, for example, can provide learning opportunities at the same time as being productive in terms of work output. Similarly, recruits may understand particular topics, such as appointment setting, more easily and more effectively when they have certain prior knowledge, such as the role of a sales person (which could come from meeting members of the sales team).

Until recruits settle in and get to know their away around they should never be left in limbo. This is especially important during the first few days and applies particularly to periods such as lunch and break times and towards the end of the day when induction sessions have ended. Encouraging their new colleagues to 'befriend' the recruits from day one will overcome this problem and help to lay the foundation of a new working relationship.

Any factors which impinge upon the effectiveness of induction training can affect the timetable and it is therefore important to review the training plan prior to each intake of new recruits.

Monitoring progress

Even though induction should be planned thoroughly beforehand, this is not to say that the plan is inflexible. Progress should be monitored continuously, from day one, to ensure that the training is effective overall for each recruit. Encouraging their active involvement in the training, through activities such as practical exercises and discussion groups, is the best way to obtain the feedback necessary to check their knowledge and understanding on an ongoing basis. This serves quickly to clear up any minor misunderstandings and to identify areas where training has not been fully effective. The remedial action required depends upon the situation. A widespread misunderstanding or lack of knowledge on a particular topic, for example, would suggest that the subject has not been covered effectively, perhaps through poor communication or cramming too much into too short a time. Individual problems could result from factors such as inattentiveness or having less experience than other recruits.

Closely monitoring progress, and noting any shortfall in training, will help to revise the induction plan before the next intake of recruits.

Monitoring performance will be examined in more detail later in this chapter.

Telephone techniques training

Telephone techniques training is suitable for all personnel who speak with customers on the telephone. Even new recruits who are experienced in the use of the telephone will benefit from this type of course as refresher training. When it is tailored to the company it will help recruits to learn how the company wants itself presented on the telephone, which is likely to be different from their previous employers, and become familiar with using company-specific information, for example on products and services.

The typical duration of an intensive course is one day. The overall objective is to ensure that individuals can make effective use of the telephone in building customer relations, which is achieved by enabling them to:

- create a good impression when answering the telephone;

- use the telephone confidently when answering customer enquiries;

- use listening and questioning techniques effectively;

- convey relevant information and offer assistance to customers in an accurate and courteous manner;

- control the content and direction of conversations;

- know how and when to end a call;

- put the techniques that have been taught into practice at every stage, through workshops and role plays.

The *content* of the course would generally cover the following areas, though not necessarily in this format.

Communication skills The need for a courteous approach when handling customer enquiries by telephone – the attitudes and qualities required; the effect and impact of the voice when using the telephone; practical voice control; the need for simple language and communicating without jargon.

Preparation and planning The need for mental and physical planning in order to optimise the opportunities presented by each call; deciding what information must be obtained and conveyed and how best to do that, anticipating reactions and deciding how to respond, selecting the most effective words and phrases; how to plan a call.

Opening statements Using the correct techniques so that a good first impression is created; establishing rapport; what to say in the first 15 seconds.

Controlling the call Using listening and questioning techniques to gather relevant information in a timely way, to show interest, encourage a response and ensure that the conversation is completely understood by both parties; controlling the content and direction of conversations; using open and closed questioning techniques; overcoming the difficulties of 'passive listening'.

Expressive and descriptive techniques Recognising the difficulties of communication when the two parties cannot see each other; using expressive and descriptive techniques to overcome these barriers to communication.

Closing the call Retaining control and concluding a call; different types of closing; using closing phrases.

Objection handling/difficult questions and customers Using listening and empathising techniques to handle irate or awkward customers tactfully; handling objections and difficult questions; determining a successful conclusion to a call.

Customer relations Identifying and understanding the importance of providing customers with first-class service; creating this level of service; building client relations; guidelines to establish client relations.

This can only be the briefest of descriptions because telephone techniques, and telephone sales skills, cannot be learned from a book. The course content, structure and method of delivery is also likely to vary considerably from one training provider to another.

Telephone sales skills training

This type of course is suitable for anyone who uses the telephone for applications such as direct sales, making appointments, market evaluation and informing customers of special promotions. The point made earlier about new recruits with experience in this area still requiring training, both as a refresher and to help them learn the company 'style', is true also of telephone sales skills training.

The typical duration of a course is two days and the aim is to enable delegates to:

- use the telephone as an effective sales tool;

- have the confidence to handle telephone sales effectively;

- use listening and questioning techniques to make a sales presentation appropriate to the target audience, for example identifying customer needs through questioning;

- build customer relations through their positive attitude;

- encourage cross-selling and up-selling;

- explore customer problems and offer effective solutions;

- put the techniques taught into practice at every stage, through workshops and role plays.

The content of the course would generally cover the following areas, though not necessarily following this format.

An introduction to selling Understanding why people buy; what makes a good sales person; the sales role and its environment; developing the right attitude and a desire to become an outstanding sales person.

Communication skills The advantages of telephone communication; dos and don'ts; the effect and impact of the voice when using the telephone; practical voice control; the need for simple language and communicating without jargon.

Preparation and planning The importance of knowing the products/ services, marketplace and competitors; translating product/service features into benefits; anticipating objections; planning for persuasive communication; the planning necessary to ensure a call will be successful.

Call structure Effective calls structures – opening, listening and questioning, the presentation, handling objections, closing positively; the sequence of a sale.

Reaching the decision-maker 'Getting through' techniques – dealing with the switchboard, a secretary or colleague to get through to the decision-maker; confirming 'buying' authority; techniques for creating a good first impression; effective opening statements.

Controlling the call Using listening and questioning techniques to gather relevant information in a timely way (such as customer needs and preferences), to encourage a positive response and to ensure that the conversation is completely understood by both parties; controlling the content and direction of conversations; overcoming the difficulties of 'passive listening'.

The presentation Using expressive and descriptive techniques to convey complicated technical information in an easily understood way; making an effective and well-targeted presentation by communicating the appropriate benefits according to information gathered during the listening and questioning stage; learning to paint a vivid verbal picture of benefits.

Closing Different types of close, and the most effective occasions and times to use them.

Objection handling Distinguishing whether or not an objection is true and making the appropriate response; preparing solutions to likely objections; handling common objections.

Cross-selling and up-selling The value of upgrading sales; techniques for cross-selling and up-selling.

Although there are many areas of overlap between telephone sales skills training and telephone techniques training, the two types of course are distinct in their objectives and approach.

On-the-job training

On-the-job training can be said to start as early as the first week of induction when, for example, recruits may be given practical tasks such as number searching. However, the term is probably more accurately applied to the training which individuals receive once they have started making live calls. It is naturally more intensive during the early weeks, when staff are still settling into their new jobs, but it should continue on a regular, scheduled basis for as long as they are employed in the telephone marketing unit.

The purpose, initially, is to help new staff integrate and put into practice everything they have learned from earlier training, so that they can fulfil all the tasks in their job description effectively. The time that this takes will depend on their previous experience, the effectiveness of the training provided and the standards of performance initially expected from them. Subsequently, the aim of ongoing training is continually to develop new staff's knowledge, skills and attitudes to meet the training objectives which have been set, which generally fall into three broad categories:

- meeting new or changing demands made on the unit;

- improving the efficiency and performance of the unit;

- providing planned development opportunities for staff.

Ongoing training is required even to maintain existing levels of performance. Telephone marketing includes many repetitive tasks and staff are very susceptible to functioning on 'automatic pilot'. Telephone marketing executives have to make every call count and they will fail in this task if they work by rote. Regular refresher training is required to ensure that they consciously use their skills to the full on every call, reminding them of what this involves, restating the standards of performance expected of them and motivating them to better performance.

Ongoing training should employ a wide variety of methods, according to the specific training needs, such as formal refresher courses, hands-on training supported by coaching, planned delegation, group training in team skills, self-study and informative visits, and presentations where learning is consolidated by practical tasks.

An often neglected opportunity for training is planned delegation, where individuals are given tasks normally done by a more senior person. Although senior staff may often delegate some of their tasks to others, perhaps when they are extremely busy, they do not usually exploit the training potential by planning the activity. Delegation can be a very valuable training opportunity. First, a person who is delegated a task will generally require some prior training to be able to do it effectively. Without giving staff that prior opportunity to learn, delegation will never function properly. Secondly, it is more practical and cost-effective to train existing staff to take on more senior roles when vacancies arise, or when the department expands, than to recruit from outside. Finally, it gives individuals an important opportunity for personal development, and provides an enormous boost to confidence and motivation.

The expectation, experience and personal benefits of all planned training are a powerful motivator and confidence-builder for staff, and each individual should know what they will be doing, when, and what they can expect to learn. Some form of planned training activity should be provided every four to six weeks, although *ad hoc* training, usually in the form of coaching, should be given whenever a suitable opportunity arises.

Management training

The development of training courses specifically for telephone marketing management is comparatively recent, although a number of telephone marketing agencies and other training organisations have now developed management skills courses. The content and emphasis of these courses varies considerably, but the following details outline courses run by one leading agency.

Planning, development and control

The content of this type of course would be suitable for telephone marketing supervisors, as well as managers, and anyone else who becomes involved in setting up campaigns and has responsibility for staff. Typically requiring three days, it should include hands-on practice, where appropriate, and is likely to cover areas such as:

- the distinction between telephone marketing and telephone sales;

- telephone marketing in the context of direct marketing;

- different telephone marketing applications, their benefits and how to apply them;

- work profiles, work scheduling and staffing;

- preparing, planning and setting up a campaign, including
    - resourcing
    - the use and structure of scripts
    - writing scripts
    - preparing a brief
    - briefing a calling team;

- effective measurement and monitoring;

- analysing campaign results.

Telephone marketing management

This type of course would be suitable for the same audience as the planning, development and control course, and is likely to last at least two days. It is essentially about managing a team of telephone marketers and should take a practical approach, including role play and discussion. The objectives may include enabling delegates to:

- understand the management function and roles of a manager;

- appreciate different management styles and examine their own;

- manage by objectives;

- set clear objectives, and individual goals and targets;

- understand the importance of motivation, and the principles and use of different techniques to motivate individuals effectively;

- understand demotivating factors;

- adapt their management style according to the level of the individual staff member;

- praise and reprimand staff at the right time, and in the right way;

- understand how to encourage and guide improved work performance;

- manage time effectively, including when, what and how to delegate;

- set priorities when arranging and attending meetings.

Training skills

Telephone marketing managers and supervisors require some level of training skill, even if they are not involved directly in running courses. They are responsible for identifying training needs on a day-to-day basis and a large proportion of the ongoing training provided is likely to be in the form of coaching by the manager or supervisor. A training skills course should be highly practical, probably lasting a minimum of two days, and aim to enable delegates to:

- understand the benefits of training and its importance as a key element in the success of an organisation;

- understand the role of the trainer and how certain qualities in trainers contribute to their effectiveness;

- identify training needs of the department and of individuals;

- determine what training may be required to fulfil a particular telephone marketing brief;

- understand how people learn to ensure that training materials are presented effectively;

- understand the various methods of training and their particular advantages;

- know when to use them for greatest effect, how to mix them, etc and therefore select the appropriate method;

- define training objectives and prepare lesson plans;

- understand the importance of, and how to create, the right training atmosphere;

- understand the benefits of various presentation aids, in order to select the most appropriate and use them well;

- deliver training materials confidently and effectively;

- answer and use questions effectively to ensure understanding;

- control and respond to various group and individual dynamics;

- understand the importance of post-course evaluation and validation, the methods available and how to use them.

Monitoring performance

The importance of monitoring progress during initial training, to ensure that it is fully effective, has already been highlighted. However, once a department is operating efficiently, it is all too easy to assume that performance will continue at this level without intervention. Performance will decline if management does not take a proactive approach. First, everyone forgets some of what they have learned, so knowledge needs to be revised, skills refreshed and attitudes realigned on a regular basis. Secondly, a *laissez-faire* attitude, where management shows no visible concern for maintaining and improving standards of performance, will gradually erode morale and motivation among staff. They are likely to feel that their contribution is not valued, that standards are not important and that, provided nothing is said, they can take short cuts to reach acceptable targets. The effort they put into applying their knowledge and skills gradually declines until, suddenly, management realises that there is a problem. At that stage it is likely that some of the damage is irreparable, especially in terms of morale. If the problem is left to fester the best staff are likely to leave.

Monitoring individual, team and unit performance provides detailed knowledge of how effectively work is being carried out, and is the first step in identifying where training and other support is required to help avoid these problems. It is also a constant reminder to staff that their contribution and the standards they achieve are important, and identifies opportunities to help individuals exploit their talents and fulfil their ambitions, both of which help to build morale and commitment.

What should be monitored?

All aspects of the work of the unit need to be monitored at individual, team and departmental levels, as all three provide information essential for maintaining and improving performance. A fall in productivity after the introduction of a new product launch campaign, for example, could be attributable to all or any of the teams working on the campaign, or to one or more individuals within any of those teams. Only by monitoring performance at each level can the focus of the problem be identified. Furthermore, productivity is only an overall indicator of performance, and does not identify specific strengths and weaknesses. The fall in productivity in this example could have been caused by several factors, such as poor product knowledge, or poor understanding of the campaign mechanics or of the target audience. Therefore, having identified the site of the problem, it is necessary to look at individual performance.

It is at the individual level that monitoring performance provides detailed information for staff training and development. This should cover the achievement of personal work objectives (detailed in job descriptions and quantified in standards and productivity targets) and the achievement of personal development plans (which may include activities outside individuals' current job descriptions). An example of aspects of a telephone marketing executive's performance which may need to be monitored is shown in Table 6.4.

Of course, if monitoring performance is to be of any use in staff training and development, all staff must already know and understand their tasks and responsibilities, and the standards they are expected to achieve.

A very significant factor contributing to the success of performance monitoring, and to staff morale, is the way in which it is perceived by staff. It should be conducted in an atmosphere of openness and trust, where it is perceived as a help to those being monitored rather than as a method of policing their work. This can be achieved by ensuring that staff understand the reasons for, and the benefits of, monitoring, and that the management style in the department engenders trust and co-operation.

Table 6.4 Possible performance criteria for a telephone
marketing executive

Monitoring performance

General approach:

Level of interest and	Level of participation
commitment	Eagerness to learn
Self-motivation	Team working
Self-discipline	Self-presentation
Coping with pressure	Confidence
Use of communication skills	

Call handling:

Voice	Sales presentation
Call structure/use of the	Closing
script	Overcoming objections
'Getting through'	Dealing with awkward
Opening	situations
Questioning	Product/service
Listening	knowledge

Attention to detail, accuracy and legibility:

Call card, eg completeness,	Call-back times
coding, grading prospect	Sales force diaries
potential	Mailing fulfilment
Call breakdown sheet	Reporting
Time sheet	Liaison

Achievement of targets:

Call rate	Conversion rate
Decision maker contact rate	Mailing fulfilment

Methods of monitoring performance

Telephone marketing provides an excellent environment for monitoring performance because one of its key features is the continuous measurement of activities. The operational systems which make this possible, described in Chapter 4, provide a framework which can be used in combination with other methods to provide an accurate picture of individual strengths, weaknesses and areas of potential. The main methods available are:

- operational systems;
- call monitoring;
- observation and discussion, and;
- team de-briefing sessions.

While much of the performance data available from operational systems is quantifiable, such as call results and the accuracy of call cards, the other methods of monitoring rely mostly on subjective judgement. It is therefore beneficial to use a simple form of measurement scale, for example with five levels, for each aspect of performance. This not only helps the person doing the monitoring to make an accurate evaluation, but it also gives staff an indication of how their performance rates against the standards expected by the company.

It is not enough simply to identify and record the level of performance. Contributing factors also need to be recorded if the information is to be of any use in helping staff to improve their performance. An individual's low call conversion rate, for example, could be due to a wide range of factors, and this is where the combined use of different monitoring methods comes into play. A supervisor could take this as a cue to listen in to some of that person's calls to help to identify problem areas. Perhaps, for example, they have trouble getting through to the decision-maker or overcoming objections. In addition, a single performance indicator can be misleading and assessments should always be confirmed. Various combinations of the following methods can be used to help ensure that assessments are accurate.

Operational systems These include call records, administration and procedural systems, each of which can provide valuable information on individual performance, as outlined in Chapter 4 (*see* pages 137–67).

Call results are obviously a key indicator of performance, but they relate to only a part of the job, and do not identify specific strengths and weaknesses. The same is true of the outcome of some administrative and procedural tasks, such as call card preparation and reporting. The great advantage, however, exemplified by call results, is that they can be quantified. Expressing results achieved as a percentage above or below target enables performance to be tracked over any time period and the trends can often provide an insight into factors contributing to any rise or fall in performance.

Call monitoring Call-monitoring equipment enables a team leader or supervisor to listen in to a call without interrupting or disturbing the conversation (for the legal implications of this, *see* Chapter 4, page 175). This an invaluable way of monitoring individuals' call handling, providing the opportunity both to offer *ad hoc* help and advice on improving technique, and to identify problem areas that may call for training. An example of the criteria that could be monitored on an incoming enquiry call, for example, is given in Table 6.5. Some equipment also allows calls to be recorded and this provides a good learning opportunity, because individuals have the opportunity to identify for themselves, with the support of a coach, ways of improving their technique.

Observation and discussion Observation of individuals at work is generally poorly used as a source of information on performance. It often results only in general impressions of individuals and work groups which, on occasion, may be totally misleading. This is a particularly important method of monitoring in the telephone marketing environment, because changes in interpersonal relationships can have an immediate and powerful positive or negative influence on performance. Disruptive influences, whether caused by problems of attitude, demotivation, personal problems, or whatever, must be avoided at all cost.

Observation is only an effective means of monitoring if it is structured and supported by other methods. Its natural companion is discussion, either with the individual or group concerned, or with others who may be affected. This helps to clarify and make an accurate assessment of the situation. Unrest and a visible lack of enthusiasm among a team booking appointments, for example, may be attributed simply to a lack of motivation. However, discussion could reveal that

Table 6.5 Example of performance criteria in handling an incoming enquiry

1. Welcome	— how the telephone was answered
2. Ask	— how the caller's requirements were evaluated
3. Supply	— what advice or solutions were offered
4. Close	— how the call was completed
5. Speed	— how quickly the call was answered
6. Voice	— the person's approach
7. Listen	— whether the call receiver listens, ie gives the caller time to explain and express interest
8. Satisfaction	— the result of the call
9. Attitude	— how professional and positive the call receiver was
10. Ownership	— did the call receiver take responsibility for the caller and see them through to the right person?

Source: The Direct Communications PORTFOLIO. The Decisions Group, 1990.

they are having difficulty in getting through to contacts, or perhaps they are disgruntled that their success rate is lower than another team, the reason being that there is greater competition in the region they are calling. Discussion can help to identify the real problem and can even sometimes resolve it without any further action being taken.

Discussion with senior members of other departments, with whom staff of the unit are in regular contact, can also provide valuable information on performance.

There are obviously unlimited opportunities for *ad hoc* discussion with individuals and teams, time permitting, but there is also a formal system which promotes constructive discussion on performance. This system is team de-briefing.

Team de-briefing sessions These are not the same as the de-briefing sessions which relate to the progress of specific campaigns and which are examined in Chapter 8 (*see* page 349). In the context of monitoring and appraising performance it refers to a regular forum for work groups to discuss their performance with their team leader, supervisor or manager. These sessions are basically group appraisal sessions and are therefore described in the next section. However, they do offer a valuable opportunity for obtaining and giving feedback on performance which helps to tie together all the other performance data which has been gathered.

Most crucial of all in monitoring performance is that performance data is recorded as it is gathered and reviewed regularly. Operational systems formalise the recording of quantifiable data, such as call results, and simple forms can be designed to record the more subjective assessments. These should provide a basis for tracking and reviewing performance on all relevant criteria at regular intervals between performance appraisals.

Performance appraisal

Performance appraisal is the process of reviewing individuals' performance and progress, and planning what will be done to help them achieve higher standards of performance and develop as individuals. Conducted effectively appraisals can achieve many things, for example they can be used to:

- help individuals to develop their self-appraisal skills by encouraging them to review critically their own performance and progress;

- reach agreement with them on their strengths, weaknesses and areas of potential;

- provide a record of their current abilities against which their future development can be measured;

- motivate individuals and encourage their commitment to their job, the department and the company, for example by highlighting the progress they have made, setting higher standards to work towards, expressing commitment to helping them develop, and restating company aims and objectives, and their role in helping to achieve them;

- plan how best to help them develop and realise their potential;

- draw up and agree a personal development plan, and;

- develop a closer and more trusting working relationship.

Performance appraisal should be a continuous process and the commonly known formal appraisal interview, conducted usually by the line manager either six-monthly or yearly, is only one of the methods available. The most effective appraisal systems combine this with more frequently used methods such as team de-briefing sessions, informal appraisals on an *ad hoc* basis and individual self-appraisal. Used together these methods help to create a culture of openness and trust in which performance monitoring and appraisal are seen to have direct benefits for the individual.

The person chosen to conduct appraisals will depend upon company policy and procedures, departmental structure and the type of appraisal. Formal appraisal interviews are usually conducted by the line manager, although the appraisee's supervisor may be charged with the task of collating performance data and putting together an assessment to discuss with the manager prior to the interview. Team de-briefing sessions should be conducted by the person who has worked most closely with individual teams. This may be the manager, supervisor or team leader(s), depending on the departmental structure and number/size of teams. Informal *ad hoc* appraisals can be conducted by anyone in the department, even telephone marketing executives appraising each other. Self-appraisal should be encouraged in all of these types of appraisal in order to help individuals develop the appropriate skills; it can therefore include input by another person.

All appraisals should have a structured basis and the formal appraisal interview provides a good model.

Formal appraisals

The frequency of formal appraisals for established staff should be at least once a year, although a six-monthly interview is the ideal. New recruits, during their probationary period, may be appraised first on a weekly basis and then monthly. The final appraisal of the probationary period is when the line manager decides whether or not the person is suitable for the job.

A common problem with formal appraisals it that the interview is viewed as an isolated event, of little practical value, which is loathed by both the manager (because of the time commitment) and the appraisee (largely because of the fear of criticism). However, both parties can be encouraged to view it as a positive, constructive event if the appropriate culture has been developed. The main features of an effective system are that:

Table 6.6 Example of the topics covered in an employee self-appraisal form

---

Employee self-appraisal

1. The company

a) How do you feel that you have progressed over the past six months within the company?

2. Personal development

a) Assess your work performance over the past six months. Do you feel that you have met the objectives which were originally set?
b) What do you feel have been your main achievements during this period?
c) Within your current position what do you feel are
   i) your strengths?
   ii) potential areas for improvement?

3. Working relationships

a) How would you assess your working relationships with your colleagues
   i)   Generally within the company?
   ii) Within your department, ie your peers?
   iii) At management level?

b) In relation to this, suggest any improvements which could enhance your working environment, ie regarding organisation of team and reporting structures.

4. Future development

a) What help do you feel you need to improve your work performance?
b) Do you feel you require any specific training in relation to this?

5. Career aspirations

a) How do you foresee your career path developing over the next six months and in the future?

- both the appraiser and appraisee fully understand the purpose of performance appraisal, and know when and how it will be conducted;
- both parties prepare for the interview;

- assessments are based on objective data, as far as possible, covering the whole of the relevant period;

- performance is assessed against clearly defined standards which have previously been agreed;

- the interview is a frank, open and constructive discussion of individuals' past performance, their concerns, expectations and future development;

- a plan of action for their future development, including learning objectives and timescales, is drawn up and agreed;

- the outcome of the appraisal is written down and agreed.

Preparation by both parties is essential for a successful interview, and organisations which operate systematic performance appraisals generally have a set procedure to standardise the whole process and ensure that all the relevant areas are covered effectively.

There are two types of form which can help with preparation. The *employee self-appraisal form*, covering the types of areas shown in Table 6.6, is designed as a working document to help the appraiser structure the employee's appraisal interview. It should be completed by the employee as honestly and frankly as possible, signed and dated, and then returned to the appraiser.

The *employer appraisal form*, covering the types of areas shown in Table 6.7, is designed to help the appraiser prepare for the interview and is used in conjunction with the employee's completed self-appraisal form. All of the available performance statistics and subjective assessments for the relevant period should be used in completing this form and, where appropriate, to supplement it. The appraiser should be able to draw on specific examples during the interview. For example, if the appraiser believes a telephone marketing executive's motivation is subject to peaks and troughs, and wants to explore this topic during the interview, then the appropriate performance data should be used as a way of helping the individual to recognise or refute this belief. If the person's call rate on a campaign has remained constant, but the conversion rate has shown a large fluctuation from week to week, the individual should be shown the figures and encouraged to suggest reasons for the fluctuation. Encouraging self-assessment serves two functions; it increases individuals' commitment to taking any action necessary to improve their performance, because

Table 6.7 Example of the areas covered in an employer's appraisal form

---

Employer's appraisal

Current salary:

Brief summary of present job description:

1. Attitude to work
a) Comment on the appraisee's general progress over the past six months, eg commitment to job and self-motivation.

2. Personal development
a) How do you feel the appraisee has performed during the past six months? Take into consideration any previously set objectives, appropriate training given and the use made of it, and highlight any areas of improvement or concern. Areas to cover include call handling, clerical work, productivity, use of resources, etc
b) What do you consider to have been the appraisee's main achievements during this period?
c) Examine the appraisee's main tasks and responsibilities and outline the main areas of
   i) Strength
   ii) Potential improvement

3. Working relationships
a) Comment on the following points:
   i) How do you feel the appraisee reacts to colleagues generally within the company?
   ii) How does the appraisee work within a team situation with peers?
   iii) In your opinion, how does the appraisee relate to colleagues at management level?
   iv) How does the appraisee work individually? Take into consideration personal time management, self-discipline, use of initiative etc.

4. Future development
a) Outline any possible future training requirements you feel the appraisee may need.
b) What form do you think any potential training should take, eg internal/external?

5. Potential progression
a) What recommendations would you make regarding promotion? Do you feel that the appraisee is now at a level to assume greater responsibility?

---

they have identified their own strengths and weaknesses, and it helps to develop their self-appraisal skills.

Exactly what is discussed during appraisal interviews will obviously depend on individuals' performance and circumstances, but it should include:

- an evaluation of performance compared with the tasks and responsibilities in the job description, and the standards previously set;

- an evaluation of progress since the previous appraisal, including the use made of the training provided;

- work to be done in the future, including targets, standards and working methods, and how these relate to past performance;

- identifying and agreeing specific areas for improvement, including the support that will be provided and timescales for improvement.

It is vital to the success of the appraisal interview that any feedback given to the individual is placed in context and is actionable. A *joint objectives form* can be used to consolidate all of the points for action to be taken by both parties. This is completed by the appraiser, in conjunction with the appraisee, at the end of the interview. It generally takes the form of statements about the appraisee, which have been agreed, under the types of headings shown in Table 6.8. The points for action should include the consolidation of areas of good

Table 6.8 Example of the areas covered on a joint objectives form

---

Setting joint objectives

1. **Attitude to work** – taking into account general performance, attitude, commitment, punctuality, flexibility, sickness record etc.

2. **Personal development** – taking into account previous objectives, achievements, strengths, weaknesses etc.

3. **Working relationships** – with colleagues, manager etc.

4. **Future development** – highlighting any future training requirements, including the support needed.

5. **Future objectives** – setting out jointly agreed, specific and measurable objectives for the appraisee for the next 6 months.

---

performance as well as overcoming any weaknesses. Once completed, the form is dated and signed by the appraiser and appraisee. A copy is kept by both parties so that they can monitor their progress in achieving the joint objectives in the period up to the next performance appraisal.

At the close of their interview appraisees should fully understand how their performance compares with what the company expects of them and be strongly motivated to taking any necessary action.

Team de-briefing sessions

Team de-briefing sessions provide a forum for the session leader to give and invite feedback on aspects of team performance. Team work can play an especially important role in telephone marketing and regular de-briefing sessions, perhaps monthly, are a valuable opportunity for each team to discuss issues such as:

- their overall success in achieving the team objectives, and their contribution to departmental and company objectives;

- the effectiveness of planning and organising team work;

- the level of co-operation and support between team members;

- the effectiveness of decision-making within the team;

- the contribution individuals have made to achieving team targets.

Like formal appraisal interviews, the participants in de-briefing sessions should prepare and have available any data required to illustrate specific points they want to make on team performance. The sessions should also be conducted in an atmosphere of openness and trust, which can be encouraged by the way in which performance is examined. After giving a broad statement of how well the team has achieved its objectives, for example, the session leader can invite comments on where the team has been particularly successful before moving on to weaker areas of performance. Each team member should be encouraged to make constructive comments on ways of improving team performance, for example elements of team work which need to be maintained and developed, and those which should be reduced or eliminated.

Whether or not individual weaknesses should be examined in detail during these sessions depends on the strength of the team, and the level of openness and trust that exists. However, it is necessary to examine specific working relationships which affect the team as a whole.

De-briefing sessions help to build a strong, successful team and provide a model for the team to appraise themselves on an ongoing basis.

Informal appraisals

There are many opportunities for discussing individual and team performance informally throughout the working day. Although this is most likely to be conducted by the manager, supervisor or team leader(s), all members of staff in the unit should be encouraged to help others improve their performance when they recognise such an opportunity, and to ask for advice when they feel they could benefit. This works most effectively when the appropriate atmosphere has been created and staff have learned, through their own appraisals, how to appraise performance effectively.

Informal appraisal is particularly important for new recruits during their probationary period, both to ensure that the maximum support is provided, and to encourage and motivate them.

Self-appraisal

All members of staff should be encouraged to continuously appraise their own performance and take appropriate action to improve it. Providing a supportive and stimulating environment helps to ensure that individuals are not reticent about asking for help when they need it.

Using a variety of appraisal methods working in synergy ensures that staff are given the maximum guidance, support and encouragement to improve their performance continuously. The result is a highly productive, committed workforce, and a unit which is more cost-effective and more flexible in adapting quickly to changing demands placed upon it.

The cost of training

Training resources traditionally have been one of the first areas to suffer cutbacks during times of recession. The more enlightened companies now recognise that continued investment in training is essential and, by helping to optimise the use of human resources, is one way of minimising the damaging effects of cutbacks in other areas.

The training investment required when establishing a new telephone marketing unit may appear excessive because of difficulties in recruiting skilled personnel. However, initial training represents only a small proportion of total set-up costs and is essential if the investment is to pay off. An ongoing training programme helps to build on these foundations, and ensures that maximum productivity and cost-effectiveness are maintained as the unit grows and develops.

Careful planning of the use of training resources and opportunities helps to reduce costs and maximise benefits. Live calling during initial training, for example, makes the team productive at an early stage. Losses in productivity during down-time can be minimised by conducting ongoing training during otherwise quiet periods. On Friday afternoons, for example, the decision-maker contact rate with outbound calls in business-to-business markets is comparatively low. Devoting this time to training would therefore have minimum impact on overall productivity. The positive impact of training on individuals' confidence and enthusiasm is usually immediately evident and, conducted regularly, can boost overall productivity.

The revenue-earning potential of a well-trained telephone marketing team quickly justifies the costs, as illustrated by Case Study 3 in Chapter 11 (*see* pages 423–26). Even where the work involved is not directly revenue-earning there are usually very tangible benefits which will justify costs. In an accounts department, for example, training can improve cash flow by enabling staff to encourage quicker payment by customers. In the area of customer service, benefits can be seen in a reduction in the number of complaints, for example, and increased repeat business. A good training programme can also significantly reduce the attrition rate, with all its associated cost-savings.

Reviewing training effectiveness

The effects of training should be monitored and reviewed continuously to ensure that it is achieving its objectives, and to justify the cost and help to identify how it could be made more effective. Improved performance, in accordance with the training objectives, is obviously the principal measure of training effectiveness, although delegates' comments on the perceived value of their training are also very important, as well as comments from the trainer(s).

All the methods of performance monitoring described earlier in this chapter can be used to measure improvements in performance by a comparison of the relevant measures before and after training. An improved conversion rate, for example, may indicate that the training on objection handling and sales presentation has been effective; this can be confirmed by call monitoring using a scale to quantify subjective judgements.

Simple evaluation questionnaires can be designed for the delegates to complete after each main training session, and this can act as a valuable motivator and stimulate their eagerness to learn. If staff are encouraged to comment honestly on their training and the perceived value to them, so that it can be improved to meet their needs more effectively, they are more likely to view training positively. The type of feedback that can be obtained from delegates includes:

- a measure of their understanding and retention, by asking questions on key aspects of the topics covered;

- what they thought of the relevance/effectiveness of
    - the content (coverage, what was missing etc)
    - the amount of time devoted to each topic (too much/too little/how much time required?)
    - the presentation (ease of understanding etc)
    - the presentation aids, handouts etc
    - the role plays, workshops and live calling;

- how they feel the training could be improved (in relation to the areas listed above);

- where they feel they need more training, for example on the course content or in related areas;

- how the company could provide more help and support for their development;

- how they think the training will help them in their work;

- how they feel about their ability to do their job as a result of the training.

The response from delegates is likely to be more positive if there has been a high level of participation, for example through workshops, role plays and live calling; they will have been actively involved in shaping the session to meet their specific needs and will have a clearer idea of how well they are equipped for their jobs. At the end of each main training session it is useful for delegates to set personal goals, ie 'As a result of this training I intend to . . .', which can be included in feedback questionnaires. Apart from reflecting delegates' overall reactions to the usefulness of their training, these statements help them to focus on how they will put into action what they have learned.

The trainer(s) can also provide information on subjects such as delegates' willingness to participate, their level of participation and enthusiasm, immediate reactions to the content and so on.

When the information from all these sources is collated and analysed, the effectiveness of each aspect of the training session can be gauged and used in the design of subsequent sessions. It may also provide guidance to the trainer(s) on ways of improving their style of presentation etc. In addition, it indicates delegates' further training needs, both real and perceived, which need to be taken into account in the training programme.

The importance of career paths

Career paths, showing lines of progression to ever more senior roles within the organisation, play a diverse role in the development of a highly skilled, committed workforce. Basically, they provide a framework which helps to plan training for succession, and clearly shows opportunities for promotion to motivate staff and encourage loyalty.

A major factor influencing the success of a training programme is people's motivation to learn and to apply what they learn. Individuals' commitment to their job and loyalty to the company also need to be encouraged if the investment in their training is to be put to good use. One of the most significant motivators in both these areas is the opportunity for career advancement within the organisation through personal development.

The ideal type of structure for a telephone marketing unit, as described in Chapter 4, creates a number of levels of responsibility which form a career path within the department; ideally, this should be linked in to other departments so that staff are able to make sideways or upward moves out of the unit. Overall, the training programme should be designed to help individuals progress step-by-step through the various levels of responsibility. Personal development

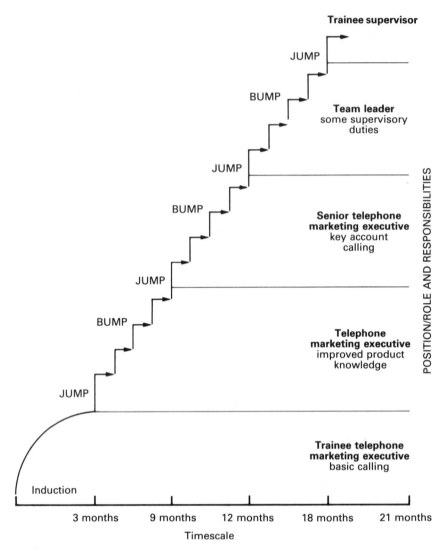

Figure 6.1 Example of bump and jump training in a skills development programme

plans, drawn up during performance appraisal interviews, define what the next step will be for each individual and what training support they will receive.

Progression within the unit obviously depends upon the acquisition of the appropriate skills, and the training provided can be divided broadly into two types – training for development within the existing role and training for a new role. These are sometimes referred to as 'bump' and 'jump' training, respectively. The key distinction is that bump training increases individuals' ability to do their existing job, while jump training introduces them to new tasks and responsibilities. The combined use of the two types of training in a skills development programme is illustrated in Figure 6.1, which also shows recommended minimum development periods for progression to higher roles.

Bump training is an important motivator because it provides the opportunity for staff to develop their skills continuously, even though there may be no immediate prospect of promotion. Job satisfaction increases as their skills improve and they become more successful in what they do, attracting more prestige and improving their chances of promotion. This also helps to create a competitive atmosphere as the more ambitious people strive to improve themselves.

The grading of roles in other parts of an organisation sometimes makes it difficult to provide concrete differentiation, for example by grade and appropriate financial rewards, between every level of responsibility in a telephone marketing unit. Team leaders and trainee supervisors, for example, may both fall within the supervisory grade. However, there are many other ways of rewarding, and thus encouraging, efforts to progress to more responsible roles, and these will be examined in Chapter 7.

A good career structure helps to encourage individuals to make the best use of the training resources available and thus increase the return on investment. By encouraging loyalty it enables the unit to develop and retain expertise which would otherwise have to be bought in at a premium.

One of the most important challenges facing organisations in the 1990s is maintaining their competitiveness in the marketplace. To achieve this they will have to ensure that their workforce possess the necessary knowledge, skills and attitudes to maintain the highest possible levels of performance, while meeting the challenges of a constantly changing trading environment. No organisation can ignore the crucial role that training has to play, particularly in telephone marketing where the competition for skilled personnel is rising rapidly.

Of course, the ability to do a job well does not automatically infer good performance; every individual has to be encouraged to use his or her abilities to the full. Training is an important method of motivating staff, but there are many other techniques which can be used within the telephone marketing environment to encourage higher performance. These will be examined in Chapter 7.

7

Motivating Staff

If staff have the knowledge, skills and resources necessary to do their work, their performance depends almost entirely upon their level of motivation. No matter how good the product or service, and the campaign design and implementation, the campaign will not achieve its full potential, and could fail miserably, if staff are not committed to applying themselves wholeheartedly to their work.

Telephone marketing is infamous for its high burnout factor and is traditionally an area of high staff turnover. The work is often repetitive, tedious and frustrating, and yet staff must try to fully exploit the potential of every call. If they lack enthusiasm they tend to become sloppy in following the call structure, and the boredom reflected in their voice is picked up by customers. No company can afford to risk alienating its customers or to lose good staff when they are in such short supply. Encouraging commitment to high levels of performance and loyalty to the company is therefore a crucial factor in determining the success of a telephone marketing campaign and, ultimately, the survival of the unit.

Because of the nature of telephone marketing applications there are some very important spin-off benefits from having a highly motivated team. The most significant of these, and paramount in today's marketplace, is an improved quality of customer service, which encourages their loyalty and helps to exploit their lifetime value. At the same time it improves the company's image and position in the marketplace.

Encouraging staff to try to achieve their best at all times is necessarily a flexible and dynamic process, and what is needed is a package of motivators which can accommodate these different and changing needs.

Whose job is it?

The most immediate influence for motivating staff is the person with direct responsibility for leading them, which is determined by the way in which leadership responsibilities are shared according to the structure of the unit. However, no one person bears all the responsibility, nor is it confined to within the telephone marketing unit. If there are team leaders, a supervisor and a manager, for example, all will play a motivating role according to their particular job responsibilities and the opportunities these provide for applying different motivational techniques. Some factors, such as pay and working conditions, will generally be outside the direct control of the unit's management, but they can still make a case to senior management for action to be taken where necessary.

Knowing when and how to apply appropriate techniques effectively requires skill, and this topic should be given particular emphasis in any supervisory training provided for staff in the unit.

Reading the signs

Whoever has responsibility for motivating staff must always be alert for signs that show individuals are lacking motivation, or that they need to make extra effort on a particular task (for example list cleaning, which can be very boring) or at a particular time (perhaps when they are flagging, such as the last hour in the morning or afternoon), so that they can provide the necessary support and encouragement. Similarly, they need to recognise when individuals are motivated and are working well so that they can reward, and thus reinforce, this behaviour.

Behaviour and attitudes which can reflect a high level of motivation include:

- consistently high performance, and results often above target;

- enthusiasm and determination to succeed;

- eager co-operation in overcoming difficulties or problems;

- willing acceptance of responsibility;

- the contribution of constructive ideas for improving the performance of the unit.

Those who lack motivation, on the other hand, exhibit symptoms such as:

- results often below target;

- apathy and indifference to the job;

- frequent failure to meet deadlines;

- a continual need for encouragement or prompting to complete tasks;

- irritability when faced with delays or problems;

- a poor record of time-keeping/absenteeism;

- frequent complaints about minor problems or difficulties;

- a negative attitude to work-related problems and lack of co-operation in dealing with them.

The operational systems required to run a telephone marketing unit enable constant monitoring of each individual's performance, but it is important to be able to identify the reasons underlying the results achieved. Using a variety of monitoring methods, described in Chapters 4 and 6, helps to distinguish properly between a problem of motivation and, say, a training need. Ideally, of course, staff should not be allowed to become demotivated to the extent that it has an impact on their performance. The majority of the techniques described below, implemented effectively and at the right time, are therefore designed to maintain an optimum level of motivation.

Methods of motivating staff

Methods of motivating staff have changed considerably during the 1980s, particularly under the influence of our changing expectations of the rewards to be gained from work. Ways of encouraging the performance of telephone marketing staff have developed particularly rapidly, due partly to the rapid expansion of the industry and to the nature of the work. The prospect of earning a high commission, which was once a staple motivator for people doing repetitive jobs requiring continuously high levels of effort and concentration (such as selling classified ads), has largely been replaced by more effective 'rewards', for example a higher basic salary plus bonuses.

Methods of motivating can be divided broadly into strategic and tactical, although the distinction is sometimes hazy and some methods can be applied in both ways. The strategic factors, such as pay structure and the working environment, are either permanent or long-term influences. Some, such as improvements in the working environment, are not powerful motivators and have a short-term effect at best, but they can cause dissatisfaction and frustration if they are inadequate. These strategic factors, which also include company policies, systems and procedures, and management style, have been included in this chapter because they provide the basic components of a motivational package. If they are inadequate, then any other methods employed to motivate staff may be ineffective. Tactical methods, such as target setting and offering incentives, provide the means by which staff motivation is boosted, on a project basis, so that it is maintained at an optimum level. They are generally applied on a short-term basis, as and when required, and are supremely important in the telephone marketing environment. If call records reveal that call rates or decision-maker contact rates fall in the last hour of the morning and afternoon work periods, for example, an incentive could be offered for the best results achieved during these periods.

There are many opportunities in the day-to-day work of a telephone marketing unit to apply tactical motivators, but not all methods are applicable in every situation. What motivates one individual may not motivate another; what encourages someone one week may hold little interest the next; and the amount of encouragement individuals need varies according to their current level of motivation and the amount of effort required for the task they are doing. The people responsible for motivating staff must therefore get to know the needs of individuals and understand what motivates them, as well as considering their frame of mind at particular times and the amount of effort required to complete their current tasks.

However, above all, it is important to remember that motivators will not be effective if action is not taken to remove any underlying cause of poor motivation, such as insufficient knowledge, poor skills or interpersonal conflict. In addition, a single demotivating influence can negate all other measures taken to motivate staff.

Working environment

The working environment can have a powerful influence on individuals' ability and willingness to work efficiently and the degree of satisfaction they derive from their work. A variety of factors shape this environment, and thereby influence staff motivation, including the physical environment, corporate policies, systems and procedures, communication, and the style of management.

Providing a physical environment which is conducive to, and supportive of, high levels of performance has been examined in Chapter 4, pages 180–83. The other factors are of a more pervasive nature; they overlap to a great extent and incorporate many of the areas covered in other sections of this chapter. General principles of good management practice obviously apply, but there are some areas where telephone marketing operations require special attention.

Corporate policies, systems and procedures   The role and importance of sound systems and procedures in the efficient operation of a telephone marketing unit have already been examined. However, they also have a significant impact on staff morale. If they are cumbersome to operate, or do not fully meet the work needs of staff, they can give rise to frustration and loss of commitment. In addition, without adequate monitoring of work activities, reward systems will be inefficient, and greater effort will go unrecognised and therefore not be encouraged. Because telephone marketing relies so heavily upon these systems and procedures, particular care must be taken in their design.

Another important factor is how the rest of the company views the telephone marketing unit. If its role is undervalued or unrecognised, the unit's staff are less likely to feel commitment to their jobs. The operational success of the unit will also be reliant, to varying degrees, upon the co-operation of others elsewhere in the company. Company-wide commitment to, and recognition of the importance of, telephone marketing is therefore essential in maintaining morale and efficiency within the unit. Everyone in the company should be made aware of this through internal PR, particularly when the unit is first established.

Management style   Telephone marketing requires a greater degree of supervision, and therefore a higher supervisor/staff ratio, than most work activities, because the nature of the work demands comparatively intensive monitoring and control. The style of supervision or management will therefore generally have a proportionately greater impact on staff morale in a telephone marketing unit than in other departments.

In the day-to-day work of the unit there is a wide range of

opportunities for the manager/supervisor to create an atmosphere which encourages staff commitment, for example in planning work so that everyone has an opportunity to work on interesting tasks, and giving staff the freedom to use their initiative. It is vitally important that these opportunities are used to the full because in-house telephone marketing operations often start out, and sometimes continue, at a disadvantage. There may be some negative feelings towards the unit, for example, and staff can often feel isolated from the mainstream activities of the company. On top of this, corporate policies may restrict the manager's freedom to use certain methods of motivating staff, such as offering incentives and providing a clear career path within the unit. It is still relatively uncommon for in-house units to enjoy the same sort of autonomy that other comparative operations enjoy, and this is bound to be picked up by staff. The style of management therefore needs to compensate actively for these potentially demoralising factors.

Communication   One way of helping to overcome any sense of isolation felt by staff in the unit is to ensure that there are efficient channels for two-way communication between the unit and all other parts of the organisation. Not only will this help to educate other departments about the role of the unit, and its importance, but it also ensures that staff are kept aware of what is happening elsewhere in the organisation. Holding monthly briefing meetings provides a good opportunity for informing staff of wider organisational issues. There is a case to be made for positive discrimination in favour of a telephone marketing unit in its first year or two of operation (*see* Chapter 9, page 375), and part of this should take the form of good PR for the unit. Publicity should be sought, for example about recent results and current campaigns, in company newsletters, at staff meetings and using any other media available. The inclusion of staff members from the unit on consultative committees and other forums, especially concerning customer care, sales and marketing, should also be encouraged.

Formal channels of communication, used at planned, regular intervals, should also exist between telephone marketing staff and the unit's management, and between the staff themselves. Briefing sessions, for example, generally cover the progress of individual teams and the contribution the unit is making to company results, as well as wider issues. In addition, regular de-briefings should be a part of any campaign, and provide an opportunity for problems and concerns to be aired and dealt with promptly. Staff can also conduct monthly brainstorming sessions, at which the supervisor or manager may be present, to address any areas of concern. Informal communication should obviously be encouraged at all times.

On the wider front, communication plays a role in the effective use of all methods of motivation, from displaying results and the incentives being offered, to ensuring that staff are aware of training and promotion opportunities.

Individual, team and departmental goals

Telephone marketing thrives on goal setting. Many of the targets for a campaign, such as the call rate and conversion rate, are easily defined and can therefore be used as personal, team and departmental targets. Because results are continuously monitored, individuals and teams can measure their level of performance against these targets at any time. When the achievement or exceeding of targets is tied in with various forms of reward, such as incentives and recognition or praise, they provide a powerful motivator. However, it is important to remember that there is a wide range of performance indicators, not only the easily defined targets, which must be monitored. A high call rate, for example, may have been achieved at the expense of accuracy in completing call records.

Targets work most effectively as a motivator when they are displayed prominently in the calling area. An easel or board is commonly used to chart the results of the team(s) and the unit, for each campaign in progress, alongside set targets, details of the campaign and any incentives being offered. This provides constant feedback and encourages healthy competition between teams. 'Public' display of the results is in itself a reward for the team(s) achieving good results. The board can be kept up to date by callers, team leaders or the supervisor. Some people advocate displaying individuals' results, but this can encourage competition between individuals which may become divisive; it can work effectively, however, if there is a strong team spirit. With some campaigns it is also possible to display the overall revenue generated and this is highly beneficial, attaching a clear value to the work and providing staff with an indication of their contribution to the company's success.

Targets should always provide a challenge, but they must be realistic and should only be raised if they are being exceeded on a regular basis. It is a good idea to involve staff in setting their own targets, as this increases their commitment to achieving them. There will often be high flyers who consistently exceed targets by a healthy margin; they can be used as pace-setters provided that this is done in such a way that the poorer performers are not discouraged.

The way in which targets are communicated plays an important role in their motivating effect. Obviously staff need to know precisely what they have to do in terms of each task, and the minimum standards expected of them, but targets should be conveyed with enthusiasm, for example a 'battle cry' to beat an earlier success on a similar campaign.

The effective use of targets as a motivator helps to create an environment where people set themselves high personal standards, provided that achievements are 'recognised' in an appropriate way. Some of the ways of rewarding good performance are examined in the following sections of this chapter.

Recognition and praise

One of the best motivators, both powerful and costing nothing, is giving recognition for work well done. Being praised for good work instils a sense of achievement and the prospect of receiving praise therefore encourages greater effort. In a well-managed department it is generally more effective than more tangible incentives. However, it is essential that good work is praised consistently and at the appropriate time, otherwise staff will not form a strong association between hard work and this satisfying reward.

Praise is a simple and quick motivator to administer, but it should be delivered with sincerity and in a way that emphasises the value to the company of the individual's achievement, for example the sales achieved during the appointments booked, or the intended use of the high-quality market evaluation data gathered. Individual and team successes should be recognised and, although some people find public praise embarrassing, it is generally more effective when reported publicly, for example when announcing the winner of a particular incentive.

Involvement and accountability

The full and active involvement of staff in the work of the unit is possibly the greatest motivator of all. Giving individuals the freedom to make important decisions associated with their work, for example, encourages their commitment to producing good results; and when they have played a more active role in achieving those results their contribution to the success of the unit becomes more tangible. But if staff are going to feel motivated by greater involvement, they must feel accountable for the contribution they are making and its effects on their own results and the results of others. Involvement and accountability therefore go hand-in-hand.

There are many different opportunities for involving staff which can be grouped under two related headings – delegation and consultation. Delegating new responsibilities to individuals encourages commitment at the same time as providing a learning opportunity. An eager trainee telephone marketing executive, for example, would welcome the opportunity to do something more interesting and challenging than list building/cleaning, such as market evaluation calls. However, staff must be fully briefed on any new responsibilities they are given and be provided with any support necessary to fulfil them, otherwise they may experience difficulties and could become demotivated as a result. Their accountability for the outcome of any new activities they are undertaking must also be stressed.

Related to accountability is the question of discipline, in its broadest sense, ie maintaining the required standards of conduct and performance. The way in which discipline is managed can have a significant impact on staff morale. Staff must know the consequences of variation from the expected standards, both positive and negative, and everyone must be treated fairly, equitably and consistently. Success in telephone marketing is totally results-based and staff who are unable to achieve the required standards, despite appropriate encouragement and support being provided, should be told to seek alternative employment. Consistently poor performance by one telephone marketing executive can easily demotivate others, particularly those who are not very competitive or confident, as well as being a potential source of friction within that individual's team.

Consulting staff regularly on issues which affect or concern them, and encouraging them to express their opinions and ideas, is another powerful motivator. Being consulted, and having the opportunity to apply their initiative, knowledge and experience, makes people feel significant and valued, particularly if they see their ideas implemented or, better still, are involved in implementing them. It also creates a sense of greater control over their own work, thereby increasing commitment, and helps to prevent misunderstandings or disputes over management decisions. Telephone marketing provides many opportunities for consultation, for example at briefings/de-briefings, callers' brainstorming sessions, and on an *ad hoc* basis; and there are many areas where the input of telephone staff can be especially beneficial, for example in reviewing and fine-tuning scripts and streamlining operational systems, because it is the callers who are at the 'sharp end'.

The results achieved within a telephone marketing unit provide a clearly tangible measure of the contribution individuals are making to the success of their team, the unit and the company. The more they are involved in determining what those results are, and the more they feel responsible for their contribution, the greater their work satisfaction and commitment to hard work.

Work planning

The nature of telephone marketing work, which is nearly always repetitive and often monotonous, makes it important to consider the impact of work planning on individuals' motivation; at the same time, however, there are excellent opportunities to provide positive motivators. Apart from involving staff in planning their own work, anything which can be done to make the work easier or enables it to be carried out more efficiently, such as streamlining operational systems, or makes it more enjoyable or interesting, will help to improve work satisfaction and motivation. Where possible, work should be delegated so that individuals' skills and talents are used to the full, and they are provided with an appropriate challenge. New staff lacking confidence, for example, can be given comparatively straightforward tasks on which they can achieve good results. In general, however, routines should be varied to avoid boredom and frustration, such as rotating monotonous tasks.

The tips on applications given in Chapter 8, pages 336–40, provide some guidance on their effects on staff motivation and these are summarised in Table 7.1.

Table 7.1 Motivational aspects of different telephone marketing applications

Application	Motivational aspects
List building/cleaning	Very monotonous; concentrate the work in relatively short bursts or rotate the job between teams; can demotivate confident new staff.
Market evaluation	Most people find this enjoyable, although it requires maximum concentration.
Pre-mail or pre-launch hype	An enjoyable task, which can be used as a reward or to provide a breather from more intense work.
Appointment setting	A self-motivating job, but feedback must be given on the outcome of appointments.
Seminar/event booking	Catering calls can be monotonous.
Direct selling	A challenging, interesting and rewarding job which is self-motivating.

Pay and remuneration

Several different types of financial reward are commonly given to telephone marketing staff – basic salary, commission, bonuses and cash incentives – and their use by agencies and in-house units has already been examined in Chapter 5 (pages 197–9). There are pros and cons to using each of these as a motivator, beyond any limitations imposed by corporate policy.

Payment of a basic salary is the essential starting point; potential employees expect it and it has advantages for the company. If a definite payment has been agreed, calculated according to the revenue the unit can reasonably generate and the cost, management can ensure that productivity and profitability are at least maintained at this level. In addition, reliance upon productivity-related payments, ie with no basic salary, encourages an aggressive hard-sell environment which is unsuitable for telephone marketing; it has a detrimental effect on long-term customer relations and can lead to a high proportion of unreliable results, for example cancelled orders, inaccurate information given by prospects, or lead qualification 'fixed' by staff. One major drawback of paying a basic salary is that, because they have a guaranteed income, it will not usually motivate staff to strive for better performance. Increases in basic pay (or better fringe benefits), in recognition of improved results, will often provide a short-term boost to motivation, but staff quickly take the increase for granted. Other types of payment are therefore used to encourage performance above the expected minimum level, although, of course, individuals' basic salary should be reviewed regularly and raised when merited.

Payment by commission alone, or high commission and a low basic salary, is not effective in the telephone marketing environment. However, a commission, paid per sale or completed questionnaire for example, can be an effective motivator when offered on top of a reasonable basic salary, provided that it is high enough to be attractive, but low enough to avoid encouraging a hard-sell approach.

Bonuses paid on top of the basic salary for productivity above an agreed level are a good motivator, although they must be set at a level which will not encourage hard-sell tactics. A bonus of between 5 and 10 per cent, according to the campaign costings, would be reasonable. If staff are being paid £6 an hour, for example, and the target is eight 'orders' per hour (ie a basic payment of 75p each), a 60p bonus could be offered for each order obtained above target, acting as a good motivator and maintaining the cost-effectiveness of the application. In some applications, however, there is a more effective way of structuring bonuses. In direct sales, for example, bonuses are best paid to reward the quality of results rather than volume. A caller who achieves a high proportion of cross-selling or up-selling, for example, is exploiting the potential of each contact more, and doing the company more good, than someone who is getting through twice as many leads, but is only achieving basic sales, perhaps using hard-sell tactics and jeopardising future sales to those leads. The former is the type of behaviour that should be encouraged, when the application allows, with bonus payments.

Cash incentives are generally not effective at stimulating overall performance within the unit, unless they are large; even then they can have an adverse effect if one team, or one high flyer, is seen to win more often than others.

Healthy competition

Good telephone marketing staff are generally competitive by nature, and this can be channelled and exploited by offering rewards of the types covered in other sections of this chapter. Competition between individuals can be divisive and should never be encouraged, but friendly rivalry between well-matched teams not only motivates individuals to work harder, so that they do not let their side down, but it also helps to build team spirit and is a reward in itself through the feelings of camaraderie it generates. It is common to place known good performers in each team to act as pace-setters and provide their colleagues with a target to aim for.

Incentives

Incentives are used widely in telephone marketing to encourage competition and motivate people to out-perform their colleagues. They are not meant as a substitute for a reasonable salary, bonuses or other financial inducements. Instead, they provide an added incentive for everyone to work harder, including those who stand little chance of achieving, say, the highest conversion rate. Incentives are awarded for the highest achievement(s) on specified performance criteria over specified periods of time, perhaps the best contact rate in a particular hour, or the highest value sale over the week. An incentive scheme needs to be highly flexible, both to ensure that there are opportunities for everyone to 'win' something and to encourage harder work where it will have most impact or when it is most needed, for example the final hour of a shift.

Incentives can be offered for individual or team performance and can be tied in with a variety of performance criteria, for example call rate, decision-maker contact rate, conversion rate, overall value of sales, highest value sale, completed questionnaires, best quality lead and so on. One approach is to not publicise what the incentive will be awarded for, so that everyone concentrates on all aspects of their work. However, whatever method is used, the operational systems obviously need to enable measurement of the selected criteria over the specified period of time.

The period over which incentives are offered depends on the value of individual incentives and the needs of different individuals. Most people would find the offer of a holiday abroad appealing but, to be cost-effective, it would have to be offered over perhaps a year and not everyone is able to take such a long-term view. In addition, it does not have the flexibility that is required of telephone marketing incentives and the large prizes are likely to be won consistently by the high flyers. If high-value incentives are offered over long periods, and they can be effective at improving overall results, then smaller incentives should also be offered over shorter periods of time. One way of accommodating the preferences of both groups of people is to operate a points system, so that they can be 'cashed in' regularly for smaller value prizes or saved for something more substantial. This also provides flexibility, because points can be awarded for highest performance on any chosen criterion. As far as results are concerned, a mixture of short-term competitions has been found to be more effective than single prizes for long-term achievement.

If top performers are seen always to win the incentives other staff will become demotivated and the purpose of the scheme will have been defeated. There are two ways around this problem. First, incentives could be awarded for the highest percentage increase in personal targets on the chosen performance criterion, so that average performers stand an equal chance of winning. Varying the performance criteria for which incentives are offered can serve a similar function; an average performer may regularly contact as many decision-makers as a 'high flyer', for example, but not achieve such a high conversion rate.

The incentives, the time period, and the performance criteria for which they are offered should be varied regularly so that everyone's interest is maintained. A mixture of daily, weekly and monthly competitions can be highly effective, provided the performance criteria and incentives are varied. However, there are some applications where incentives should only be used with care, if at all. It is not advisable to offer them for lead generation and qualification, for example, as callers may be tempted to misgrade the potential of leads. And if they are used in appointment setting, the team approach should be used rather than individual incentives.

To encourage competition, details of the incentive(s) on offer should be displayed prominently alongside the results being achieved, although sometimes a 'mystery prize' may be offered. Awarding the prizes in public, for example at weekly staff meetings, adds significantly to their perceived value.

There is a wide variety of suitable incentives; they do not need to be costly, provided that they are perceived by staff as 'valuable' in relation to what they have achieved. Possibilities include hand-made chocolates, a bottle of wine, perfume or cologne, vouchers, a pair of theatre tickets, dinner for two, sports equipment, club memberships, electrical equipment and travel. Whatever is chosen, however, should be of good quality and ideally be something that staff would normally buy, or like to buy or receive. It can be difficult to find incentives which will appeal to staff of differing ages and circumstances. If practical, it is useful to consult them on what they would like as prizes, within cost guidelines and perhaps offer winners a limited choice. Cash incentives may be offered, although they need to be substantial if they are going to have the desired effect.

Incentives are taxable benefits and companies using them are wise to consider offering to pay the tax due as a part of the incentive. However, although the taxation of benefits is becoming increasingly stringent, the Inland Revenue has to consider the cost-effectiveness of collecting these taxes.

A well-structured and efficiently managed incentive scheme is an essential part of a motivational programme for telephone marketing staff. Although company-wide schemes are becoming more sophisticated and flexible, it is likely that a separate incentive scheme would have to be created for a telephone marketing unit.

Training and development

According to a UK survey commissioned by Lifeskills Management Group, sent to over 5,000 trainers and senior managers throughout commerce and industry, 85 per cent of companies felt that the opportunity for staff to develop their skills was the single biggest motivator in the retention of staff.

Training and motivation in the telephone marketing industry go hand-in-hand, and the wider role of a training and development programme in the motivation of staff has already been covered in Chapter 6. For example, one of the greatest demotivators is a lack of confidence in one's abilities; good initial training instils a great deal of confidence, which is then maintained by constant on-going coaching and regular top-up training courses. A clear indication of the prospects for advancement, in the form of a career path, is an important element in a skills development programme. The prospect of promotion, and with it an increase in salary, prestige, and the challenges and satisfactions of the job, is an excellent motivator, particularly for the more ambitious staff.

On a wider front, most people value the opportunity to develop their skills, and this is particularly important in telephone marketing where rapid growth of the industry is creating a severe skills shortage

Table 7.2 Motivating and demotivating influences in the telephone marketing environment

Motivation in telephone marketing	
Demotivating	**Motivating**
Long stretches doing monotonous, unchallenging tasks	Variety; short-term tasks; tasks which offer a stimulating challenge
Lack of clear goals; targets which are unchallenging or beyond reasonable expectations for the individual	Realistic targets – stretching but achievable, communicated clearly and enthusiastically; known good performers as pace-setters within each team
Absence of feedback on performance, eg not knowing how their work contributes to the success of the unit and the company	Public display of targets and ongoing results; regular feedback on an individual, team and campaign basis
Lack of recognition for good work, especially that resulting from extra effort	Consistent recognition and praise for good work, especially that resulting from extra effort
Anything which reduces individuals' confidence in their abilities	A comprehensive, ongoing training and development programme
Lack of involvement; limits placed on individual's freedom to use their initiative in applying their knowledge and skills, ie little responsibility	Active involvement in the work of the unit; being consulted regularly on issues which affect and concern them; delegation of new responsibilities and clear accountability for the outcome
Inadequate physical resources and working conditions	Good resources and a pleasant working environment
Cumbersome or inadequate operational systems	Effective, monitorable operational systems
Resentment of telephone marketing by staff outside the unit	Company-wide commitment to, and recognition of the importance of, telephone marketing
Feelings of isolation from the rest of the company	Awareness of what is happening elsewhere in the company and how the unit is contributing to its success
Fierce competition between individuals	Friendly rivalry between well-matched teams
The absence of material incentives; an incentive scheme where the high flyers are seen to 'win' consistently	A well-structured incentive scheme which gives everyone an opportunity to 'win'
No prospects for skills development, advancement and promotion	The opportunity to develop personal skills and gain a chance of promotion; a clear picture of the opportunities for advancement within the unit and elsewhere in the company
Fear of the consequences of not achieving the levels of performance demanded	Good management, creating an atmosphere which encourages and rewards hard work

and escalating the salaries that experienced personnel can command. Therefore, the training and development programme should not be centred on levels and roles, but should provide staff with opportunities to further their careers and to develop their long-term prospects. The result of providing these opportunities is a highly skilled, committed workforce who are likely to remain loyal to the company, given other appropriate inducements.

What to avoid

Most of the factors which can demotivate staff have been mentioned or implied in earlier parts of this chapter. Of particular importance, because they are often forgotten, are the less tangible factors such as poor communications or an iron grip by management. Working successfully in telephone marketing requires a great deal of creativity, despite the emphasis on productivity, and the atmosphere created should encourage staff to use their natural flair, backed up by their knowledge and skills. If the motivational aspects of these wider issues are not addressed, then more direct efforts to encourage high performance will fall on less receptive ears.

Perhaps one of the most powerful demotivators is a sudden 'change for the worse' in a particular aspect of the work. This could range from the appointment of a new supervisor who gives little responsibility to staff, to the sudden cessation of incentives. Where change is inevitable, and it is often highly beneficial, staff should be involved at the earliest possible stage so that they understand the reasons for change, and have an opportunity to express and discuss their ideas or concerns.

Finally, 'fear' is used as a motivator only by those who lack the skill and confidence to lead a team of people effectively. It is counter-productive on all fronts, causing resentment, loss of commitment, a slide in efficiency and productivity and, ultimately, the loss of good staff.

Telephone marketing staff have contact with more customers and prospects than anyone else in a company, and if they feel dissatisfied, bored or undervalued it can cause irreparable damage to the company's profile and future success. A well-planned and efficiently managed motivational package, taking account of the types of factors summarised in Table 7.2, is therefore essential. One of the most notable characteristics of a successful telephone marketing operation is an atmosphere which is buzzing with the activity of committed, highly motivated staff. If that can be achieved, a telephone marketing unit can become the company's most valuable asset.

8

Planning, Implementing and Managing a Campaign

A telephone marketing campaign is a set of planned and controlled activities centring on the use of the telephone to achieve a specific objective or set of objectives. The telephone may be the only medium used, but it is often used in combination with other sales and marketing activities all aimed at achieving the same objective(s).

Planning, implementing and managing a campaign is the ultimate test of the level of understanding of how telephone marketing works. This chapter refers to many topics examined in other parts of the book which are not necessarily described again; it will be most clearly understood, therefore, if those parts have already been studied by the reader.

Although using the telephone for communication is an everyday experience, a telephone marketing campaign requires extensive planning and close control if it is to be successful. Many of the activities involved are interdependent; some activities are undertaken concurrently and some may necessitate revising earlier work. The headings used in this chapter, shown graphically in Figure 8.1, therefore simply refer to key processes. The way in which these processes are handled is determined by factors such as the structure, size and operational role of the telephone marketing unit, and the nature of the application. Agencies and very large in-house units, for example, are likely to have more substantial management infrastructures than the average in-house unit and this will influence the way in which activities are delegated.

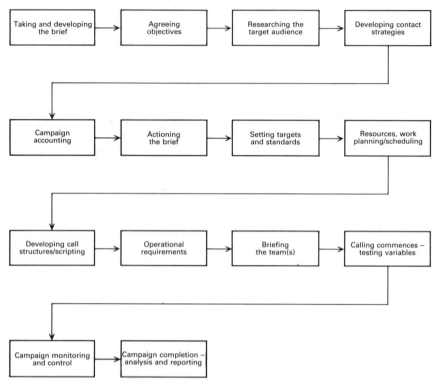

Figure 8.1 Key processes in planning, implementing and managing a telephone marketing campaign

Taking and developing the brief

Taking the brief is the starting point for campaign planning. An in-house telephone marketing unit may have many different internal 'clients' for its services (called the user for the purposes of this chapter) and the people involved in briefing the unit could vary from campaign to campaign. It is important, therefore, that these people have the authority to sanction the expenditure of resources of the proposed type and order of magnitude, and that the telephone marketing manager has the complete picture of current and future work commitments.

It is the responsibility of staff working in or with the unit to guide the user through the briefing process and obtain all the relevant information. It is an exploratory process during which the telephone marketer can begin to visualise the type of campaign that will achieve the user's objective(s) under the given set of circumstances. The amount of freedom the telephone marketer has to determine the nature of the campaign will generally depend on how the unit fits into the company's sales and marketing operation. A good brief is essential for the success of a campaign and responsibility for taking briefs should be assigned to those with the appropriate experience. Working with a good agency can provide valuable experience of this process.

Although much of the information required may be obtained during an initial meeting, briefing may happen over an extended period, in the form of close liaison with the user, as the campaign is developed. The type of information required has already been described in Chapter 3 (*see* pages 113–20), and is summarised in Table 8.1. This will vary according to the type of campaign that is visualised. Staff in the unit will quickly become knowledgeable about many of these areas, for example company products and markets, but it is dangerous to take this information for granted. A change in marketing strategy affecting target markets, for example, can change the whole perspective of a campaign.

An ideal minimum period of around six weeks should be allowed between taking the initial brief and the launch of a campaign, unless, of course, there is an urgent need to achieve the campaign objective(s). Some agencies can plan and implement a campaign in a matter of days, but this is possible only because they have the necessary expertise and resources. Until in-house staff have acquired appropriate experience, it is always advisable to employ an agency for campaigns which have to be implemented quickly, either to run the whole campaign or to set up and test it prior to bringing it in-house.

The initial briefing creates a framework around which the campaign can be designed. Ultimately, however, there may be several briefing documents which convey relevant information to each of the parties involved, perhaps telephone marketers and field sales personnel, and define their role in the campaign when the brief is actioned.

The aims and process of briefing will become clearer when reading about subsequent aspects of planning.

Agreeing objectives

Clearly defined objectives are essential both as an aid to planning, and to provide a yardstick against which to measure the progress and, ultimately, the success of the campaign. The user initially may state the

Table 8.1 Summary of areas that may be covered during the briefing process

---

Briefing in a campaign

- **'Client' or user background**
  - details of the company, past and present
  - details of product/service/event
  - details of the marketplace

- **Campaign details**
  - aims and objectives of the campaign
  - what information is to be captured?
  - broadly, how should this be achieved?
  - how will the information be recorded?
  - how frequently will data and results be reported?
  - how will it be reported at the end?

- **Other factors**
  - processing orders and liaison
  - representatives' diary availability and liaison
  - mailing schedules and liaison

- **Targets**
  - number of leads available, if any
  - presentation format of leads
  - quality of leads
  - type and extent of information on leads
  - original source of leads
  - number of workable leads
  - number of mailings
  - number of calls to be made/received
  - number of appointments/sales/attendees/completed questionnaires required
  - possible call rate
  - target call rate

- **Deadlines and scheduling**
  - leads available when?
  - user approval of campaign details (process and timing)
  - briefing callers (how and when?)
  - de-briefing callers (how and when?)
  - last call (when?)
  - communications, reporting
  - report presentation

- **Definition of success**

---

objective in fairly vague terms, such as to generate leads for a special promotion, and the telephone marketer has to probe deeper to find out precisely what the campaign has to achieve. The user may not have sufficient experience to realise the full potential of a campaign in terms of additional objectives that could be achieved, for example that appointment booking calls could also be used to gather valuable information about contacts for use later.

The objectives of a campaign evolve during the planning process, but agreement should be reached early in the briefing process on the primary objective of the campaign, for example to generate 'x' number of qualified leads. Ultimately, however, this will be stated as an answer to the question, 'What does the user want to happen as a result of each contact made?'. This may be for a succession of contacts with each individual, perhaps by mail, then telephone, then a sales visit, depending on the structure of the campaign. Each communication seeks to take the individual one step nearer to an ultimate objective, such as placing an order or attending a product launch, while achieving its own set of objectives. Stating objectives in this way helps in many aspects of planning, including developing contact strategies and designing the content of communications.

Targets, for example the number of decision-maker contacts and/or appointments to be made, ultimately form part of the campaign objectives. During the initial briefing the telephone marketer will be able to give the user an indication of what it is possible to achieve, although accurate figures may not be available until after the campaign has been tested. There must be early agreement, however, on what will constitute an acceptable outcome, ie a definition of success. The user may have unrealistic expectations of what can be achieved, for example, and the telephone marketer will also need to know what level of resources are likely to be required.

Eventually the objectives of each element of the campaign (ie each contact opportunity) can be stated in the following terms.

- **What** has to be achieved (for example encourage readers of a trade magazine advertisement to telephone the company)?

- **Why** does the user want to achieve this objective (for example to provide leads that can be screened by telephone marketers to determine whether booking an appointment or direct mail is appropriate)?

- **How** will this objective be achieved (for example selecting a magazine with an appropriate readership/target audience, the advertisement copy, a special offer, use of an 0800 number)?

- **What outcome** should be sought (for example a minimum number of respondents to the advertisements)?

- **What standard** of outcome should be achieved (for example a minimum percentage of respondents qualifying for an appointment)?

- **By when** should this be achieved (for example the closing date of a special offer)?

Each of the departments involved, for example sales, marketing, telephone marketing, PR, will have their own set of objectives for the campaign which contribute to the achievement of the ultimate objective.

When setting objectives it is vital to ensure that they can be achieved and serviced with the resources available. Are there sufficient telephone marketing executives to answer the expected number of inbound calls, for example, and can the sales force service the expected number of appointments? These types of questions have implications for campaign planning, for example scheduling of media advertisements and work planning within the telephone marketing unit.

Researching the target audience

A good knowledge of the target audience(s) is essential for planning an effective campaign. The dominant theme is accurate targeting to ensure that an appropriate message is delivered to the right person, in the right way, at the right time.

The objective(s) of the campaign will determine the type and profile of the target audience. Sometimes the contacts will already be defined, as in list cleaning and servicing customer accounts. Often, however, the target audience has to be defined in terms of what characteristics they should have in order to achieve the campaign objective(s). Generating orders, for example, will require contacts who have bought, or are likely to buy, from the company. This type of approach has important implications for campaign planning. Direct response advertising, for example, has to be targeted at those people who are most likely to respond in the way required, for example to request information or place an order. The development of a marketing database, examined in Chapter 9 (*see* pages 361–76), is an invaluable aid in targeting, helping to identify both known contacts who are most likely to respond positively and the characteristics to look for in unknown contacts, for example on bought-in lists.

Knowledge of the characteristics of the target audience helps to determine, among other things:

- where potential contacts' details are most likely to be found, for example customer records, the best type of list to buy in, the best magazine to advertise in;

- how they can best be contacted, for example by telephone or by mail;

- when they can best be contacted (where relevant), for example day (am/pm), evening, weekend, season, event-related (perhaps after a house purchase);

- their potential value and consequently the amount that can be spent on communicating cost-effectively with them, for example the most cost-effective medium and offer;

- whether all will qualify for an offer and, if not, how they qualify;

- their prior knowledge of, and contact with, the company;

- the type of marketing message that is most likely to appeal to them, for example the offer;

- what objectives could be achieved when contact is made, for example primary – an order; secondary – additional information on them; tertiary – greater awareness of the company and its products; and consequently the style of the response mechanism that may be needed (for example coupon details, call structure);

- what information they may require/request;

- what objections may be raised or questions asked.

The sources of contacts' details will determine what information is available about them and consequently will influence many of the factors listed above. These sources are examined in Chapter 9 (on pages 363–71) and include company records, commercial databases, mailing lists, responses to mailings, targeted media advertising, trade and telephone directories, and miscellaneous sources such as professional and trade organisations.

Many of the factors which must be considered in sourcing contacts, because they have a bearing on campaign planning, have been examined in Chapter 3 in connection with 'briefing in a campaign' (pages 113–20). They include:

- the number of leads available, if any;

- in what form the leads are available, for example on tape or disk, and how they will have to be processed before use;

- the quality of the leads in terms of meeting the targeting criteria (for example company size, budget) and accuracy of the information (for example age of the list);

- the information available on leads, for example basic contact details, previous contact/purchase history;

- the original source of the leads;

- the number of workable leads, for example after removing those with insufficient information and duplicates;

- when the leads will be available.

Table 8.2 Calculating the number of leads required in an appointment booking campaign

The number of leads required		*Number of leads required per week*
Number of qualified appointments required per week	= 80	*(80)*
Proportion of contacts likely to be reached (according to the market, seniority and completeness of contact details)	= 65%	*(123)*
Proportion of leads meeting the targeting criteria	= 72%	*(171)*
Estimated conversion rate (proportion of decision-maker contacts resulting in an appointment)	= 13.5%	*(1,266)*
Contingency margin	= +20%	*1,520*

Using this type of information it is possible to calculate things such as the number of leads required for a particular campaign or part of it, as shown in Table 8.2. A similar type of calculation can be used to determine approximately the number of appointments that could be booked with a limited number of leads. The number of leads that have to be telephoned each week can later be used to calculate the number of callers required or, alternatively, the number of leads that can be processed, and appointments booked, by the callers available. A margin of additional leads is always built in to accommodate contingencies, for example unexpected difficulty in making contact.

Developing contact strategies

Having identified and analysed the target audience, the next step is to decide how the company will communicate with them. The increasing successful use of direct marketing methods is a reflection of the philosophy that the best way to gain and keep customers is to establish and maintain a personal dialogue with them. Each communication is designed to exploit growing knowledge of the target audience to deliver timely, personalised marketing messages to maximise their value at every opportunity. A contact strategy is simply a planned series of communications designed to achieve this objective in the most cost-effective way.

The methods which can be used to establish and develop this personal dialogue include direct response advertising (coupons and telephone), door drops, direct mail, telephone marketing and face-to-face meetings. Which methods are used on which occasions will depend upon a number of factors, for example:

- the availability of contacts' details – if their name, address and telephone number are not available then personalised mail and telephone communications are not possible, but targeted direct response media advertising could be used;

- the objective of the communication – to make a sale, book an appointment or gather information; booking an appointment by mail, for example, is impractical, and having the sales team gather prospect information is too costly;

- the margins on the products or services being offered, ie expensive contact media generally cannot be used cost-effectively where profit margins are low;

- prior contact, purchase history and position in the product life-cycle – using an inexpensive medium (mail) to contact borrowers three months before the expiry of their loans, to alert them to the possibility of a further loan, and a more personal but expensive method (telephone) one month before expiry to sell a new loan;

- the business or market segment – some, such as travel agents, receive so much direct mail that it receives little or no attention;

- the extent and nature of the communication – highly complex products and services are best described in person or in writing, rather than over the telephone;

- the urgency of the response required – if it must be obtained the same day then the telephone is the best medium;

- whether or not a response must be guaranteed;

- geographical constraints – face-to-face meetings, even offering the prospect of a fairly high return, may not be cost-effective for single contacts in remote locations;

- the budget available, ie cost constraints may prohibit the use of the most effective medium in a particular situation.

These factors, taken together, help to identify the best contact strategy in a particular situation. A fictional example of how they come together is given in Table 8.3 (real examples are contained within the case studies in Chapter 11). A contact strategy may be relatively simple, as in cycling re-selling calls to existing customers, or it may be highly complex, as in large-scale database-driven marketing. Within a specific target audience there may be a number of different groups or segments which, to obtain the best response, need to be treated differently, ie to have different contact strategies.

Contact strategies should remain flexible and be modified or changed wherever there is an opportunity to increase cost-effectiveness. Continuous testing, examined later, helps to identify where improvements can be made.

The overall aim of a contact strategy is to maximise the value of each individual by building an increasingly strong and profitable relationship through a series of communications. These cannot be viewed in isolation; each communication builds upon the previous one, and the strategy should define how each contact will be treated according to previous contacts and responses to them. It is vital,

Table 8.3 Example contact strategy

Company: A car manufacturer

Target market: User/chooser company car drivers of a certain value in London, SW19.

Aim: To establish a strategy that enables car dealers to offer the right car, at the right time, to the right person.

Stage One The company needs to source potential buyers in the SW19 area. They could mail companies' personnel offices, enclosing a questionnaire and asking them to fill in the relevant contact names, but this would be time-consuming and with no guaranteed quality response. They decide to call these people, as it is quicker, will generate a more immediate response and information will be of a higher quality. Using the telephone in this way will also enable them to evaluate other factors that will have a bearing on later contact strategies:

- level of decision-maker (influencer and buyer)
- how frequently they change their cars
- what, if any, company car policy they employ
- how they like to be contacted

A telephone campaign is set to build an up-to-date list of company car drivers and establish when they are due to change their cars, ie

0–3 months	3–6 months	6 months–1 year	1 year plus

Stage Two These details are entered on to a bespoke marketing database so that they can be graded for future contact, enabling contacts to be pulled off at the appropriate time.

Now they are ready to contact the companies on the database and inform them of their service.

The form of contact depends on how much information needs to be imparted. Highy technical or complex products/services which rely heavily on the visual image to make their point, must allow the potential buyer to look at or read about the product/service at an early stage in the contact strategy.

Personalised direct mail is the right solution in this case. If the message is simple, clear and lends itself easily to a conversation, then a telephone call is probably the answer. Ultimately a combination of both may be used for following up or pre-hyping activity.

Stage Three In this case, direct mail must convey the image of the product in order to sell it on a long-term basis. The 6-month plus contacts are mailed with information on the new range of cars including a response device, ie 0800 and/or reply-paid coupon.

Stage Four At the same time, 0–6 month's contacts are called offering them test drives or more information from their local dealers who have been matched to them by their postcode on the database. Those who don't want to test drive are either sent a personalised mail piece or archived for future activity.

Stage Five The 6-month plus prospects will thereby mature and immediately go back into Stage Four.

This contact strategy is also backed up by advertising on a local and national level so that each mailing and phone call is building upon a conscious awareness.

Based on an example in The Direct Communications PORTFOLIO, The Decisions Group, 1990.

therefore, to keep a record of all contacts made and the outcome. The most efficient way of tracking individuals, and deciding how and when they can best be contacted again, is by developing a marketing database. The use of such a database in planning and driving marketing communications is examined in Chapter 9 (*see* pages 361–76).

There are five other factors that can influence the design of contact strategies – the marketing mix, the offer, timing, continuity and follow-up.

The marketing mix

The ways in which different sales and marketing activities are combined in a contact strategy can have a dramatic effect on results and overall cost-efficiency. The role of the telephone as a part of this mix is examined in Chapter 2 (*see* pages 39–43). For example, it obviously makes sense to telephone a lead whose value is unknown before a sales visit; this call can be used to screen the lead, to determine potential value and book a qualified appointment, if appropriate. The selection of the best mix ultimately rests upon the effective use of information about the contact.

The offer

The word 'offer' is used here to refer to that part of a communication which encourages the recipient to respond positively. At the simplest level this may be an explanation of why the person is being mailed or called, such as, 'I would like this information so that I can send precisely the information you need', in that this fulfils some of the contact's needs. At a higher level it may include the offer of favourable credit terms if the person responds within a specified time limit.

The offer being made, by whatever method of communication is being used, can determine the nature, volume, speed and completeness of responses. Any or all of these may be crucial to achieving the objective of the communication, as follows.

- A special promotion may be expensive to stage and only cost-effective if there is a large volume take-up; the offer therefore has to be sufficiently attractive to the target audience to stimulate this volume of response.

- Prospective attendees at a seminar may note the final, distant date for booking and payment and take advantage of it – leaving the organiser uncertain of whether or not it will be fully booked; an offer of a substantial reduction for early booking and payment, though reducing total income, can prove more cost-effective by generating bankable income and allowing more time to ensure full attendance.

- People filling in questionnaires or answering questions may make little effort to be accurate or complete if there is no tangible benefit in them doing so, for example a better service, 'free' entry in a prize draw.

The primary factor in determining the appeal of an offer is its perceived value to the target audience ('What's in it for me?'). This appeal may be tangible, such as the offer of a free gift, or fairly abstract, as in a promise to donate a sum of money to charity if the person responds. The monetary value of 'free' gifts is usually perceived by the target audience as being much higher than the actual cost to the company, for example because of bulk purchasing. However, even relatively expensive goods or services can be offered provided that they generate sufficient business to make them cost-effective. Offering a free test drive to anyone who cares to telephone in response to a television advertisement, for example, may appear to be an expensive way of generating interest, yet one European car manufacturer used this method widely because they estimated that around 20 per cent of all those who accepted a test drive would eventually buy the product. Another way of increasing the perceived value of an offer is to match it to the current needs, interests or aspirations of the target audience. This type of offer can range from the free modelling knife taped to the hobbyist magazine, to the supplier who offers companies a photo-copier on loan for 12 months provided they purchase consumables from them. Timing can also influence the attractiveness of an offer; discounts on a new kitchen will appeal more to people who need a new kitchen, for example, perhaps after a house move.

Another factor to consider is the trade-off between the effort required in responding and the 'reward' for doing so. Anything which increases the effort required, unless that itself has some intrinsic 'value' (for example phone-in competition promotions), generally detracts from the appeal of the offer. Response mechanisms should therefore be designed for ease of response, ie keeping questions short and simple, providing a reply-paid coupon and a free 24–hour phone line. Conflict within the offer must be avoided. For example, it is pointless emphasising speed of response by the company ('immediate despatch of our brochure') if the response mechanism chosen is slow (a coupon).

With the growth in the use of direct marketing the population has become increasingly discerning. Targeting is the key to making an effective offer and the more information available about the target audience the more personalised and appealing the offer can be made, ie their specific circumstances and needs can be addressed. Its importance cannot be overestimated. As an example, the mailing test results summarised in Table 8.4 show that the quality of the list and the quality of the offer can make a sixfold and a threefold difference in response rates, respectively; when the other major variables are taken into account, the best combination can result in an amazing 58 times more respondents than the worst.

Table 8.4 Factors affecting mailing response rates

Mailing test results	
Factor	*Difference between best and worst*
List	x 6.0
Offer	x 3.0
Timing	x 2.0
Creative	x 1.35
Response	x 1.2
The best combination is 58 times more responsive than the worst!	

Timing

The timing of communications can be important at a number of levels. The connection with the appeal of an offer has been mentioned already, but accessibility (for example by telephone), communication cycles and the mechanics of the marketing mix (for example mail/ telephone) must also be considered.

The times when contacts are accessible by telephone, and sometimes mail, can vary according to the target market and the time of the day and year. In business-to-business markets, for example, calls generally should be made within office hours and when the contact is likely to have time to talk. Just before 9.00am, or slightly earlier in some businesses, can be a good time, because the interruptions of the day (like meetings) have generally not started. It does depend on the vertical market though. Publicans, for example, generally prefer to take calls during their opening hours (because rest periods are precious), although not during their busiest periods; doctors, on the other hand, are usually unavailable during surgery hours. Popular holiday periods are another time when the decision-maker contact rate can fall considerably, or during major events of special interest (for example phoning car fleet managers during a motor show).

The best time to call consumer markets depends on the lifestyle of individual contacts, ranging from the type of work they do, to hobbies or interests that may take them out of the home at certain times. It is not only a case of catching them at home, but also calling them at a time that is convenient. Many of the codes of practice for telephone marketing, examined in Chapter 10, include what are termed 'reasonable hours'. However, even this does not guarantee convenience for the consumer, for example telephoning a mother as the children come in from school. The preferred time for telephoning any contacts is obviously when call rates are cheapest, but to do this and ignore these other factors is usually far less cost-effective. Accessibility by mail is less time-sensitive, although response rates can drop if there is a gap between the date of the mailing and receipt by the contact, for example if they arrive back from holiday to find a pile of direct mail waiting for them.

The cycle of direct communications with each contact should be planned in a logical way so that each communication is timely. What is timely can depend upon a large range of factors, such as the profile of the target market, the product/service offered and the contact's position in its lifecycle, corporate budgeting and so on. Ultimately, however, it should seek to maintain regular contact in a way which meets individuals' current needs and fully exploits their long-term potential (the fictional contact strategy in Table 8.3 provides an example of a well-planned cycle of communications). The time between successive communications can have a critical impact on response rates. As an example, Figure 8.2 shows the effect of the

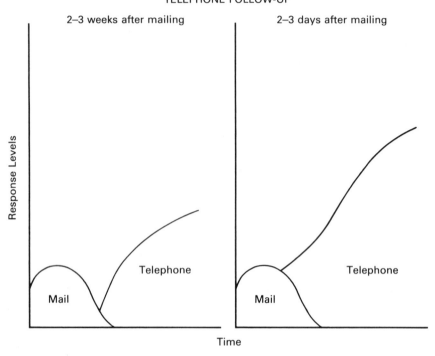

Figure 8.2 Effect on response levels of the timing of telephone follow-up to a mailing

timing of telephone follow-up to a mailing. In this case, the earlier follow-up ensures that any interest generated by the mailing can be fully exploited.

Continuity and follow-up

The reason for establishing a contact strategy – a planned series of communications – is to develop and exploit the business relationship. Obviously this is less successful if there is a deviation from this plan. Devising appropriate operational systems, which are examined later, is one way of ensuring that the strategy operates efficiently. At the simplest level this means ensuring that the company does what it has promised, for example a brochure is sent out or a member of the sales team keeps an appointment. But research conducted by the UK agency Colman RSCG Direct* suggests that many companies fail even at this level.

---

* *Direct Response Advertising: The Other Side*, July 1990, report compiled by Omer-Li Cohen PR for Colman RSCG Direct.

Table 8.5 Efficiency of follow-up on direct responses from advertising

---

Response to advertisements pursued:
Receiving a response = 69%
No response   = 31%

Breakdown of those receiving a letter/brochure after initial enquiry:
Wrong information received   = 33%
Received follow-up information = 25%
No follow-up   = 71%
Unpersonalised letter   = 25%
Follow-up telephone call   = 8%

Breakdown by market sector of those not responding to the initial enquiry:
Auto   = 10%
Financial   = 20%
Personal and leisure = 42%
Business   = 50%

Breakdown by market sector of those not making further contact with the respondent after sending an initial letter/brochure:
Auto   = 55.5%
Financial   = 100%
Personal and leisure = 71%
Business   = 100%

Percentage of letters sent to 'Dear enquirer' or non-personalised:
Auto   = 10%
Financial   = 25%
Personal and Leisure = 50%
Business   = 60%

Average number of days taken to send the initial information requested:
Auto   = 12
Financial   = 7
Personal and Leisure = 6
Business   = 3.5

Synopsis of conclusions: In responding to an advertisement that has actively asked for a response, and provided a response mechanism:
Chance of receiving any information   = 70%
Chance of getting the information wanted or needed = 45%
Chance of not being contacted again   = 70%
Chance of receiving a follow-up telephone call   = 5%
Chance of being written to as 'Dear Enquirer'   = 25%
Average time for information to arrive   = 1 week plus

Source: Direct Response Advertising: The Other Side, July 1990, report compiled by Omer-Li Cohen PR for Colman RSCG Direct. Reprinted with permission.

The agency conducted a survey to find out how efficiently companies in the auto, financial, leisure/personal and business markets handled sales enquiries as a response to press advertisements bearing a coupon and/or 0800, 0345 or 0898 telephone number. A total of 35 advertisements were followed up, including 28 featured in national and Sunday newspapers and supplements over a one-week period in May 1990. The results of the survey are summarised in Table 8.5. There was only a 70 per cent chance of respondents receiving information and the majority of those (70 per cent) were never contacted again. Only 5 per cent of all respondents received a follow-up telephone call. Apart from damage to potentially profitable relationships, this is clearly a waste of money; estimated expenditure* on direct response advertising in newspapers and magazines in the UK in 1990 was around £470m. The Colman report concludes that:

> 'there seems to be an irresponsible use of response handling mechanisms in advertising. These are precisely the ones that will effect a direct line between an advertiser and its market place. These are precisely the lines that are at worst being damaged and at best not being cared for effectively.'

There are clearly many factors to consider in developing effective contact strategies and operating them efficiently. They are at the heart of a direct marketing campaign and, being dynamic, it is necessary continually to monitor results and test different variables to determine the most effective approach. Establishing and developing a marketing database is a growth area because it helps to automate this process and deploy valuable resources in the most efficient way.

Campaign accounting

Estimating and monitoring costs versus benefits, and actual expenditure versus predicted expenditure, is a continuous process which begins at the planning stage and continues until completion of the campaign. One of the attractions of direct marketing methods is that they are accountable – the cost and benefits of each and every contact

---

* *Direct Response – The Market Map*, a quantitative analysis of the UK direct response industry, 1990. Commissioned from Research Associates by the Colorgraphic Group.

made can be calculated. At the planning stage, however, predictions, particularly of benefits, have to be made based on experience or knowledge of previous similar campaigns (whether run in-house or with an agency), or the expertise of an agency. Accounting at this stage also helps to compare the likely cost-effectiveness of different strategies and tactics. Once the campaign reaches the testing stage the accuracy of these cost/benefit predictions can be gauged and the campaign fine-tuned to achieve the best results. Continuous monitoring of results and cost analysis as the campaign progresses helps to ensure that these targets are maintained. Analysis of results once the campaign is completed provides figures for the actual cost/benefits, which can be compared with the initial predictions and the budget.

Actioning the brief

All the people involved in a campaign will need to know precisely what they have to do, and this is defined in briefing documents for specified individuals in each of the key areas of activity, for example sales, marketing, telephone marketing, external agencies. By using these documents, each of these individuals will be able to plan, implement and manage the contribution they and their staff or associates will make to the campaign.

Briefing documents are key components in the success of a campaign. To ensure that all activities are co-ordinated, they must include sufficient details of others' roles, particularly the deadlines they are working to, for example a telephone marketing campaign manager will need to know when mailings go out, or when the sales manager plans to have the sales team available to fulfil appointments. The contents of the documents obviously vary according to the nature and extent of the campaign, but they may include information such as:

- campaign title;

- a brief statement of the objective(s);

- campaign manager (telephone marketing unit or marketing department);

- campaign sponsor (user);

- launch and completion dates;

- target audience(s), for example customers, prospects, distributors, retailers and their 'profile';

- number in the target audience;

- personnel resources, for example telephone marketers, national accounts team, dealers;

- training required, for example products/services, mechanics of the application (if new);

- media being used, for example telephone, mail, media advertising;

- media schedules, ie when different media are being used;

- the offer(s) being made;

- budget;

- success criteria, for example number of orders, appointments, leads;

- reporting – type and frequency/dates;

- contact strategy.

Although the responsibility for planning the finer details of a campaign may rest with separate departments serving the relevant functions, close liaison between all parties is essential. If direct response advertising is involved, for example, whoever is assigned the task of identifying the best medium for, and the creative content of, the advertisement will need to liaise with someone in telephone marketing if the telephone is being used as a response mechanism. Knowledge of the content of advertisements is obviously essential in planning how incoming calls will be handled, when the lines will have to be staffed and so on. Similarly, those planning the advertisements will need to know what it is possible to achieve on an incoming call, for example the extent of information that can be obtained or given, so that this can be balanced with the content of the advertisements.

Methods and frequency of liaison between appointed persons are built into the briefing documents so that each department is quickly alerted to unexpected delays elsewhere which may impinge upon their own work. It is also vital that everyone involved in the campaign understands the lines of command and reporting. Conflicts or confusion over who to contact, and from whom to take instructions or advice, can quickly lead to disaster.

Setting targets and standards of performance

Clearly defined targets and standards of performance play a key role in the monitoring and control of telephone marketing activities. To be effective they must be realistic (ie attainable), measurable (quantity, quality, time) and fully understood by those who are working to achieve them. Key areas of activity for which targets and standards must be set are listed in Chapter 4 (*see* page 166); these include call handling, achieving the objectives of the call, calling statistics, recording responses and associated tasks such as diary maintenance.

The way in which targets and standards are defined depends upon the activity being measured. Some, like call rates, are easily defined in terms of calls to be made per hour. Others, like the use of a script, require a more subjective approach and rely largely upon the skills of the supervisor to determine whether or not they are being achieved. Those areas where targets and standards can be most clearly defined include:

- call rate (expressed as a number of calls per hour);

- decision-maker contact rate (contacts per hour);

- conversion rate (the percentage of calls where the objective has been achieved);

- applying qualification criteria (expressed as a percentage of properly qualified contacts);

- minimum standards of information to be collected (expressed in absolute terms);

- accuracy of information recorded, for example call cards, diaries (expressed as a maximum permitted error rate);

- following procedures, for example
  - call-backs (expressed as a maximum permitted variance from the time agreed with the contact)
  - fulfilment (expressed as a maximum permitted delay)
  - reporting (expressed in absolute terms of what, when and how to report).

What activities can be measured and defined as a target or standard will obviously vary according to the campaign. The level at which they are set depends upon previous experience of similar campaigns and/or the results achieved when the campaign is tested. Any initial estimates may be revised up or down after testing. Achievable targets generally rise during the first few days of a campaign, both through fine-tuning and the telephone marketers becoming more familiar with the campaign. Clearly displaying targets in the calling area, and charting the achievement of the team, can act as a motivator and this has already been examined in Chapter 7. If existing targets are regularly being exceeded they should be raised, though not to a level which is unattainable. Operational systems, examined later, are the means by which the achievement of targets and standards are monitored during a campaign. Some examples of realistic call rates are given later in the chapter in 'Tips on applications'.

Resource expectations, work planning and scheduling

The type and order of magnitude of resources required to achieve the campaign objectives will often be apparent during the initial briefing, but the calculations are continually refined as the campaign develops. At the same time, the campaign objectives, strategy and tactics may be tempered by the availability of resources and/or budget.

Even a comparatively straightforward campaign like handling calls generated by direct response advertising involves accounting for a wide range of resources. In addition to telephone lines, advertising media, equipment and documentation, the staff resources (both company and external) will range from media planning and creative work (art/copywriting) to call handling, supervision and administration.

Departmental priorities and the scheduling of different campaign elements also have to be considered to determine whether or not there will be any conflicting demands on fixed resources. Sometimes these can be avoided by careful scheduling of work or, alternatively, outside resources may be bought in. Some resources may not be available in-house, or a decision may have been made to buy in a higher level of expertise or capacity. If the company has insufficient trained telephone marketing executives to handle the expected volume of calls, for example, an agency may be employed to provide additional, temporary support staff, either on-site, or on the agency's own premises. This is also a cost-effective solution when there is a sudden increase in demand on resources during a campaign. An unexpectedly successful product launch or special promotion, for example, may overload in-house resources and risk losing valuable opportunities. Many well-established agencies can supply fully trained and briefed callers, and a project manager, within 24 hours to ensure that these opportunities are exploited to the full.

Careful work planning and scheduling is essential for the efficient deployment of resources, and improving the overall cost-effectiveness of the campaign. This process involves:

- defining all the tasks that have to be completed;

- assessing the resources required for each, their availability (quantity, quality, location, time) and how they will be acquired;

- creating a schedule for completion of each task, showing where they are interdependent or critical to overall progress;

- deciding how tasks will be assigned or delegated to make optimum use of available resources, including individuals' skills and qualities;

- drawing up contingency plans to be implemented, if necessary, to ensure that critical tasks are completed on time.

Some aspects of planning and scheduling work in a telephone marketing unit have been examined in Chapter 4, pages 130–32, in connection with staffing levels. The range of factors to be considered will depend upon the complexity of the campaign, but in general terms the following type of information may be required:

- When the first and last calls will be made, or are expected to be received, may be dependent upon:
  - availability of leads
  - time required for preparation of leads
  - success criteria (for example a fully booked seminar, sufficient appointments each week for the sales team)
  - user approval of campaign details (and any outside approval required, for example from the Takeover Panel)
  - origination of advertisements/direct mail, call structures, documentation
  - lead times for publishing/broadcasting/distributing direct response materials
  - publication dates/transmission times/posting dates
  - the speed/delay of the target audience in responding
  - other demands on telephone marketing resources.

- The rate at which calls have to be made, or incoming calls handled, over the duration of the campaign may depend upon:

- number of successful calls required (which may be time-dependent, for example appointment booking)
- number of leads available/direct responses expected
- medium of direct response (for example telephone or coupon for telephone follow-up)
- required speed of telephone follow-up of coupon responses (ideally the same day)
- proportion of leads meeting the targeting criteria
- estimated conversion rate
- variation in contact availability according to the time of day/day of the week/season
- variation in inbound call rates according to the time of day and day of the week (or volume of coupons received per day)
- estimated call length (according to call structure/script) and time for associated activities
- number of times unavailable contacts will be re-called.

This information enables the telephone marketing supervisor or manager not only to determine the staffing levels required over the duration of the campaign, but also to identify critical dates for the start/completion of certain activities, for example briefing and de-briefing staff. Activity levels can only be estimated until the campaign has been tested, but these are sufficient for work scheduling. The campaign design can help in making the most efficient use of resources. Direct response advertising, for example, can be spread over time to generate a steady, manageable flow of incoming leads, rather than creating peaks and troughs of activity.

Once a schedule of activity has been drawn up, showing the start and completion dates of all tasks, it should be circulated to all key personnel involved in the campaign.

Developing call structures/scripting

One of the most crucial aspects of campaign development is planning how calls will be handled. The guiding influence in developing conversation frameworks, or call structures, are the objectives to be achieved within each call. Scripts are often used to help staff follow the call structure that has been created. Although these are not essential, except under special circumstances, they can provide certain benefits.

Benefits and drawbacks of using scripts

A major benefit of the telephone over other methods of communication such as direct mail is its intimacy. Anything which detracts from the personal nature of a telephone conversation reduces its value in helping to establish or develop a profitable relationship. One of the major dangers of the unskilled use of a script is that it will sound like a prepared speech. A script is designed to be used as a framework for a conversation, incorporating appropriate 'prompts' to help the telephone marketer concentrate on communicating; it is not meant to be read word for word.

Using a script can provide many benefits, as shown in Table 8.6, but it is counter-productive if not written and used skilfully. Scriptwriters must be able to create a framework within which individuals can employ their own skills and style to steer the conversation and achieve the most productive outcome. Telephone marketers need to be able to follow the structure and key content of a script while making the conversation sound spontaneous. To do this they must be given the freedom to ad lib within the framework of the script. These points apply equally to designing call structures.

The choice of whether or not a script is required depends upon the complexity of calls and the level of experience of call handlers. An experienced team working long term on a single application, for example, may have been given extensive training so that they do not need any prompting to follow the required call structure. Even where a script is used, experienced telephone marketers often dispense with it, except for reference, once they have become familiar with the campaign. An example of where scripts are particularly useful is when an incoming call may be one of several different types, and the telephone marketer has to treat each one differently. There may also be situations where using a script is essential, either because the company needs to know and approve what information is being given or because outside approval is required. An example of the latter situation is in shareholder communications where there are strict guidelines on how the campaign must be conducted (*see* Chapter 10, page 390).

Content and structure

The content of a script, or that built into the call structure, depends upon many of the factors discussed so far, such as the objectives of the

Table 8.6   The benefits and drawbacks of scripting

Benefits

Focuses the conversation on achieving the call objectives

Provides control over what is being said and creates consistency

Can be approved, if necessary, by internal departments (eg legal) and external bodies (eg Takeover Panel)

Helps to ensure that information given is accurate

Embodies a range of expertise brought to bear on each call

Provides guidance on features, benefits and unique selling points

Provides ready counters to common objections and answers to questions

Helps to ensure that all the information required is gathered

Helps to guide the conversation, leaving staff free to concentrate on communicating with the contact

Can shorten training time because essential information is contained within the script (eg on products/services)

Improves the quality of communication, particularly of the weaker communicators and the less experienced

Helps to limit the length of the call by using only essential information

Provides a framework for testing to optimise results and set targets

Results can be predicted more accurately because call handling is more consistent

Provides a structured medium for training new staff

Drawbacks

Can detract from the communication process eg sounding impersonal, inhibiting creativity

Limits flexibility and the freedom to take advantage of opportunities that may arise (eg up-selling or cross-selling)

Can hinder the better communicators by defining the information they should use

Has to be used with skill and confidence to be effective

Requires good scriptwriting skills

---

call, the offer and the target audience, while the structure is designed to put the content into a conversational framework. The following types of questions together help to identify what the script or call structure should cover:

- What is the overriding purpose of the call?

- What are the benefits to the contact of making a positive response, for example product benefits, a better service, quick resolution of a problem?

- What will a positive response cost the contact, namely how much money or time?

- When, if ever, did the company last communicate with these contacts?

- How and why did they communicate, and what was the outcome?

- What else is known about these contacts, if anything, and is any of this information relevant to the purpose of this call?

- What does the company want the contacts to do/what will the company do after the telephone conversation?

- What information will each party require to do this?

- Are the company's actions dependent upon contacts' qualifying criteria?

- What other information would it be valuable to exchange?

- What else could the company achieve with this telephone call and what are their respective priorities?

- What other information might contacts request, such as product/ service literature, miscellaneous questions?

- How will the company fulfil these requests?

- What objections might contacts raise during the conversation and how can they best be answered?

- What market information might be relevant to this target audience and to the conversations with them?

When planning a script or call structure it is important to remember that every call can achieve something, for example gather information and promote the company, even if the main objectives cannot be achieved. Whatever the purpose of the call, but particularly where products or services are involved, it is necessary to create a list of features, benefits and unique selling points (USPs). The most important of these, with reference to the contacts' needs, may be incorporated into a script, while the complete list will provide valuable background and reference information for the telephone marketer.

Particular care must be taken when planning for inbound calls because the nature of calls may vary. Prospects telephoning in response to an advertisement, for example, may have a range of requests beyond those which the ad has been designed to stimulate. It may tell people that they can phone for a brochure, and some readers may ask for the name and address of their nearest stockist. These possibilities must be accommodated within the script or call structure to ensure that each type of request is handled efficiently and consistently. In some applications, such as a customer helpline, the range of enquiries and requests can be even greater. Under extreme circumstances the number of variants on incoming calls can be so great that they can only be handled efficiently using a sophisticated computerised 'script'. Computerised telephone marketing systems can be especially advantageous in these situations, enabling call handlers to move quickly around the script or conversational framework and call up any information required, such as the caller's nearest dealer. Extra care must be taken, therefore, when planning call structures for inbound calls. There must be guidelines on how to handle each type of call that can be expected, and call handlers should be able to locate quickly the relevant part of the 'script'. An example of such a script is described in the Comet case study in Chapter 11, pages 427–32. Outbound call structures are usually less complex, though not always, but they still need careful planning if they are going to be used successfully.

The variations on content and structure are unlimited and there is no 'model' script or call structure even for specific telephone marketing applications. It is not possible to give comprehensive guidance here on what they should contain and how they should be structured, but all scripts/call structures should contain the following elements whose proportions vary according to the nature of the application.

The opening The beginning of a call obviously differs depending on whether it is outbound or inbound, but it should always aim to create a strong positive impression in the first 15–20 seconds. For outbound calls the first task is to get through to the decision-maker. With business-to-business calls this may entail going through the switchboard, where the caller may want to check the name, job title and address of the decision-maker. It is vital on all outbound calls to ensure that the decision-maker has been reached before continuing the call. If unavailable, or the call is inconvenient, a call-back date and time should be arranged. On reaching the decision-maker the caller should start with a polite greeting and a statement of the caller's name, company name and purpose of the call. Then the decision-maker should be asked if the call can be continued and this can be done most positively by mentioning an important benefit. The opening may also include reference to the previous occasion on which the person was contacted, if at all.

The first words spoken when an inbound call is received will depend upon the purpose for which the telephone line is being used, for example the switchboard or a dedicated customer service line. The first task then is to capture NAT (name, address and telephone number) details and determine the reason for the call. This will then determine the call structure applicable to the remainder of the call.

Questioning Asking structured questions is the means by which the telephone marketer guides the conversation. Apart from being used to gather valuable information, for example on the decision-maker's situation and specific needs, appropriately worded questions can be used to encourage the type of response required. In appointment booking, for example, it is more positive to ask *when* it would be convenient for a sales representative to call than to ask *if* a rep could call.

Open-ended questions (usually beginning with the words who, what, when, which, why, how or where) demand a more comprehensive response than a simple 'yes' or 'no', and are therefore very useful for gathering information, for example, 'What type of car do you drive?', or 'Why did you choose to buy at this particular time?'. These types of questions encourage the contacts to do most of the talking and are especially important in finding out about their needs and preferences.

Closed questions encourage a 'yes' or 'no' response, for example, 'Does your department currently use our widget?'. Although the opportunities for using closed questions constructively is more limited than for open questions, they are obviously useful for obtaining a definite response, for example, 'Now you know the benefits of our product, will you be attending our product launch?'.

Another type of questioning technique is to encourage the contact to choose from two or more alteratives, such as, 'Which day of the week would suit you best for an appointment?', or 'Would it be easier for you to attend the London or the Brighton seminar?'. These are particularly useful at the closing stages of a conversation.

Finally, loaded questions can be useful under certain circumstances, but they must be used with care. Compare the following two loaded questions. 'I'm sure you would like to order another two packs and take advantage of our volume discount for five packs or over, wouldn't you? It will save you 15 per cent on the cost of your order.' 'You wouldn't like to miss out on this important opportunity, would you? All of your competitors will be there.' The first question presents a clear benefit, while the second has negative connotations and would almost certainly be counter-productive.

The effectiveness of questions obviously depends on the telephone marketer's ability to pose them correctly, to listen and analyse the responses, and to respond appropriately. Hesitancy in saying 'yes' to an invitation to visit the company's showroom and meet a representative, for example, could indicate that the person will not show up, thereby wasting an opportunity for that rep to meet someone else. A further question could be used to probe deeper to help confirm the contact's intention, for example, 'What time should I telephone you on Tuesday morning to check that you are still able to attend in the afternoon?'. However, when probing questions are used too much, or are spoken in anything approaching an aggressive manner, it can appear like an interrogation and this must be avoided.

Questions should be used, above all, to provide the contact with opportunities to talk about their needs, preferences and intentions. This means that the telephone marketer must allow time for the contact to respond and have an appropriate mechanism within the script, or documentation reflecting the call structure, to note responses.

The presentation   This is basically the 'sales pitch'. Whether or not the call is sales-orientated it will include an offer of some sort which must be presented positively by stressing features, benefits and USPs relating to the decision-maker's needs. These are not necessarily limited strictly to products and services and can include information such as the company's profile, position in the marketplace and so on. Features, benefits and USPs have to be incorporated carefully into call structures to provide just the right amount of information to generate sufficient interest to achieve the call objective. If it is a pre-mail call to determine interest in attending a product demonstration, for example, it is a waste of time giving a detailed description of the product, although the telephone marketer should have information to hand to answer any questions the contact may ask. This may be in the form of a benefit sheet or brochures, for example, to which the telephone marketer can refer as required.

Objection handling The type and number of objections to giving a commitment that contacts may raise will depend largely upon the effectiveness of the presentation and the stressing of benefits, ie poor 'selling' creates objections. Of secondary importance are the business relationship with them (for example, previous communications and transactions) and the purpose of the call (for example, market evaluation or sales).

Ideally, the style and content of the script should pre-empt likely objections. Common reactions to a market evaluation call, for example, may be 'How long will this take?' and 'Why do you need this information?'. Both of these 'objections' can be avoided by answering them in the opening of the call. Lack of perceived value is what most often gives rise to objections, and the less apparent or lower the value the more tenaciously contacts hold on to their objections. Selective use of features, benefits and USPs, according to the needs and preferences of each contact, are therefore the best way of either pre-empting, if possible, or overcoming objections. For direct sales calls the sales team is often the best source of information on likely objections and how to overcome them effectively.

Handling objections, which can arise at any point in a conversation, is one of the most difficult aspects of call handling. To do this successfully telephone marketers require training and appropriate support in the form of the script or call structure, a benefits sheet and a list of 'likely objections' with appropriate responses. Often, however, the contact may not give the real reason for not wanting to make a commitment, or may not voice an objection directly, and it is the telephone marketer's job to probe and identify the reason. Sometimes it is apparent that there is little chance of overcoming an objection and it is generally wise to close the call politely. Apart from avoiding wasting time, it is possible that another call to the contact at a timed later date will elicit a more positive response.

Closing The way in which a call is closed depends upon its purpose and what has been said during the conversation; it can range from traditional sales closing techniques to simply thanking people for their time. Several different closes may be written into the script so that the telephone marketer can select the one appropriate to the conversation that has taken place. Knowing the best time to close, for example setting a date and time for an appointment, or confirming delivery and invoice address for goods, is something that is learned through training and experience. All calls, however, should end on a positive note, whatever the outcome, so that no resistance to any subsequent communication is created.

Scripts should be written in a conversational style and, where appropriate, create vivid verbal images of features and benefits to compensate for the lack of illustrations or photographs. Call structures should help telephone marketers to achieve the same effects. Courtesy and politeness are obviously extremely important, and this should also be reflected in the style of the script or call structure. They should also conform to the codes of practice, and sometimes legislation, relevant to the type of call. Market research calls made in the UK, for example, should conform to the Market Research Society's Code of Conduct and the ESOMAR Guidelines, and all telephone sales/marketing calls should conform to the British Direct Marketing Association's Telephone Marketing Guidelines (*see* Chapter 10).

Scriptwriters

Writing good telephone marketing scripts, or creating good call structures, requires a rare combination of skills and knowledge. Not only must scriptwriters understand how to exploit the sales and marketing potential of a telephone conversation, and translate it into words on paper or screen which are easy for telephone marketers to follow and use, but they also require considerable background knowledge of telephone marketing, the campaign objectives and mechanics, the products or services being promoted, and the target audience and marketplace. Neither copywriters of brochures, direct mail and advertisements, nor senior sales and marketing executives are likely to meet these requirements individually. Scriptwriting should therefore generally be a collaborative effort. With the information gained from briefing, and subsequent research and planning, a suitably skilled telephone marketer, usually the campaign manager or handler, should be able to construct a script or call structure which can then be developed and refined by calling on the expertise of others in the sales and marketing department. Subsequently, the people who will have to

Table 8.7 Dos and don'ts when writing telephone marketing scripts

Scriptwriting Dos and Don'ts

Do

Ensure that the right person has been reached and confirm details as appropriate, eg status, function, needs

Open by stating the caller's name, company, purpose of the call and asking to continue

Include an important benefit in the opening

Aim to create an impact in the first 15–20 seconds

Allow for inserting into the script personal information about each contact, where appropriate/available

Keep to the point and use short sentences

Ask open-ended questions regularly, eg to obtain information, clarify responses when necessary

Use closed questions sparingly, where commitment or confirmation is to be encouraged

Incorporate prompts for callers to cope with all responses, eg to arrange a more convenient time to call, to close, to move to another part of the script if necessary

Incorporate all the likely answers to questions in the script (these are used by the telephone marketer to note responses and prompt contacts if necessary)

Ensure that all information to be checked or gathered is detailed and that it can be recorded with minimum effort

Prepare separate documents with likely objections/how to overcome them and product/service features, benefits and USPs

Write in a conversational style and test this by reading the script aloud

Adhere to any codes of practice or legislation applicable to the campaign

Don't

Use 'hard-sell' techniques

Use phrases that telephone marketers may find unnatural or difficult to say

Use jargon, eg relating to the company's business, products etc

Use excessively effusive language

use the script or follow the call structure should be asked to review it and advise on any details which they believe, from their experience, could be improved. It may be revised again during the testing phase of the campaign. In addition, the user may ask to see and approve the script or call structure at any one or all of these stages.

A brief list of dos and don'ts in scriptwriting is given in Table 8.7, although not all of these may be relevant to all call types. Examples of a script and associated documentation, such as benefit and objection sheets, are shown in Chapter 4 (*see* pages 140–58). The way in which scripts or call structures are presented varies. Sometimes a flowchart structure is used to help the telephone marketer move quickly from one part of the 'script' to another, and some people prefer to use overlapping cards taped on to a board which can be flipped over as required.

Scripts and call structures are a part of the operational systems which help to ensure that a campaign is managed efficiently.

Operational requirements

The range and functions of operational systems needed to run a telephone marketing operation are examined in detail in Chapter 4 (*see* pages 137–67), where they are categorised as recording and administration systems, procedures and standards. Overall, they serve to ensure that all activities required to achieve the campaign objective(s) are completed as planned, in terms of quality, quantity and timing. This is achieved principally by formalising the flow of information between all the parties involved, so that it can be acted upon as appropriate. An appointment-booking campaign, for example, would involve callers, sales representatives, telephone marketing and sales management, prospects, possibly support staff, for example for mailing fulfilment, and maybe others. The activities formalised by the operational systems in this situation would need to include:

- grading customers and prospects according to the qualification criteria and processing them as appropriate, for example book an appointment, target for immediate mailing or for later communication;

- capturing any additional information required about the contact;

- updating sales representatives' diaries and monitoring their availability;

- sending appropriate information on contacts to representatives;

- confirming appointments with customers or prospects;

- informing mailing fulfilment of contacts' details as appropriate;

- updating customer and prospect records;

- recording the outcome of appointments;

- processing the outcome of appointments, for example an order, further information/visit required;

- collecting, monitoring and collating calling statistics for telephone marketing management;

- collating call results for sales management;

- collating appointment results for sales and telephone marketing management;

- two-way reporting between
  - callers and telephone marketing management
  - representatives and sales management
  - telephone marketing and sales management and, perhaps,
  - callers and representatives.

Some of the functions to be served by operational systems are the same for all campaigns, such as monitoring call statistics. Those specific to a particular campaign will generally become apparent during the planning of the contact strategy. The more complex a campaign the more demands are placed upon these systems; many different activities are being undertaken, often interdependently, and each requires and generates different information which must be communicated and utilised efficiently. Detailed questioning of the information management requirements can be used to help ensure that all the appropriate functions are incorporated within the operational systems and that the information is used effectively. This entails answering questions such as the following.

- What specific activities does the campaign involve?

- What information is required to complete each of these activities?

- From whom will that information be obtained, and how?

- When will that information be available/required?

- What valuable information could be acquired during the completion of each activity?

- Who needs this information, and when?

- Who, in addition, would find it useful to know, and when would they use it?

- How will management ensure that information is gathered, communicated and used as efficiently?

The design of operational systems should aim to make the most efficient use of information, ie avoiding duplication and being well integrated by an overall information management strategy. They should be simple and quick to use and, ideally, as 'transparent' to the user as possible, ie the way they function is unobtrusive. Automation, examined in Chapter 4 and elsewhere, greatly enhances operational efficiency.

All operational systems must obviously be in place before the campaign is launched, and may be amended as a result of testing.

Briefing the team(s)

The final task prior to the start of telephone activity is to brief the staff involved, including those who will fulfil supporting roles. Briefing can be viewed as a training session designed to enable staff to apply their skills to best effect in a campaign. More specifically, for telephone marketing staff, it serves to:

- provide information and guidance on
  - the campaign objectives and structure
  - the role of telephone marketing in the campaign
  - the user
  - features/benefits and unique selling points of the product/service/event
  - the offer
  - profile(s) of the target audience
  - likely objections and ways of overcoming them
  - likely questions and how to answer them
  - the marketplace
  - the competition;
- inform staff of

- — any special operational requirements, for example for monitoring, reporting and reviewing activities
- — timings, schedules and deadlines
- — any contingency plans which exist;

- highlight similarities with previous campaigns of which staff have experience;

- familiarise them with the script or call structure and other documentation;

- inform them of targets, standards and success criteria;

- delegate tasks, as required;

- give staff an opportunity to ask questions, clarify their understanding and make constructive comment;

- generate a high level of commitment and enthusiasm for the campaign.

The depth of coverage of each of these areas, and the time devoted to them, will depend upon the level of staff knowledge and experience of the particular type of campaign. Effective briefing generally takes around two to four hours and it should be conducted as near as possible to the launch of telephone activity, so that staff are still charged with enthusiasm.

A variety of presentation and training methods may be employed in a briefing, according to the needs of the campaign, but it should include role playing – to familiarise staff with the script and give practice in objection handling, answering questions and utilising background knowledge. Background knowledge is extremely important, helping to instil staff with confidence in their ability to deal with whatever type of situation might arise during a call. Providing printed information, either specially prepared or in the form of brochures etc, is often valuable, particularly for reference, and, in some circumstances, staff may benefit from seeing products/demonstrations.

The briefing should be conducted by a senior member of the telephone marketing staff, perhaps the supervisor or project manager, who will understand more clearly the needs of telephone staff. The user may also be present, to answer any questions and/or make a short presentation.

Staff should be encouraged to take an active part in the briefing,

Table 8.8   Tips on operational and staffing factors for different telephone marketing applications

Application	Operation	Staff elements
List building/ cleaning	Call rates will vary depending on: • accuracy of list • level of decision-maker • number of contact names • 'responsibility for', rather than job titles • whether information has to be gained at switchboard or departmental level • whether additional information is required. Average call rate about 10–12 per hour. Should quality-check a minimum of 10% of calls.	Very monotonous and therefore demotivating: • concentrate the work over short periods of time or rotate teams • use incentives. The emphasis is on accuracy – spelling, handwriting/ keyboard skills – and speed. A good job to start a new caller who requires a gentle lead in. Can have an adverse effect on confident new staff if they are given a mundane task.
Market evaluation	Call rates vary tremendously, eg 3–10 per hour, depending on: • the number of questions • the complexity of answers required. Remember that this is not 'research', as the information is likely to be used later for sales and marketing purposes. It is generally best to use any computer resources available for recording/ analysing data. Plan in advance what system will be used for analysis if this is to be done manually – the format of recording can aid analysis. 'Questionnaires' will require checking, which is very time-consuming. There is a high emphasis on reporting.	Mainly uses skills in the areas of questioning, assimilating and listening. Requires maximum concentration. Requires a certain level of continuity for best results. Most callers find this an enjoyable task. All calls need to be well administered and it therefore needs a thorough and methodical approach.

Lead generation and qualification	The yield will be comparatively low, but each lead will have a high potential to convert to a sale. When appointment setting, it is important to consider other leads identified, eg an appointment in 3–6 months. Assessment of campaign effectiveness should encompass the sales ability of the field sales personnel. It is important that all involved are clear about, and agree on, what is a qualified lead, ie the parameters for screening leads. Call rates average 6 per hour. A 'comments' section in the call card is important.	Uses the majority of skills. Always use a minimum of 2 callers for comparison of results. A fairly comprehensive briefing will enhance the results. It is advisable to use experienced callers. Giving feedback to callers is of prime importance, particularly for motivational purposes. This is not a good application for which to use incentives as callers may be tempted to misgrade the potential of a lead.
Pre-mail or pre-launch	Difficult to quantify its effect and therefore it is important to ensure agreement on the expected outcome. Timings are of key importance – the wrong timing can decrease the effectiveness of the call. Call rates vary depending on market factors, eg 2–7 per hour. Call content and call card should be designed to capture maximum feedback to the call and message; this will help in drawing final conclusions. It is important to be aware of all other recent contact with the people called.	Personality counts in this type of work. The job is enjoyable and can be used as a reward/ breather. The team needs a warm-up session rather than a thorough briefing.

Appointment setting	This is more effective if there is a close working relationship between callers and the representatives. Representatives' sales areas should be clearly defined and sufficient availability must be ensured. It is best if appointments are booked no more than 2–3 weeks in advance. Callers should ascertain the length of each appointment. Requires tight lead control. Call rates vary depending on market factors, eg 3–6 per hour. It is best to run campaigns with small teams over a longer period of time. Monitor conversion rates and other responses closely, especially large numbers of literature requests and 'not interesteds'. Obtain feedback on quality from representatives, ie time-wasting appointments.	Closing techniques are critical for maximum effect. A useful job to train staff – with a combination of experienced and inexperienced callers. The job is self-motivating. If using incentives, use the team approach rather than individual incentives.

Seminar/event booking	Can be approached in two ways: 1. Call–mail–call–(catering call) 2. Mail–call–(catering call). This is not a foolproof method of guaranteeing attendance; it will only give an accurate guide if timed correctly. If the call is a follow-up to a mailing (method 1), the chances are that a free seminar or event will attract a large proportion of free-loaders. If there is a charge, or attendees require qualification, a larger number of calls will be required. Call rates on initial calls vary from 5–7 per hour, and on catering calls from 8–12 per hour. Close (hourly) monitoring of conversion rates is required to ensure that the event is not over-booked. Example response rates for a non-paying event are: * 400 unqualified leads * 200 qualified and personalised invitations sent out * 80 acceptances at catering call stage * 60 final confirmations * 50 attendees. The number of leads required is best calculated from the number of attendees required.	Initial calls are the hardest, particularly when there is a charge or attendees need to be qualified. Because of genuine fall out, these are possibly the easiest calls to 'fix', especially the catering calls; continuous taping is therefore advisable. Catering calls are easy but can be monotonous. If using method 1, it is a good idea to keep the same team and, ideally, have individuals doing their own call backs. If a manual system is being used, handwriting has to be good to ensure that invitations can be personalised accurately.

Direct selling	Campaigns run over longer periods of time are more successful.	Requires skilled/experienced callers.
	Strong links are required into distribution and production.	Full briefing is required on special offers, discounts and free trials, eg when and to whom they can be offered.
	Realistic targets should be set and agreed with the sales department; it is important to ensure that the level of return (£ for £ spent) is acceptable.	A challenging, interesting and rewarding job. Self-motivating.
	A test campaign should not be run on a commission-only basis – initial enthusiasm to earn high commission could give misleading results.	

Note: Call rates and response rates are highly dependent upon factors such as the quality of the lead source, the accessibility of the target contacts, and the complexity of the call.

answering questions posed by the leader to ensure their understanding, asking questions to clarify their role and making constructive comments where they feel the campaign could be improved. A high level of involvement helps to generate commitment.

As a result of briefing, all staff should understand clearly what it is they have to do, to what standard and by when, and be fully committed to, and enthusiastic about, achieving their personal work objectives.

Tips on applications

This is a convenient point to look at some of the operational and staffing issues that need to be considered when planning and managing specific telephone marketing applications. The charts in Table 8.8 are by no means comprehensive, but they illustrate the range of knowledge that can be brought to bear in running a successful campaign. Companies lacking experience of a particular application can improve their chances of success by consulting an agency, either to run a test or the full campaign; this also provides a valuable learning opportunity for subsequent, similar applications.

Calling commences – testing variables

Testing is the process of evaluating the effect on results of changing different campaign variables in order to use those which optimise results. It takes the form of a mini-campaign conducted prior to full launch or roll-out.

Telephone marketing testing can be used at different levels. First, it can be used to justify the use of telephone marketing as opposed to another activity, for example to test whether direct sales calls to accounts generating a certain level of revenue are more cost-effective than visits by the field sales force. At another level it can be used to determine how well different activities, such as direct mail and telephone marketing, work together. Finally, it can be used to find the optimum set of variables within a single activity or combination of activities.

The changes made to a campaign as a result of testing can range from minor alterations, such as the timing of telephone follow-up to a mailing, to a complete rethink of the campaign strategy, for example the mix of activities or the target audience. However, provided appropriate expertise has been brought to campaign planning, testing generally results in refinement rather than major strategic changes.

Continuous monitoring of results enables fine-tuning of a direct marketing campaign at any time, but it is always advisable to conduct a test before roll-out, when it becomes very costly to make anything more than minor changes. It also provides an accurate costing for the campaign, upon which roll-out may be conditional. Testing is best conducted immediately prior to roll-out, since the campaign is already up and running for the test, and the telephone marketers are into their stride.

One of the major benefits of telephone marketing is that, because of the immediacy of response, the effectiveness of different elements of a campaign can be tested and changed more quickly than other direct marketing methods. Broadly, testing enables the company to:

- determine what strategy and tactics which will be most cost-effective in achieving the campaign objectives;
- calculate the return on investment for the full campaign;
- make a limited commitment of resources until the return is known;
- obtain benchmark (ie optimum attainable) results which can be used as targets for this and similar campaigns;

- predict more accurately what resources are required and deploy them more efficiently;

- fine-tune the operational systems.

Testing inbound campaigns is conducted infrequently compared with outbound campaigns, but the need is far greater in one respect. It is vital to get a realistic estimation of the volume and rate of incoming calls that can be expected so that the number of lines and staff required can be planned effectively, ie to answer all calls without unreasonable delay, but not to have staff sitting idle waiting for the telephone to ring.

Effective testing entails a considerable amount of work and it should be written into the campaign schedule at an early stage, otherwise there will either be insufficient time to test and achieve optimum results, or roll-out will have to be delayed. The testing process can be divided into a number of stages:

- selecting variables to be tested;

- setting targets;

- selecting the test sample;

- test preparation, for example setting test conditions and establishing monitoring systems;

- collating and analysing results;

- interpreting results and making recommendations for roll-out.

If a company has a marketing database, which enables highly sophisticated testing on large numbers of variables, most of these stages can be automated – from identifying variables with the biggest impact to analysing the results of the test (marketing databases are examined in Chapter 9, pages 361–76). However, a campaign can be tested effectively without the aid of a marketing database, provided it is given sufficient thought and care. Contracting a good agency to run the test (examined in Chapter 3, pages 80–82) is another alternative which is particularly useful for companies with little experience of telephone marketing or for those planning a new application.

Selecting variables

In order to plan a test effectively it is vital, first of all, to be clear about what is being tested. Some of the key variables that can be tested are:

- list/lead source;

- geographical location;

- socio-economic factors/company type (for example market, size);

- contact level in business-to-business markets, for example influencer, specifier, decision-maker;

- marketing mix;

- offer;

- creative approach/tone;

- timings.

Within each of these areas a large number of factors can be tested and their influence on results evaluated. At the strategic level, by calculating what it costs using current methods to achieve a particular objective, such as gain a customer or make a sale, it is possible to design tests to determine whether there are more cost-efficient alternatives, for example testing direct response advertising compared with direct mail and telephone follow-up. At a more tactical level, it is possible to test business-to-business lists, for example, by measuring the results obtained by targeting contacts according to vertical market, company size or geographical location. Similarly, the influence of the offer made to consumers could be tested against socio-economic factors or the creative approach.

In an ideal world every element of a campaign would be tested and evaluated, in all combinations, but this is impractical both in terms of time and cost. What should be tested are those elements which are most likely to make a significant difference to the results achieved. The first step is to detail all the elements of the campaign and then try ranking them in order of their expected level of influence. Previous experience of similar campaigns to the same or a similar target market may help, or, if it is a new market/type of campaign/product or service, the research conducted to help plan the campaign. Examples of some of the factors which could be tested in a direct marketing campaign are shown in Table 8.9. The two most important factors in

Table 8.9 Possible variables for testing

Some direct marketing campaign variables				
Telephone marketing	*Mailing*	*Direct response advertising*	*Contact strategy*	*Pricing*
Lead sources	List sources	Media	Mix of media, eg telesales vs field sales	Discounts
Speed of reaction to leads	Offer	Positioning on page	Non-respondee follow-up	Levels, bundling
Male/female caller	Creative – letter enclosure envelope	Positioning of coupon	Segmentation of respondees by: speed of response level of interest/usage, previous contacts made	Service, maintenance agreements/ guarantees
Script approach	Timing	Length of coupon		Payment terms and period

Source: The Direct Communications PORTFOLIO, The Decisions Group, 1990.

telephone marketing are the list quality/targeting and the script or call structure.

Setting targets

Setting targets for a campaign was examined earlier in this chapter and it is basically the same for testing, except that the cost of different variables becomes more important in the calculation. Since the aim is to find the most cost-effective method of achieving a particular objective, the cost of different variables needs to be considered if the comparison of results is to have any meaning. The difference in cost between offering a 10 per cent and a 15 per cent discount, for example, would have to be made up in the value of any extra responses generated. Target response levels would therefore be different. Areas where costs are particularly important include bought-in lists, the offer, direct response media and advertisement size/duration, mix of media and pricing.

Costing the use of different variables helps to determine whether the targets that need to be achieved, to make their use cost-effective, are realistically attainable. If not, there is little value in testing them; if they are, then a target can be set.

Selecting the sample

Ideally, the test sample chosen from the marketplace should meet three criteria:

- it should enable the testing of one variable at a time;
- it should mirror the target market and market conditions of the roll-out; and
- it should be of sufficient size to provide significant and meaningful results.

If more than one variable is changed at a time it will be difficult to assess the effects of each one independently. If the test is designed to measure the effectiveness of an inbound response line compared with coupon response to direct mail, for example, then the copy, the target market and the timing should be identical for both. This can prove difficult. Two samples selected from a target market, for example, can never be identical; there will always be a variation in some of their characteristics. The answer is to try to ensure that the factors likely to have the largest impact on response rates (other than the variable being tested) are as close as possible in both samples.

There are many factors which can make it difficult to guarantee that a test will mirror the target market and market conditions. With direct response advertising, for example, it may be difficult to predict the influence of factors such as penetration and saturation of the target market. And selecting samples from contact lists must be done carefully if they are to be representative of the whole list. A random sample may not be representative unless it is of sufficient size. Markets can also change rapidly, which is one reason for testing immediately prior to roll-out.

Sample size can have a major impact on the results achieved and the perceived cost-effectiveness of different variables. The larger the sample, if chosen at random, the more likely it is to be representative of the target market, although there are practical limitations to the size of a test sample. A marketing database is very useful for selecting a representative sample of a manageable size; this is done by analysis rather than at random.

There are also other factors to be taken into account in terms of sample size. Take the example of a test of appointment booking by telephone given in Table 3.5 (page 97). A test of 25 hours resulted in a cost of £253 per appointment booked, compared with £57 for a test of 100 hours (a recommended minimum duration for testing outbound telephone marketing applications). The decision-maker contact rate and conversion rate both rise as the campaign progresses, and set-up costs are spread more widely, with the result that perceived cost-effectiveness rises. There are statistical methods of calculating an appropriate sample size under different circumstances, but common-sense estimates, taking into account the major influencing factors, will suffice.

Test preparation

A test clearly differs from roll-out in some important respects and this is reflected in the preparation. In particular, the recording, monitoring and control systems need to be more comprehensive. Once the test conditions have been established they must be monitored to identify any changes which occur during the test and, where possible, controlled. If callers fall behind in following up coupon responses, for example, the delay could influence the results. This change can be controlled by stepping up the number of callers, although this will have to be accounted for in the subsequent cost/benefit analysis.

Some changes cannot be accommodated, however, and these will have to be noted so that their impact can be assessed when the test results are analysed. Recording systems, together with those for collating and monitoring results, must therefore be designed to capture information on all the campaign variables which could impact upon results. In addition, of course, data must be captured to enable a calculation of the cost-effectiveness of the different variables being tested, as well as any information which could help with further refinement of a variable, such as responses to scripted questions. A clear understanding of why a variable is being tested helps to determine what data must be captured.

The selection of telephone staff to conduct a test is also an important factor in setting the test conditions. Where two teams are testing different variables, for example, they must be comparable in their collective ability, otherwise any differences in results cannot be attributed solely to the effect of the variable.

Collating and analysing results

Once a test is under way, and some results have been collated, there may be a temptation to opt for immediate roll-out or to discard a particular variable. This would negate much of the rationale behind the design of the test and should be resisted. Even if the final decision is negative, the cost of the full test is justified by the value of the detailed information gathered, which can be used in planning future activity.

When the full results have been collated, the actual test conditions should be compared with those planned to determine whether any changes occurred which could have influenced the results. These must be taken into account when the results are analysed.

Analysis of the results of anything more than a very simple test can require complex statistical techniques, but there are software applications packages available (dedicated statistical packages and standard spreadsheets) which automate this process. A marketing database with testing facilities, if available, will also analyse results automatically.

Interpretation and recommendation

Analysis of the test results, showing planned/actual targets and cost/benefits, may provide a clear indication of which variables should be implemented at roll-out. Results may not be clear cut, however, and decisions may have to be made based on subjective value judgements, or the results may pose more questions than they answer and the best course of action will be further testing.

The more variables that are tested, the more difficult it is generally to interpret the results and make recommendations for changes, if any, prior to roll-out or further testing. There are always pitfalls for the unwary, and considerable experience in the appropriate field is required to make the best use of test results. An obvious trap is to identify two variables which, independently, produced results exceeding the target, and to recommend that they are combined at roll-out. Although the test results may be reproduced, or even exceeded, under some circumstances there are situations where the reverse is true. It is important that recommendations for changes are made with reference not only to the test results, but also to the rationale behind the use of particular variables. At a very simple level, for example, questions from two scripts may seek to achieve the call objective in different ways. If they are mixed because of the test results obtained, the logical call structure may be destroyed. If there is any doubt about a particular interpretation of results then a further test should be designed rather than risk disaster at roll-out.

Thorough testing is cost-effective, despite the work involved, particularly for large-scale campaigns. It is also an investment in the future development of the telephone marketing operation. Setting up a library of test results creates a valuable resource to help build continuously on previous successes.

Once a satisfactory test has been conducted and all the preparation work has been completed, such as the revision of documentation and work scheduling, the campaign is ready to be rolled out. Despite the success of a test, however, it is essential to monitor the campaign continuously , and take action as appropriate, to ensure that the results being achieved on a continuing basis compare favourably with the benchmarks set during testing.

Campaign monitoring and control

Once a campaign is under way there are many factors which can influence the results achieved, ranging from staff becoming bored with a monotonous task to external influences such as strikes and changes in the marketplace. Optimum results will only be maintained if the campaign is closely monitored and controlled, until its completion, to ensure that work progresses as planned and, if not, to take appropriate action.

It has been stressed earlier that telephone marketing provides an ideal environment for monitoring and control of work activities, and the systems and methods used have been examined in detail elsewhere (in particular, the use of 'Operational systems' in Chapter 4; 'Monitoring performance' in Chapter 6; and 'Motivation' in Chapter 7). In summary, the range of activities involved, carried out variously by telephone marketing executives, team leaders, supervisors and managers, includes:

- ongoing gathering and collation of calling statistics, for example call/decision-maker contact/conversation rates;

- monitoring individual and team performance, for example call handling, achievement of call objectives, calling statistics;

- quality checking
  - recalling a percentage of contacts (usually around 10 per cent)

- checking all call records for quality and minimum standards of information;

- monitoring achievement of targets and deadlines;

- staff de-briefing, often held for the first time on the second day of the campaign;

- fine-tuning the campaign, as appropriate;

- regular assessment of progress against planned targets, and costs where appropriate;

- adjusting targets as required, for example raising them if they are being exceeded consistently;

- reporting and analysis – planned and ad hoc as required;

- resource monitoring and control, for example
  - stepping up/down the number of callers
  - revising schedules, such as concentrating calls when decision-makers are most easily contacted;

- motivating staff;

- on-the-job training.

De-briefing is particularly important, both as a means of identifying possible ways of improving the campaign and by encouraging staff commitment by enabling them to contribute their ideas and therefore ultimately affect their own results. A de-briefing is basically a brainstorming session where the team(s) and the supervisor or manager use their experience of the campaign so far, such as call rates and contacts' reactions to the call content, to come up with ideas for fine-tuning it. Sometimes the user will also take part. One or two sessions are commonly held, often on the afternoon of the second and third days of the campaign.

The success of each of the activities listed above in helping to maintain optimum results is naturally dependent upon the skills of the people carrying them out. Within companies where telephone marketing is coming to play a more prominent role in the sales and marketing strategy there is increasing emphasis being placed on the quality of human resources. While operational systems provide the framework for gathering data on performance, it is the skill of staff in utilising these systems that determines the success of a campaign. The importance of building the skills resource within a telephone marketing unit has important implications for how monitoring and control is conducted. A short-sighted view would be to consider the results of a campaign as the be-all and end-all. Equal consideration must be given to the development of individual staff members and the team as a whole. It is during a campaign that the most valuable learning opportunities arise, and skilled supervision and management is required to make the most of these opportunities and thus help to guarantee the success of future campaigns.

Campaign completion – analysis and reporting

The end of a campaign presents an opportunity for both the user and telephone marketing management to learn a great deal. One of the things to come out of the briefing process is a specification of precisely what information the user wants about and from a campaign, which is contained in one or more final reports prepared by the telephone marketing unit. In addition, telephone marketing management will often prepare internal reports to help improve efficiency in terms of both campaign design and operations.

What it is possible to include in a user report is obviously determined by the information captured during a campaign, for example via a script. It is also influenced by the positioning of the telephone marketing unit within the company. They may not be able to produce a full cost/benefit analysis, for example, in a campaign involving other sales and marketing activities. Similarly, detailed analysis of a database-driven campaign will often be a separate function, in which case a report may be prepared *for* telephone marketing management. The task of analysing results is made easier by the design of efficient operational systems, whether these are automated, such as computerised telephone marketing linked into a marketing database, or whether they rely upon human analytical skills.

Basic information in a final report to a user might consist of the following.

Introduction

- background to the campaign;
- the target market, source and number of leads;
- aims and objectives;

- targets – expected call and conversion rates and campaign duration;
- the budget.

Results

- changes implemented during the campaign, with reasons;
- breakdown of effective calls by coding (number and percentage of total);
- analysis of results/conversion rates by coding (number and percentage of total);
- breakdown of results by response to scripted questions (type of response, number and percentage of total);
- analysis of costs – per call and effective call.

Conclusion

- achieved targets – call and conversion rates, number of effective calls;
- non-effective calls and leads – factors contributing to achieved targets, for example number of leads available, number searches, prospect unavailability;
- summary and prospect attitude towards campaign – reflections on the campaign and what contributed to its success etc;
- analysis of job titles and business types;
- recommendations for future contact strategies and tactics;
- tables and graphic analyses.

This information, although comparatively basic, can provide valuable information to help plan future sales and marketing activities. In a campaign run for a building society, for example, the question was asked, 'What factors did you consider/are you considering with regard to taking out a mortgage at another bank or building society apart from *name?*'. The results showed that the top four factors, in order of priority, were the interest rate being offered; a special deal or discount; recommendation; and convenience. This provides a clear indication of the type of marketing strategy that is likely to appeal to this group of prospects. Similarly, responses to questions about how prospects became aware of the company would provide information on levels of awareness created by different marketing activities. An analysis of how callers felt prospects reacted to the call also provides information on the acceptability of the method(s) of communication used.

While computerised systems are a great boon to analysing work activities, for example inbound call patterns and staff response times, simple paper-based systems can be designed to capture data on almost any type of activity, provided it is considered at the planning stage. The importance of early specification of what information needs to be captured cannot be underestimated. Ultimately, detailed analysis and reporting, combined with documentation on the planning process itself, provides the basis upon which future successes will be built.

The close of a campaign should be taken as an opportunity to give staff due praise and thanks for their efforts and, together, to review their work on the campaign as a learning exercise.

Companies new to telephone marketing should not be daunted by the extensive planning and level of expertise required to mount a successful campaign. As an alternative to recruiting the necessary expertise, external resources are widely available to help companies over this first hurdle. The extensive documentation which results from a campaign, for example initial research data, the operational systems and results, then enables it to be repeated again and again. Taking advantages of the training courses in telephone marketing management available from some agencies will help to develop the in-house resource. As staff expertise grows, the company will be able to exploit its knowledge of its own business and marketplace in the refinement of earlier campaigns, and the development of new ones, becoming increasingly less reliant on external services.

9

Development and Growth

Telephone marketing is a fast-moving industry and companies using the medium cannot afford to be complacent, even in the face of past successes. Simply in terms of efficiency and productivity there is always room for some improvement, for example by developing a more highly skilled and motivated workforce, improving campaign planning and management, and streamlining operational systems. On the broader scene, telephone marketers are refining techniques, developing new applications to take advantage of market opportunities, devising more tightly integrated marketing strategies to optimise the value of each element in the marketing mix, and capitalising on new information technologies to improve efficiency and aid innovation.

Telephone marketing is a dynamic medium and companies should be constantly reappraising how they can best deploy and develop their resources to achieve maximum benefit, whether these are in-house, at an agency, or both. Some of the key areas for consideration are:

- developing applications and exploiting opportunities;

- improving information management;

- developing and using a marketing database;

- telecommunications.

It is worth while re-emphasising here that, under most circumstances, telephone marketing agencies who regularly undertake a broad cross-section of work for clients in different markets are the richest source of expertise on how best to exploit the medium. With in-house operations, however large and sophisticated they may be, there is inevitably a tendency towards focusing on what is happening in the company's own markets. Cross-fertilisation between methods and techniques used in widely different markets is an important source of ideas for innovative and profitable applications. Working with an agency, even on an occasional basis, can help to prevent the company becoming blinkered to opportunities. As telephone marketing becomes a staple in the marketing mix, it will be the companies breaking new ground who will remain ahead of the competition.

Developing applications and exploiting opportunities

Given the flexibility of telephone marketing and a constantly changing market environment, there are always opportunities for companies to enhance the way they are using the medium. These can be divided, arbitrarily, into five groups.

New applications These are applications chosen because telephone marketing has proved to be the most cost-effective way, or the only way, of achieving a particular objective.

Improving the effectiveness of current applications The majority of this book is devoted to ensuring that efficiency and productivity are maintained at an optimum level. This can range from more effective recruitment, training and motivation of staff, to continuous testing of elements of a campaign to determine the most effective combination.

Complementary applications Many applications can be run more efficiently when they work hand-in-hand. First, individual calls can achieve more than one objective and so some applications can be combined. Lead generation and qualification calls, for example, can be used to contribute to building and maintaining a database simply by adapting the call structure to incorporate appropriate information-gathering objectives. Secondly, simple applications working in combination can help to achieve higher level objectives. Appointment setting and servicing customer accounts, for example, can be incorporated into a customer care or loyalty-building programme.

Integrating telephone marketing with other activities The use of telephone marketing to improve the efficiency of other individual sales and marketing activities has been examined in Chapter 2. However, its complete integration into the sales and marketing strategy provides the highest level of benefits and is a major trend in the industry.

Opportunist applications These can include tactical applications, such as capitalising on a competitor's price increase, and more long-term, strategic applications, such as exploiting a new market trend. Some of the other applications that may be classed as opportunist include those designed to take advantage of, or minimise the damaging effects of:

- market events, for example new products and services, new entrants into the market;

- 'crises', for example product failures and contamination, takeover bids, disputes affecting key customers;

- changes in corporate strategy, for example distribution policy, account handling;

- changes in legislation, for example tightening of restrictions on above-the-line advertising.

The range of opportunities for exploiting telephone marketing is enormous, but recognising and exploiting them requires companies to be constantly aware of the potential of the medium. Many opportunist applications, for example, benefit from contingency planning so that campaigns can be implemented quickly when the opportunities arise. Similarly, establishing a marketing database, when taken in isolation, is a huge commitment. Considered in the long term, however, as a driving force and analytical tool for exploiting market opportunities, it is almost essential in today's competitive marketplace.

Companies also need to look outside for new opportunities. There is a growing trend towards non-competing companies collaborating, for example, in areas such as joint promotions and developing a marketing database as a shared resource.

It is also important to keep an eye on trends in the telephone marketing industry and related areas, particularly in terms of what competitors are doing. Research commissioned by the Colorgraphic Group* on the UK direct response industry predicts the following trends during the period 1990 to 1995:

- the greatest growth will be in the telephone marketing and computer package (for direct marketing) sectors;

---

* *Direct Response – The Market Map*, a quantitative analysis of the UK direct response industry, 1990. Commissioned from Research Associates by the Colorgraphic Group.

- the Single European Market is seen as the major growth opportunity for companies supplying direct mail and telephone marketing services;

- the most promising sectors for growth within telephone marketing (agencies) are database development and customer care;

- within database development there are opportunities to develop psychographic databases (these will be explained in the next section);

- inbound consumer calling (handled by agencies) is likely to increase as more retailers and fast-moving consumer goods companies turn to direct response;

- there is growing interest in international outbound telephone marketing campaigns;

- there are opportunities for improved business, international and specialist lists, to meet the trend towards niche marketing.

New entrants to telephone marketing obviously cannot take advantage of all the opportunities at once, but those who have not even started to use the medium have probably already been left behind by the competition. Building up the necessary resources is a gradual process. Many companies, having started with a single application and having recognised the potential, now consider telephone marketing as an integral part of their plans for business development. Table 9.1 shows how a company might develop this resource. Not all companies decide to set up an in-house operation, but among those that do there are many who also use agency resources. Agencies remain the most accessible route for any company wanting to enter the fast moving world of telephone marketing. Large numbers of companies who have sampled success in this way then go on to develop their own telephone marketing resources.

Information management

The potential

Throughout the 1980s growing recognition of the potential value of long-term customers encouraged many companies to concentrate more and more of their resources on direct communications. With

Table 9.1 Example development of a company's telephone marketing operations

	Phase one	Phase two	Phase three
New applications	Lead generation and qualification; Appointment setting/diary management	Prospecting; Back-up servicing of customer accounts; List building, cleaning and testing; Building and maintaining a database; Market research and test marketing	Customer care/loyalty building; Response handling; Opportunist tactical (eg crisis management) and strategic (eg responding to market trends) applications
Resources	Applications serviced by an agency	Agency does list work and market research; in-house unit established to service remaining applications	Agency provides the capacity for opportunist tactical work and handles direct response calls; in-house handles remaining applications
Integration	Liaison with the sales force	Personalised mailings sent out by the in-house unit	Direct response advertising used to generate calls to the agency; database-driven direct communications programme established by the in-house unit

advances in database technology they were able to exploit detailed customer and prospect information, using timely, personalised communications to help build long-term relationships and realise their lifetime value. The ability to measure costs per result accurately proved highly desirable at a time when marketing departments were coming under increasing pressure to become more accountable.

Continued advances in information technology, combined with falling computing costs, are likely to revolutionise the management of sales and marketing information in the 1990s. Automation of many aspects of gathering, managing and exploiting market information offers the prospect of greater efficiency and productivity, together with improved decision-making leading to better strategic use of sales and marketing resources.

Production costs in manufacturing industries have already been slashed by automation. Moriarty and Swartz of Harvard University have noted* that, as a result of automation, direct labour costs now account for only 8 to 12 per cent of production costs. Michael Dell, founder of the US personal computer manufacturer, Dell Corporation, commented in an interview with the *Financial Times*† that, 'There is so little labour content in our product that even if we used robots provided free it would hardly affect our costs'. Further savings on production labour costs therefore offer little scope for increasing profitability, whereas automation of sales and marketing activities, which account for an average 15 to 35 per cent of total corporate costs, offers enormous potential.

Among the examples of marketing automation cited by Moriarty and Swartz are a US$7bn electronics manufacturer and a US$8m printing company, both of which achieved a first-year return on their investment of more than 100 per cent. The printing company, for example, invested US$80,000 in a minicomputer and telephone marketing software; the result was a 25 per cent increase in sales and investment payback in less than six months. Despite the obvious potential for improving productivity, the authors write that, 'Few companies have automated any part of their marketing and sales functions. Even fewer appear to understand the significant strategic benefits that can accrue from marketing and sales automation.'

A wide range of software packages is already available for automating tasks in areas such as telephone marketing, direct mail and sales and marketing management; many of these are relatively inexpensive and the enormous power and low cost of modern personal computers means that even the smallest companies can automate at least some of their sales and marketing activities. Although the full benefits of automation are achieved when it integrates an organisation's entire sales and marketing operation, the

---

* Reprinted by permission of the *Harvard Business Review*. Excerpt from 'Automation to Boost Sales and Marketing' by Rowland T Moriarty and Gordon S Swartz (January–February 1989). Copyright 1989 by the President and Fellows of Harvard College.
† *Financial Times*, 20 September 1990.

process can start with single activities such as planned telephone marketing campaigns. There are several excellent software packages incorporating telephone activity which provide an environment for integrated information management (*see*, for example, the features of TOPCAT, page 70, and Pro.file, page 168).

At the core of these systems, which Moriarty and Swartz call marketing and sales productivity (MSP) systems, is the marketing database (examined in more detail in the next section). Access to the data held enables sales and marketing personnel to optimise the value of every contact they have with customers and prospects. Anyone in a company talking to customers on the telephone, for example, could instantly access data about them, to personalise the conversation, and update the information as necessary. Any person with access to the system who makes contact with that customer even minutes later would have access to the new data. A fully integrated system would gather information from all sales and marketing activities, building historic records of all contact made with every customer and prospect. As the data is continuously enriched and refined it becomes increasingly useful as a tool for planning and driving sales and marketing activities (as an example, *see* Table 9.4 on page 370).

Automation boosts productivity by improving the efficiency of sales and marketing personnel, and by increasing the effectiveness of marketing communications. Moriarty and Swartz point out that 'efficiencies gained through task automation and improved marketing management are interdependent and reinforcing'. Task automation results in the collection of more complete market information which management can then use to make more informed decisions about how to deploy sales and marketing resources more efficiently and maximise profitability.

Grasping the opportunity

So how does a company go about automating sales and marketing activities? First, throwing money at the problem is not the solution. Planning is the key to achieving the best results, not the level of investment, and this requires a re-evaluation of the management of sales and marketing activities. The fundamental issue is information management.

We will take the telephone as an example. How many companies are realising the full potential of the telephone contact they have with their customers and prospects? Any contact in a sales or marketing context provides an opportunity for a profitable dialogue, for example queries on deliveries or accounts, credit control, service requests and complaints, as well as traditional sales and telephone marketing activities. The first step in making efficient use of sales and marketing resources is to maximise these opportunities, for example by:

- setting minimum standards of information which must be gathered from each type of contact (bearing in mind the needs of all those who may want to access and use the information subsequently);

- establishing a system for recording this information in a standard format, storing it and making it readily accessible to those who could make profitable use of it in their contact with customers and prospects;

- establishing a tracking system and contact strategies which determine when and how customers and prospects will be contacted, according to the data held about them;

- developing ways of analysing the data held to help plan marketing strategies and tactics;

- helping staff to acquire the knowledge, skills and attitudes required to make the best use of the resources available to them.

All contact with customers and prospects should be rationalised by addressing these types of issues, laying down rules and guidelines for gathering, managing and exploiting information. There are many opportunities for automating individual elements of this type of system, but the full benefit is achieved by having all activities linked via a central database which sits in the background. Modern information management systems are highly flexible so that the front end can be designed to suit individual roles. A telephone marketing executive, for example, would use the system in a different way to a credit controller or a regional sales executive, but they would each be accessing and feeding information into the same database. The managers of various sales and marketing functions would similarly draw on this central resource, which is being continuously updated.

There are huge benefits of economy and synergy in establishing this type of integrated system. The strategic use of telephone marketing, exemplified by some of the case studies in Chapter 11, is one example of the effectiveness of the information management approach. Rapid growth in the use of strategic telephone marketing at the beginning of the 1990s suggests that more and more companies are recognising the fundamental importance of an overall strategy for gathering, managing, and exploiting customer and prospect information. Automation plays a key role in the success of such a strategy and appears to offer sales and marketing departments their biggest opportunity, and challenge, for the 1990s.

Developing and using a marketing database

Here is a piece of information – 9365 – which is of no particular value to you until you know how to use it. To me it has a very real value as it is my Barclaycard PIN number. A simple illustration of the point that information is only effective when you know what it can be used for. . . .

Consider a database as an inert, lifeless beast. What breathes life into it, from my point of view, is its use as part of a direct marketing campaign or strategy.

Glenn Hurley, marketing director of The Decisions Group

With increasing competition to find, acquire and keep customers, more efficient targeting of marketing communications, making the right offer, to the right people, at the right time, has become the key to profitability. One of the factors which has stimulated the growth of database marketing (Table 9.2) is the increasing fragmentation of

Table 9.2 Factors stimulating the growth of database marketing

Why database marketing has evolved
• Mass markets breaking down into segments
• Media fragmentation and differentiation
• Increasing recognition of customer value
• Need for accountability
• More confidence in direct marketing methods
• Decreasing cost of computer technology
• Increasing cost of television advertising (production and airtime)
• Increasing competition/competitive threat

markets, creating a greater diversity of buying groups with different needs, tastes and aspirations. Direct marketing has grown rapidly because, unlike mass marketing media, it enables companies to communicate personally with individuals, and to show that they recognise and can cater for these differences.

Telephone marketing, like other direct marketing methods, is more cost-effective and profitable the more accurately it is targeted. Good targeting is essential for taking advantage of its benefits (for example personal and flexible) and minimising or avoiding its drawbacks (for example comparatively high cost and low volume, intrusive). Whether the application is inbound (for example taking calls stimulated by press advertisements) or outbound (for example setting appointments with prospects), the more the company knows about the target audience, the more effective calls become. One of the earliest stages in planning a campaign is researching the target market and sourcing contact details and, in the longer term, building a marketing database is the most efficient way of doing this.

The marketing database has evolved as a tool for helping to gather, store, manage and analyse data about customers and prospects to automate the targeting process. At the same time it has greatly increased the opportunities for exploiting market information in direct marketing. Companies building a marketing database should note, however, that the gathering, storage and use of personal data in the UK, as in many other countries, is governed by the Data Protection Act 1984 (*see* Chapter 10, 390–92).

While a database alone can be considered 'an inert, lifeless beast', in use it is a dynamic resource which is continuously evolving. Developing and using a marketing database can be divided into a number of broad, interdependent processes:

- building the database;

- customer profiling and segmenting the database;

- sourcing new contacts;

- exploiting the database.

The symbiotic relationship between the telephone and the marketing database has already been examined in Chapter 2 (*see* pages 44–5); the remainder of this section looks at some of the ways in which customer and prospect data can be acquired and exploited.

Building the database

The inherent value of a marketing database rests in its composition of accurate, relevant data; using inappropriate or inaccurate data wastes marketing resources and can lead to heavy losses, both financially and in terms of customer confidence. The planning involved in establishing a database, outlined in Chapter 4 (on pages 167–72), includes answering two key questions: 'What information will the database hold?'; and 'Where will the information be obtained?'. The criterion for deciding what information to gather should be its value (or potential value) to the company in planning and driving its sales and marketing activities. A database can hold an enormous range and volume of information on consumers and/or businesses, but it is wasteful of resources and inefficient to store data of little value.

A newly established database will usually consist of information collated from various parts of the organisation to form individual records for each customer (past and present), and each prospect (such as from enquiries) etc. Subsequently, every contact with these people, by telephone, sales visits, mail, coupons etc, should be exploited in a planned and controlled way to gather, update and exploit database information (the importance of this strategy has already been highlighted in the previous section on information management). A reactive approach, utilising normal contact opportunities such as incoming enquiries, is obviously less expensive than proactive methods such as cold calling, and telephone contact provides the most valuable opportunity for obtaining precisely the information required because of the flexibility of the dialogue.

Details of new contacts will obviously be required to help obtain new customers and develop new markets. There are several different sources of this type of information, such as commercial databases and lists (this will be examined later), but the company needs to be able to calculate the potential value of these prospects if contacting them is going to be cost-effective. This is achieved by profiling existing good customers (ie noting their characteristics) and using this information to choose the best sources of prospect names. Profiling also enables the existing database to be segmented so that different 'value' contacts can be identified automatically; combined with their profile characteristics this helps to plan the most cost-effective way of exploiting their value.

Customer profiling and segmenting the database

A marketing database's *raison d'être* is to help find, acquire and keep customers, and the first step is to use it to identify the characteristics of a 'customer'. By analysing the data held on customers it is possible to identify their relative value to the company, using criteria such as how much they spend, how often, what they buy and what proportion of their budget for that type of product or service they spend with the company. By also analysing the characteristics of the best customers, such as (for businesses) the size of the company, their vertical market or business type, and geographical location, and (for consumers) age, sex, hobbies and lifestyle etc, it is possible to define a 'user profile' for each product or service.

The company now knows who its best customers are and what characterises them, so other people showing these characteristics could also possibly become good customers given the right encouragement. However, there may be a large number of criteria which determine customer value and not all good customers will necessarily exhibit the same set of characteristics. A method is needed which will distinguish the relative importance of these criteria in determining the customer's tendency to buy. This is achieved by assigning a points value to each of the chosen characteristics, for example more points for regular than irregular purchases, less points for companies in industries that use less of a product than others and so on.

Every customer can be analysed in this way, a process known as 'scoring' the database, so that their overall score represents their value to the company. Now the database can be analysed and divided into market segments representing different levels of customer value. Even though a large number of characteristics may be scored on a huge number of contacts, analysis is quick and straightforward because the process is automated by scoring.

A market segment is simply a group of buyers or prospects sharing common characteristics, influencing their propensity to buy, which differentiate them from other groups. Segmentation of the database turns it into a very powerful tool for targeting marketing communications. The characteristics of high-value customers in one segment, for example, could be used to identify potential customers for the same products or services from commercially available lists. Similarly, as the database is developed, another segment may consist of prospects who use a competitor's products and could be targeted with a special offer on the company's products.

However, segmentation is neither static nor clearly defined. Individual contacts may fall into three or four segments, for example, because they score highly on the key criteria used to define those segments. The scoring of contacts on different criteria, and their segmentation, also fluctuates dynamically as new information about them is added to the database. If a prospect company has opened a new manufacturing plant, for example, its scoring on criteria such as the number of employees and total budget for a product can change. Responses to sales and marketing approaches recorded on the database will have a similar effect.

In addition, the marketplace is in a state of constant flux and the effectiveness of a particular segmentation for targeting can alter with changes in tastes, the social climate, affluence, the availability of improved products and so on. All of these changes in scoring reflect changes in customers' value and the way in which the next communication with them should be planned and executed. So effective segmentation is a process of continuous refinement, testing the results of using different clusters of profiling criteria to segment the database and target specific marketing activities.

There are, however, a number of standard ways of profiling and segmenting buyers for targeting which have developed within the direct marketing industry. These include:

- **geographic** – targeting is based on location, for example by region and postal code;

- **demographic** – where socio-economic factors such as age and status are used to identify suitable contacts;

- **geodemographic** – which combines the targeting criteria used in geographic and demographic methods;

- **psychographic** – where lifestyle or behavioural data is overlaid on geodemographic data (also known as psychodemographic targeting).

The methods which provide the most accurate targeting are first psychographic and then geodemographic profiling. There are a number of widely known proprietary geodemographic profiling systems for the consumer market, such as Mosaic, Acorn and PiN, which companies can use to segment their own database.

The growing importance of more accurate targeting is reflected in the Colorgraphic research predictions of a shift in market share for

Table 9.3 Predicted changes in profiling methods employed within database development and management in the direct response industry

Profiling method	Market share (%)	
	1989	1995
Demographic	29	20
Geographic	29	20
Geodomographic	29	20
Psychographic	13	40

Source: Direct Response – the Market Map. Reprinted with permission

different profiling methods (Table 9.3). The trend towards niche marketing is a major driving force behind the predicted growth in the use of psychographic profiling methods.

The most valuable method of profiling is one tailored to the company's own business, taking into account its products and services, operational structure, markets and business development plans. Modern information technology enables companies using such bespoke profiling methods still to utilise external data sources employing different profiling methods. Commercial organisations maintaining databases and providing contact lists use profiling methods of different levels of sophistication, but, chosen carefully, using the company's own knowledge of its user profiles, these can be an excellent source of new contacts.

Sourcing new contacts

Once a company has segmented its database, it has a valuable tool for identifying the best sources of new contacts with appropriate characteristics. These sources are targeted with varying precision and one of the factors that may be important in selection is what type of marketing activity will be used initially to target them. A more accurately targeted list would be required for telephone marketing than for an inexpensive mailing, for example, because of the comparatively higher cost. Conversely, a source may be selected and then an appropriate marketing activity chosen according to the potential value of the contacts.

Where the company has decided on a particular marketing activity, then obviously the chosen source must provide the information on contacts required for that activity. Many mailing lists, for example, do not include all or, in some cases, any contacts' telephone numbers, and could not be used for telephone marketing without number searching. In the past this has been labour-intensive and was therefore very expensive. However, with the advent of Phone Base, Phone Disc and Electronic Yellow Pages from British Telecom (*see* page 378), this process can be automated, although not all contacts on the list may be listed in the directory and the matching process will still require valuable computer time.

The overall cost of acquiring the data required is obviously an important consideration, whatever its source. The accuracy and quality of data is generally reflected in the price, whether it is from renting a select mailing list or the cost of placing a direct response advertisement in a highly targeted trade magazine. It should be borne in mind that a short but expensive list of highly targeted contacts could be more valuable to the user than a longer, less expensive list which is poorly targeted.

Another factor which must be considered in the selection of data, particularly on consumers, is whether the data provider has complied with the Data Protection Act 1984 in the gathering and storage of the data, and whether it can be used for the purpose which the company intends (the implications of the Act for telephone marketers are explained in Chapter 10, pages 391–2). If the data is to be used for a mailing then it is pertinent to ask whether it is cleaned against the Mailing Preference Service database, and for telephone marketing whether it is cleaned against the Telephone Preference Service database, when it becomes operational (*see* Chapter 10, pages 394–5).

Three important questions should be asked of all suppliers of contact data (this applies equally, by the way, to internal sources of contacts): 'What was the original source of the data (for example membership forms, questionnaires)?'; 'When was it gathered initially?'; 'How often is the information updated?'.

In the BDMA survey* of the agency sector of the UK telephone marketing industry, the sources of lists of prospects and customers

---

* *Survey of the UK Telephone Marketing Industry* (1988), prepared by the Telephone Marketing Committee of the British Direct Marketing Association, 1990.

cited by respondents were, in order of frequency mentioned: computerised databases; other databases; direct mail response; list brokers; directories; and press leads.

Databases There are a growing number of psychographically profiled consumer databases, such as the National Consumer Database, Lifestyle Selector and BehaviourBank, built by specialist companies who use questionnaires to gather data regularly from millions of households across the UK. The National Consumer Database, maintained by ICD Limited, for example, holds information on 43 million individuals and 22 million households (in 1990), including data on the people, their homes, wealth, location and lifestyle. Detailed classification of consumers enables users of these databases to identify prospects most likely to buy their products and where to contact them. In the business-to-business market the number of commercial databases is also growing, and these use various profiling criteria such as vertical market, company structure and decision-maker authority.

'Mailing' lists The market in renting (and occasionally selling) lists of consumer or business names and addresses for direct marketing has grown rapidly in recent years. According to the Colorgraphic research, the volume in the UK market in 1989 was 1,000 million names. Lists are available either directly from list owners (such as professional organisations), compilers or list brokers.* In July 1990 there were reportedly more than 4,200 commercially available business and consumer mailing lists in the UK.†

Lists vary enormously in size, from many millions down to about a dozen names, but the number of names on individual lists is decreasing in line with the trend towards more accurate targeting and the ability of the industry to provide more selective lists.

Directories There is a wide range of publications providing a wealth of information on businesses and, of course, the telephone directories

---

* The UK professional body representing list brokers is the British List Brokers' Association (address in Appendix C).
† The Direct Marketing Organisation maintains a database of mailing lists available for rental in the UK which is hired out to direct marketing companies (address in Appendix C). There are also a number of other companies providing information on available lists, including the BDMA.

for consumers and businesses. Trade directories, such as *Kompass* and *Kelly's*, include details of a large number of UK companies, including the names of selected personnel and their function. Similar publications are available for many other countries.

Random dialling of consumers from telephone directories is not recommended. It is used for direct selling by less reputable companies, but it has a very low success rate and can easily damage a company's image, as well as that of the telephone marketing industry as a whole. The BDMA Telephone Marketing Guidelines (Appendix B, pages 443–5) states that 'sales and marketing calls should not be generated by random or sequential dialling manually or by computer'. Telephone directories are useful, however, for number searching when targeted contact lists are incomplete.

Targeted media advertising The UK direct response advertising market grew by 91 per cent between 1985 and 1989, according to the Colorgraphic research, and is expected to increase by 62 per cent from 1989 to 1995. The market share of the different media is predicted to change little during this period; in 1989 the figures for the major sectors were radio – 13 per cent, television – 27 per cent, and newspapers and magazines (off-the-page) – 60 per cent. Posters and the cinema account for a tiny proportion of the total market.

There are thousands of opportunities for using the media, particularly in the trade and special interest magazine sectors, to stimulate responses by mail and/or telephone from consumers and businesses. The media operators, in general, can supply highly detailed data on the audiences they reach, which companies can use to identify their most promising target audience.

Other sources There are a variety of other sources of contacts which may be valuable under different circumstances. These include professional organisations, trade bodies, and consumer and trade exhibitions. The organisers of trade exhibitions generally produce lists of exhibitors and visitors which can be purchased. With the increasing segmentation of this market, these lists can be a valuable source of contact details.

Whatever source or sources of information are used, it is vital that the data acquired is processed, both to avoid duplication and to improve targeting. Duplication is one of the quickest ways to destroy the effectiveness of a mailing or telephone call, whether it is to the

Table 9.4 Example uses for a marketing database

Uses for a marketing database
• Customer/prospect profiling and contact targeting • Market segmentation • Lead generation, qualification and tracking • Identifying prospects • Accessing complete customer histories • Testing variables to enhance effectiveness and determine optimum marketing mix • Sales and marketing activity prompts • Sales force diary management • Pre-call briefing of sales team • Maximising face-to-face selling time • Generating contact correspondence and reports • Response/results analysis and cost management • Prediction of campaign response rates • Tracking and analysing contact histories • Targeting use of resources according to known value of customers/prospects • Sales territory planning • Account monitoring, eg re-order cycles, contract renewals, repeat purchases, opportunities for cross-selling and upselling, usage of competitors • Sales personnel and third party (eg distributors, agents) performance and target monitoring • Tracking sales and marketing effectiveness • Analysis of market trends locally and nationally • Market testing • Customer loyalty programmes • Product/service development through analysis of customer feedback • Developing new products and services to offer customers • Identifying new market opportunities • Data-driven strategies for integrated marketing • Reporting for long-term development

same person or two or more 'related' people in a company or household. In addition, of course, the sourced data may include contacts already on the company's database whom it may not be appropriate to treat in the same way as new contacts.

Newly acquired lists should be merged with each other, and the existing database, and purged of duplicate and irrelevant information. Different methods of de-duplication can be tested, sorting on any combination of data that suits the company's objective for the contacts.

Exploiting the database

Some of the applications of a marketing database are listed in Table 9.4, but database technology has advanced almost to a point where the potential applications are limited only by the imagination of those developing and using it.

Referring back to the 'ladder of loyalty' in Chapter 2 (page 74), the overall aim of database marketing can be viewed as identifying suspects, and then establishing and maintaining a personalised dialogue with them to drive them up the ladder so that they become prospects, then customers, then clients and finally advocates. At each step of the way, the relationship with the individual is monitored, and knowledge of them is used to prompt, plan and deliver a timely, personalised marketing message to maximise their value at every opportunity.

Analysis of the database enables a company to determine the most cost-effective method of communicating with each market segment (for example face-to-face, telephone marketing or direct mail), according to the objective of the communication (for example qualify/screen a lead, provide product information or close a sale) and the potential value of contacts within the segment. An example of how different methods of communication may be planned in this way is shown in Table 9.5. Of course, factors other than customer value influence this system; geographical location, for example, may make it impractical to have regular face-to-face contact with some high-value customers; the type and range of products or services the company supplies, its pricing structures, and many other factors may also influence the choice of communication channels. The database helps to analyse the relevant criteria to determine the most appropriate course of action.

At a simple level, a knowledge of existing customers can be used to

Table 9.5 Example of using different methods of communication according to the potential value of the contact and the objective of the communication

Potential value	High	Medium	Low
Objective **Generate lead**	Direct mail	Direct mail	Direct mail
Qualify/ screen lead	Telephone marketing	Telephone marketing	Direct mail
Pre-hype for sale	Face-to-face	Telephone marketing	Direct mail
Close sale	Face-to-face	Telephone marketing	Direct mail

help identify good prospects and to determine the type of approach that might encourage them to make their first purchase. If a customer buys a certain product from the company infrequently, but is known to use more of that product, perhaps indicated by the business type or the proportion of their budget they spend with the company, this information can help to plan what type of approach to make to increase their purchasing value. Analysis of buying habits can also identify opportunities for cross-selling or up-selling. If the members of one group of customers regularly buying product A also tend to buy product B, for example, then new customers for product A can also be targeted for product B. At a more sophisticated level, some companies, particularly in the financial services industry, use the database to analyse their knowledge of their customers in order to help develop new products and services which will appeal to them.

Analysis of the database can be highly sophisticated. A company using regular mailings, for example, could send them out on a weekly cycle and measure the response at, say, three and seven weeks. Once recorded, these results could be used to predict future response rates. Statistical analysis of the data may incorporate well over a hundred variables (including contact characteristics, timing, the offer etc), each assigned a value according to the earlier responses. The results of analysis can be used in a variety of ways, such as to optimise the timing, the offer and the targeting. If a certain response rate is required, for example to provide a certain number of leads or make a special offer cost-effectively, then the target audience can be selected, according to the value of the variables, to provide the required response rate.

Modern databases can track millions of contacts throughout their buying life, noting and helping to analyse all characteristics and events which can be exploited to maximise their value and automatically selecting those ripe for a particular sales or marketing activity. A financial services company, for example, could be tracking customers' product usage history; those who have reached a certain level of repayment on loans could be targeted at times when extra cash may be required, such as a change of address, children starting school, or booking times for annual holidays. Every single variable for every name on the database can be analysed, in relation to a particular product or service, in order to identify when and how to approach them to achieve a positive response. The more relevant information companies have about their customers and prospects, the more effective this process becomes.

A marketing database, as a part of a sales and marketing information management system, is also invaluable in helping to manage some of the problems which arise in operating 'hybrid marketing systems'. This term has been coined to describe marketing operations where new channels or methods of direct communication have been added to the existing strategy. Whereas previously a company may have sold only through its field sales force and dealers, for example, if it adds new methods, such as telephone marketing or direct mail, perhaps to target new customers or market segments, it creates a hybrid marketing system.

As companies strive to increase market coverage and find more cost-effective methods of selling, the creation of hybrid systems, by adding new methods incrementally, is almost inevitable. However, Moriarty and Moran of Harvard University have highlighted difficulties in managing such systems.* 'Such actions', they say, 'typically result in

---

* Reprinted by permission of the *Harvard Business Review*. Excerpt from 'Managing Hybrid Marketing Systems' by Rowland T Moriarty and Ursula Moran (November–December 1990). Copyright 1990 by the President and Fellows of Harvard College.

conflict and morale problems inside the marketing organisation and confusion and anger among distributors, dealers, and customers on the outside.' The authors go on to explain the main difficulties and provide guidance on methods of overcoming or containing them.

The key to a successful hybrid system is to distinguish clearly between the marketing tasks that have to be achieved (such as lead generation and qualification), which the authors say are the basic building blocks of the system, and the methods available to achieve them (such as direct mail and telephone marketing). The analysis of these basic components enables the effective design and management of the system, creating customised strategies to satisfy the needs of different market segments in the most cost-effective way.

Moriarty and Moran use what they call a 'hybrid grid', with the marketing tasks and ways of achieving them on adjacent axes, to show how this analysis works. When using the grid to decide how a particular task should be achieved, a balance has to be struck between the costs of different methods and their effectiveness in satisfying the needs of customers in each market segment.

Conflict arises inevitably when a new method of direct communication is added to the marketing system. First, those using established methods will resist any change that could increase the competition for customers and thereby possibly lose them revenue. Second, those outside the company, whether they are customers, prospects, dealers, or whatever, can easily become confused and alienated when multiple offers of the same products are made to them. Some conflict is desirable, as it reflects good market coverage, but it is potentially destructive and Moriarty and Moran suggest that it can be controlled, once the amount and location of conflict has been identified, by 'establishing clear and communicable barriers and specific and enforceable guidelines that spell out which customers to serve through which methods'.

Areas where barriers and guidelines cannot be defined, such as large companies with both centralised and decentralised buying policies, need to be communicated clearly to marketing personnel, so that they are aware that there will be internal competition. Beyond that, however, there are a number of 'natural' boundaries, principally customer characteristics, geographical location and products, which can be used to decide how specific customers will be served, and thus control and contain the conflict.

The introduction of a hybrid marketing system inevitably involves a variety of organisational changes, for example in structure and policy, and Moriarty and Moran provide two helpful administrative guidelines, although they point out that each system will present unique management challenges. First, the effectiveness of potential strategies should be gauged by asking the following questions.

- Will it satisfy customers in the most cost-effective way?

- Will it maximise coverage and control throughout the system?

- Will it limit destructive conflict inside the organisation?

Secondly, when new methods are introduced, the timing of changes should take into account revenue flows. A new method is unlikely to make a significant contribution to overall revenue in its first year, particularly in a large organisation, and management should therefore discriminate positively in favour of the new method during the transitional period. The authors point out that 'companies with hybrid systems rely heavily on compensation policies to reinforce new boundaries and routinely subsidise new activities during transitional periods'. As an example, compensating the field sales force for loss of commission is one way of introducing positive discrimination to allow the new method time to grow.

Apart from the need to control conflict, the operational success of a hybrid system depends upon the effective management of information on customers and prospects. This is where the marketing database, used as a centralised resource, can play an important role. Apart from helping to plan customised approaches for different market segments, the database helps to co-ordinate activity within and between each channel of communication. Not only does this improve efficiency, but it also ensures that the transition between one marketing task and another, often undertaken by different units within the company, is transparent to the customer.

In their conclusion, Moriarty and Moran write:

Many signs indicate that hybrid systems will be the dominant design for going to market in the 1990s. How a company manages its systems will help determine its fate in the marketplace. A company that designs and manages its system strategically will achieve a powerful advantage over rivals that add channels and methods in an opportunistic and incremental manner. A company that makes its hybrid system work will have achieved a balance between its customers' buying behavior and its own selling economics. A well-managed hybrid system enables a marketer to enjoy the benefits of increased coverage and lower costs without losing control of the marketing system. Further, it enables a company to customise its marketing system to meet the needs of specific customers and segments.

It is not only direct marketing communications which benefit from the marketing database. Sophisticated analytical tools are available which provide a wealth of management information on current and future markets to help plan sales and marketing strategies and tactics. As the database develops, companies can become more proactive in exploiting opportunities, for example by identifying and tracking market trends, and creating new products for new markets. In a constantly changing trading environment the database, as the core of a sales and marketing information management system, can become one of a company's greatest assets.

Telecommunications

The second half of the 1980s witnessed great advances in telecommunications technology, and associated products and services. New developments, particularly in the field of digital technology, have opened up immense opportunities in the way that business communications can be conducted. Telephone marketing operations will undoubtedly be a beneficiary of new telecommunications technologies in the 1990s, in areas ranging from quicker connection of calls and clearer lines, to more sophisticated call handling and visual communications. Many of these opportunities are already available, while others are in advanced stages of development. Telephone marketers will need to monitor developments in this key area closely in order to avoid missing opportunities which could keep them ahead of the competition. The following descriptions provide a flavour of the opportunities opening up in this field.

Integrated services digital network (ISDN)

The introduction of ISDN provides a high-speed, high capacity transmission route via a single digital connection over the public telecommunications network. Offering direct dial on national and international routes, this enables companies to send and receive high-quality data, images, text and voice with the ease of making a phone call. ISDN is already available to many business customers in several countries, and by the end of 1991 British Telecom (BT) expect it to be available to all business centres and high streets in the UK. BT has been working with international network operators, and by the end of 1990 were providing an international service to about a dozen countries; by 1993 they plan to be serving the whole of the European Community as well as Australia, Singapore, Hong Kong, Sweden and Canada. ISDN could reach consumers by the end of the twentieth century. National ISDN calls are currently no more expensive than ordinary phone calls, but international calls are charged separately.

The key benefits of ISDN are greater quality and speed of communications, at low cost, and the possibility of a new range of applications. These benefits arise from:

- faster call set-up, quieter and clearer lines, and more reliable connections;

- high-speed data transmission without the need to lease costly, dedicated private lines and without the need for a modem (ie direct connection of computers to the network);

- high quality and colour text and image transmission;

- video image transmission;

- simultaneous voice/data/image transmission over a single connection.

Some of the applications of these features which could benefit telephone marketing operations include:

- simultaneous access to a local or remote database while talking on the telephone, ie all of a company's staff using the telephone for contact with customers and prospects, wherever they are located, could access and update a single, central marketing database;

- remote generation of contact correspondence, for example in the country of origin of a call;

- the ability to transmit photographs of products;

- a new breed of fax machines, ten times faster than current ones and producing laser printer quality;

- desk-to-desk videophones;

- helplines which enable the operator to talk callers through problems using voice and images, for example sharing a computer screen;

- high-quality stereo audio for audiotex applications;

- a videotex industry.

A number of suppliers are developing products to take advantage of ISDN and, as the network rapidly reaches more and more businesses, and probably eventually consumers as well, improving the quality and flexibility of communications will represent an increasingly important opportunity for businesses as we move towards the 21st century.

Products and services

There is a growing range of products available, or in various stages of development, which will enable some telephone marketing operations to improve their efficiency and/or the sophistication of their applications. The following examples are only a small selection.

Phone Base, Phone Disc and Electronic Yellow Pages   Number searching has always been a time-consuming and costly exercise which telephone marketers try to minimise. Until recently the only alternative to BT's directory enquiries service, limited to two numbers per call and for which a charge was introduced in April 1991, was to search laboriously through local telephone directories. However, in March, BT introduced three new computer-based services. Phone Base is a service which provides subscribers with access to the computerised database used by BT's own directory enquiries staff. This can be accessed via modem from an office PC and lists 17 million entries which are continuously updated. Phone Disc holds these entries on compact disc, updated quarterly, which are accessed using an IBM-compatible PC and compact disc player. Electronic Yellow Pages is BT's computerised database of 1.8 million businesses and services, which subscribers can access via modem from an office PC.

BT suggest that Phone Base is the most cost-effective choice for those making around 20–300 directory enquiry calls a week. There is no rental charge or connection fee, just a charge for the period it is used (in October 1990 these charges, including VAT, were under 13p a minute peak rate, 10p standard rate and 6p at other times). Phone Disc is offered as an alternative for those making over 300 directory enquiries a week. The cost, excluding VAT, was £2,200 a year in

October 1990. Electronic Yellow Pages is charged in the same way as Phone Base, and is obviously better suited to locating business telephone numbers.

Because these three products/services are PC-based, they can help to automate the search for the telephone numbers of contacts on bought-in lists, although obviously they do not include ex-directory numbers. A variety of other techniques may be useful in analysing and exploiting Phone Disc data, for example in identifying regional target audiences by sorting on locality, although it should be remembered that random dialling has little or no merit ethically or commercially.

Voice messaging Voice messaging enables a caller to leave a voice message, for example when a person is unavailable or the line is engaged, which the intended recipient can listen to later. That person can be alerted by a pager or can simply call the service to check whether any messages have been left.

BT's Voicebank message handling system is an example. Users are provided with a dedicated telephone number for their Voicebank mailbox and, using any multi-frequency dial tone telephone, can access calls left for them by entering their PIN number. Messages can be played back, deleted, or saved for up to 72 hours.

Voice messaging is of limited benefit to telephone marketers and is open to abuse, should users' numbers become widely known, by companies whose use of the telephone already borders on the unethical. However, the facility is likely to gain increasing popularity with the spread of personal (pocket mobile) telephones and increasing emphasis on accessibility of company staff. As a result, it may become useful where companies have already built up a good relationship with their contacts who are then more likely to be receptive to telephone marketing calls received in this way.

Interactive fax Systems are already available which enable an individual to use a dial tone telephone to request a company's fax machine automatically to send specific information to the caller's fax. The system can be configured to meet individual companies' requirements and provide a range of information available to callers on request. In some applications, particularly where speed is essential, this can provide a valuable alternative to coupon or telephone responses for contacts to acquire information easily.

Videophones Until recently, video telephones have only been able to provide a still image, updated four or five times a minute. With the arrival of ISDN, however, desktop videophones providing a live, moving image are about to become a commercial reality. A number of telecommunications companies have developed high-quality desktop videophones, including BT and the electronics giant Philips, which could be commercially available in 1991. The videophone will undoubtedly prove valuable in many jobs, and could become increasingly popular as the cost falls and more companies gain access to ISDN. When their use becomes widespread it could prove useful for telephone marketers in showing customers certain products, as well as generally enhancing the personal nature of telephone communication.

Interactive television The modern cable network, using 'broadband' cables, is of high capacity and is capable of carrying telecommunications traffic as well as TV signals. Some cable companies predict that two-way telecommunications will be their major source of revenue by the end of the 1990s. Cable television has already been used as a training medium, enabling two-way communication between the trainer in a studio and trainees in their homes. Early predictions of the growth of the cable network have been extremely optimistic. Only around 700,000 UK households had access to broadband cables by the end of 1990, with fewer than 20 per cent of these subscribing to the service. However, interactive television could become a useful medium for telephone marketers, particularly on a localised basis, as the cable industry gains momentum during the 1990s.

Deregulation and competition

A restructuring of the UK telecommunications industry, breaking the duopoly of BT and Mercury Communications, could have important implications for telephone marketing. The review of UK telecommunications policy in November 1990, by the Department of Trade and Industry, seems certain to lead to far more players in the market and increased competition. Both BT and Mercury have their own telephone marketing agencies and at least one other agency has been exploring the possibility of collaborating with telecommunications suppliers to lay its own cables. In general, however, telephone marketing operations are likely to benefit from a fall in prices, particularly on international calls, as new operators compete, and possibly from the introduction of new telecommunications products and services.

The 1990s will be a decade of opportunities for exploiting telecommunications, with cheaper, more reliable and more sophisticated products and services. The standardisation of communications protocols will facilitate international traffic and encourage the use of telecommunications in exploiting overseas markets. Companies wanting to exploit these opportunities will have to monitor technological advances closely, as a part of their overall strategy, to determine where they can be used to improve sales and marketing efficiency, and establish new initiatives.

No company can afford to ignore opportunities for improved profitability, expansion and growth. Telephone marketing is no longer a minor in the marketing world. It has matured and gained a track record and pedigree which is enticing more companies into the fold every day. The horizon of opportunities continues to expand rapidly and, whatever a company's business objectives, professionally planned and implemented telephone marketing can help to improve the effectiveness of existing operations, aid business development and often provide the basis for new initiatives. Any company which has not yet dipped a toe into the water should consider as a matter of urgency how they can exploit the benefits that this powerful marketing tool has to offer.

10
Legislation and Good Practice Initiatives

Ever since there has been co-ordinated discussion between telephone marketing practitioners, the industry has taken the view that self-regulation is far preferable to government legislation. This applies in almost all countries where the industry has achieved recognisable status. Self-regulation allows companies more freedom, within strict codes of conduct, to develop and adapt to meet the challenges of changing economic, social and technological conditions. It encourages creativity and innovation which are vital to an industry which is still developing.

The industry has been able to forestall legislation to a large extent by reacting swiftly to criticisms over misuse of the medium, and through continued discussions with relevant regulatory authorities, and consumer and government watchdogs. Self-policing takes place largely through codes of practice developed and published by national telephone marketing trade associations, to which members subscribe. These guidelines, which are updated regularly, are designed to encourage professional use of the medium and thereby squeeze out the 'cowboys' whose unethical, and sometimes illegal, conduct gave the industry a particularly bad consumer image in its earlier years. In addition, the trade associations play a wider educational role, promoting both the medium and its professional use.

National trade associations seem to have gained the confidence of legislative bodies in their efforts to police the industry, even though they fight a constant battle to prevent, or at least influence, the introduction of additional legal restrictions; and they are likely to become more influential as the industry develops and becomes more competitive. Companies who do not adhere to these codes of practice will be under increasing pressure. Not only will they lose business through lack of professionalism, they will also fail to gain the support of mainstream telephone marketing operators. However, many unsolicited and unprofessional calls are still being made to consumers, even though, comparatively, the numbers are reducing.

It is perhaps not surprising that, despite the efforts of the trade associations, the amount of legislation affecting telephone marketing operations is gradually increasing throughout Europe, the US and other major developed countries. Each country obviously has legislation of a general nature designed to protect consumers, for example from fraudulent or negligent action, which all businesses must observe and which vary in stringency from country to country. In the UK, for example, it is illegal to make false statements of fact to induce someone to enter into a contract. The originator of the message (such as an agency's client) is even liable if misleading information is given in error; agencies, on the other hand, would not be liable under these circumstances provided they had exercised proper care and skill in carrying out their work.

Each country also has laws which, though not necessarily designed with telephone marketing in mind, and sometimes with total disregard for the practical implications, place more specific restrictions on telephone marketing. Legislation of this type will be outlined later in this chapter. The national trade associations have, in some instances, brought their knowledge of the industry to bear during the formulation of these laws, as well as lobbying for their amendment and/or clarification with regard to telephone marketing. However, in the UK at least, there are some areas of dispute which have yet to be resolved.

Despite the obvious need to observe the law, and the commercial benefits of adhering to codes of practice, companies using telephone marketing in-house show a surprising lack of knowledge of what this involves – at least in the UK. This was the British Direct Marketing Association's (BDMA) finding in its 1988 survey. Only 13 per cent of the companies responding claimed knowledge of BDMA activities relating to telephone marketing, for example, and only 3 per cent of those using trained and dedicated telephone marketing staff were members of the BDMA. The results of the survey of agencies were equally surprising. When questioned about awareness of BDMA activities, only 53 per cent of respondents spontaneously mentioned the Association's Telephone Marketing Guidelines; and the figure only rose to 65 per cent when prompted. This is further confirmation that there is an enormous job of education still to be done about what constitutes good, professional telephone marketing.

The United Kingdom

The telephone marketing industry in the UK has had considerable success in forestalling legal restrictions. However, recent additions to the legislature, such as the Data Protection and Financial Services Acts, have caused concern over the implications for the industry. The BDMA continues to lobby and negotiate with the relevant legislative bodies to ensure that unnecessary and unrealistic restrictions are not added to the statute book, as well as pursuing a wider role of educating people in professional and ethical conduct.

BDMA Telephone Marketing Guidelines

The BDMA's Telephone Marketing Committee was formed in 1979 and set about drawing up good practice guidelines for telephone marketing operators. The Telephone Marketing Guidelines, first issued in October 1980, were revised in February 1988.

These guidelines, reprinted in Appendix B (pages 443–5), were the result of discussions within the industry and with the Office of Fair Trading (OFT – which has endorsed the latest revision). They define professional and ethical conduct in the use of telephone marketing, in both consumer and business-to-business markets, and cover the areas of disclosure, honesty, reasonable hours, courtesy and procedures, and restriction of contacts. Members of the BDMA have agreed to comply with the guidelines; when selecting an agency it is therefore advisable to ask whether they are a member and, if not, whether they subscribe to these guidelines.

The guidelines have been included in the rules of conduct for companies subscribing to the Telephone Preference Service (TPS), described later, and will therefore have a much wider take-up when the TPS becomes operational.

Office of Fair Trading (OFT)

The OFT is the UK's trading practices government watchdog. In 1981, concerned to protect consumers from sharp practices, they began to investigate instances of unethical and unprofessional conduct by telephone marketers. In October 1984, four years after the BDMA Guidelines were introduced, they published a report called *Selling by Telephone*. Many of the guidelines included in this report coincide with those from the BDMA, who had worked closely with the OFT during its preparation. These guidelines are reprinted in Appendix B, on page 446.

The OFT continues to take an interest in telephone marketing practices and to play a role in shaping voluntary codes of practice through its discussions with the industry. They were involved, for example, in early discussions on the introduction of a TPS (*see* page 394).

British Telecom (BT)

BT, as the principal telecommunications network operator in the UK, announced, in February 1989, that it would disconnect all premium rate 'chatline' services run by independent companies. Although this proved that BT has considerable power in preventing use of the telephone for certain purposes, the decision was only taken after unprecedented publicity and extensive lobbying. Outcry from parents about excessive bills run up by their children, often talking for hours at a time on the chatlines, apparently made it imperative that BT took action. With the provision of greater safeguards (*see* later, under 'ICSTIS'), these services have now been reinstated. The ability of BT to disconnect users was a source of indignation in certain quarters of the telephone marketing industry – that a private company with an effective monopoly on the provision of telecommunications services could appoint itself arbiter and take this action unchallenged.

There are, of course, other regulations concerning the content of telephone calls. The British Telecommunications Act 1981 prohibits the making of calls whose content is 'grossly offensive', or which are 'indecent, obscene or menacing in character'. It is also illegal knowingly to send a message which is false in order to cause 'annoyance, inconvenience or needless anxiety'. Telephone marketing calls which are exceptionally aggressive or untruthful would fall into this category.

ICSTIS

The Independent Committee for the supervision of Standards of Telephone Information Services (ICSTIS) was formed in September 1986. Earlier that year, BT had introduced its premium rate (0898) service and subscribers were required to observe a Code of Practice in relation to programme content. ICSTIS, which took over the Code, was formed to avoid the possibility of conflicts of interest between BT and service providers on the acceptability of content. The committee's terms of reference are to supervise both the content of, and promotional material for, premium rate telephone services. Extracts of the May 1991 edition of the Code are reprinted in Appendix B, pages 447–51.

Separate ICSTIS rules exist governing 'Live Conversation Services', which include Chatline services (enabling more than two people to conduct a conversation) and Live Conversation Message services (either one-to-one, where the customer talks to the service provider, or subscriber-to-subscriber, where two customers talk to each other). Chatlines and One-to-One services were formerly governed by two separate sets of rules, but a single set of rules applying to all Live Conversation services became operative on 1 August 1990. In 1991 ICSTIS was considering producing a revised code which, among other things, would incorporate these rules into the main body of the Code of Practice.

The network operator's standard contract for the provision of premium rate services obliges customers (the service providers) to comply with the ICSTIS Code of Practice. Any breach of this Code may result in their service being withdrawn. Providers of live services are also required to contribute to either the Chatlines Compensation Fund (enabling contributors to operate only Chatlines) or to the Live Conversation Services Compensation Fund (contributors to which can operate any of the live conversation services). These funds are administered to compensate telephone subscribers, to meet the costs of ICSTIS in preparing, revising, applying and administering the Code and to finance the fitting of call-barring equipment on telephone subscribers' premises (or the obtaining of call-barring at the exchange as appropriate) in circumstances where there has been unauthorised use of that person's telephone to gain access to these services. ICSTIS also operates a free 24-hour complaints line on 0800 500 212 to help police these services.

The Consumer Credit Act 1974

Since a 1985 amendment to the Consumer Credit Act 1974, all credit agreements entered into during a telephone call, and where there is no face-to-face contact, must be followed by posting of the necessary documents for the applicant's signature. However, this does not apply to the use of credit cards for mail order.

Financial Services Act (FSA)

The Financial Services Act, governing the provision of advice on investment and life insurance, came into force in 1986. It is designed to prevent unprofessional or fraudulent action by advisers giving investment advice and has important implications for telephone marketing agencies handling this type of business.

Scope The FSA covers any investment product, including life assurance with a savings or investment element and health insurance if it covers a term of five years or more, with some exceptions. 'Alternative investments', for example stamps and works of art, and building society or bank or National Savings accounts are excluded.

Stipulations The FSA requires that companies carrying on investment business must be authorised through membership of one of the regulatory bodies formed by the Act, such as the Securities and Investments Board (SIB) and LAUTRO. Authorised companies can appoint representatives to act for them, but those representatives cannot act for any other company in that particular field of investment.

The Act operates on the principle of suitability of the advice provided. People who are authorised must be able to provide best advice, which entails having sufficient knowledge of the products and services offered, disclosing all relevant implications of the proposed transaction, and ascertaining information about the potential investor's circumstances to give best advice. Those acting as representatives of an authorised company would have to satisfy that company that they are fully capable of giving 'best advice'.

Implications for telephone marketing The Act presents little difficulty for investment companies operating telephone marketing in-house, since company authorisation will cover all their business activities. However, the situation for telephone marketing agencies is more complex. In June 1991 SIB issued guidance notes on *Telephone selling by telephone marketing agencies*, interpreting the position of agencies which are not themselves authorised under the Act. These state that, in relation to any call, three issues must be considered separately:

whether the call is unsolicited; whether it amounts to an investment advertisement; and whether it involves an activity which raises the need for authorisation.

Unsoliticted calls (that is, made without *express* invitation) made by any person with the aim of encouraging those called to enter into an investment agreement must comply with the Financial Services (Unsolicited Calls) Regulations 1987 made by SIB. If these calls are made by an agency on behalf of a client, the calls must, in effect, also comply with that company's authorising body's rules on unsolicited calls.

The contents of investment advertisements must be approved (or 'signed off') by an authorised person as complying with the Act. Agencies must consider whether the calls they intend to make will amount to 'advertisements'. In SIB's view, pre-recorded messages are likely to be advertisements and can be signed off by an authorised client. However, 'free form' and scripted calls are unlikely to be advertisements. If these calls involve authorisable activities then the agency would either have to be authorised or be a representative of an authorised company.

Three of the activities constituting investment business, for which authorisation is required, are: dealing in investments; arranging deals in investments; and giving investment advice. In SIB's view, an agency would be dealing in investments if it accepted instructions for the purchase or sale of investments. If it makes arrangements with a view to a client selling or buying investments, or the people called buying or selling investments, it is also likely to be viewed as arranging deals. However, calls without any promotional content, such as live operators recording callers' requests for a brochure, are unlikely to amount to arranging deals. Conversely, telephone marketers inviting contacts to make an appointment with a company representative are likely to be involved in arranging deals.

Companies have to meet very stringent requirements to become authorised and it is unlikely that a telephone marketing agency would seek authorisation. Even acting as a tied representative would require a very substantial investment in resources and would also limit the agency's potential client base.

The SIB's interpretation of the Act is more stringent than the industry had hoped, and the BDMA will continue to lobby for a more favourable view. If there is no change it is likely that growth in this area will be confined largely to in-house operations.

The scope of the FSA also extends to shareholder communications during takeovers and mergers, which is seen as an investment decision.

The City Code on Takeovers and Mergers and Substantial Acquisitions

In addition to the Financial Services Act, the City Code on Takeovers and Mergers and Substantial Acquisitions includes guidance on the correct and legal use of the telephone in shareholder campaigns. These are contained in Rule 19, which stipulates that, in campaigns of this type:

- anyone other than staff of the financial adviser requires the consent of the Takeover Panel;

- information supplied must be previously published, accurate and not misleading;

- shareholders must not be pressurised but encouraged to consult their professional advisers;

- the script, to which callers must adhere, must be approved by the Panel;

- the financial adviser must be involved in the briefing and supervising of calling;

- if callers divulge information other than that scripted, it must be made immediately available to all shareholders.

The part of Rule 19 governing telephone campaigns is reprinted in Appendix B, page 452–3.

Data Protection Act 1984 (DPA)

The Data Protection Act 1984 came fully into force in November 1987, since when the Data Protection Registrar has issued a series of guidance notes interpreting and clarifying the scope of the Act. It gives individuals various rights concerning the data about them held on computer.

Scope The DPA covers any organisation collecting and storing on computer, or collecting for storing by another party, data about individuals.

Stipulations The DPA requires registration, on the Data Protection Register, of companies who hold data about individuals on computer.

It lays down eight principles of good practice in relation to the collection and use of personal data (reprinted in Appendix B, page 454). The key stipulations are that:

- data must be accurate, relevant and up to date in relation to its intended use;

- individuals have the right to know if data is held about them, to see a copy of the data and, where appropriate, to have it corrected or erased;

- personal data must be obtained and processed fairly and lawfully.

This latter stipulation was clarified in Guideline 4, published in February 1989, issued as a result of a rise in the number of complaints made to the Data Protection Registrar. It requires that, when obtaining data from individuals, they should be told clearly and honestly, before they give any information:

- what information they provide will be held as personal data;

- the intended user of that data;

- who else will be able to use it; and

- the purpose for which it will be used.

The registrar acknowledges, however, that in the majority of cases there would be no need for this information to be given specifically, because it would be clear from the circumstances under which the data are collected. An order coupon in an advertisement would not need to state, for example, that the name and address supplied would be used by the company to deliver the product ordered, or to send further promotional material on other similar products. In practice, the need to provide the data subject with a separate statement covering, say, the intended purposes or users will arise only where such purposes or users are substantially different from what the data subject would otherwise assume. Where different data will be put to different uses, or be available to different users, the individual must be informed how each piece of data will be used and by whom – before they provide it.

Implications of the DPA for telephone marketing Although direct marketing was not specifically referred to in the original Act, it has direct and very serious implications for the industry. While most people in the industry agree with the principle of data protection, for their own benefit as well as that of consumers, it is seen as severely and unfairly limiting in some areas. For example, compliance with the Act renders some forms of data collection by telephone impractical. Having to pre-empt a conversation with a caution about the uses to which personal data may be put will make it more difficult to hold a reasonable conversation and will increase the length and cost of a telephone call. Since data gathering is now often a secondary objective of many types of telephone marketing call, this has broad implications for the economics of many of its applications.

When renting or buying a contact list a company should check, with the list supplier, that individuals on that list were informed, at the time their personal data was collected, that the data may be passed to a third party, so that they have been given an opportunity to object.

Not surprisingly, the most recent interpretations of the Act have aroused strenuous opposition from the BDMA, as well as the Post Office, but the recent, second edition of the Advertising Association's Code of Practice brings the two sides together on all but one issue (*see* below).

The Advertising Association (AA)

The AA's Code of Practice Covering the use of Personal Data for Advertising and Direct Marketing Purposes was first published in March 1987 and revised in June 1990. It provides guidance to help users comply with the data protection principles and covers duties of the data user, the eight data protection principles, and additional rules, as well as providing a model 'Subject access request form'.

Relevant sections of the Code are reprinted in Appendix B on pages 455–60. Of particular interest are the foreword, preface, recommendations in sections 3.1.7–9 (on the collection of data) and sections 3.1.11–12 (on the acquisition and use of lists).

The AA, and the guidelines in the code, disagree with the Data Protection Registrar on the issue of the 'fair obtaining' of personal data as required by the first principle. The difference of opinion has arisen because it is not always practical to inform the data subject, at the time of data collection, how that data might be used subsequently. Where the future use of the data is not obvious, for example by the nature of the transaction through which it is obtained, the Data

Protection Registrar requires that the data subject must be informed of future use and users. However, the AA says that there should be allowance for the possibility of changes in data use subsequent to collection, provided that the data subject is given the opportunity to object. When theatre tickets are purchased by credit card over the telephone, for example, or any other short transactions, it is often impractical to explain how the personal data gathered may be used. The guidelines in the code allow for the data subject to be informed later if that data is going to be put to significantly different use. For example, the fulfilment pack, when the theatre tickets are sent, would inform the data subject of the intended use and provide a response mechanism should they wish to object. The registrar does not feel that this would fulfil the legal requirements but, at present, the issue could only be clarified in court.

Among the organisations committing themselves to observing the AA code, and making its observance a condition of membership, are the BDMA and the British List Brokers' Association.

The Office of Telecommunications (Oftel)

Oftel is an independent body set up under the Telecommunications Act 1984 to monitor and regulate telecommunications in the UK. As the official watchdog, it monitors consumer reaction to telephone sales calls, through regular surveys, and has considerable influence over legislative proposals intended to curtail misuse.

In a report published in 1988, Oftel stated that two-thirds of the people surveyed had received telephone sales calls within the previous 12 months. A large majority of these objected to the calls (which were most often of the type made by companies selling double glazing and fitted kitchens) and wanted action taken to curtail them. As a result, Bryan Carsberg, the director general of Oftel, said he would 'keep the development of this phenomenon under review'. The report also stated, however, that these comments were not representative of general public opinion, and implied that there is not widespread objection to professionally made telephone marketing calls. Their input on future legislation is therefore likely to be beneficial to the industry as a whole.

Oftel has also been closely involved with the development of the Telephone Preference Service, which will be an appointed agent of the Office. All telephone subscribers in the UK, individuals and organisations, must observe the extensive regulations laid down in the Class Licence for the Running of Branch Telecommunication Systems (also called the Branch Systems General Licence – BSGL). A revised edition of the licence was published by Oftel on 8 November 1989. This contains, for the first time, clauses which stipulate that, a) individuals can inform companies that they do not wish to receive further sales calls from them, and that this must be complied with; and that, b) a register be kept, by a 'specified person', of those people who do not wish to receive unsolicited calls and which callers must observe. This latter stipulation refers to the Telephone Preference Service being set up by the BDMA. The relevant parts of the Licence (Condition 9) are reprinted in Appendix B, page 461–2.

Telephone Preference Service (TPS)

The BDMA's proposals for a TPS are expected to be approved by the director general of Oftel, Bryan Carsberg, in 1992. It is a scheme similar to the Mailing Preference Service (MPS), originated by the BDMA and established in 1983, whereby members of the public can apply to have their details removed from mailing lists.

Discussions between the BDMA and the OFT on the design of a TPS began in 1986. In April 1989, when the association had submitted detailed plans, Oftel took over negotiations and their slightly different approach led to a revision of the proposals. Subsequently, news that the Branch Systems General Licence (BSGL) was to be revised, and would include reference to telephone marketing, resulted in further negotiations and amendments. Final proposals were submitted in March 1990.

When established, probably around six months after approval, consumers will be able to apply to have their names recorded on a central register, maintained by the TPS, if they do not wish to receive unsolicited calls. Regular updates of the register will be supplied to subscribers to the TPS, so that they can remove from their lists the names of those people who do not wish to receive unsolicited calls. Any telephone marketer who makes an unsolicited call to someone on the register will be in breach of their licence, which could lead to court action and, ultimately, suspension of the telephone service.

The BDMA had intended the TPS as a voluntary system, like the MPS, but the new licence brought the concept under statutory control. However, the association is happy that the scheme they have devised will sit comfortably within the regulatory structure of the licence. There was, initially, considerable debate over the definition of an 'unsolicited' call referred to in the licence. The director general of Oftel originally wanted this to apply to all calls, except those to current customers of the company. However, agreement appears likely to be reached on the types of calls which would fall within the scope of the TPS, ie any calls which are made by a company which has the names and telephone numbers of the people other than because they are, or have recently been customers, or because they have made an enquiry about the company's products or services. Basically, this means any calls made to people with whom the company has had no prior contact. Therefore, rented or bought lists, or those compiled from registers or directories, would have to be cleaned against the TPS register.

Rules of conduct have been drawn up for companies using the TPS and these incorporate the BDMA Telephone Marketing Guidelines. The TPS is being established as a separate company and will be funded, eventually, by payments from the organisations who want to receive updates to the register. Effectively, this should be everyone who uses telephone marketing to a consumer audience – otherwise they cannot guarantee compliance with their Branch Systems General Licence.

At the end of February 1991, more than seven years after it was established, the MPS register contained details of about 300,000 individuals and was receiving some 12,000 new applications per month. It may be that, since the telephone is generally regarded as more intrusive than mail, the TPS will prove more popular. This would increase the risk to non-TPS users of making unsolicited calls to those on the register. However, there will be a clear commercial benefit to subscribers once the TPS is well established. It will reduce the number of unfruitful calls – saving money and reducing the dispiriting effect of rejection on callers.

The Market Research Society (MRS) and Industrial Marketing Research Association (IMRA)

The MRS and IMRA are the representative bodies of those engaged in marketing or social research in the UK. One of their aims is to ensure that professional standards are maintained throughout the industry and they first introduced a self-regulatory Code of Conduct in 1954. The latest edition became operative in January 1991.

The introduction to the code states:

> Assurance that research is conducted in an ethical manner is needed to create confidence in, and to encourage co-operation among the business community, the general public and others.

Rules laid down within the code cover the following areas:

A. Responsibilities to informants
  - Assurances must be honoured
  - Confidentiality must be guaranteed
  - Adverse effects must be avoided
  - Special care shall be taken in interviewing children

B. Responsibilities to the general public and the business community

C. The mutual responsibilities of clients and agencies
  - Basis of trading
  - Confidentiality
  - Fieldwork
  - Reporting
  - Retention of records
  - Circulation of results

D. Conditions of membership and professional responsibilities

The code contains some direct references to the use of the telephone for market research, but, since it defines what constitutes professional conduct for market researchers, most of the guidelines apply to telephone research. There is one stipulation of particular relevance in terms of telephone marketing operations – the collection of data for sales activities under the guise of market research is prohibited. This has also been incorporated into the BDMA Telephone Marketing Guidelines. The most pertinent sections of the code are reprinted in Appendix B, pages 463–6.

The January 1991 edition of the code incorporates for the first time references to the Data Protection Act, and adherence to the code will help to ensure that research is conducted in accordance with the principles of data protection encompassed by the Act. The MRS and IMRA have also produced separate guidelines which explain the implications of the Act for market researchers, and provide indications of good practice.

ESOMAR

The European Society for Opinion and Marketing Research (ESOMAR) has issued guidelines on Distinguishing Telephone Research from Telemarketing. These guidelines highlight the potential problems that telephone marketing could create for the market research industry, and make recommendations for action to help maintain the public's confidence in the integrity of market research.

The main danger areas for market research are identified as public confusion between the two activities, public irritation at the rise in the number of unsolicited telephone calls of all kinds, and the trend towards legal restrictions on all forms of intrusion on privacy. The recommendations cover four areas:

- a ban on market researchers making outbound sales calls to consumers;

- the clear separation of market research and telephone marketing activities;

- good practice for telephone research;

- actions by local market research associations.

The full text of the ESOMAR Guidelines is reprinted in Appendix B, pages 467–72.

Continental legislation and initiatives

Like the UK, other European countries have relied largely on self-regulatory codes of conduct to avoid restrictive legislation. However, in some, such as West Germany, there is already legislation which severely restricts telephone marketing operations. As the industry grows and more calls are made, some European governments are showing an increased interest in even greater statutory control.

The chart in Table 10.1 summarises the key guidelines in the codes of conduct of some European countries. The chart is not comprehensive and, since the codes are designed to be followed in spirit as well as literally, they have a broader significance than may be apparent from the chart. Anyone intending to use telephone marketing to, or within, these countries should therefore obtain a copy of the relevant code from the national trade association, the addresses of which are given in Appendix C.

Table 10.1 Summary of European countries' codes of practice for telephone marketing

Country	Code applies to	Disclosure	Termination of call on request	Need to ask 'is the call convenient?'
UK	consumer and business-to-business	name of principal, promptly – repeated on request; purpose of call, at start; details of calling company or principal on request; if by recommendation, third party identified promptly	promptly and courteously at any stage	when initiated by a company or representative; offer to ring back at more convenient time
West Germany	consumer and business-to-business	name of principal, and purpose of call before the conversation starts		
France	consumer calling	name of principal, repeated on request; reasons for contact, at start; NAT of principal if requested		
Italy	consumer and business-to-business		promptly and courteously	time must be appropriate; must be available to call back at more convenient time
Sweden	Consumer and business-to-business	name of agency or principal at start, except in market research where different rules apply	must be respected	
Norway	consumer calling			
Holland	consumer calling	name of principal, immediately; purpose of call; rights and commitments when goods or services offered	if inconvenient	yes

Country	Call content	Honesty	Cooling off period	Reasonable hours
UK	restricted to matters directly relevant to purpose of call	must not evade truth or deliberately mislead	at least 7 days and contact to be so informed	avoid unreasonable hours; may vary by region, household and business; 9pm latest
West Germany		principles of truth and clarity apply		9am–8pm Mon–Sat; Not Sundays or public holidays
France		script must describe offer precisely and accurately	can return or refuse any article within legally prescribed time	9am–9pm Mon–Fri; 11am–9pm Sat.
Italy	consistent with stated reasons for call	must not evade truth or deliberately mislead		must take account of regional usage and custom; time must be 'appropriate'
Sweden				
Norway				9am–9pm Mon–Fri; 9am–6pm Saturday; Not Sundays
Holland		information must be exact and true; no improper or misleading approach	7 days unless shorter time agreed during call	within acceptable hours, according nature of the call

Country	Restriction of contacts	Name removal (from lists)	Sales calls	Market research
UK	no calls knowingly made to unlisted/ex-directory numbers; no calls to consumers at work unless invited; calls must not be generated by random or sequential dialling	on request; must subscribe to Telephone Preference Service (when established)	must not use high pressure tactics	sales and marketing calls not allowed under guise of research; where the words 'survey' or 'research' are used, info cannot be used for a sales approach
West Germany	no calls to private individuals unless requested; no sales calls which may disturb work, unless in accordance with business requirement	lists must be surrendered to client or destroyed by agency after project	not to use hard-sell tactics	no survey, market public opinion or social research to be feigned
France		immed on request – prospects and customers		information gained not to be used for sales, or resold
Italy	client lists must not be used for other clients or other purposes without permission; lists must be of maximum quality and targeted as closely as possible	on request	must not attempt to pressurise in any way	same as UK

Norway	may not use bought-in consumer mailing lists; employers' address lists, existing lists and tel. directory may be used			
Holland		comply as soon as possible – no later than 3 months after written request		*see* footnotes

Country	Minors	Automatic dial recorded message players	Other provisions
UK	avoid sending information, accepting order or appointments	either introduce as a computer call on behalf of . . . , or have live operator introduce call if of personal nature	when making appointments, contact point to be given for cancellation or amendment; orders to be confirmed in writing
West Germany			must observe legal regulations in force, particularly rules of fair trading and consumer data protection; client info is strictly confidential; their names can only be divulged with consent; *see* footnotes
France		*see* footnotes	must not use automatic calling for commercial solicitation; methodology and script are joint responsibility of agency and client
Italy	avoid obtaining orders, unless authorised by parent	either introduce as a recorded call on behalf of. . . , or have live operator listening in	when making appointments contact point to be given for cancellation or amendment; company must take responsibility for statements made by callers; campaign details not to be divulged without client's consent
Sweden			when closing, caller must ensure recipient understands consequences of the call; should comply with guidelines agreed with Dept of Consumer Affairs; relations with clients should meet accepted good business standards
Holland		*see* footnotes	telephone marketing should comply with the law

Footnotes:

West Germany: This stringent Code of Ethics also covers the following areas:

- must follow the recommendations of the Federation of German Chambers of Industry and Commerce and of the German Direct Marketing Association
- can only take orders for which they have the necessary expertise and facilities to handle
- performance deadlines and charges must be realistic and they must endeavour to keep them
- must continually endeavour to improve their knowledge, abilities and operational techniques
- human relations with customers and employees must be given highest priority next to the work itself
- must comply with data protection; this still applies to employees after they leave the agency; data must not be passed on to a third party
- documentation from in-house operations must be destroyed on completion of the campaign
- only trained personnel may be used; a minimum 3-day course with information on legal regulations and conduct on the telephone, including practical telephone training; training must also be given in marketing (according to the assignment), management, direction, organisation and operation
- campaign objectives must be given to the client in writing; the client must be informed if these cannot be attained
- all essential statements will be set out in guidelines and callers must observe and not deviate from these
- supervision must be guaranteed, with special provisions where commissions are paid to callers.

France: Automatic call-making equipment is not to be used in the context of 'commercial solicitation', in line with the National Commission of Information and Freedom. The telephone marketing trade association condones its use provided that any request from a private individual to stop transmission is recognised immediately. And it is only permitted if they have given express written agreement in advance. The originator and the principal must be identified in the message. Users of automatic calling equipment have to be registered with the National Commission of Information and Freedom.

Holland: Fully automatic calls are implicitly not allowed because the call cannot be terminated if and when recipients say they wish to end the call. It is implicit, in the statement 'improper and misleading approaches are not allowed', that sales calls may not be made under the guise of market research.

The legislation in European countries which impinges upon tele-phone marketing activities is far too varied to cover here in depth. In many countries there are laws which impose similar restrictions to those in the UK. However, some countries have stricter laws which could pose problems if it is decided to 'harmonise up' and provide one legislative structure for the Single European Market. In West Germany, for example, where probably the most stringent restrictions are imposed, the equivalent of the UK's Data Protection Act prohibits cold calling; consumers can only be contacted at home when a business relationship already exists. The German 'Unfair Competition Law 1909' and consumer protection laws also have far-reaching implications. There is also a growing trend in France, supported by very strong lobbying, towards greater legislation to protect con-sumers. Although Italy has various pertinent legislation, such as that governing the types of product that can be used as premiums for mailshots, it does not yet have data protection laws. Technically, therefore, data cannot be transferred to Italy from, say, the UK, because it contravenes the UK data protection laws. Only 7 of the 12 members of the European Community currently have legislation on data protection.

The inconsistency of the laws throughout Europe therefore imposes restrictions of which companies must be aware when they move across national boundaries. It also means that, currently, it is impossible to create a truly pan-European direct marketing campaign which can efficiently achieve common objectives in each country. The alterna-tives are either to develop different campaigns for those countries with similar legislation, or to compromise and develop a single campaign with less targeted objectives. Advice on legislation specifically affect-ing telephone marketing can usually be obtained from the appropriate national trade association (*see* Appendix C).

The prospects for Europe post-1992

There are already indications that there may be some form of European legislation governing telephone marketing in the Single Market. The European Commission, for example, has already called for a study of consumer sales calling and it has been suggested that there may also be a European instruction on the times that calls can be made.

Many people in the industry believe we are now seeing the tip of the legislative iceberg emerging. A preliminary draft of a European directive on data protection was issued in June 1990. Leaked information had suggested that this would opt for self-regulation rather than harmonising up to match the strict laws in force in countries like West Germany. It was expected that the directive would reinforce the Council of Europe's 'Recommendation on the protection of personal data used for the purposes of direct marketing', and encourage those countries which had not ratified this convention to do so quickly. This would have safeguarded consumer interests without imposing severe restrictions. The published draft has proved more alarming, in that it opts for legislation. The proposals include:

- data subjects must be notified of what personal data will be held and how it will be used when it is first collected;

- data subjects must explicitly authorise the use of their data, such authorisation being revocable at any time;

- data subjects can claim compensation if their data is misused or causes damage;

- data can only be transferred to another country if legislation in that country provides the same level of protection as the country in which it was collected;

- a consultative committee of government representatives should be established to recommend alterations to, and provide interpretations of, the directive.

Although, overall, the directive favours self-regulation, the base-line will be legislation close to that existing in West Germany. Tony Coad, a member of the task force set up by the European Direct Marketing Association (EDMA) to tackle the directive (before its publication), says that this legislation is so restrictive that it leaves no scope for self-regulation. The task force had been conducting a survey of direct marketing across Europe to help in formulating a workable self-regulatory code of conduct. Many European trade associations will undoubtedly now be pressing for amendments. In the UK, for example, the BDMA is lobbying the government and the Confederation of British Industry. Failure to secure changes will pose a major threat to the European direct marketing industry.

In another area, a new European directive is proposed on distance selling. Much of this is already law in the UK, but it will also give consumers in all member states a 'cooling-off' period after making decisions in their home. The BDMA Guidelines already recommend a seven-day cooling-off period for agreements made over the telephone.

Also in the European context, the BDMA will be encouraging other European countries to establish a Telephone Preference Service. This will provide a network, as is happening with the Mailing Preference Service, whereby countries wanting to use pan-European telephone marketing could clean their list against the TPS register of the target countries.

As regards the possibility of a European code of conduct for telephone marketing, the views of the industry are mixed. Although it may help to prevent further legislation, it would be difficult to formulate a single code which was acceptable to all countries. Even if a code were to be agreed, it could prove difficult to police effectively because it would involve major changes to some countries' existing codes.

The United States of America

There are two reasons for looking across the Atlantic at the laws and good practice initiatives governing telephone marketing in the US. First, any company wishing to tap successfully into the American market using this medium will have to observe the law and, if they are going to compete on equal terms with American practitioners, conform to good business practice for the industry. Secondly, it is generally accepted that developments in many business sectors in the US are anything from two to five years ahead of Europe. It has therefore become common practice to look to the US when trying to predict and plan for developments in Europe. However, it should be remembered that the US has more of a telephone culture. The level of unsolicited consumer calling there is currently vastly greater than in any European country, and is likely to remain so.

There are bills in almost every US state relating to telephone marketing although, surprisingly, little has been passed into the legislature. The reason seems to be the extensive self-regulation by the industry, although there are laws which bear peripherally on tele-phone marketing and help to enforce good practice in specific areas. The method of state legislature means that there is little consistency across the country and users of telephone marketing have to ensure that, when working in different states, local restrictions are observed. The principal restrictions in the US are as follows.

The Asterisk Bill   This bill has so far only become law in one state – Florida, in 1987. The name originates from the mechanism by which, originally, consumers could indicate that they did not want to receive unsolicited sales calls – an asterisk next to their listing in the telephone directory. Now they can have a line added, for a small fee, saying, 'No sales solicitation calls'. Each breach of this law makes the caller liable to a heavy fine.

Automatically Dialled, Recorded Message Players (ADRMPs)   Some states have guidelines for the use of ADRMPs. These were drawn up largely in response to complaints that the equipment prevented emergency calls being made. Because equipment does not disconnect when the recipient of the call hangs up, the line is engaged and tied up until the end of the message. The basic recommendation is that an operator introduces the call.

Registration   In some states, telephone marketing operations have to be registered with the state and are required to submit details of their business. The US Direct Marketing Association (DMA) has lobbied to have its members exempted from registration, with some success. They have argued that membership indicates that a business is legitimate.

Good business practice   As in other countries, there are many laws, both federal and state, which are designed to protect consumers. Although these were not designed with telephone marketing specifically in mind, or even direct marketing, they do regulate business practices, for example in the area of data protection. These are referred to in the guidelines issued by the DMA.

DMA guidelines   The US DMA's Guidelines for Telephone Marketing provide principles of conduct intended to bring the medium in line with other marketing media. They cover the following areas:

- prompt disclosure – name of 'sponsor' and purpose of call – no sales or fund-raising calls in the guise of research or surveys;

- honesty – including the need to substantiate claims, if necessary;

- terms – disclosure of costs, terms, conditions etc prior to commitment by customers;

- reasonable hours;

- use of automatic equipment – prohibiting the use of automatic dialling equipment unless it immediately releases the line when the called party disconnects – must not be used as automatic dial, recorded message players;

- taping of conversations – requires all-party consent or the use of a beeping device;

- name removal;

- minors;

- prompt delivery – should abide by the Mail Order Merchandise (30 day) Rule for prepaid goods;

- cooling-off period – three days;

- restricted contacts – including prohibition of random and sequential dialling;

- laws, codes and regulations – should operate in accordance with laws and regulations of the US Postal Service, Federal Communications Commission, Federal Trade Commission, Federal Reserve Board and other applicable federal, state and local laws.

The DMA also issues Guidelines for Ethical Business Practices, which provide basic guidance for all forms of direct marketing.

Telephone Preference Service (TPS)   In 1985 the DMA set up a TPS, which operates in the same way as the service being established by the BDMA in the UK. Consumers who do not wish to receive unsolicited calls can have their details added to a register, which is distributed quarterly to subscribing telephone marketing operators.

A copy of the DMA guidelines, and up-to-date information on legislation in the US, can be obtained from the DMA at the address given in Appendix C.

Legislation is constantly evolving and it is almost inevitable that some of these changes will have implications for telephone marketing.

However, the industry's trade associations will continue working to forestall legislation through effective self-regulation. Through liaison with the appropriate legislative bodies, they will also try to ensure that any laws which are introduced accommodate the needs of the industry as well as the people they are designed to protect.

11

How Others Have Done It – Case Studies

Each of the case studies in this chapter is a summary of a project carried out by a telephone marketing agency for one of its clients. They were selected because they provide excellent examples of the successful planning and implementation of telephone marketing in varied applications. However, it was equally important to demonstrate how companies are using the medium as an integral part of their corporate sales and marketing strategy. This is the central theme of two of the case studies which are intended to illuminate the concept of information management, where the strategy is designed to exploit sales and marketing information on an ongoing basis. More and more companies are capitalising on the benefits of this type of integrated approach, but the same principles can be applied to the use of information gathered from more straightforward telephone marketing campaigns, such as lead qualification and appointment setting. The more efficiently sales and marketing information is managed, the more cost-effective and profitable the process becomes.

Briefly, the case studies are as follows.

Case Study 1 Database marketing of business class air travel between London and Amsterdam. *Client*: Transavia Airlines. *Agency*: The Decisions Group.

Case Study 2 Sales lead management in the personal computer industry. *Client*: Zenith Data Systems. *Agency*: Telemarketing Link.

Case Study 3 Consultancy, staff selection and training for a newly established business development unit in the financial sector. *Client*: Abbey National Personal Finance. *Agency*: The Decisions Group.

Case Study 4 An electrical retailer's LinkLine 0800 Customer Helpline to allay consumer fears about an impending 'crisis' situation. *Client*: Comet. *Agency*: The Decisions Group.

Case studies are documented with the permission of the client.

Case Study 1: Database marketing

Client: Transavia Airlines.

Agency: The Decisions Group.

Transavia Airlines, the large Dutch charter airline, was granted its first scheduled route, between London Gatwick and Amsterdam Schipol airports, in 1986. There were already two operators on this route – British Airways (BA), offering four flights a day out of Gatwick, including the first and last of the day (the busiest period), and KLM offering seven flights. Transavia entered the market with four flights, the same as BA.

Competing with the existing operators on this route, well-established in the marketplace, presented an enormous challenge. Undercutting on price was not a realistic option, because of the nature of the industry, and Transavia chose a broad-based above-the-line marketing campaign. A budget of around £100,000 a year was earmarked for activities in areas such as exhibitions, trade magazine advertising and posters at the airports. Even so, building market share in the face of the stiff competition proved extremely difficult. After a year the airline was operating the route at an average 40 per cent capacity, when the break-even point was around 75 per cent, and incurring considerable losses.

Transavia then made a series of decisions aimed at filling more seats and securing their continued operation on this route. This included opening a Gatwick office to complement the one at Schipol airport, concentrating on providing a service to business class travellers where the profit margin was higher, and switching the whole of their marketing budget to below-the-line activities. The latter was a bold decision and the company decided to employ specialists, The Decisions Group, to ensure that the strategy had the best possible chances of success.

The overall aim was to build market share among business travellers who fly regularly between London and Amsterdam. A customer loyalty programme, based on incentivised travel, would form the core of the campaign and would be used to exploit the target market on an ongoing basis. The Decisions Group designed, implemented and managed an integrated campaign incorporating telephone marketing, direct mail and database marketing. The strategy for the campaign, which began in March 1988, was to:

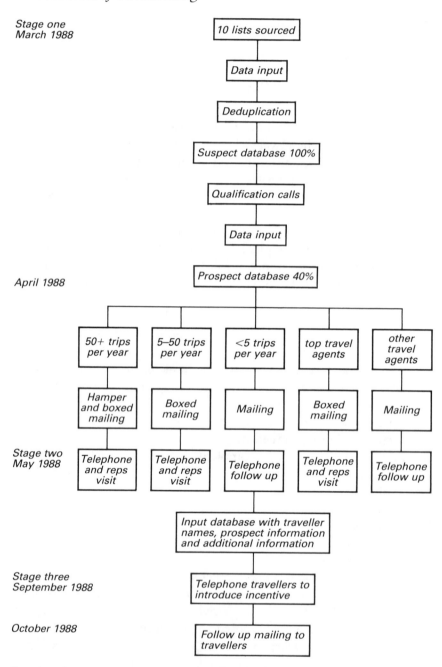

Reprinted with the permission of Transavia Airlines

Figure 11.1 Transavia Airlines database marketing strategy

- identify the potential market;

- establish individual business travellers' needs;

- develop regular communication between the airline and individual travellers.

There were three stages in the first year of the campaign, which are represented graphically in a simplified form in Figure 11.1.

Stage 1 The first step was to establish the target market in order to build a database. Ten different lists were sourced of companies who might have some connection with Holland, and therefore possibly have a travel requirement, and were based within the Gatwick catchment area. After deduplication these lists formed a database of 'suspects', which Decisions then qualified by telephoning the companies to obtain information such as:

- the name of the person responsible for arranging air travel within the company, who was then asked ...;

- whether anyone in the company flies to Holland on business and, if yes, ...;

- the airport they normally fly from;

- the airline they fly with, and the reasons;

- the method of booking travel and the details of their travel agent, if used;

- the number of trips made to Amsterdam per year; and

- awareness of Transavia's Gatwick–Amsterdam service.

This market evaluation exercise enabled Decisions to segment the database into three categories, consisting of companies whose personnel made:

    ... more than 50 trips per year;
    ... between 5–50 trips per year;
    ... less than 5 trips per year.

Another target market consisted of the travel agents used by these companies, numbering around 400, which could be segmented according to the revenue they obtained from business class flights in the previous year.

The outcome at this stage was a prospect database containing name, address and telephone number (NAT) details of 1,000 companies, and the names and job titles of 800 travel organisers.

At this time there was a low awareness of Transavia Airlines in the marketplace and they were otherwise perceived as a charter airline. Expensive, high-quality mailings were chosen as one of the main vehicles for raising awareness and presenting an image consistent with the needs of their target market – business travellers – who wanted a regular, reliable and high-quality service. Two different mailing packs – a boxed presentation and a flat pack – were used, together with hampers, and the distribution was determined by the segmentation of the database:

- those making more than 50 trips per year – a hamper, together with the boxed presentation, delivered personally by the sales manager;

- 5–50 trips per year – the boxed presentation delivered personally by the sales manager;

- the top 10 travel agents (in terms of revenue) - the boxed presentation;

- less than 5 trips per year and the remaining travel agents – the flat pack.

Overall, the mailings were delivered personally by the sales manager to the top 12 per cent, while the remaining 88 per cent were told in their mailing to expect a follow-up telephone call.

Stage 2 The next step was to build a customer (traveller) prospect database, by obtaining information from the travel organisers and agents. The sales manager was able to gather information from the top 12 per cent of prospects when delivering the mailings, while the remaining 88 per cent were telephoned by Decisions. The most important information to obtain from the organisers was the names of individuals for whom they booked travel, but it also included:

- feedback on the mailing pack;

- whether they intended booking air travel with Transavia in the near future;

- how they would prefer to be contacted in the future;

- the names of other travel organisers in the company; and

- confirmation of previous details.

Information obtained from the travel agents differed slightly in that they were asked how they did, or would, book travel with Transavia, and to name two or three clients for whom they regularly booked flights to Amsterdam. Overall, 1,500 travellers' names and job titles were added to the database, together with additional profiling information on the organisers and agents.

At this stage of the campaign Transavia had increased sales of business class tickets on the route by 90 per cent. This was largely to the detriment of KLM who, as a result, decided to pull off the Gatwick–Amsterdam route from 1 June 1988. This provided an excellent opportunity to utilise information on the database. Transavia were able to gain a competitive advantage over the remaining operator, BA, by quickly informing users of KLM of the company's decision.

Stage 3 The third stage of the campaign was an ongoing process, using regular communication by telephone and mail to continuously develop the database, and enable more accurate profiling and targeting of the market. This provided the basis for a programme of personalised communication offering appropriate travel incentives to help build customer loyalty.

Decisions first telephoned all travellers to establish a dialogue and introduce the incentive scheme. They were then sent personalised mailings which were followed up by another call. The main objective of this call was to find out more about individuals' personal travel needs and to prioritise them according to how often they flew to Amsterdam and whether or not they were in the Gatwick catchment area. Each traveller on the database could then be placed in one of six 'priority' groups which were used to determine the type of incentive that individuals were offered.

Various items were included in the travellers' mail packs at different stages, for example an illustrated Transavia brochure, a flight time-table, a shopping guide to Amsterdam, a free phonecard for use at Schipol airport railway station, a prize draw for one of three weekends for two in Amsterdam and various questionnaires eliciting information which would be used to develop the database. There was also a weekly prize draw over a six–week period, for a magnum of champagne, which travellers entered by leaving their business card at the departure gate at Gatwick. This provided further information for the company prospect database.

A sample of 200 travellers who did not respond to each mailing were telephoned to encourage replies to the questionnaire and gain other feedback. The sequence of call/mail/call was repeated on a regular basis, using the feedback gained on each cycle to fine-tune the next communication. Overall the response rate was excellent, at up to 30 per cent, with around 10–12 per cent of all travellers returning their questionnaires.

Decisions also booked appointments by telephone for Transavia representatives to visit travel organisers and agents, targeting specific geographical areas each month. The objectives of the visit were outlined during the call so that both parties would achieve the maximum benefit. Basically, these visits were designed to encourage involvement in the customer loyalty programme.

This part of the campaign ran from September 1988 until May 1989, when it was suspended for the summer low season. The database had now grown to 1,200 companies with at least two traveller's names per company, and there had been a dramatic 120 per cent increase in Transavia's sales of business class tickets since the campaign began.

The campaign achieved industry recognition when it was awarded the 1988 Direct Response Innovation Award. According to the judges for the award, made by *Direct Response* magazine, The Decisions Group had

> produced a well documented campaign with a clear strategy to achieve a set of objectives. Considering the total reliance on the below-the-line marketing the success of this campaign was outstanding, furthermore the ongoing nature of data collection and the continued application of this worthwhile strategy is particularly noteworthy.

Commercial success encouraged Transavia to continue the customer loyalty programme from September 1989 to June 1990, during which time the size of the database was doubled. Transavia had now gained 54 per cent of the market, overtaking BA on the route, with 30 per cent of those on the database flying regularly with the airline. The company had also signed up their largest client, revenue from which covered the cost of all their telephone marketing activity.

With the value of experience with an agency, and the planned expansion of scheduled services, the decision was taken to undertake database design and maintenance in-house. This process was completed step by step, converting the travel organisers first of all and then the travellers. Design and maintenance do require high levels of dedication, but the value of an in-house operation is the control and insight that is immediately available to the user. Transavia commenced this part of the operation in September 1990.

One of the key factors in the success of this campaign has been the use of the database, in conjunction with the telephone, mail and sales visits, to develop a personal relationship with customers. Transavia Airlines has been able to build substantial customer loyalty, displacing the previous market leader, by targeting its limited promotional spend where it has most impact.

Case Study 2: Sales lead management

Client: Zenith Data Systems.

Agency: Telemarketing Link.

Personal computer manufacturer Zenith Data Systems, part of Groupe Bull, receives more than 1,000 sales leads a month by post at its Slough (UK) offices and many more by telephone. The majority of these leads are end-users responding to an aggressive marketing communications programme which encompasses advertising, direct marketing, exhibitions and PR.

The personal computer market has become increasingly competitive, and high-speed processing and monitoring of leads is essential to minimise the risk of losing valuable business to competitors. Zenith originally employed a part-time member of staff to enter limited details of the sales leads into a database. These were then printed out by sales territory and passed to the appropriate member of the sales team. After that, however, no track was kept of the outcome of the leads. This meant that sales and marketing management had no detailed information, such as who was buying and how they became aware of the company's products, on which they could base their planning of future sales and marketing activities.

Rapid growth in demand for Zenith Data Systems' desktop and portable PCs meant an increasing volume of leads and a proportionately greater risk of losing business. In April 1989 the company decided to make sales lead management a priority, and thus began a period of dynamic change in their sales and distribution activities.

Only two groups can buy direct from the company in the UK – three authorised Zenith distributors and around 50 authorised Zenith dealers (or Value Added Resellers – VARs). The VARs are so called because they offer their customers (the end-users) a complete solution to their computing problems, not just hardware products. Any dealer who is not authorised, and there are a total of around 8,000 computer dealers in the UK, has to buy from one of the three distributors. Zenith recognised that some of these dealers, though not selling large enough volumes to buy direct, do buy on a regular basis. However, this is usually only when they have an order from an end-user; they rarely hold stock and do not actively promote any particular manufacturer's products. Zenith wanted to encourage them to become proactive in marketing the company's products, ie order makers rather than order takers.

Most computer manufacturers have a fund available to support the promotional activities of their VARs, but this arrangement would be impractical for non-authorised dealers, because they don't deal directly with the manufacturer. So Zenith conceived another type of programme which would help to achieve its objective. This was the registered dealer programme, whereby Zenith would guarantee to supply qualified leads in return for the non-authorised dealers buying two items of demonstration stock and undertaking one marketing project, for which the company would provide practical advice and ongoing support. At the time Zenith had no contact with these dealers and, to make the programme work, they needed to establish a direct dialogue. This would be achieved through outbound and inbound telephone support.

The company decided to employ outside specialist help to run the programme, both to free staff to concentrate on their key tasks and to provide the necessary degree of flexibility. The primary consideration was to select a company which could provide rapid turnaround, because sales leads die quickly in the PC business, and tight control of the operation. This called for one-stop shopping with a supplier who could provide both efficient lead management and the necessary telephone marketing services. Telemarketing Link (TML) met these criteria. The only reservation, from some of the company's sales management, was having sales leads in the hands of outsiders. However, TML's reputation for security soon dispelled any such fears and the agency was appointed in June 1989 to handle the project.

Up until this time leads were being received by telephone via an 0800 number serviced by British Telecom's Connections in Business, based in Bristol, and directly at Zenith's offices, while written leads were received at a PO box facility in Slough, where both TML and Zenith are based. All of these leads were now to be channelled through TML, who operated a system whereby, once lead details had been entered, a personalised letter was generated automatically to be sent with company and product details to each lead. The system also sorted the leads automatically to determine whether they should be passed, for follow up, to:

- the recently established major accounts sales force at Zenith;

- authorised dealers (VARs); or

- the newly termed registered dealers (via distributors).

There were three main sorting criteria for the leads – the number of company employees, the budget available and location. The critical factor is generally the number of employees, which determines the potential number of PCs that may be required, even if not immediately. If a lead was a company employing over a certain number of employees it would be passed on to the major accounts sales force. Most large corporate buyers prefer a dialogue with the manufacturer and the major accounts team, although they do not sell direct, would pitch for the business and, if they were successful, then nominate a suitable VAR to supply and service the account. Leads from slightly smaller companies would be sent direct to VARs, while details of the smallest companies would go to registered dealers, who were ideally placed to supply one or two units. The other important sorting factor was the postcode of the lead, which was used to identify automatically the appropriate member of the major accounts team or the nearest VAR or registered dealer.

Coinciding with the appointment of TML, Zenith had redesigned their sales lead form to include far more detail than previously about each contact, including the source of the lead, the current equipment used, company size, intended purchase time, name of the decision-maker, SIC (standard industry code), name, address and telephone number. Once the TML system had sorted the leads it would automatically generate the sales lead forms, together with personalised letters, to the appropriate VARs and registered dealers. It had previously taken two weeks to process leads. Now, within two to three days of leads arriving at TML, they had been informed personally that their enquiry was being dealt with and the appropriate Zenith outlet had full details to follow it up immediately.

TML telephoned VARs on a four–weekly cycle to follow up the leads they had been sent, which enabled them to provide Zenith with a regular status report. If anyone had experienced any problems with an end-user, for example, a member of the Zenith sales force serving the VARs could arrange a visit. The registered dealers were followed up as part of the registered dealer programme.

One way in which Zenith encouraged registered dealers to promote the company's products was to provide them with a manual designed to help and support them in their promotional efforts. Apart from listing the major features, benefits and unique selling points of Zenith products, this manual, *The A-Zenith Directory*, contained a wide range of information offering practical advice on promotional activities.

Most of the dealers were, after all, small companies whose experience and priorities were in sales rather than marketing. The directory included information on how to use direct mail, sources of mailing lists, fulfilment services, advertising, example advertisements, how to arrange and run seminars, likely costs, and all aspects of marketing suitable for the small PC dealer.

Zenith realised that a direct dialogue was essential to encourage dealers to use this directory and, through their promotional activities, to position themselves as the local centre for Zenith Data Systems products. The vehicle for this dialogue was the the Zenith Care Line, established at TML, and operated by a person specially recruited for the job, who had a knowledge of marketing information technology products. He would call every registered dealer on a four–weekly cycle to talk through any promotional activities they were undertaking, to offer ideas and advice on activities suitable for their type of company, and generally try to keep the directory at the forefront of their minds. The prospect of a call each month provided gentle persuasion for the dealers to carry out some promotional activity on Zenith Data Systems products.

The Care Line was designed to provide a very personal service where the dealer principals would be on first-name terms with their contact at TML. They also knew that they could call their contact direct if they required any additional help or advice. Zenith set an upper limit of 150 dealers to be included in the programme, or about 50 per distributor, because any greater number would have reduced the personal nature of the service. This figure was achieved by mid-1990, when the database had effectively grown from 0 to 150 dealers since the start of the programme.

The monthly calls to dealers were also used to establish what results they were achieving with their leads and identify any problems they might be experiencing with end-users. Regular reports to Zenith meant that the sales force serving the distributors (who supply the dealers) would know which dealers needed a visit. Instead of calling on an *ad hoc* basis, they could now manage their time more efficiently.

Distributors are generally reticent about revealing the names of their customers to the manufacturers, but this was necessary for Zenith to supply leads directly to the dealers. However, the distributors have benefited. Previously the dealers had tended to telephone round all three Zenith distributors, when they had an order to fill, looking for the best price. Now, because they are getting added value, in the form of more help with their business, they tend to use one distributor. So the distributors have gained a more loyal customer base of best-selling Zenith dealers. In addition, with the names of the dealers and the data from the Care Line, Zenith can now plan to target those dealers more effectively in their sales and marketing programme.

The fairly radical changes in Zenith's sales and distribution policy were aimed at achieving two objectives:

- to ensure that every sales lead was exploited to its full potential; and

- to provide better service and support to those selling the company's products, so as to encourage them to think of Zenith Data Systems before any other computer manufacturer.

To achieve these objectives the company developed an integrated communications strategy encompassing lead generation media, direct mail, telephone marketing and personal visits. This strategy has proved highly successful and is being continuously monitored and developed to maintain optimum use of resources.

Case Study 3: Consultancy, staff selection and training

Client: Abbey National Personal Finance Ltd.

Agency: The Decisions Group.

The introduction of the Financial Services Act in 1986 permitted widespread changes in the ways that financial companies could service their markets. Communications serve a vital role in times of rapid change, both to avoid confusion arising from the changes and to take commercial advantage of them. Not surprisingly, therefore, the use of the telephone by the financial services industry increased dramatically during the late 1980s.

Abbey National plc has been marketing-led since the mid-1980s and, as competition intensified, the company began a major re-organisation in 1989, aimed at providing customers with a better service. Part of the programme, due to be completed in 1992, consists of removing administration from the branches so that 75 per cent of floor space can be dedicated to serving customers. All administration will be handled at 40 regional centres linked by a new generation multi-million pound computer system. The reorganisation, which has included the whole of the Abbey National sales and marketing operation, provides the structure necessary to support the company's marketing push into the increasingly competitive 1990s.

In 1988 Abbey National was moving towards flotation and a change in status from a building society to a bank, major changes which offered an enormous opportunity to gain competitive advantage. When looking at ways of capitalising on this opportunity, the company decided to establish a Business Development Unit (BDU) within one of its subsidiaries, Abbey National Personal Finance (ANPF), based at Milton Keynes.

The principal aims of the BDU were to use telephone marketing to:

- offer further loans to customers who needed them;

- resell personal finance facilities to customers with maturing loan accounts; and

- follow up accepted customers who had not returned their application.

ANPF carried out a pilot programme in-house. This pilot identified the potential to produce in excess of £1m of incremental business per year for each telephone marketing executive working a $3\frac{1}{2}$-hour day. However, the company recognised that telephone marketing expertise was required to ensure smooth implementation of the unit and to provide a sound foundation for future growth and development. As a result, The Decisions Group were appointed in February 1989 to select staff, design and deliver training and provide consultancy support.

The most successful time for calling had been found, during the test, to be the evening, and it was intended to set up a team of eight telephone marketing executives (TMEs) and one supervisor to work from 5.00–8.30pm five days per week. Decisions' brief, basically, was to select and build a strong team, developing each individual's telephone marketing skills so that they could confidently achieve predetermined targets.

TMEs and the supervisor were to be selected, and trained initially, together, and selection took place in March/April 1989. It had been decided to target the recruitment advertising, placed in the local press, at young women with children who wanted to return to work. This was for two reasons. First, Milton Keynes had a zero unemployment rate and this sector of the labour market therefore offered good opportunities for recruiting staff of a high calibre. Equally importantly, however, women returners were more likely to portray the desired stable and professional approach to their work.

The selection procedure consisted of a number of stages. Decisions first created a personal profile of the ideal candidate for recruitment, using the job descriptions to determine the abilities and qualities required. From these, a list of assessment criteria was compiled which were incorporated into a variety of easy-to-use forms for the interviewers.

Three types of interview were employed – telephone screening to produce a short list, then a group interview, which served to identify the best candidates and a person who may be suitable for the supervisor's role, followed by one-to-one interviews. Thirty-five women telephoned the number appearing in the press advertisements and professional screening of these calls resulted in a shortlist of 25 candidates to attend the group interview. Of these, 14 were subsequently selected for one-to-one interviews. Offers were made to 12 candidates, of whom 9 accepted – making up the required 8 TMEs and 1 supervisor.

After selection, there were two main areas of training to address: product training, which would be carried out by ANPF, and telephone skills training, to be carried out by Decisions. As the overall objective was to build a highly effective, dedicated team, it was felt that the ideal location would be Abbey National's training department, as opposed to Decisions' own training facility, which would reinforce the introduction of corporate culture during induction.

The structure of the training programme, which was designed by Decisions to maximise its effectiveness, consisted of:

- two days' product training;
- two days' telephone marketing training;
- one day of product training, to include live calling on the final evening.

Decisions designed a highly interactive telephone marketing course specifically to match the unit's initial needs. Because all delegates were returning to work, it was felt that it should consist of short learning modules with a strong bias towards workshops and role plays, tailored around ANPF and its products, aimed at developing individuals' skills and team building. Seven training modules were designed:

- an introduction to selling;
- communication skills;
- preparation and planning;
- call presentation, and features and benefits;
- overcoming objections;
- closing;
- coaching individuals during their first live calls.

Various visual aids were incorporated, including OHPs, slides and films, along with telephone simulators to enable delegates to put theory into practice.

In view of the intensity of the training, which meant developing nine people from scratch to become proficient in both product and skills, it was thought beneficial to have two trainers to improve the trainer/delegate ratio, and thus improve training effectiveness and make it easier to monitor learning levels. Training took place in June 1989.

After each day's training, all delegates were issued with an evaluation questionnaire to measure their understanding and retention. This enabled Decisions to provide ANPF with a report on individual delegates' skills level and the skills delegates felt they needed to acquire, together with recommendations for appropriate follow-up training.

One month later, Decisions provided follow-up training covering:

- closing for customer satisfaction;

- practice in handling objections;

- presentation skills;

- upselling and downselling.

This course was followed by a session with the trainer listening in to live calls. Like the earlier course, all delegates were issued with an evaluation questionnaire. Subsequently, Decisions prepared a report identifying specific individual and departmental strengths and weaknesses, and making recommendations for future action.

Feedback from the course delegates, given on the evaluation forms, showed that the training had instilled an enormous amount of confidence in their ability to do the job, as follows.

'Extremely relevant training – I feel much more confident now I have done this course'

'Excellent – it expanded my limited knowledge beyond what I possibly could have expected'

'I feel most inspired and eager to be successful'

The unit has proved extremely successful, exceeding targets for generating business from the start, for example:

June – December 1989   137 per cent of target;
January – April 1990   125 per cent of target.

Sufficient business was generated in the first six months to make a small contribution to profit after the initial set-up and operating costs were deducted. ANPF attributes this success to the quality of training provided by The Decisions Group, who were subsequently contracted to provide *ad hoc* refresher and development training for the unit's staff, as well as training and consultancy in other areas, including credit control and investor relations.

The size of the BDU has been increased from the initial 9 staff to 15 in November 1990 and, through constant testing, measurement and control, the aim is continually to improve the unit's performance.

Case Study 4: 0800 customer helpline

Client: Comet.

Agency: The Decisions Group.

All businesses faced a tough economic climate in 1990 and electrical retailers were no exception. Comet is one of the UK's leading electrical retailers, with a trading policy of offering a wide choice of goods at competitive prices, at conveniently located stores, and supported by comprehensive customer service guarantees. During a decade of intense competition, the company had identified the fact that those retailers likely to succeed would be those who offered the best customer service.

On 3 November 1990, British Satellite Broadcasting (BSB) and Sky Television announced that they were merging to form British Sky Broadcasting. Although fierce competition between the two satellite television companies had long been in evidence through particularly aggressive, high-profile media advertising, the merger was totally unexpected and attracted massive news media coverage. The new company stated that all satellite TV transmissions would be broadcast ultimately via the ASTRA satellite used by Sky and transmissions via the Marcopolo satellite used by BSB would cease. However, typical of most 'crisis' situations, there was no information available on how this would affect those who had bought or were renting BSB satellite receiving equipment. As a result, there was a great deal of speculation which only served to compound the confusion and anger of consumers who realised that their BSB equipment would become redundant.

Comet quickly recognised the need to take a proactive stance, both to protect the interests of its customers and to limit any commercial disadvantage arising from customers' frustration and anger. The first step was to suspend sales of BSB equipment immediately following the merger announcement.

Secondly, Comet's strategy was to provide customers with easy access to the most up-to-date information as it became available, and to explain where they stood as a result of the merger. The best method of communication to meet these needs was the telephone, and Comet decided to establish a helpline. The Decisions Group was contracted to establish and run this service.

The Comet Satellite Helpline, using a LinkLine 0800 (call free) number, with five lines, went 'live' on Saturday, 10 November 1990, just a week after the merger announcement. It was open from 9.00am until 5.00pm, seven days a week, and outside these hours an answerphone advised callers to ring again between 9am and 5pm. Details of the Helpline were advertised on posters in Comet stores and on Ceefax. In addition, a letter from Comet's managing director was made available, from 10 November, in all of the company's stores. This explained the aims of the Helpline and gave the number to call for advice and information, as well as reassuring customers that Comet was pressing British Sky Broadcasting for clarification of the situation. It informed customers that the latest information was available on the Helpline.

Because of the uncertain nature of the details of the merger, and the aim to provide the most up-to-date information available, the Helpline operators needed comprehensive guidance on how to answer customers' enquiries. It was also recognised that people other than Comet customers might want information on the effects of the merger for a variety of reasons. The operators faced two problems – the need to be able to answer accurately enquiries from people with a range of concerns and to deal effectively with calls, the nature of which would be largely unpredictable.

A scripted approach under these circumstances, where a wide range of information would be needed to answer enquiries effectively, can be difficult for operators to manage when the service first goes live. However, it was decided that this was the best way of ensuring that the needs of all callers could be satisfied as fully as possible.

The script was designed to provide all the information required (and available at the time), for each type of call expected, in a form that would help the operators to advise each caller efficiently. It was predicted that callers would fall into five groups.

A   Those who had bought their satellite receiving equipment from Comet.
B   Those who bought their equipment from another source.
C   Those renting equipment from a rental supplier.
D   Non-satellite equipment owners who were interested members of the public.
E   Members of the press.

The largest number of calls was naturally expected from people in group A. However, the situation was further complicated by the fact that Comet offers a 14-day product exchange period, as part of their

Comet Customer Pledge. This means that, during that period, customers returning goods in their original packaging to the store where they were purchased, together with the receipt, can claim a full refund. Comet decided to extend this pledge to all customers who had bought BSB satellite equipment during the two weeks prior to the merger announcement, ie on all purchases after 20 October.

The script was presented in clearly defined sections so that operators could find the information required to answer each type of enquiry quickly. Where appropriate, these sections included variations of a core statement, expressing sentiments similar to those in the managing director's letter, which read along these lines:

> Comet is doing everything it can to promote your interests with the newly merged company. We feel that the vague statements made by British Sky Broadcasting about a transitional period and swop-over to ASTRA equipment are unsatisfactory and we are pressing the new company to outline in detail its obligations to purchasers of BSB equipment.
>
> The position is that since the equipment [purchased from Comet] is not faulty, obviously your complaint is that it may be redundant because the service originally promised by BSB will not be available in the future. This may mean that you have a claim against BSB and you should consider taking advice on this.

The introductory section of the script was designed to ascertain into which group each caller fell and then the appropriate information and advice was offered, as follows:

Customers who purchased BSB satellite receiving equipment from Comet **before** *20 October 1990*   It was explained to these callers that the 14-day product exchange period had expired and they were no longer covered by the Comet Customer Pledge. The core statement was then conveyed, followed by reference to the managing director's letter. Finally, callers were invited to leave their name, address and telephone number – so that they could be contacted as soon as any further news affecting their situation was available – or to call the Helpline again later.

Customers who purchased BSB satellite receiving equipment from Comet **after** *20 October 1990*   These callers were informed that if their equipment was still in its original packaging they were covered by the Comet Customer Pledge and could return it, together with the receipt, and claim a full refund. If the equipment had been installed already, and the pledge was therefore invalid, callers were informed the same as customers who had purchased before 20 October.

Callers who purchased their satellite equipment from another source
Operators advised these callers to check the situation with the retailer from whom they bought their equipment. However, they were also advised that, according to the information available, Comet understood that they had no claim against the retailer. Reference was then made to the managing director's letter available at all Comet stores and its content was conveyed. Finally, callers were invited to call the Helpline again when more information might be available.

Members of the public who do not own or rent satellite receiving equipment
The operators explained to these callers that the Helpline was only for people who have BSB satellite receiving equipment and that the company could not comment on other satellite issues. If callers persisted they were invited to write, with their detailed queries, to Comet's communications department, the address of which was supplied.

A member of the press Operators were to advise any member of the press calling the Helpline to ring Comet's press office on the number supplied.

In addition to these categories the script contained further information to help the operators in 'if asked' situations. This information covered callers' queries on the following topics:

Movie Channel query The core statement was conveyed to these callers and they were invited to call the Helpline again when more information might be available.

Extended warranties (Comet customers only) Callers enquiring about extended warranties on BSB satellite receiving equipment, purchased from Comet, were given the name and address of the company handling Comet warranties.

Credit purchases Comet's store credit card is operated by Timecard and one of the possible queries from callers was whether they could stop their monthly payments for satellite receiving equipment purchased using this card. This question was answered, first, with an explanation of how such a credit operation works, with the credit company purchasing the equipment from the retailer on behalf of the customer. It was then explained that no comment could be made on Timecard's position, but that the customer should consider taking advice concerning any claim they might have against BSB.

Callers who rent their satellite equipment from a rental supplier   Comet does not supply equipment on a rental basis and these callers were advised to check the situation with their rental company. They were also informed of the managing director's letter available at all Comet stores and the operator outlined its contents. Finally, callers were invited to call the Helpline again when more information might be available.

From the day that the Helpline went 'live', on Saturday, 10 October, Comet had informed many of the callers (according to the group into which they fell) that either the operator would call them back as soon as further information was available, or they could call the Helpline again later. In addition, of course, there were likely to be people calling the Helpline for the first time until its planned closure, once the position had been clarified with British Sky Broadcasting.

On Friday, 16 November, an addition to the script was issued explaining events that had happened in the previous few days. The home secretary, David Waddington, had said in a speech in the House of Commons that the merger was a 'clear breach of contract' and was a matter for the Independent Broadcasting Authority (IBA – the government's broadcasting regulatory body) and the Office of Fair Trading (OFT – the government body regulating mergers and acquisitions). The IBA had subsequently announced that it intended to revoke BSB's programme licence. The addition to the script also expressed Comet's belief that the IBA would be anxious to secure the interests of consumers who had purchased BSB equipment, and mentioned that callers might want to consider registering a complaint in writing directly with the IBA, the OFT or their local MP. If they wished to send a letter, the operator could supply the addresses of the IBA and the mergers branch of the OFT.

The Helpline was still open at the time this case study was written, but in the 11 days from 10–20 November 1990, a total of 1,964 calls had been received. These were broken down as follows:

A   1,493   (bought equipment from Comet);

B   345   (bought equipment from another source);

C   42   (renting equipment from a rental supplier);

D   83   (interested non-satellite equipment owners);

E   1   (member of the press).

Most of the callers with BSB satellite receiving equipment expressed dissatisfaction with BSB and were confused about what was happening, for example whether their equipment would be swapped for ASTRA equipment free of charge. Many also said they were pleased that the 0800 Helpline had been set up and made good use of it by calling more than once to check if any further information was available.

When the situation is finally resolved, Comet will mail the customers who have bought BSB equipment from them, and have given their name and address on the Helpline, with details of the outcome.

The damage that could have been caused to Comet's customer base by the merger announcement, had Comet not taken this proactive stance, cannot be assessed. However, the popularity of the Helpline demonstrated that, even when a relatively small proportion of customers are involved, there are considerable benefits to be gained by directly addressing the issues in crisis situations.

Unlike many crises, the satellite television debacle was not of Comet's making and the company had no control over the outcome of the situation, other than bringing their influence to bear on British Sky Broadcasting. By acting quickly in providing the Helpline, Comet was able to demonstrate a caring approach not only to its own customers but to all consumers who had an interest in the situation. This audience included competitors' customers and so helped the company to establish a dialogue with prospective Comet customers. In addition, the fact that callers were told of the availability of the managing director's letter in all Comet stores provided an inducement for them to visit one of the stores.

Comet turned a crisis situation to its advantage and reinforced its caring approach to customers. In addition, the company enhanced its position with the media in being the main retail source of up-to-date information.

Appendix A

Suppliers of Telephone Marketing Services

UK Suppliers

There were over 100 suppliers of telephone marketing services in the UK at the end of 1990 and this list is not comprehensive. A proportion of suppliers cease trading each year, while new ones enter the market, and some of the details given below may have changed. The names of new suppliers, as well as those not included in this list, sometimes appear in the marketing press (*see* Appendix C). Companies marked with an asterisk (*) are members of the British Direct Marketing Association (BDMA) and it is a condition of their membership that they operate to the standards of ethical and professional conduct laid down in the BDMA's Telephone Marketing Guidelines (*see* Appendix B, pages 443-5).

(**Note:** Inclusion in, or omission from, this list does not infer any recommendation or otherwise by The Decisions Group, the publishers or the author. Every effort has been made to provide accurate and, where possible, complete information. Readers are referred to Chapter 3, pages 100-11, about the importance of careful selection of a supplier; in particular, the quality of service provided should be a major consideration when comparing quotations/charges.)

Abacus Telephone Marketing
204 Queensway
Bletchley
Milton Keynes MK2 2ST
Tel: 0908 270099

*Adkins Wheeler Partnership
St Georges House
40–49 Price Street
Birmingham B4 6LA
Tel: 021-359 8081

*Adlink
West Link House
981 Great West Road
Brentford
Middlesex TW8 9DN
Tel: 081-560 3199

*Aspen Direct
28/32 Shelton Street
London WC2H 9HP
Tel: 071-836 0055

Aspect Marketing
St Mary's Green
Chelmsford
Essex CM1 3TU
Tel: 0245 492828

*Audiotext
Pembroke House
Campsbourne Road
Hornsey
London N8 7PT
Tel: 081-348 4294

*Ayton Marketing Systems
52a High Street
Stokesley
Middlesbrough
Cleveland TS9 5AX
Tel: 0642 711477

*BCC Marketing Services Ltd
Belgrade Business Centre
Denington Road
Wellingborough
Northamptonshire NN8 2QH
Tel: 0933 443322

*BPS Associates Ltd
First House
Sutton Street
Holloway Head
Birmingham B1 1PE
Tel: 021-666 6161

Brann Direct Marketing
(*see* Contact 24)

*BT Connections in Business
Walpole House
18–20 Bond Street
Ealing
London W5 5AA
Tel: 081-567 7300

The Business Extension Ltd
13 Princeton Court
55 Felsham Road
Putney Bridge
London SW15 1AZ
Tel: 081-780 1766

Business Services Agency
Fourth Floor
Charlton House
Chester Road
Old Trafford
Manchester M16 0GW
Tel: 061-873 7161

Callplan International Ltd
45–47 Monument Hill
Weybridge
Surrey KT13 8SF
Tel: 0932 859666

Cans Marketing
2–7 Mancetter Square
Werrington
Peterborough PE4 6BX
Tel: 0733 76967

*CCN Systems Ltd
Talbot House
Talbot Street
Nottingham NG1 5HF
Tel: 0602 410888

*Chapter One Direct plc
Green Lane
Tewkesbury
Gloucestershire GL20 8EZ
Tel: 0684 850040

*Colorgraphic Group
(*see* The Decisions Group)

*Commercial Breaks
13/29 City Business Centre
Hyde Street
Winchester
Hampshire SO23 7TA
Tel: 0962 841131

Concept Telemarketing Ltd
118 Elderslie Street
Glasgow G3 7AW
Tel: 041-226 3994

The Connect Corporation
Sterling House
Browning Street
Ladywood
Birmingham B16 8EH
Tel: 021-452 1797

Contact 24
Fifth Floor
Finance House
Stokes Croft
Bristol BS1 3QY
Tel: 0272 429261

*Control Marketing Ltd
40 Mill Green Road
Mitcham
Surrey CR4 4HY
Tel: 081-640 6722

**The Corporate Group of
Companies**
Gills Green Oast
Gills Green
Hawkhurst
Kent TN18 5ET
Tel: 0580 754000

*Dalman & Dalman
Top House
Woodcote Green
Bromsgrove B61 9EF
Tel: 0562 777000

*Datamail Direct Advertising
34 Alexandra House
140 Battersea Park Road
London SW11 4NB
Tel: 071-720 1202

*Dataplan Direct Ltd
44 London Road
Newbury
Berkshire RG13 1LA
Tel: 0635 38336

*Datapoint UK Ltd
Datapoint House
400 North Circular Road
London NW10 0JG
Tel: 081-459 1222

*The Decisions Group
19 Worple Road
Wimbledon
London SW19 4JS
Tel: 081-879 7766

Direct Communications
Alexander House
Station Road
Aldershot
Hampshire GU11 1BQ
Tel: 0252 312494

*Direct Marketing Services
66 St George's Place
Cheltenham
Gloucestershire GL50 3PN
Tel: 0242 584175

Expedite Group
Britannia House
50 Great Charles Street
Birmingham B3 2LP
Tel: 021-233 2777

Factel
Third Floor
Monaco House
Bristol Street
Birmingham B5 7AS
Tel: 021-622 6841

FKB Telephone Marketing
Third Floor
The Chambers
Chelsea Harbour
London SW10 0XF
Tel: 071-376 5466

*Golley Slater Telephone Marketing
9–11 The Hayes
Cardiff CF1 1NU
Tel: 0222 388621

Henniker Hodder & Worstall
37 St Georges Road
Cheltenham
Gloucestershire GL50 3DU
Tel: 0242 226100

Hotlines Telemarketing Ltd
2 Iffley Road
Hammersmith
London W6 0PA
Tel: 081-741 9596

*IBIS Information Services Ltd
Waterside
Lowbell Lane
London Colney
St Albans
Hertfordshire AL2 1DX
Tel: 0727 25209

In-Touch Telesales
25A Kings Road
Guildford
Surrey GU1 4UW
Tel: 0483 300289

*Judith Donovan Associates Ltd
Phoenix House
Rushton Avenue
Bradford BD3 7BH
Tel: 0274 656222

*Keywords Direct
162 High Street
Southampton
Hampshire SO1 0BT
Tel: 0703 225062

*Kingston Communications
Broadway House
105 Ferensway
Hull
North Humberside HU1 3UN
Tel: 0482 26161

Latchwise Advertising & Marketing Ltd (LAM)
56 Westcliff
Preston
Lancashire PR1 8HO
Tel: 0772 50303

*Ledger Bennett Direct Marketing Ltd
Haywood House
Lake Street
Leighton Buzzard
Bedfordshire LU7 8RS
Tel: 0525 383883

*Leiderman & Roncoroni Ltd
8 Barnard Mews
London SW11 1QU
Tel: 071-738 2424

Lynton Glenthorn Direct
Angel House
7 High Street
Marlborough
Wiltshire SN8 1AA
Tel: 0672 514477

*Mailcom plc
Snowdon Drive
Winterhill
Milton Keynes MK6 1HQ
Tel: 0908 675666

McColl McGregor
17 Napier Square
Houston Industrial Estate
Livingston EH54 5DG
Tel: 0506 31244

*Merit Direct
Merit House
Timothy's Bridge Road
Stratford Upon Avon
Warwickshire CV37 9HY
Tel: 0789 299622

Michael Hope Partnership
Gainsborough
The Findings
Farnborough
Hampshire GU14 9EG
Tel: 0276 34814

Newbury Marketing
47 Aylesbury Road
Thame
Oxfordshire OX9 3PG
Tel: 0844 261777

On Line Marketing (Europe)
Suite 4
121 Cold Bath Road
Harrogate
North Yorkshire HG2 0NU
Tel: 0423 520240

PDT Telemarketing
28 West Street
Marlow-on-Thames
Buckinghamshire SL7 2NB
Tel: 06284 76937

Parade Telemarketing Ltd
Parade House
Rovex Business Park
Hay Hall Road
Tyseley
Birmingham B11 2AF
Tel: 021-706 2020

*Passmore International
Raglan House
St Peter Street
Maidstone
Kent ME16 0ST
Tel: 0622 765454

*Payne Stracey
73–75 Goswell Road
London EC1V 7ER
Tel: 071-490 7555

PBA Group
The Courtyards
Hatters Lane
Watford WD1 8YH
Tel: 0923 55544

*PHM Integrated Direct Marketing
Oakwood House
St John's Estate
Penn
High Wycombe
Buckinghamshire HP10 8HQ
Tel: 0494 816551

*Price Direct Business-to-Business Direct Marketing
505a Norwood Road
West Norwood
London SE27 9DL
Tel: 081-761 7612

*Procter & Procter Direct
20 Fulham Broadway
London SW6 1AH
Tel: 071-381 8889

Profiles Telephone Marketing
59 Harrow Lane
Maidenhead SL6 7NY
Tel: 0628 32828

*Programmes UK Ltd
Edinburgh House
7 Corporation Street
Corby
Northamptonshire NN17 1NG
Tel: 0536 400444

*PSP Marketing
248–250 Lavender Hill
London SW11 1LJ
Tel: 071-228 6730

Ralton Group Ltd
Stephenson Road
Groundwell Industrial Estate
Swindon
Wiltshire SN2 5AN
Tel: 0793 726000

*RCF Marketing Group
20–22 Grosvenor Gardens Mews
North
Belgravia
London SW1W 0JP
Tel: 071-823 5269

Readycall
1 Stanley Road
Bromley
Kent BR2 9JE
Tel: 081-460 6006

*Response Analysis & Mailing Ltd
Unit 8&9
Crusader Industrial Estate
Hermitage Road
London N4 1LZ
Tel: 081-802 4140

*Richmond Response Ltd
Richmond House
Otley Road
Guiseley
Leeds LS20 8BS
Tel: 0943 870202

*RSVP Marketing
Gunhill House
Gunhill
Dedham
Colchester CO7 6HP
Tel: 0206 322333

Rushton Response
Spring Mill
Earby
Colne
Lancashire BB8 6RN
Tel: 0282 844455

*Helena Stevens & Associates
52–54 Cricklade Road
Gorse Hill
Swindon
Wiltshire SN2 6AA
Tel: 0793 614486

*Stormark Ltd
Stormark House
30a Horsefair
Banbury
Oxfordshire OX16 0AE
Tel: 0295 268143

*Systems Market Link Ltd (SML)
Windsor House
Spittal Street
Marlow
Buckinghamshire SL7 3HJ
Tel: 0628 890100

*Telecom Information
4th Floor
Royal Oak House
Prince Street
Bristol BS1 4QE
Tel: 0272 293898

Teleconsult (Ogilvy & Mather Direct)
Knightway House
20 Soho Square
London W1V 6AD
Tel: 071-437 9878

*Teledata Ltd
Unit 3
Aircall Business Centre
Colindeep Lane
London NW9 6BX
Tel: 081-205 0005

Telelab Limited
Greater London House
Hampstead Road
London NW1 7QP
Tel: 071-380 6969

Telemark Communications Ltd
Wimborne House
4 Stanley Park Road
Wallington
Surrey SM6 0EY
Tel: 081-773 1313

*Telemarketing Link Ltd
804 Oxford Avenue
Slough
Berkshire SL1 4LN
Tel: 0753 696161

Telemarketing Network Europe (TNE)
Stennack Road
Holmbush Industrial Estate
St Austell
Cornwall PL25 3JQ
Tel: 0726 72235

*Telephone Database Services Ltd
Tech West 10
Warple Way
London W3 0UE
Tel: 081-746 2626

Teletactics Ltd
18 Hogfair Lane
Burnham
Buckinghamshire SL1 8BU
Tel: 06286 61605

*Timms Triefus Maddick
7 Soho Square
London W1V 6JE
Tel: 071-494 0582

TMP Telephone Marketing
Palmsaa House
Uphall Road
Ilford
Essex IG1 2UF
Tel: 081-514 1072

*UK Connect Ltd
24a Gold Street
Saffron Walden
Essex CB10 1EJ
Tel: 0799 516020

*Wunderman Worldwide Ltd
Greater London House
Hampstead Road
London NW1 7QP
Tel: 071-380 6666

International telephone marketing database

The European Telemarketing Federation, in conjunction with Philip Cohen, one of Europe's telephone marketing gurus, maintains a database of telephone marketing companies in more than 20 countries outside the USA. It includes the address, telephone and fax numbers, size and speciality (inbound/outbound; consumer/business-to-business; specific competence; computerisation etc). Further information can be obtained from:

Philip Cohen
Consultant AB
Stationsgatan 3
S-931 Skelleftea
Sweden
Tel: +46 910 19988
Fax: +46 910 16838

Appendix B

Legislation and Industry Codes of Conduct

This Appendix contains documents outlining the legislation and codes of conduct, referred to in Chapter 10, which relate to telephone marketing activities undertaken in the UK. Many of these are updated regularly and confirmation of the latest revisions can be obtained from the appropriate organisations, whose addresses are given in Appendix C.

(**Note:** Many of these documents are given in extract only. They are reproduced here only to supplement Chapter 10 in providing a basic understanding of the legislation and codes of conduct affecting UK telephone marketing operations. The extracts cannot be relied upon to reflect the true scope or spirit of the documents and it is recommended that anyone intending to undertake telephone marketing activities in the UK first obtains complete copies from the appropriate sources and ensures that they fully understand their implications. The same applies to anyone intending to make calls to or within other countries, so as to ensure that they observe all the relevant legal requirements and good practice initiatives.)

The following documents are covered:

- British Direct Marketing Association Telephone Marketing Guidelines.

- Office of Fair Trading Guidelines.

- ICSTIS Terms of Reference and Code of Practice.

- Extract from Rule 19 of the City Code on Takeovers and Mergers and Substantial Acquisitions.

- The Data Protection Principles of the Data Protection Act.

- Extracts from the Advertising Association's Code of Practice Covering the use of Personal Data for Advertising and Direct Marketing Purposes.

- Extract from the Class Licence for the Running of Branch Telecommunication Systems (Branch Systems General Licence – BSGL).

- Market Research Society Code of Conduct.

- Distinguishing Telephone Research from Telemarketing: ESOMAR Guidelines.

British Direct Marketing Association (BDMA) telephone marketing guidelines

Introduction

The British Direct Marketing Association Guidelines for Telephone Marketing Practices are intended to provide organisations involved in direct telephone marketing to both consumers and businesses with principles of ethical and professional conduct.

All members of the BDMA shall comply with any relevant legislation which may supersede these guidelines. In addition, all members shall comply with the following guidelines in respect of activities not covered by specific law, or when legal requirements are less restrictive than the guidelines.

Disclosure

1. The name of the company on whose behalf a sales and marketing call is made or received should be voluntarily and promptly disclosed, and this information repeated on request at any time during the conversation.
2. The purpose of the call should be made clear at the start, and the content of the call should be restricted to matters directly relevant to its purpose.
3. The name, address and telephone number of the company responsible for the call should appear in the telephone directory, or be available through directory enquiries, or be readily available through another source. This information shall also be given on request.
4. If a telephone marketer is acting as an agent of a company, the name, address and telephone number of the agent should be disclosed upon request at any time during the conversation.
5. If a person phoned was recommended by a third party, the identity of the third party should be voluntarily and promptly disclosed.

Honesty

1. Telephone marketers should not evade the truth or deliberately mislead. Any questions should be answered honestly and fully to the best of the knowledge available.
2. Sales and marketing calls should not be executed in the guise of research or a survey. In cases where the words 'research' or 'survey' are used the information obtained must not be used to form the basis of a direct sales approach either during or after the call.
3. Companies should accept responsibility for statements made by their sales staff or agents.

Reasonable hours

1. Telephone marketers should avoid making sales and marketing calls during hours which are unreasonable to the recipients of the calls, bearing in mind that the OFT recommends that calls to consumers should not be made later than 9.00 pm unless expressly invited and that what is regarded as unreasonable can vary in different parts of the country and in different types of households or businesses.
2. When sales and marketing calls are initiated by a company or its representatives, telephone marketers should ask whether the timing of a call is convenient. If it is not, they should offer to ring back at a more convenient time.

Courtesy and Procedures

1. Normal rules of telephone courtesy should be observed. Telephone marketers should avoid the use of high pressure tactics which could be construed as harassment.
2. Telephone marketers should always recognise the right of the other party to terminate the telephone conversation at any stage, and should accept such termination promptly and courteously.
3. If, as a result of a telephone contact, an appointment is made whereby a representative of a company is to visit a consumer at home, the consumer should be provided with a clearly identified contact point in order to facilitate possible cancellation or alteration of the appointment.
4. Confirmation of an order placed should be sent to the customer and any documents forwarded in accordance with the prevailing legislation.
5. Telephone marketers should take particular care not to seek information or to accept orders or appointments or invite any other action from a minor.
6. When consumer sales and marketing calls are made by a company or its representatives, there should be a cooling off period of at least seven days for oral contracts resulting from such calls, and the recipients of the calls should be so informed.

Restriction of Contacts

1. Sales and marketing calls should not be generated by random or sequential dialling manually or by computer.
2. Sales and marketing calls should not knowingly be made to unlisted or ex-directory numbers.
3. Unless expressly invited consumer calls should not be made to individuals at their place of work.

4. Members should subscribe to the Telephone Preference Service (when it becomes available).
5. Members should delete from their telephone contact lists those persons who have specifically requested not to be contacted by telephone for sales or marketing purposes.
6. When sales and marketing calls are initiated by a company or its representatives and automatic message and recording equipment is used, it is necessary, subject to the requirements of the Branch Systems General Licence, either to:

a) Immediately effect an introduction on the lines of 'This is a computer call on behalf of . . .' or to

b) Have a 'Live' operator introduce the call under those circumstances where the nature of the call is of a personal or a sensitive nature.

Definitions

1. **Business calling:** Sales and marketing calls, for an individual as a representative of his or her company.
2. **Consumer calling:** Sales and marketing calls for an individual not as a representative of his or her employer or company.
3. **Sales & marketing call:** A call designed to generate a sale of a product or service, or to lead toward a sales of a product or service to the specific company or consumer as a result of the information given during a telephone conversation.

BDMA February 1988

Source: British Direct Marketing Association, reprinted with permission.

Office of Fair Trading Guidelines

The Office of Fair Trading considers that all firms responsible for initiating or making unsolicited telephone approaches to consumers should ensure that calls comply with the following guidelines:

The call

1. Callers should ask whether the timing of the call is convenient. If it is not, they should offer to ring back at a more convenient time. Calls should not be made after 9.00pm.
2. The caller's name and that of the company responsible for the call should be given at the start of the call and repeated at any time if requested.
3. The purpose of the call should be made clear at the start, and the content of the call should be restricted to matters directly relevant to its purpose. Calls should never be made under the guise of market research nor combined with the offer of unrelated goods and services.
4. Callers should not mislead, be evasive, exaggerate or use partial truths and they should answer questions honestly and fully. Companies should accept responsibility for statements made by their sales staff or agents and take appropriate disciplinary action if breaches of these guidelines occur.
5. The caller should always recognise the right of the person called to terminate the telephone conversation at any stage and should accept such a termination promptly and courteously.
6. The caller should provide the person called with a clear opportunity to refuse any appointment or offer.
7. If the caller makes an appointment for someone to visit the consumer's home, he or she should provide a contact point in order to facilitate possible cancellation or alteration of the visit by the consumer.

General

8. Unsolicited calls should not be made to people at their place of work.
9. Callers should ensure that they do not obtain information, appointments or orders from minors, and that they do not call unlisted telephone numbers.
10. Consumers should be sent copies of all the relevant documents, including agreements, contracts and statements of their legal rights if they place an order. A cooling-off period of at least seven days should apply following receipt of such papers during which the consumers could, if they wished, cancel their order and be entitled to a refund of any payment which they have made.

Extract from the report, *Selling By Telephone*, October 1984.
Source: The Office of Fair Trading, reprinted with permission.

ICSTIS Terms of Reference and Code of Practice

Terms of reference

To supervise both the content of, and promotional material for, premium rate telephone services and to support the Network Operators in the enforcement of the Code of Practice.

The Independent Committee for the supervision of Standards of Telephone Information Services is appointed to undertake the following tasks:

a) to set standards relating to the content and the promotion of premium rate telephone services and to keep such standards under review;
b) to monitor such services to ensure that both the content and promotional material comply with these standards;
c) to investigate complaints relating to the content and the promotion of premium rate telephone services;
d) to recommend measures designed to achieve compliance where breaches of the Code have been identified; and
e) to provide occasional reports on the numbers and categories of complaints received and the action taken.

This Code of Practice has been produced by the Independent Committee for the supervision of Standards of Telephone Information Services (ICSTIS) and relates to the provision of premium rate services provided by means of a public telecommunications network.

All decisions made by ICSTIS in pursuance of the application of this Code will be made at the discretion of the Committee.

The Code
Part One
Content of Communications

All services

1.1   Communications must not contain false, out-of-date or misleading information.

1.2   Communications must not be of a kind that are likely to:
a) encourage or incite any person to commit a criminal offence;
b) cause grave or widespread offence by reason of their sexual or violent content;
c) debase, degrade or demean;
d) induce or promote racial disharmony;

e) encourage, incite or suggest to any person the use of harmful substances;

f) encourage or incite any person to engage in dangerous practices;

g) induce an unacceptable sense of fear or anxiety;

h) result in any unreasonable invasion of privacy;

i) mislead any person with respect to the content or cost of the service being offered;

j) prolong or delay the service unreasonably.

Expert or specialist services

2.1 Communications containing information or advice involving the skill and judgement of an expert or specialist, must indicate clearly the identity, current status and any relevant professional qualifications and experience of the person(s) supplying the specialist information or advice at the beginning of the communication.

2.2 Where specialist services contain advice, the communication must be prefaced with a statement that the recipient of the communication should not act upon such advice without first consulting a suitably qualified practitioner in the particular field of the relevant specialism.

2.3 All specialist communications should be conveyed in a manner that properly reflects the seriousness of the subject matter of the advice.

Religious and political communications

3.1 Communications which reflect a particular religious or political viewpoint must pay due regard to the sensibilities of those who may reasonably be expected to hold differing religious beliefs or political opinions.

Children and young persons and other dependent persons

4.1 Communications, either wholly or in part, designed for, aimed at or intended for an audience of children and young persons must not include:

a) references to sexual practices that a reasonable parent would not wish his or her child to know about;

b) language that a reasonable parent would not wish his or her child to hear.

4.2 Communications must not involve any invasion of privacy of any child or young person, or any mentally disordered or mentally handicapped person, or of any other dependent person, having regard to the special protection needed for such dependent persons.

4.3 Communications must not encourage children and young persons, or any other dependent persons, to ring additional telephone numbers.

4.4 Communications aimed at, or intended for an audience of children or young persons should be prefaced by a short statement explaining that the service is more expensive than an ordinary telephone call and should only be used with the agreement of the person responsible for paying the telephone bills.

Charities

5.1 Communications aimed at raising revenue for charitable purposes should be prefaced with a statement identifying the fund raiser, the name of the charity and the charitable object to which the funds are being donated.

Part Two
Promotion and Advertising

All promotional material

The following provisions apply to all forms of promotion and advertising where the intent is, either directly, or indirectly, to encourage the use of premium rate services.

Printed material

6.1 This Code incorporates the provisions of the British Code of Advertising Practice (BCAP) and the British Code of Sales Promotion Practice (BCSPP).

6.2 The Service Provider shall ensure that the charge for calls to each service advertised is clearly stated on all material. Prices shall be noted in the form of a price per minute (or part of a minute), inclusive of VAT.*

6.3 So that the reader may readily appreciate the cost of these services, the pricing information must be legible, prominent and horizontal.

6.4 The identity and address of the provider of the service shall be clearly stated on all material.

---

* Televoting services lasting no more than one BT unit of time will not be considered to be in breach of the Code if they fail to comply with this provision.

6.5   The promotional material in relation to specialist services must clearly indicate the current status and relevant professional experience of the person(s) involved in providing the specialist service.

6.6   The promotional material must not be misleading in relation to the service actually provided.

6.7   Advertisements must not contain pictures or words indicating violence, sadism or cruelty, or which are otherwise of a repulsive or horrible nature.

6.8   Advertisements for erotic or sexual entertainment services must not contain pictures or words which suggest or imply the involvement of children or young persons.

6.9   Advertisements which appear in generally available publications (other than 'top shelf publications'*) must not contain pictures or words of a sexually suggestive nature which are unacceptably offensive.

6.10   Advertisements for erotic or sexual entertainment services must not appear in free or unsolicited publications.

Children and young persons

7.1   Promotional material aimed at, or intended to be readily accessible to an audience of children or young persons, should include a statement (which is no less distinctive than the main message) explaining that the service is more expensive than an ordinary telephone call and should only be used with the agreement of the person responsible for paying the telephone bills.

7.2   Furthermore, BCAP – Section C.X paragraph 1.1 states that 'Direct appeals or exhortations to buy should not be made to children unless the product advertised is one likely to be of interest to them and one which they could reasonably be expected to afford themselves'.

---

* For the purpose of this provision, 'top shelf publications' are publications which by reason of their erotic, indecent or sexually entertaining or explicit content, are normally placed on the top shelf by newsagents.

Other forms of promotion and advertising

8.1   Promotional material on radio, television, cable, telephone or other forms of transmission will be required to observe these rules to the extent reasonable and appropriate to the technology employed.

Source: ICSTIS, reprinted with permission.

Extract from Rule 19 of the City Code on Takeovers and Mergers and Substantial Acquisitions

19.5   Telephone campaigns

Except with the consent of the Panel, campaigns in which shareholders are contacted by telephone may be conducted only by staff of the financial adviser who are fully conversant with the requirements of, and their responsibilities under, the Code. Only previously published information which remains accurate, and is not misleading at the time it is quoted, may be used in telephone campaigns. Shareholders must not be put under pressure and must be encouraged to consult their professional advisers.

Notes on Rule 19.5

1. Consent to use other callers

   If it is impossible to use staff of the type mentioned in this Rule, the Panel may consent to the use of other people subject to:

   a) an appropriate script for callers being approved by the Panel;
   b) the financial adviser carefully briefing the callers prior to the start of the operation and, in particular, stressing:

      (i)   that callers must not depart from the script;
      (ii) that callers must decline to answer questions the answers to which fall outside the information given in the script; and
      (iii) the callers' responsibilities under General Principle 2; and

   c) the operation being supervised by the financial adviser.

2. New information

   If, in spite of this Rule, new information is given to some share-holders, such information must immediately be made generally available to shareholders in the manner described in Note 3 on Rule 20.1.

3. Gathering of irrevocable undertakings

   The Panel must be consulted before a telephone campaign is conducted with a view to gathering irrevocable undertakings to accept an offer. Rule 19.5 applies to such campaigns although, in appropriate circumstances, the Panel may permit those called to be informed of details of a proposed offer which has not been publicly announced. Attention is, however, drawn to General Principles 2 and 4.

4. Financial Services Act 1986

The provisions of the Financial Services Act 1986 (such as Section 56, relating to unsolicited calls) and also rules made by the Securities and Investments Board or other regulatory bodies may be relevant to the telephoning of shareholders. Any view expressed by the Panel in relation to such telephoning can only relate to the Code and must not be taken to extend to that Act or to any such rules.

25.10.90

Source: The Panel on Takeovers & Mergers, reprinted with permission.

The Data Protection Principles of the Data Protection Act

The first principle: The information to be contained in personal data shall be obtained, and personal data shall be processed, fairly and lawfully.

The second principle: Personal data shall be held only for one or more specified and lawful purposes.

The third principle: Personal data held for any purpose or purposes shall not be used or disclosed in any manner incompatible with that purpose or those purposes.

The fourth principle: Personal data held for any purpose or purposes shall be adequate, relevant and not excessive in relation to that purpose or those purposes.

The fifth principle: Personal data shall be accurate and, when necessary, kept up to date.

The sixth principle: Personal data held for any purpose or purposes shall not be kept longer than is necessary for that purpose or those purposes.

The seventh principle: An individual shall be entitled:
a) at reasonable intervals and without undue delay or expense:
   i) to be informed by any data user whether he holds personal data of which that individual is the subject;
   and
   ii) to have access to any such data held by a data user;
   and
b) where appropriate, to have such data corrected or erased.

The eighth principle: Appropriate security measures shall be taken against unauthorised access to, or alteration, disclosure or destruction of, personal data and against accidental loss or destruction of personal data.

Source: Office of the Data Protection Registrar, reprinted with permission.

Extracts from The Advertising Association's Code of Practice covering the use of Personal Data for Advertising and Direct Marketing Purposes (Second edition, June 1990)

Foreword

... The First Principle also requires that information to be contained in personal data shall be fairly obtained. The Advertising Association's view of how this requirement can be met, which is included in Section 3.1 of the Code, differs from my own.

In order to meet the fair obtaining requirement, I take the view that, when obtaining information for direct marketing purposes a data user should inform the person supplying the information as to whom the information is for, why the information is required and for what purposes the information will be used or disclosed. Armed with this information, that person can then decide whether to provide the information or not.

If the identity of the data users and all the intended uses and disclosures are clear from the context in which the information is being supplied, no further explanation should be necessary. In some cases, however, there may be additional uses and disclosures which the person supplying the information could not reasonably be expected to know about. Then, the duty to obtain information fairly requires steps to be taken to make him aware of the true position. This will usually be done by briefly explaining the intended uses, disclosures and users. A general description will usually be sufficient.

My view does not generally demand that individuals should be given the opportunity to opt out of the use, for direct marketing purposes, of the information they provide. However, the provision of an opt out can be helpful and may be necessary in some circumstances. I welcome the fact that a number of organisations carrying out direct marketing activities are now offering an opt out to individuals when they first collect information from them. This is a helpful standard for the industry to set. ...

The Registrar has a duty to promote the observance of the Data Protection Principles and to consider any complaints that they may have been breached. In considering the case of any data user on its merits, I shall have regard to whether, and how, the data user has sought to abide by the appropriate parts of this Code. However, observance of this Code does not guarantee that I will accept that a particular data user has complied with the Act.

February 1990

Eric J Howe
Data Protection Registrar

Preface

... over the last three years, the views of the industry and those of the Registrar have moved apart on one particular aspect of 'fair obtaining' of personal data as required by the First Principle, and that fact is highlighted in ... the Registrar's Foreword. There has been a vigorous debate on the points involved, both privately between the AA's Data Protection Committee and the Registrar's Office, and in the press, causing a shift in emphasis away from reliance on register entry as the sole source of information for data subjects about data users' purposes and activities.

This shift has led to a revision of S.3.1 of the Code which now requires, in certain circumstances defined in Sub-Section 3.1.8, that data subjects be given specific information about 'significantly different' uses which data users intend to make of their personal data, and also that they be given the opportunity to object to such use.

There is no difference of opinion between the Registrar and the Advertising Association about the transparent nature of the vast majority of commercial transactions involving the use of personal data, and the predictability of what use will be made of such data in the course of a developing commercial relationship. The difference arises in connection with the timing of any notice given to data subjects of the intention to put personal data to 'significantly different' use. The position of the Advertising Association, reinforced by the Council of Europe *Recommendation on the Protection of personal data used for the purposes of direct marketing*, R(85)20), is reflected in Sub-Section 3.1.9 ...

Revised Guideline 4, published by the Registrar in February 1989, ... lays stress on the need for the data subject to be clearly informed of the data user's identity and intentions at the time of data collection. There is the implication that, in the absence of such clarity, personal data may be used only for purposes which were transparent at the time of collection.

This view runs counter to the AA's view that fair collection must include the possibility of changes in the use of data subsequent to the act of collection, as long as data subjects are given notice and the opportunity to object.

The question will not be resolved until a case is decided by the courts. In the meantime, the AA stands by the Code but wishes its members to be aware of a freely acknowledged difference in the interpretation of the First Principle between the Registrar and itself.

Part I Introduction

2 Duties of the Data User

2.5 The Council of Europe *Recommendation on the protection of personal data used for the purposes of direct marketing,* whilst directed at protecting the privacy of the individual in the face of the growing use of data processing in direct marketing, also recognises that the use of personal data is essential to the maintenance and development of direct marketing. The Data Protection Act does not prevent the use of personal data for legitimate direct marketing purposes provided that the data user is properly registered and complies with the Data Protection Principles. Nothing in this code is intended to restrict the proper use of personal data for direct marketing. It is of the essence of this Code that its provisions are intended to safeguard the rights of data subjects in such a way that good customer relations and good business practice coincide.

2.6 Nowhere is this coincidence more clearly demonstrated than in the case of data subjects who do not wish to receive unsolicited marketing approaches as a consequence of their personal data being put to uses which they could not have foreseen at the time those data were collected, and to which they would have objected had they known. These are the very prospects data users will wish to pin-point in order to avoid.

2.7 Data users' duties to the data subject (as described in this Code) include therefore:

    a) reminders at appropriate times of the existence of the Register and the Data Protection Act;

    b) particular care in cases where it is intended to pass personal data to third parties so as to give data subjects an opportunity to object;

    c) the installation and maintenance of facilities for recording and honouring objections to direct marketing approaches whether received direct or via the Mailing Preference Service.

Part II Principal Provisions

3 The Principles

3.1 *The First Principle* **The information to be contained in personal data shall be obtained, and personal data shall be processed, fairly and lawfully.**

3.1.7 There are however circumstances in which the requirement of fairness in the collection of personal data calls for additional measures. In such cases (see 3.1.8 below) data users to whom this Code applies should at an appropriate point in their communications, and subject to the conditions set out in 3.1.9 below, advise data subjects in general terms of the uses and/or disclosures that are intended to be made in the particular circumstances, and how data subjects may object thereto.

3.1.8   A statement as mentioned in Section 3.1.7 above must be made to data subjects in all cases in which, at the time that personal data are collected, data users intend to put their personal data to a significantly different use, namely

a) to disclose their personal data to third parties for direct marketing purposes; or
b) to use or disclose their personal data for any purpose(s) substantially different from the purpose(s) for which they were collected and which data subjects could not reasonably have foreseen and to which it is probable that they would have objected if they had known; or
c) in any other case in which, but for the making of such a statement, harm to data subjects would be likely to occur.

3.1.9   For the purpose of the foregoing Section, an appropriate point will

a) in all cases be at the time of collection of the personal data; or
b) at any other time prior to the intended use or disclosure, provided that the notice is so served as to allow the data subject adequate opportunity to object to such use or disclosure.

3.1.10 Data users must comply with any objections from data subjects to their personal data being put to any significantly different use.

3.1.11 Fairness and lawfulness apply also to antecedent possession and collection, and data users should therefore, as far as is practicable, ensure that personal data they propose to acquire or to use comply with this Principle. In many cases, the data user will have to be satisfied with a formal warranty from the supplier that they do.
The warranty from the list owner should include undertakings that

a) he is registered as a data user;
b) the data were fairly and lawfully obtained;
c) the list was updated on a specified date or during a specified period. This undertaking should be accompanied by a statement of the respects in which the data have been updated;
d) requests from data subjects for the correction or deletion of data have been complied with;
e) received and disputed data have, where appropriate, been so marked;

f) the purpose or purposes for which the data are registered are compatible with their disclosure to the intending user and his proposed use of them;

g) the data have, where applicable, been collected, held and processed in compliance with the Code.

The warranty should also state whether the list has been MPS cleaned, and if so, during what period this was last done.

3.1.12 The supplier of any such list as aforesaid should in turn require from the prospective user undertakings that

a) the data will be used only for the purpose or purposes authorised by the supplier;

b) where the prospective user is required to be registered under the Act, those purposes are within the terms of the prospective user's registration;

c) no disclosure will be made to any third party, except as expressly permitted by the supplier, and provided always that any such disclosure is covered by the terms of the prospective user's registration;

d) any request for access, correction or deletion received by the prospective data user from a data subject will, when appropriate, be referred to the supplier.

Part III Additional rules

5 Miscellaneous Provisions

The foregoing rules define the obligations of data users and, where appropriate, bureaux in relation to the Principles governing data protection. In several cases they afford benefits that go beyond the requirements of the Act. But they do not exhaust the wider social obligations of data users. Further rules applicable to the conduct of direct mail advertising and marketing are set out in this section.

5.1   Data users must comply with the provisions of the British Code of Advertising Practice, the British Code of Sales Promotion Practice and the sectoral codes to which they subscribe (e.g. those promulgated by the Association of Mail Order Publishers, the British Direct Marketing Association, the Mail Order Traders' Association, the Direct Mail Producers' Association and the British List Brokers' Association).

5.2   Even though the Act does not state that data subjects have a right to have their names excluded from mailing lists, the Council of Europe's

Recommendation on data protection and direct marketing proposes that such a facility should be made available. Accordingly, data users to which this Code applies must comply with the requirements of the Code of Practice of the Mailing Preference Service and should, where possible, use the recommended method of not erasing the name, but of retaining it on file with a suppression marker.

Source: Advertising Association, reprinted with permission.

Extract from Class Licence for the Running of Branch Telecommunication Systems (Branch Systems General Licence – BSGL – published November 8 1989, by Oftel)

Condition 9

Restrictions on advertising and supply activities

9.1 Where the Licensee conveys Messages by means of a connection between an Applicable System and a Specified Public Telecommunication System for the purposes of the advertising or the offering for supply or provision or the supply or provision of goods, services or any other thing, and receives from any person who runs a telecommunication system by means of which he receives such Messages a request to cease sending them to a telecommunication system run by that person, the Licensee or any member of its Group shall:
a) forthwith cease sending such messages to any telecommunication system run by that person and identified to the Licensee by reference to a number which is used to make calls to that system;
b) maintain, or secure that there is maintained, a record giving particulars of the persons and the Numbers referred to in subparagraph (a) above and shall make that record available for inspection on reasonable notice by the Director.

9.2 Where:
a) in respect of a telecommunication system run by him or on his behalf a person has notified a Specified Person that he does not wish to receive unsolicited calls (whether of a general or a particular kind) made for the purpose of the advertising or the offering for supply or provision or the supply or provision of goods, services or any other thing; and
b) a Specified Person keeps a list of such notifications in a form specified by the Director and made available for inspection by the public.

The Licensee or any member of its Group shall not make such unsolicited calls to the telecommunication systems so listed.

9.3 Paragraph 9.2 shall only have effect where the Director has determined the description of unsolicited call to which the paragraph shall apply and the description of persons who shall be entitled to notify a Specified Person under the paragraph in relation to any such description of unsolicited call and the Director may determine different descriptions of unsolicited call and different descriptions of persons in relation to such calls.

9.4   In this Condition:

'Number' has the meaning set out in Condition 22.8;

'Specified Person' means a person who so consents specified by the Director for the purpose of keeping and making available for inspection by the public a list as specified by the Director of telecommunication systems in respect of which a person has notified the Specified Person that they do not wish to receive unsolicited calls made for the purpose of the advertising or the offering for supply or provision or the supply or provision of goods, services or any other thing.

Source: Crown Copyright, reproduced by kind permission of OFTEL.

Extracts from The Market Research Society & Industrial Marketing Research Association Code of Conduct (January 1991)

Relationship with other Codes

This Code is broadly compatible with the Codes of AMSO (Association of Market Survey Organisations), and the ICC/ESOMAR International Code of Marketing and Social Research Practice.

It does not take precedence over national law. Members responsible for research overseas shall take its provisions or those of the ESOMAR Code as a minimum requirement and fulfil any other responsibilities set down in law or by nationally agreed standards.

Basic principles

Research is founded upon the willing co-operation of the public and of business organisations. It depends upon public and business confidence that it is conducted honestly, objectively, without unwelcome intrusion and without harm to informants. Its purpose is to collect and analyse information, and not directly to create sales nor to influence the opinions of anyone participating in it. It is in this spirit that the Code of Conduct has been devised.

The general public and other interested parties shall be entitled to complete assurance that every project is carried out strictly in accordance with this Code, and that their rights of privacy are respected.

In particular, they must be assured that no information which could be used to identify them will be made available without their agreement to anyone outside the agency responsible for conducting the research. They must also be assured that the information they supply will not be used for any purposes other than research and that they will in no way be adversely affected or embarrassed as a direct result of their participation in a research project.

Finally, the research findings themselves must always be reported accurately and never used to mislead anyone, in any way.

Rules

A.   RESPONSIBILITIES TO INFORMANTS

   Assurances must be honoured

A.1   Any statement made to secure co-operation and all assurances given to an informant, whether oral or written, shall be factually correct and honoured.

Confidentiality must be guaranteed

A.2　No information which could be used to identify people or companies shall be revealed to anyone, except to those who need it to check the validity of the data or who are engaged in the processing of them. These people must not make any other use of this information or pass it on to anyone else. All persons (including interviewers) involved in handling data must be familiar with, and have agreed to abide by, the relevant provisions of this Code.

It is only with the permission of the informant that the above requirement may be altered. If such permission is given it must be recorded by the interviewer at the time.

This rule applies to all forms of research including participant observation studies. The informant may not be aware that he has participated in a research project but he is still fully entitled to have his identity protected, and the responsible member must ensure this.

A.3　To preserve the confidentiality of the information provided by informants, members must ensure that all reasonable care is taken to keep questionnaires and data files secure, whether they are held in hard copy or on computer.

A.5　Where there is a possibility that a respondent may be identifiable even without the use of his name or address (eg because of the smallness of the population being sampled), then this must be made clear to him and he must be given the opportunity to withdraw from the research.

A.6　Where informants represent an organisation, or are speaking for a function (eg marketing manager, managing director) then their organisation may be listed in the report if it is essential to indicate sample coverage. It shall not, however, be possible for any piece of information obtained directly from an informant or otherwise provided in confidence to be related to any particular organisation, nor for any individual informant to be identified, either directly or indirectly, without his explicit permission.

Adverse effects must be avoided

A.7　All reasonable precautions shall be taken to ensure that the informant, and others closely associated with him, are in no way adversely affected or embarrassed as a direct result of any interview, including product test participation, or any other communication concerning the research project.

A.8　Where use of the information that will be contained in the survey report might have an adverse effect directly on the informant's organisation (eg when interviewing a competitor or a potential competitor), it is imperative that the nature or sponsor of the survey be revealed before the relevant information is collected.

A.10 A leaflet, card or letter giving the name of an organisation and a telephone number must be left with, or sent to, the informant so that he may check that the interview is genuine. This should include thanks to the informant and if appropriate a minimal explanation of the principles of research.

In the case of telephone surveys, at the end of the interview the interviewer should offer the name of the agency or client, a telephone number, and a contact name. He must also offer the informant the opportunity of verifying that the survey is genuine in a way that does not lead the informant to incur any cost.

A.13 The informant's right to withdraw, or to refuse to co-operate at any stage, shall be respected. No procedure or technique shall be used to coerce or imply that co-operation is obligatory. If the research is being conducted under statutory powers the possible consequences of refusal shall be explained to the informant.

A.16 In the case of telephone interviews it is not necessary to tell the informant that the call is being monitored by a supervisor or executive of the agency when this is solely for the purpose of quality control. If visitors wish to monitor a telephone interview they shall only be permitted to do so if they are familiar with, and have agreed to abide by, the relevant provisions of this Code.

A.17 If an informant wishes to withdraw from a survey he has the right to have his questionnaire destroyed. In the case of telephone interviews the research agency shall write to the informant confirming that this has been done. As with all points relating to telephone interviewing, this applies equally to surveys using hard copy questionnaires and to computer-aided telephone interviewing methods.

A.18 No calls in person or by telephone shall be made to a domestic household before 9.00 am weekdays, 10.00 am Sundays, or after 9.00 pm any day, unless by appointment. For those carrying out overseas research the conventions of the country in which the research is being carried out should be followed.

Special care shall be taken in interviewing children

A.19 Before children under the age of 14 are interviewed, or asked to complete a questionnaire, the permission of a parent, guardian, or other person responsible for them, such as a teacher, shall be obtained. In obtaining this permission the interviewer shall allow the responsible person to see or hear the questions which will be asked, or, if this is not practicable, shall describe the nature of the interview in sufficient detail to enable a reasonable person to reach an informed decision, ie not only should the subject matter of the interview be described, but any sensitive or embarrassing questions, scale items, techniques or other material, should also be brought to the attention of the responsible person. The responsible person shall also be specifically informed if it is intended to ask the children to test any products or samples.

Throughout this Code reference to the informant shall be read as references to the parent or other person responsible for the child, either instead of, or in addition to, the child.

A.20   Members must be alert to circumstances where the sensitive nature of the research requires that this procedure should also be followed with young people aged 14–17 years.

A.21   For any research carried out among those aged under 18 years, the criterion must be that when the parent or guardian hears about the interview no reasonable person would expect him to be upset or disturbed.

B.   RESPONSIBILITIES TO THE GENERAL PUBLIC AND THE BUSINESS COMMUNITY

B.1   Public confidence in research shall not be intentionally abused.

B.2   No activity shall be misrepresented as research. Specifically, the following activities shall in no way be associated directly or by implication, with the collection of research data:

a) enquiries whose objectives are to obtain personal information about private individuals per se, whether for legal, political, private or other purposes;

b) the compilation of lists, registers or data banks of names and addresses for non-research purposes (eg canvassing or fund raising), unless this is done from already available sources other than market research;

c) industrial, commercial or any other form of espionage;

d) the acquisition of information for use by credit-rating or similar services;

e) sales or promotional approaches to the informant;

f) the collection of debts;

g) direct or indirect attempts, including the framing of questions, to influence an informant's opinions or attitudes on any issue.

Source: The Market Research Society and Industrial Marketing Research Association, reprinted with permission.

Distinguishing Telephone Research from Telemarketing: ESOMAR Guidelines (February 1989)

Introduction

Both market research and telemarketing are in themselves legitimate activities in most countries. However, telemarketing presents some growing dangers for market research and the two activities need to be clearly differentiated. Telemarketing must not be carried out under the banner of market research or in any way confused with it.

The ICC/ESOMAR International Code of Marketing and Social Research Practice stresses the importance of maintaining the public's confidence in the integrity of market research and sets out responsibilities towards informants and the public generally. In particular:

1. Article 2 emphasises that survey informants' rights to anonymity must always be strictly observed and their names and addresses must not be used for non-research purposes.
2. Article 13 specifies that among the activities which 'shall in no way be associated, directly or by implication, with Marketing Research interviewing or activities' are
   – 'the compilation of lists, registers or data banks for any purposes which are not Marketing Research'
   – 'sales or promotional approaches to the Informant'.

Any associations of these kinds are likely to damage the public's image of market research as such and to lead to increasing levels of non-cooperation in research surveys (and possibly to legal restrictions on the freedom of survey research).

We must not compromise on these principles and jeopardise the public's cooperation with us.

ESOMAR is a Society with individual membership, and it spans a wide range of countries with different social and legislative systems. For these reasons it would be very difficult for the Society to introduce a mandatory Code governing the activities of organisations as such. It can however set out Guidelines as a recommended framework for action at national level. This is the purpose of the present document. There are certain countries, such as the Federal Republic of Germany, where some of the recommendations are already mandatory requirements under local laws or regulations. However, as with other problems, ESOMAR believes that in general self-regulation is preferable to legally-enforced restrictions imposed by courts of law. The ESOMAR Council hopes that by following these Guidelines, the market research profession can avoid the difficulties which often result from restrictions imposed from outside. The recommendations should be regarded as the minimum requirements necessary in those countries which do not already have stricter local legislation. Although many of the points inevitably relate to the activities of organisations as such, individual Members of the Society will usually have the authority or influence needed to put the recommendations into effect.

What is telemarketing?

This term covers a range of telephone activities which are intended to result in a sale of some product or service to an identified potential customer – either immediately or at some later date. By definition it involves the obtaining by the seller of the name and address of the person to whom the sale is to be made. These activities are therefore clearly in conflict with Articles 2 and 13 of the International Code. They may also create other difficulties for the market research profession.

'*Inbound*' telemarketing (where the *customer* initiates the telephone call, usually as the result of having seen some advertisement or as part of some more regular ordering procedure) poses no problems for market research. The customer is under no illusions of participating in a market research survey; and he need disclose his name and address only if he chooses to do so, knowing the likely consequences of this.

'*Outbound*' telemarketing (where the *seller* initiates the call) may be:

a) *business to business*; or
b) *business to private consumer*.

In either case, it may involve:

1) a *database call*, where the objective is to compile, update or 'enrich' a sales list for use on some later occasion; or
2) a *selling call*, where the purpose is actually to make a sale.

Business-to-business activities are less likely to cause problems for market research. Most are clearly identified as a marketing operation and use the name of the selling company. The respondent will probably be used to receiving such calls and accept them as standard business practice. Problems can however arise:

– if the call is made under the pretence of carrying out a market research survey (more likely in the case of database calls)
– if the respondent is a member of a 'high-risk' group which is the target of an unacceptably large number of these calls, such as doctors, specialists, purchasing managers.

Business-to-private-consumer telemarketing is the field where most problems arise for market research. Certain higher-value goods and services (eg durables, household improvements, financial services) are increasingly being marketed in this way. There are far greater dangers that such activities will be confused with market research and that they will irritate the public generally.

What problems does telemarketing create for market research?

The rapid growth of telemarketing internationally is happening at the same time that an increasing proportion of market research worldwide is being carried out by telephone. Both these trends will continue.

The *main dangers* which arise for market research are:

1. *Confusion* in the minds of the public between telemarketing and genuine market research. At worst, less scrupulous telemarketing operators may use a pseudo-research approach in making their calls ('sugging', or selling-under-the-guise-of-research). Even without this element of deliberate deception, a respondent may find it difficult to distinguish between a genuine research call – with all the attendant safeguards under our Code of Practice – and a telemarketing call asking for personal information of the kinds needed for a sales database. This confusion may well reduce public willingness to cooperate in market research surveys.
2. An increase in the total number of unsolicited telephone calls of all kinds, leading to growing public *irritation* and therefore again to unwilling-ness to cooperate in genuine research. This is especially a danger among high-risk groups such as senior business executives, professional people such as doctors, or people living in more affluent neighbourhoods.
3. There is in any case a trend for public authorities and courts of law to restrict activities which involve any perceived 'intrusion on privacy', and to control the collection and holding of personal data of different kinds. Confusion between market research and telemarketing, and growing irritation with unwanted telephone calls, could lead to *restrictions or even a ban* on the use of the telephone for both research and selling.

These dangers are not hypothetical. They have already created difficulties for market research in the US and are showing signs of doing the same in certain countries in Europe and elsewhere.

Action

National market research associations are urged to follow up the recom-mendations set out below, adapting and strengthening them as appropriate to their national situation. In doing this it will be important to take into account the view both of local researchers and also of others working in marketing, including telemarketing itself. The best hope of minimising the problems discussed in these Guidelines will be to work as closely as possible in cooperation with telemarketing organisations, encouraging the latter to develop their own compatible Codes to differentiate their activities from those of market research and also – if and when they themselves diversify into market research – to follow the principles set out here and in the main ICC/ESOMAR International Code.

Recommendations

1. *Ban on Direct Selling Calls, Outbound, to Consumers*

   It is recommended that no market researcher will be engaged in selling calls (as previously defined) to the private consumer, even if he or she should be directly or indirectly linked to a non-market research organisation, the business of which may involve telemarketing or database marketing.

2. *Separation of Activities*

   In a growing number of cases, market research and telemarketing are carried out within the same organisation or group of organisations. In order to differentiate clearly between the two types of activity:

   2.1 *Different organisation names and addresses* should be used in conducting the different activities even where the same telephone installation is used. The names should be very clearly differentiated to avoid any possible confusion. Names such as 'ABC Telephone Research' and 'ABC Telemarketing' can easily be confused by the public, and some alternative such as 'XYZ Telemarketing' should be used instead. Telemarketing company names should also avoid the use of words with a research connotation.

   2.2 The two types of activity should be conducted *by different principals*.

   2.3 Where the same telephone installation is being used for both, *different telephone numbers* should be allocated and publicised for the different activities.

   2.4 It is preferable that *different staff* are used for the tasks of telephone interviewing and telephone selling (in any case, the skills required are often different). If, for any reason, any of the same people are used, they should be *clearly instructed* in the different objectives and procedures involved, and the two types of project clearly separated operationally.

   2.5 The use of the telephone for *compiling lists of 'business prospects'* (or for adding to the file of information on an existing list), where the lists are then used for sales or other non-research purposes, is *not* a market research activity (Article 13 of the International Code). Market research organisations must always fully safeguard the *anonymity of respondents* when carrying out market research.

In a growing number of countries *a clear separation of the two types of activities is in any case increasingly likely to be necessary in order to comply with data protection legislation.*

3. *Telephone Research – Good Practice*

Telephone research calls should of course conform to general good research practice, but the practical aspects of telephone contact make certain considerations even more important. In particular:

3.1 It is essential to make clear to the respondent at the outset that the call is concerned only with *a research survey* and that no element of selling is involved (either immediately or in the future).

3.2 Respondents should be clearly told how they can *check* the bona fides of the research organisation, or raise any other queries about it or the research, at no cost to themselves.

(FREEFONE numbers operated by the research organisations, individually or jointly, are one possible tool for this).

3.3 Since many people are worried at receiving an unexpected telephone call from a complete stranger, it is important to be able to give a clear and convincing *explanation* of why the particular respondent's number is being called, and how it has been selected. This is critical if any selection procedure is used which leads to calling a proportion of non-listed (ex-Directory) numbers. The use of automatic dialling equipment which continually recalls a given number until the respondent replies to the call is *not* acceptable.

3.4 Calling should be restricted to 'sensible', acceptable *interviewing hours*. Given the lack of personal contact, additional care may be needed to make the experience an interesting and pleasant one for the respondent.

4. *Actions by Local Market Research Associations*

The local market research association(s) in each country should consider what steps are necessary and appropriate to maintain public and governmental support for the practices of bona fide market research. In particular:

4.1 *Establishing links with the local telemarketing association,* or relevant groups of telemarketing companies, in order to encourage the adoption by the latter of suitable codes of practice designed to
   – outlaw 'sugging'
   – reduce the more general dangers of confusion between selling and research

  – minimise the possible irritation effects of unsolicited calling.
  Such steps are of course also in the interests of the clients for both
  types of activity.

4.2 *Increasing public and official awareness of the safeguards provided by the*
  ICC/ESOMAR International Code and any relevant national codes,
  especially in
  – banning the use of market research interviews for direct selling
  – guaranteeing the security of any personal or confidential information supplied by respondents
  – guaranteeing respondent anonymity.

4.3 *Introducing a free 'hotline' facility for respondents,* or the public generally,
  to call with any complaints or queries (this facility already exists in a
  few countries).

4.4 *Periodically monitoring* the extent and nature of any public dissatisfaction with unsolicited telephone calling so that, if necessary, further
  remedial action can be taken.

Appendix C

Further Information

This Appendix includes details of organisations referred to in the body of the book together with other sources of information, advice, products and services for telephone marketing and related activities.

(**Note:** Inclusion in, or omission from, this list does not infer any recommendation or otherwise by The Decisions Group, the publishers or the author. Every effort has been made to provide accurate and, where possible, complete information.)

UK Organisations

The Advertising Association
Abford House
15 Wilton Road
London SW1V 1NJ
Tel: 071-828 4831/2771

Association of Mail Order Publishers
1 New Burlington Street
London W1X 1FD
Tel: 071-437 0706

British Direct Marketing Association
Grosvenor Gardens House
35 Grosvenor Gardens
London SW1W 0BS
Tel: 071-630 7322

British List Brokers' Association
16 The Pines
Broad Street
Guildford
Surrey GU3 3BH
Tel: 0483 301311

Chartered Institute of Marketing
Moor Hall
Cookham
Maidenhead
Berkshire SL6 9QH
Tel: 06285 24922

Colman RSCG Direct
35 Bedford Street
London WC2E 9EN
Tel: 071-379 6292

Colorgraphic Group
Response House
Christopher Mews
Saxby Street
Leicester LE2 0ND
Tel: 0533 556373

Direct Mail Producers Association
34 Grand Avenue
London N10 3BP
Tel: 081-883 9854

Direct Mail Services Standards Board
26 Eccleston Street
London SW1W 9PY
Tel: 071-824 8651

The Direct Marketing Agency Register Ltd
12 Harley Street
London W1N 1ED
Tel: 0992 501805 (administration)

The Direct Marketing Centre
1 Park Road
Teddington
Middlesex TW11 0AR
Tel: 081-977 5705

The Direct Marketing Organisation
21a Caroline Street
St Paul's Square
Birmingham B3 1UE
Tel: 021-233 9553

ICSTIS
(The Independent Committee for the supervision of Standards of Telephone Information Services)
4–12 Lower Regent Street
London SW1Y 4PE
Tel: 071-925 0110

Mailing Preference Service
1 Leeward House
Plantation Wharf
London SW11 3TY
Tel: 071-738 1625

The Market Research Society
15 Northburgh Street
London EC1V 0AH
Tel: 071-490 4911

Office of Fair Trading
Field House
15–25 Bream's Buildings
London EC4A 1PR
Tel: 071-242 2858

Office of Telecommunications (Oftel)
Export House
50 Ludgate Hill
London EC4M 7JJ
Tel: 071-822 1600

Office of the Data Protection Registrar
Springfield House
Water Lane
Wilmslow
Cheshire SK9 5AX
Tel: 0625 535777 (enquiries)
Tel: 0625 535711 (administration)

The Panel on Takeovers and Mergers
PO Box No 226
The Stock Exchange Building
London EC2P 2JX
Tel: 071-382 9026

Securities and Investments Board (SIB)
Gavrelle House
2–14 Bunhill Row
London EC1Y 8RA
Tel: 071-638 1240

National and international trade associations

The organisations listed in this section can generally provide information about codes of conduct and legislation relating to telephone marketing in and to their respective countries.

Australia

Australian Direct Marketing Association
10th Floor
52–58 Clarence Street
PO Box 3982
Sydney NSW 2000
Australia
Telephone: +61 2 247 7744
Telex: 70842
Fax: +61 2 262 2435

Austria

Direct Marketing Verband/ Esterreich
Südrandstrasse 7
Postfach 100
1232 Vienna
Austria
Telephone: +43 1 67 0996
Fax: +43 1 67 6633

Belgium

Vlaamse Direct Marketing Vereniging (VDMD)
Bierbeekstraat 14
3001 Louvain
Belgium
Tel: +32 16 23 3109
Telex: 72080
Fax: +32 16 29 1809

Association du Marketing Direct (AMD)
142 Rue de Stalle
1180 Brussels
Belgium
Tel: +32 2 332 0375
Fax: +32 2 332 1070

Canada

Canadian Direct Marketing Association
1 Concorde Gate
Suite 607
Don Mills
Ontario M3C 3N6
Canada
Tel: +1 416 391 2362
Fax: +1 416 441 4062

Denmark

Dansk Markedefoeringsforbund
(Danish Direct Marketing Association)
Vesterbrogade 24 4
1620 Copenhagen V
Denmark
Tel: +45 31 22 1782
Fax: +45 31 22 4688

Europe

European Direct Marketing Association
34 Rue du Gouvernement Provisoire
B-1000 Brussels
Belgium
Tel: +32 2 217 6309
Fax: +32 2 217 6985

European Telemarketing Federation
(as above)

European Society for Opinion and Marketing Research (ESOMAR)
JJ Viottastraat 29
1071 JP Amsterdam
The Netherlands
Tel: +31 20 664 2141
Telex: 18535
Fax: +31 20 664 2922

Finland

Suomen Suoramarkkinointiliitto Oy
(Finnish Direct Marketing Association)
Henry Ferdin Katu 5M
SF Helsinki
Finland
Tel: +358 0 663 744
Fax: +358 0 663 772

France

Union Française du Marketing Direct
60 rue la Boétie
75008 Paris
France
Tel: +33 1 42 56 3886
Telex: 642367
Fax: +33 1 45 63 9195

Germany

Deutscher Direktmarketing Verband EV
Schiersteiner Strasse 29
6200 Wiesbaden
West Germany
Tel: +49 6121 84 3061
Telex: 4186131
Fax: +49 6121 80 7921

Hong Kong

Hong Kong Direct Mail and Marketing Association
PO Box 7416
Hong Kong
Tel: +852 5 681177
Fax: +852 5 884 1381

Italy

Associazione Italiana per il Direct Marketing (AIDIM)
Corso Venezia 16
20121 Milan
Italy
Tel: +39 2 76 00 1534
Telex: 353151
Fax: +39 2 76 00 4958

Japan

Japan Direct Marketing Association
32 Mori Building 4–30
3chome Shibakoen
Minato-ku
Tokyo 105
Japan
Tel: +81 3 434 4700
Fax: +81 3 434 4518

The Netherlands

Direct Marketing Instituut Nederland
Weerdestein 96
1083 GG Amsterdam
The Netherlands
Tel: +31 20 642 9595
Telex: 15594
Fax: +31 20 644 0199

New Zealand

The New Zealand Direct Marketing Association Inc
PO Box 937
Aukland
New Zealand
Tel: +64 9 499 329
Fax: +64 9 497 455

Norway

Norsk Direckte Markedsforing Forening
c/o DMB&B Lund & Lommer A/S
Postboks 7645
Skillekekk
0205 Oslo 2
Norway
Tel: +47 2 43 0480
Fax: +47 2 43 0438

South Africa

The South African Direct Marketing Association
PO Box 3891
8000 Cape Town
South Africa
Tel: +27 21 252 690
Fax: +27 21 419 5780

Spain

Asociacion Espanola de Marketing Directo (AEMD)
Provenza 238 3.3
08008 Barcelona
Spain
Tel: +34 3 323 4061
Fax: +34 3 454 0795

Sweden

Swedish Direct Marketing Association (SWEDMA)
PO Box 14038
Strandvagen 7B/3
104–40 Stockholm
Sweden
Tel: +46 8 661 3910
Telex: 12442
Fax: +46 8 662 7612

United Kingdom

British Direct Marketing Association (BDMA)
Grosvenor Gardens House
35 Grosvenor Gardens
London SW1W 0BS
Tel: +44 71 630 7322
Fax: +44 71 828 7125

United States of America

Direct Marketing Association Inc (DMA)
11 West 42nd Street
New York
NY 10036
United States of America
Tel: +1 212 768 7277
Fax: +1 212 768 4547

Periodical publications

Periodical marketing publications are an excellent source of information on telephone marketing and related activities, often including news on trends and innovations, examples of applications and details of new service providers. The following list is selective.

The Direct Communications PORTFOLIO
The Decisions Group
19 Worple Road
Wimbledon
London SW19 4JS
Tel: 081-879 7766
Fax: 081-879 7700

Direct Marketing International
4–8 Tabernacle Street
London EC2A 4LV
Tel: 071-638 1916
Fax: 071-638 3128
(includes a quarterly insert called *Teledirect*)

Direct Response
4 Market Place
Hertford
Hertfordshire SG14 1EB
Tel: 0992 501177
Fax: 0992 500387

Directions
Direct Marketing Association
Inc (DMA)
11 West 42nd Street
New York
NY 10036
United States of America
Tel: +1212 768 7277
Fax: +1212 768 4547

Marketing
30 Lancaster Gate
London W2 3LP
Tel: 071-413 4150
Fax: 071-413 4504

Marketing Week
Centaur Communications Ltd
St Giles House
50 Poland Street
London W1V 4AX
Tel: 071-439 4222
Fax: 071-439 9669

On-the-line
4 Market Place
Hertford
Hertfordshire SG14 1EB
Tel: 0992 501177
Fax: 0992 500387

Precision Marketing
St Giles House
50 Poland Street
London W1V 4AX
Tel: 071-439 4222
Fax: 071-439 8065

Information technology for the marketing industry

The Association for Information Systems in Marketing and Sales (AIMS) maintains and publishes a register of information technology-related products and services supplied by member companies. Further details can be obtained from:

**The Association for Information
Systems in Marketing and Sales
(AIMS)**
c/o Melanie Thorogood
Workstations Ltd
Abbey Court
90–96 High Street
Burnham
Buckinghamshire SL1 7JT
Tel: 0628 603284

Suppliers of telephone marketing software

The number of suppliers of software applications packages which support telephone marketing activities is growing rapidly. This brief list includes those supplying products mentioned in the body of the book and a selection of others.

Alpha-Numeric
Walton House
The Courtyard
West Street
Marlow
Buckinghamshire SL7 2LS
Tel: 06284 75661

Callscan Limited
Callscan House
32 Granville Street
Birmingham B1 2LJ
Tel: 021-631 4101
(supplier of telephone traffic
management software)

CCS Pippbrook Ltd
Computer House
Bradford Road
Cleckheaton
West Yorkshire BD19 3TT
Tel: 0274 875858

Data General Ltd
Data General Tower
Great West Road
Brentford
Middlesex TW8 9AN
Tel: 081-758 6000

Datapoint (UK) Ltd
Datapoint House
400 North Circular Road
London NW10 0JG
Tel: 081-459 1222

Mercury Management Software
Mercury House
10 Parade Mews
London SE27 9AX
Tel: 081-674 8898

Merit Direct
Merit House
Timothy's Bridge Road
Stratford Upon Avon
Warwickshire CV37 9HY
Tel: 0789 299622

Norsk Data Ltd
Benham Valence
Newbury
Berkshire RG16 8LU
Tel: 0635 35544

Prospects For Business Ltd
148 Shoreditch High Street
London E1 6JE
Tel: 071-739 4804

Sanderson CFL Ltd
CFL House
Manor Road
Coventry CV1 2GF
Tel: 0203 555466

Space Computer Systems Ltd
Suite 45
Beaufort Court
Admirals Way
Waterside
South Court
London E14 9XL
Tel: 071-537 3727

Systematics International
Essex House
Cherrydown East
Basildon
Essex SS16 5BT
Tel: 0268 284601

Telesystems Europe
Dinjselburgerlann 1
Postbus 601 – 3700 AP
Zeist
Netherlands
Tel: +31 3404 66911
Fax: +31 3404 55203

Voice processing equipment suppliers

The development and supply of voice processing systems is a rapidly expanding industry which now regularly holds exhibitions attracting large numbers of exhibitors. The following suppliers are listed as a source of information on the features available in commercial voice processing systems.

Acumen Technologies
41 North Road
Islington
London N7 9DP
Tel: 071-607 6766

Marconi Speech and Information Systems
Airspeed Road, The Airport
Portsmouth
Hampshire PO3 5RE
Tel: 0705 661222

Newbridge Information Systems
Coldra Woods
Chepstow Road
Newport
Gwent NP6 1JB
Tel: 0633 413600

Periphonics
Albany Court
Albany Park
Camberley
Surrey GU15 2XA
Tel: 0276 692083

Telsis Ltd
Barnes Wallis Road
Segensworth East
Fareham
Hampshire PO15 5TT
Tel: 0489 885877

Texas Instruments Ltd
Manton Lane
Bedford MK41 7PA
Tel: 0234 270111

TISL Ltd
172–184 Bath Road
Slough
Berkshire SL1 3XE
Tel: 0753 33399

Audiotex service providers

Again, this is a rapidly expanding industry and it is not possible to provide a comprehensive list of managed service providers here. Good sources of information on the industry and service providers are the publications *Audiotex Briefing* and *World Telemedia*, both published by Triton Telecom (*see* below). There are a number of consultancies specialising in audiotex, including the following.

Halcyon Solutions
292a Burdett Road
London E14 7DQ
Tel: 0860 384409

Teleconnect Industries
65 Maygrove Road
West Hampstead
London NW6 2EH
Tel: 071-328 3258

Triton Telecom Ltd
45 Kings Terrace
Camden
London NW1 0JR
Tel: 071-911 6002

Another good source of information is the industry trade association.

**Association of Telephone
Information and Entertainment
Providers Ltd (ATIEP)**
Longcroft House
Victoria Avenue
Bishopsgate
London EC2M 4NS
Tel: 071-621 9573

The following list is a small selection of companies providing an audiotex bureau service, some of whom specialise in sales promotion.

Bell Audiotex
c/o Bell House
31–33 Ansleigh Place
London W11 6DW
Tel: 071-221 3141

British Telecom
Callstream Services
8th Floor
Tenter House
45 Moorfields
London EC2Y 9TH
Tel: 0800 282 282

Broadsystem Ltd
The Elephant House
Hawley Crescent
London NW1 8NP
Tel: 071-485 5964

Cablecom
35 Hay's Mews
Berkeley Square
London W1X 7RQ
Tel: 071-409 1002

Legion Telecom
4 Greenland Place
London NW1 0AP
Tel: 071-267 6777

Tardis
19 Quarry Street
Guildford
Surrey GU1 3UY
Tel: 0483 300200

Telecom Express
211 Piccadilly
London W1V 9DL
Tel: 071-548 9950

Telecom Information
4th Floor
Royal Oak House
Prince Street
Bristol BS1 4QE
Tel: 0272 293898

**Telephone Information Services
plc**
24 West Smithfield
London EC1A 9DL
Tel: 071-975 9000

In addition, there are a growing number of telephone marketing agencies investing in technology for audiotex, which is likely to accelerate growth in the diversity and sophistication of marketing applications.

Index